THE BETROTHED OF DEATH

D0068714

Recent Titles in
Contributions in Comparative Colonial Studies

Science and Social Science Research in British India, 1780–1880: The Role of Anglo-Indian Associations and Government
Edward W. Ellsworth

Journalists for Empire: The Imperial Debate in the Edwardian Stately Press, 1903–1913
James D. Startt

Imperial Diplomacy in the Era of Decolonization: The Sudan and Anglo-Egyptian Relations, 1945–1956
W. Travis Hanes III

The Man on the Spot: Essays on British Empire History
Roger D. Long, editor

Imperialism and Colonialism: Essays on the History of European Expansion
H. L. Wesseling

The Racial Dimension of American Overseas Colonial Policy
Hazel M. McFerson

Meeting Technology's Advance: Social Change in China and Zimbabwe in the Railway Age
James Zheng Gao

U.S. Imperialism in Latin America: Bryan's Challenges and Contributions, 1900–1920
Edward S. Kaplan

The Kingdom of Swaziland: Studies in Political History
D. Hugh Gillis

The Bringing of Wonder: Trade and the Indians of the Southeast, 1700–1783
Michael P. Morris

Policing Islam: The British Occupation of Egypt and the Anglo-Egyptian Struggle over Control of the Police, 1882–1914
Harold Tollefson

India: The Seductive and Seduced "Other" of German Orientalism
Kamakshi P. Murti

THE BETROTHED OF DEATH

The Spanish
Foreign Legion
During the
Rif Rebellion,
1920–1927

José E. Álvarez

Contributions in Comparative Colonial Studies, Number 40

GREENWOOD PRESS
Westport, Connecticut • London

Library of Congress Cataloging-in-Publication Data

Álvarez, José E., 1955–
    The betrothed of death : the Spanish Foreign Legion during the Rif Rebellion,
    1920–1927 / José E. Álvarez.
        p. cm.—(Contributions in comparative colonial studies, ISSN 0163–3813 ; no. 40)
    Includes bibliographical references and index.
    ISBN 0–313–30697–4 (alk. paper)
    1. Rif Revolt, 1921–1926.   2. Spain. Ejârcito. Legiân—History.   3. Spain—History,
Military—20th century.   4. Spain—Foreign relations—Morocco.   5. Morocco—Foreign
relations—Spain.   I. Title.   II. Series.
    DT324.5 A48   2001
    946'.074—dc21   99–055222

British Library Cataloguing in Publication Data is available.

Copyright © 2001 by José E. Álvarez

Library of Congress Catalog Card Number: 99–055222
ISBN: 0–313–30697–4
ISSN: 0163–3813

First published in 2001

Greenwood Press, 88 Post Road West, Westport, CT 06881
An imprint of Greenwood Publishing Group, Inc.
www.greenwood.com

Printed in the United States of America

The paper used in this book complies with the
Permanent Paper Standard issued by the National
Information Standards Organization (Z39.48–1984).

10 9 8 7 6 5 4 3 2 1

To the Legion on its 80th anniversary

Contents

Illustrations   ix
Chronology   xi
Abbreviations   xiii
Preface   xv
Acknowledgments   xvii

1. Introduction   1
2. Creation of the Legion, 1919-1920   13
3. First Operations of the Legion, 1921   37
4. Legion Operations, 1922-1923   75
5. Xauen, 1924   113
6. The Alhucemas Bay Landings and Abd-el-Krim's Defeat   163
7. The Finale: Ajdir, Targuist, and Peace, 1926-1927   191
8. Conclusion and Epilogue   219

Appendix A: Organization of the Legion   225
Appendix B: Table of Battle Casualties   235
Appendix C: The Legion's Creed   237
Appendix D: Songs of the Legion   239
Appendix E: A Brief Biography of José Millán Astray y Terreros   245
Appendix F: A Brief Biography of Francisco Franco Bahamonde   247
Appendix G: Chart of Enlistment Bonuses   251
Appendix H: List of All Forces at Alhucemas Bay, September 1925   253

Bibliography   257

Index   267

A photo essay follows Chapter 3

Illustrations

MAPS

All maps listed below were drawn by the author.

1. The Spanish Protectorate 5
2. The Western Zone; The Yebala and Gomara, 1920-1921 24
3. The Melillan Command, 1921 43
4. The Reconquest of the Melillan Command, 1921-1924 48
5. The Retreat from Xauen 127
6. The Alhucemas Bay Landings 171
7. The Liberation of Kudia Tahar 173
8. The Campaigns of 1926 195
9. The Campaigns of 1927 203

TABLES

1. Organization and Equipment of the *Tercio* 17
2. Organization and Equipment for a *Bandera* 18

Chronology

1859-1860	First Moroccan War
1893	First Melillan campaign against the Riffians
1898	Spanish-American War
1909-1910	Second Melillan campaign against the Riffians
1911-1912	Third Melillan campaign against the Riffians
1911	*Regulares* founded by Dámaso Berenguer Fusté
1920	Spanish Foreign Legion founded by José Millán Astray y Terreros
1921	The Annual disaster
1922	Antonio Maura's government was replaced by the Conservative
1923	José Sánchez Guerra, which in turn was replaced by the Liberal Manuel García Prieto
1923	General Miguel Primo de Rivera's *Pronunciamento*
1924	Ben Tieb incident and the withdrawal from Xauen
1925	Alhucemas Bay landing
1926	Abd-el-Krim surrenders to French forces
1927	Peace of Bab Taza—end of the Rif Rebellion
1930	Primo de Rivera resigns
1931-1936	Spanish Second Republic
1934	Spanish Army of Africa (the Legion and *Regulares*) crushes the Asturian miners' uprising
1936-1939	Spanish Civil War. Legion joins in the overthrow of the Second Republic

Abbreviations

AGM	Archivo General Militar (Segovia)
CL	Colección Legislativa del Ejército (Legislative Collection of the Army)
DO	Diario Oficial del Ministerio de la Guerra (Official Diary of the Ministry of War)
DOL	Diario de Operaciones de la Legión (Serrallo de la Legión, Plana Mayor del Tercio, Archivo General, Ceuta)
OC	Orden Circular (Circular Order)
PM	Plana Mayor (Staff)
RD	Reales Decretos (Royal Decrees)
RO	Real Orden (Royal Order)
ROC	Real Orden Circular (Circular Royal Order)
SHM	Servicio Histórico Militar (Madrid)

Preface

The purpose of this book is to introduce the reader to the origins of the Spanish Foreign Legion from its inception in 1920, through the start of the Rif Rebellion in 1921, to the pacification of the Spanish protectorate in 1927. This text focuses on why the Legion was created, how it was similar to or different from the French Foreign Legion on which it was patterned, and how the Legion was organized within the army. The text also considers the Legion's impact on the reconquest of the territory lost after the Annual disaster. Here, the Legion is examined as the cradle of the coterie of generals who "saved" the Second Republic from a Soviet-style revolution in October 1934 in Asturias, but who rose up against the Republic in July 1936, touching off the bloody Spanish Civil War. There was a vital need in the protectorate for *fuerzas de choque* (shock troops) capable of fighting the natives on their own terms and terrain, as well as being able to reduce the growing number of Spanish reservists and conscripts who were perishing in the pacification of the protectorate. Professional soldiers or mercenaries willing to die for Spain formed the backbone of the Legion, thus replacing lowly, poorly trained conscripts. As the Legion's founder, José Millán Astray, noted, each Legionary would serve a dual role: He would take the place of a Spanish conscript while at the same time provide a fighting man to fill the ranks. This policy greatly appealed to the people of Spain whose sons filled the ranks of Spain's army in Morocco. Particular consideration is given to the personalities who forged this unlikely group of volunteers into an elite fighting force and led them in the most important battles of the Riffian War.

Acknowledgments

I t goes without saying that a work of this scope necessitates the input and assistance of many interested parties. I would like to take this opportunity to most gratefully thank the following people and institutions for their kind assistance. None of the following pages would have been possible without the help of professor Peter P. Garretson, who guided and encouraged me, my editors at Greenwood Press, Heather Ruland Staines, Emma Moore, and Frank Saunders, as well as Carolyn P. Boyd, James W. Cortada, Shannon E. Fleming, Judith Keene, and David B. Mock for reviewing the manuscript and providing me with excellent advice and comments. In Spain, I am most deeply indebted to the following for their kind assistance and friendship: Colonel of Infantry and former Legionary, Ramón Moya Ruiz, presently of the *Servicio Histórico Militar* in Madrid for the use of his personal photographs of the Legion; the staff of the *Archivo General Militar* in Segovia; General Manuel Villoria Font, C.L. José ("Pepe") Herrero Iglesias, and the members of the *Hermandad de Antiguos Caballeros Legionarios* (Madrid chapter). In Ceuta, the former commanding officer of the 2nd *Tercio* ("Duque de Alba") Colonel of Infantry José Enrique Domínguez Martínez de Campos and the officers and Legionaries of the IVth and Vth *Banderas*; Major Manuel ("Manolo") Pérez Pajuelo, former director of the *Museo de la Legión*, who befriended me and gave me complete access to all the holdings of the museum; my dear friend, retired Legion Captain C.L. Alejandro Zamacola Monis, and former Legionary Captain Francisco ("Paco") Sacristán Romero for his outstanding comments and remarks. I would also like to thank Captain Miguel Ballenilla y García de Gamarra, formerly the CO of the 1st Company of the Ist *Bandera* of the 1st *Tercio* ("Gran Capitán") for all his help and encouragement. Finally, a special thanks goes to my old friend John P. Dunn, to my mother, Hayda Álvarez, and to my wife, Caroline, for her invaluable help with the maps, tables, and text formatting.

Chapter 1

Introduction

Spain's modern military and diplomatic involvement with Morocco began in 1859 when troops sent by General Leopoldo O'Donnell crushed a revolt by Moroccan tribesmen against Ceuta, a Spanish *presidio* since 1578.[1] Following this brief six-month war, which resulted in a series of Moroccan defeats, Spain was forced by Great Britain and its own tenuous international position to accept a series of treaties that, while extracting concessions from the Moroccan sultan, limited its territorial ambitions and restored to some degree the antebellum stability. This stability remained intact until the early 1890s. Moreover, Spain was able to secure the city of Tetuán until a monetary indemnity was paid off by the Moroccans. Tetuán would later become the capital of the Spanish protectorate.[2]

The next Spanish-Moroccan military conflict occurred in 1893, outside the boundaries of Melilla (a Spanish *presidio* since 1497) where laborers were building a small fort near the city (at Sidi-Guariach) on Spanish territory. Because they considered the construction a violation of local sovereignty, local Riffian tribesmen killed several workers. Spanish troops engaged the tribesmen but were repelled with losses. Before reinforcements could be mustered, the tribesmen attacked, inflicting further losses on the Spanish, including the death of their commander, General Juan García Margallo. General Arsenio Martínez de Campos required 15,000 men to repel the Riffians and restore order.[3]

Militarily, Spain's defeat in the Spanish-American War of 1898, known in Spain as *El Desastre*, brought to light before the international community and the people back home the deplorable state of the Spanish military. Conscripts died abroad in the thousands through disease and neglect. The fault lay with a government that failed to equip and supply the troops properly (a nagging problem that would continue well into the 20th century) and with an officer corps that refused to reduce its bloated ranks.[4] Geopolitically, the loss of her overseas empire to the United States left Spain with only her Moroccan *presidios* and Rio de Oro, Ifni, and Equatorial Guinea in northwestern and central Africa, respectively. At a time when overseas possessions were a mark of a great, powerful nation and Great Britain, France, Germany, and even Italy, Belgium, and Portugal had colonies abroad, Spain had lost most of hers. This international humiliation had a powerful impact on Spain's national psyche, but it was most strongly felt within the ranks of the armed forces. The loss of these overseas colonies took away the opportunity for active service and therefore deprived the army and navy of any chance of restoring the loss of prestige and honor that the troops had suffered. It appeared as if opportunity for military adventure outside Spain was lost, along with any chance of gaining promotion and wealth that campaigning could provide. For officers of the regular army, it seemed as if their future would be spent performing wearisome garrison duty throughout the peninsula.[5]

This national disgrace, the Disaster, strengthened the nation's resolve to hold on tenaciously to what was left in Africa. This was not the attitude in all of Spain, however. Public opinion on the whole was disinterested in colonial enterprise and, after the debacle of 1898, vaguely opposed to it. *Africanismo* (African imperialism) found its most fervent supporters in such tiny groups as the *Real Sociedad Geográfica*, the *Centros Comerciales Hispano-Marroquies*, and the *Liga Africanista Española*. Although outspoken, none of these groups had much of a following.[6]

France, the major player in the Maghreb, was slowly but methodically expanding from Algeria into Morocco. The French government realized that to proceed with this expansion it had to recognize Spain's interests in Morocco and its strategic position between North Africa and France. In 1904, France, with British encouragement, decided that Spain should join her in the self-appointed assignment of protecting the sultan of Morocco. Spain was to be permitted to expand into the area surrounding Melilla and Ceuta, and in October, Liberals and Conservatives in the Spanish parliament approved this French-Spanish treaty. By this agreement, two of Europe's major powers, France and Great Britain, recognized Spain's interests in Morocco. France made it possible for Spain to play an active role in Moroccan affairs while at the same time keeping her place in the concert of Europe.[7]

The situation in Morocco once again heated up on 9 July 1909, when a force of Riffian tribesmen attacked a military outpost protecting Spanish workers building a railway to serve the iron ore mines outside Melilla.[8] Four workers and one sentry were killed. This was the chance Spanish colonialists had been anticipating. On 13 July, 6,000 Riffians attacked a force of 2,000 Spaniards; ten days later, the tribesmen engaged Spanish forces for a third time. The campaign began disastrously for the Spaniards when the 1st Madrid Chasseurs under the command of the reckless General Guillermo Pintos Ledesma were ambushed in the *Barranco del Lobo* (Wolf's Ravine). In the *presidios* at the time, only 15,000 soldiers could be called upon for combat, so the government decided to reinforce its meager colonial forces with 40,000 reserves. This mobilization for a colonial conflict led to anti-war protests that were particularly strong in Barcelona. The authorities suppressed these protests harshly, and the period in late July and early August 1909 came to be called the "Tragic Week."[9]

The "Tragic Week" episode visibly demonstrated the government's commitment not only to remain in Morocco for political purposes by reinforcing the number of troops posted there but also to expand from its *presidios* toward the interior.[10] Moreover, the event brought to light the deep divisions that existed in Spain between those who advocated overseas colonization and those who opposed it. What brought about such outpouring of resentment toward the government, especially in Barcelona, was the call-up of reservists for service in Morocco. The bulk of those who served in the ranks of the army were conscripts and reservists, who came primarily from the peasantry and the working class—two segments of the Spanish population who supplied the cannon fodder for Spain's ambitions in Morocco. They were poorly trained, equipped, and led. There was also little sympathy for the officers who served in Morocco, as they were volunteers rewarded with *méritos de guerra* (merit promotions based on battlefield heroics, not seniority) and decorations for risking their lives against the Moroccans; conscripts and reservists did not have that option.[11]

With the arrival of thousands of fresh troops in Melilla during 1909-10, Spanish forces were able to move from Melilla to occupy an enclave that stretched from Cabo Tres Forcas to the southern shore of Mar Chica and ranged about ten kilometers into the interior. This campaign gained new territory for Spain, which had been losing it around the world for the last 200 years, and provided the Spanish army an opportunity to gain glory, respect, and promotions.[12] However, these African adventures were extremely costly in lives and resources. Militarily speaking, the 1909 campaign served as a wake-up call for the army. Two important lessons were learned: First, native troops under the leadership of Spanish officers (the *Regulares* founded in 1911 by Dámaso Berenguer Fusté, the future High Commissioner of the protectorate), were better acclimated to the terrain of the protectorate than were peninsular troops. Second, there emerged a new crop of junior officers who would go on to play pivotal roles in Spanish history up to the 1970s. Untainted by the defeats of 1898, these men would, from their beginnings in 1909, earn their stars in combat with the *Regulares* and the Spanish Foreign Legion. They would go on to command armies on both sides of the Spanish Civil War, though mostly on the Nationalist side. Francisco Franco Bahamonde, Emilio Mola Vidal, Miguel Cabanellas Ferrer, Agustín Muñoz Grandes, José Varela Iglesias, Juan Yagüe Blanco, Francisco García Escámez e Iniesta, José Asensio Cabanillas, and Vicente Rojo Lluch are but a few of the leaders who emerged.[13]

After 1910, the situation in Melilla calmed down and the focus of attention shifted to the western sector. In mid-1911, the French tried to seize Larache, which was clearly in the Spanish sphere of influence. The French were, however, dissuaded by the arrival of two Spanish warships, the armored cruiser

Cataluña and the transport *Almirante Lobo,* which disembarked troops under the command of Lieutenant Colonel Manuel Fernández Silvestre (who would be commander in chief of all forces in the Melillan sector ten years later). On 8 June, Silvestre occupied Larache without bloodshed. Spain proceeded to occupy large portions of territory around Ceuta by peaceful means and through agreements with local chieftains.[14]

The situation in Morocco quickly shifted back to Melilla on 24 August 1911, when Riffian tribesmen on the eastern bank of the Kert River attacked a General Staff cartographic unit. The local sheikh, El Mizzian, declared *jihad* (holy war) against the Spanish Christians. Spanish forces moved westward from Melilla and crossed the Kert River, about twenty miles east of Melilla. Poor weather and enemy resistance led to a Spanish retreat to the *presidio* and halted the campaign. Again, Riffian tribesmen threatened Melilla itself. The war continued until spring 1912, when Spanish forces pushed the Riffians across the Kert River and El Mizzian died in battle, leaving his men without an effective leader.[15]

The Moroccan sultan, Moulay Abd-al-Hafid, was forced to sign the Treaty of Fez in 1912, which established the French and Spanish protectorates. Spain was to administer the northern one-fifth (another source gives the area as "roughly a quarter"), the less economically profitable zone, with Tangier being declared an international city (see Map 1). The Spanish protectorate consisted of roughly 18,000 square miles inhabited by sixty-six indigenous tribes subdivided into various clans and subclans that constantly fought among themselves. The two most warlike of these tribes, especially in resistance to colonial domination, were located within the Spanish zone. They were the tribes of the Yebala in the west under the rule of Sherif Muley Ahmed el Raisuli (aka er Raisuni) and of the Rif in the east. Hypothetically subordinate to the khalif, the sultan's deputy in Tetuán, capital of the Spanish Protectorate of Morocco, the protectorate's rural tribes basically ignored the sultan and were even more opposed to domination from foreign "infidels."[16]

Having acquired this new colony, Spanish forces attempted their first pacification of it in 1913 when they moved to occupy the region around the sacred city of Xauen in the western zone of the protectorate. In bitter combat with the tribes of the Yebala, Spanish troops were forced back to Tetuán, where they remained until an armistice could be hammered out with el Raisuni.[17] Under the leadership of General Felipe Alfau Mendoza, the protectorate's first High Commissioner, and Colonel Manuel Fernández Silvestre, Spanish forces advanced into the Yebala and engaged in numerous small-scale battles with el Raisuni's forces. El Raisuni was clearly a worthy adversary who kept the Yebala tribes in line through a combination of charisma and terror. Eventually, protectorate officials and el Rasuini reached a modus vivendi and he became a temporary friend of Spain's.[18]

During World War I, the Spanish protectorate remained relatively quiet. However, German influence peddling and gun running occurred in an effort to instigate indigenous opposition to French authority in the Maghreb. This was

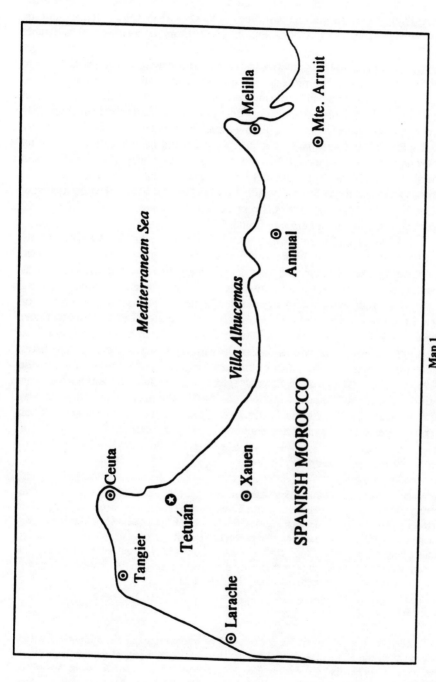

Map 1
The Spanish Protectorate

especially the case in the Spanish protectorate. "He [Abd-el-Krim Sr.] had during the war smuggled arms into the Riff, been in touch with German mining interests, and come to realize that there were in his territory deposits of considerable value."[19]

To understand the great need for a well-trained and dedicated force to fight Spain's battles in the protectorate, it is imperative that one be aware of the dismal state of the Spanish army in Morocco. The Spanish army had been in decline since the Spanish-American War. Following the aforementioned 1909 campaign, Spanish journalists asked how a modern (perceived to be well trained, well disciplined, and adequately equipped) army could be so easily frustrated by Moroccan irregulars lacking modern organization, heavy weapons, or professional leadership. Army leaders were hard pressed to explain why their forces in Morocco were not up to the task. Although the General Staff prepared a manual dealing with irregular warfare, officers in the field ignored the written rules, preferring to lead with their *cojones* (guts).[20]

At the time, the army was in a deplorable state. As Ron Vaughan noted, the officer corps was corrupt and inefficient. The majority of the officers were stern disciplinarians who ignored their duties, and quite a few went on leave at the beginning of a campaign, leaving sergeants to run the companies. Money intended for supplies and the paymaster was pocketed by the officers and the sergeants, and much of the equipment sent to Morocco never made it to the front: Entire warehouses full of supplies were sold to smugglers, who in turn sold the goods to the natives. "It was reported that half of the cartridges were filled with sawdust!" Factionalism permeated the ranks of the junior officers and the noncommissioned officers (NCOs). The average Spanish soldier was an illiterate peasant conscript insufficiently trained, poorly disciplined, badly equipped, and supported by deficient medical and commissary services. "Many carried obsolete rifles which had never been cleaned since they were first issued years before!"[21]

Captain Mellor's professional assessment of the army, and especially of its officers, read as follows:

Every one in Northern Morocco knew that many of the Spanish officers spent their time whoring and gambling in Melilla [in Ceuta, Larache, and Tetuán, too]; knew what happened to stores and the fate of the men's pay. Some officers never saw their regiments, but contented themselves with parading like peacocks through the streets while the half-starved youths of Spain in shoddy, torn clothes wandered miserably through the Riff hills, not knowing where they were going or even why they were engaged in this fantastic adventure. Their one desire was to return to Spain and their own homes.

Mellor went on to state:

The Spanish army was in a terrible condition. The troops were quite untrained and hardly knew in which end of the rifle to put their cartridges. None of the usual military precautions were taken. This is no exaggerated picture, and these points were many of them noted by correspondents at the time and admitted in the Cortes [Spanish parliament] after the disaster [Annual].[22]

In "Bridegrooms of Death: A Profile Study of the Spanish Foreign Legion," John H. Galey summed up the situation when he wrote:

Several factors had combined to retard the development of Spanish military science. After its crushing defeat in the Spanish American War of 1898, Spain remained isolated from the mainstream of European industrial progress. Then, since Spain had not participated in the first world war, its armed forces did not acquire the new military skills and improved techniques gained at such terrible cost by the belligerents. Finally, the rapid turnover in Spanish ministers of war prevented them from putting through various projected reforms and innovations in the armed forces.[23]

The poor fighting qualities of the regular army did not extend to the *Regulares*. In the beginning, Moroccan troops were distrusted and Spanish officers assigned to the *Regulares* were unsure of them and inexperienced. Officers followed the French example of command as Berenguer had been taught in French North Africa. In the 1912 Melilla campaign, however, the *Regulares* proved themselves by fighting with great tenacity and resolve while suffering heavy casualties. By 1919, there were only four *tabores* (battalions). When fighting began in the Yebala region, the *Regulares* formed the vanguard. The officers of the *Regulares* had the highest casualty rates of any unit in the army, but those who survived their wounds became the elite of the *africanistas* (career officers serving in Africa). The *Regulares* thus became the birthplace for the top officers of Spain's army in the protectorate. Whether they remained with the *Regulares*, as did Santiago González Tablas, Emilio Mola Vidal, and José Varela Iglesias, or joined the Legion, as did José Millán Astray, Francisco Franco Bahamonde, Rafael Valenzuela Urzaiz, and later Juan Yagüe Blanco, or became generals of the regular army, like José Sanjurjo Sacanell and Dámaso Berenguer Fusté, the *Regulares* meant recognition and promotions.[24]

The method of pacification the military employed was for the *Regulares* to do the lion's share of the fighting while the regular army would hold the newly conquered territory by means of a string of *blocaos* (blockhouses).[25]

While the *Regulares* performed admirably in the Spanish protectorate, a new organization was in its formative state in 1919. The brainchild of an ex-*Regulares* officer, Major José Millán Astray, the soon-to-be-created Spanish Foreign Legion was to serve with the *Regulares* as the shock troops of the Spanish army. Millán Astray's proposal for a Foreign Legion, based on the more famous French Foreign Legion, would have a dual purpose: First, it would be made up of hardened professional soldiers, and second, it would spare a Spaniard from having to be shipped off to Morocco.[26] The most perspicacious opinion for the creation of the *Regulares* and the Spanish Foreign Legion comes from Diego Abad de Santillan in the prologue to General Juan Picasso González's *Expediente Picasso* when he declared:

What would the professionals in the military do without Morocco? A solution appeared in an organization independent of the ups and downs of Spanish politics, with its own identity, and there, one had the Foreign Legion. Combined with the *Regulares*, it would become a powerful organization, mercenary, strongly disciplined, and whose moral existence was expressed in the euphoric cry of, "Long live death!"

The casualties in such formations did not have any repercussions on Spanish morale; these were adventurers from all backgrounds who were paid to kill, and to die. This was the brilliant inspiration of general Sanjurjo, of Millán Astray, and of Francisco Franco. Thus the Legion quickly became the key to Spain's control of Morocco. Also, more than once in Spain itself, the Legion was a dependable instrument against rebellions, and the protests of radical organizations. Finally, it was a "military academy" for converting the Spanish armed forces into like-minded units.

In the future, the *africanista* party could not be silenced or ignored, neither in Morocco nor in the peninsula, and it was impossible to govern without it and less against it.[27]

NOTES

1. For more on the 1859-1860 campaign, see Robert Rezette, *The Spanish Enclaves in Morocco*, trans. Mary Ewalt (Paris: Nouvelles Editions Latines, 1976), 50; Ignacio de Abenia Taure, *Memorias sobre el Riff* (Zaragoza: Imprenta de Antonio Gallifa, 1859); J. Hardman, *The Spanish Campaign in Morocco* (Edinburgh, 1860); Shannon E. Fleming, "North Africa," in *Spain in the Nineteenth-Century World: Essays on Spanish Diplomacy, 1789-1898*, ed. James W. Cortada (Westport, CT: Greenwood Press, 1994), 91-102; *Enciclopedia Universal Ilustrada*, 1958 ed., s.v. "Marruecos"; and R. Gil Grimau, *Aproximación a una bibliografía española sobre el Norte de África (1850-1980)* (Madrid: Ministerio de Asuntos Exteriores. Dir. Gral. de Relaciones Culturales, 1982).

2. Raymond Carr, *Spain, 1808-1975* (Oxford: Clarendon Press, 1982), 261. See the following for details of the peace agreement between the sultan and the Spanish government regarding territory, The Army War College, Course at the Army War College, *The Present Situation of Spain in Morocco*, by Brigadier General Allison Owen, La. N.G., Memorandum for the Director, G-2 Division, The Army War College, 11 October 1924. Washington Barracks, D.C.; The Army War College Curricular Archives, File #288A-80, 2.

3. Rezette, 51. In *Annual*, Eduardo Ortega y Gasset (Madrid: Rivadeneyra, 1922), 188, wrote that the 1893 incident gave Cuban rebels, who had been deported to Melilla, the impetus to rise again against the Spanish authorities in 1895 after having seen "examples of immorality, disorganization and ineptitude" within the Spanish army. Translation by the writer. Henceforth, all translations by the author unless indicated otherwise. In 1893, the Riffian chieftain, Maimon, chased Spanish forces under the command of General Margallo, all the way back to the town of Melilla just as Abd-el-Krim would do to General Silvestre's forces in 1921. See José María Bueno Carrera, *Uniformes de las unidades militares de la ciudad de Melilla* (Madrid: Aldaba Militaria, 1990), 20. As a consequence of the defeats the Spanish military had suffered around Melilla, the army

adopted the Mauser Model 1893 rifle (the most advanced at the time) as its primary battle rifle, supplanting the 11 mm/.43-cal. Remington rolling block, which used black powder. The five-round, clip-fed "Spanish" Mauser in 7 mm, using smokeless powder, would serve the Spanish army for the next fifty years. The Model 1893 rifle with the Simson bayonet was carried by Spanish infantrymen during the Spanish-American War, the Rif Rebellion, and the Spanish Civil War. It was replaced in 1943 by the Model 43 Mauser, but in the then more popular European caliber of 7.92 mm. For more on the Model 1893 Spanish Mauser, see José Boado y Castro, *El fusil Mauser español, modelo de 1893; descripción, municiones, accesorios, funcionamiento, nomemclatura, desarme, cuidados que exige, noticias de su fabricación, reconocimientos, tiro de precision, marcas y empaques, propiedades balísticas y datos numéricos* (Madrid: Tipográfico, 1895); Ludwig Olson, *Mauser Bolt Rifles*, 3 rd ed. (Montezuma, IA: F. Brownell & Son, 1976); and Robert W. D. Ball, *Mauser Military Rifles of the World* (Iola, WI: Krause Publications, 1996), 217-218.

4. John Keegan, *World Armies* (London: MacMillan Press, 1979), 644. For more on the problems, as well as the powerful influence of the Spanish army on the government, see Gabriel Cardona, *El poder militar en la España contemporánea hasta la Guerra Civil* (Madrid: Siglo XXI de España Editores, 1983); Julio Busquets, *El militar de carrera en España* (Barcelona: Editorial Ariel, 1984); and Miguel Alonso Baquer, *El ejército en la sociedad española* (Madrid: Ediciones del Movimiento, 1971).

5. Walter B. Harris, *France, Spain and the Riff* (London: Edward Arnold & Co., 1927), 50.

6. Shannon E. Fleming, *Primo de Rivera and Abd-el-Krim: The Struggle in Spanish Morocco, 1923-1927* (New York and London: Garland Publishing, 1991), 12. A similar sentiment was expressed by Antonio Azpeitua in *Marruecos, la mala semilla: Ensayo de análisis objetivo de como fue sembrada la guerra en África* (Madrid: 1921), 68-69, when he wrote:

The military occupation of Morocco was conceived shortly after the loss of Cuba and the Philippines. In Africa they were looking for a place to employ the excessive numbers of army officers and the formidable bureaucratic apparatus which, after the Treaty of Paris, were left without a purpose.

Today, Morocco is a new Cuba, with the only difference being that Cuba was rich, it had coffee plantations, sugar and tobacco plantations, while Morocco is poor, and, all that devours [;] that monstrous bureaucracy-military, takes from Spain, from the peasant, from the industrialist, from the worker.

7. For an in-depth study of Spain's policies vis-à-vis Morocco during the early years of the 20th century, see Shannon E. Fleming, "The Disaster of Annual: Spanish Colonial Failure in Northern Morocco, 1902-1921," (Master's thesis, University of Minnesota, 1969); and George Hills, *Spain* (New York: Praeger Publishers, 1970), 114. For more on the treaties between France and Spain (1902-1904), see Fleming, *Primo de Rivera*, 22-28.

8. For information on Spanish and German iron ore mining interests in the Rif, see Pessah Shinar, "Abd al Qadir and Abd al Krim: Religious Influences on Their Thought and Action." *Asian and African Studies*, Vol. I, Annual of the Isreali Oriental Society (Jerusalem, 1975), 161; James Joll, *The Origins of the First World War* (New York: Longman, 1984), 132; and J. D. Fage and Roland Oliver, eds., "Morocco," *The Cambridge History of Africa*, Vol. VII (London and New York: Cambridge University Press, 1975), 7, 300.

9. Hills, 114. See also Rezette, 53-54. The author states that a young Abd-el-Krim, then working as an interpreter for the *comandancia general* (general command) of Melilla, saw the impotence of Spanish forces during the 1909 uprising. Captain F. H. Mellor, *Morocco Awakes* (London: Methuen Publishers, 1939), 37-38; Joaquín Arraras, ed., *Historia de la Cruzada Española* (Madrid: Ediciones Españolas, 1939), 38-42. An excellent account of the 1909 campaign around Melilla and the "Tragic Week" draft riots can be found in Stanley G. Payne, *Politics and the Military in Modern Spain* (Stanford, CA: Stanford University Press, 1967), 105-112, and in Joan Connelly Ullman, *The Tragic Week: A Study of Anti-clericalism in Spain, 1875-1912* (Cambridge, MA: Harvard University Press, 1968). See also Alal al-Fasi, *The Independence Movements in Arab North Africa*, trans. Hazem Zaki Nuseibeh (New York: Octagon Press, 1970), 92; Robert B. Asprey, *War in the Shadows: The Guerrilla in History* (New York: Doubleday & Co., 1975), 402; and Chapter 10 of Tomás García Figueras, *Marruecos: La acción de España en el Norte de África* (Barcelona: Ediciones Fe, 1939).

10. Sebastian Balfour, *The End of the Spanish Empire, 1898-1923* (Oxford: Clarendon Press, 1997), 200-201, noted that "the threat of French intervention to restore order forced a reluctant [Prime Minister Antonio] Maura to order troops into the interior beyond the coastal enclaves."

11. Carlos Blanco Escolá, *La Academia General Militar de Zaragoza (1928-1931)* (Barcelona: Labor Universitaria, 1989), 82-83.

12. Fleming, "Disaster of Annual," 17-18.

13. J. Ramón Alonso, *Historia politica del ejército español* (Madrid: Editora Nacional, 1974), 455; and Balfour, 187. The Spanish *presidio* of Melilla became the birthplace of the *Regulares*, founded on 30 June 1911. The *Grupo de Fuerzas Regulares Indigenas de Melilla Nº 1* was led by Lieutenant Colonel Dámaso Berenguer Fusté and was composed of one battalion of infantry (with four companies) and a cavalry squadron. See Bueno, 41. For more on the *Regulares* and the *Mahal-la Jalifiana* (different from the former in that the men and most of the officers were Moroccan), see Ron Vaughan, "The Forgotten Army: The Spanish in Morocco." *Savage & Soldier*, 16, no. 2, (April/June 1984): 2. It is interesting to note that when the idea for the *Regulares* was proposed, Berenguer was sent to Algeria and Tunisia to study how the French used native troops; Fleming, "Disaster of Annual," 46. Eight years later, Millán Astray would travel to Algeria to study the French Foreign Legion before setting up the Spanish Foreign Legion.

14. Fleming, "Disaster of Annual," 25; Mellor, 38; Rezette, 54; and Arraras, ed. (1911), 52-58. For more on the two Spanish ships, see *Jane's Fighting Ships*, ed. (1923), 324 and 332, respectively.

15. David S. Woolman, *Rebels in the Rif: Abd el Krim and the Rif Rebellion* (Stanford, CA: Stanford University Press, 1968), 44; Payne, 113-114; and Fleming, "Disaster of Annual," 26-28. The newly founded *Regulares de Melilla* killed El Mizzian in battle.

16. Vaughan, 2. The "roughly a quarter" is from Hills, 118. See Fage and Oliver, 288-289. Harris on 59, described the tribes of the Spanish protectorate as follows: "The people of the Riff and the Jibala are considered to be the best fighting-men in all Morocco." Therefore, in the Franco-Hispano Agreement of 1912, Spain was allotted the worst agricultural terrain and the most bellicose subjects. El Raisuni has been described by some as a brigand and a kidnapper, but it could be said that he was also a survivor. In 1908, he backed Mulay Hafid for the sultanate of Morocco and was richly rewarded for that support. He swore an oath to him, and the new sultan reinstated el Raisuni as governor of the Yebala and part of the Lukus, as well as pasha of Arcila. He was both feared and respected by the tribesmen of the Yebala. With his wealth and power, he built palaces in Tangier, Tetuán, Xauen, Arcila, Larache, Zinat, and Tazarut. Until his capture by Abd-el-Krim, he was a power to be reckoned with by both the Spaniards and the tribesmen of the Yebala. See Woolman, *Rebels in the Rif*, 50-53. For more on Ahmed el Raisuli, see Rosita Forbes, *El Raisuni, the Sultan of the Mountains: His Life as Told to Rosita Forbes* (London: Thornton Butterworth, 1924). El Raisuni became internationally infamous in 1904 for kidnapping an American citizen Mr. Pedicaris. As President Theodore Roosevelt said at the time: "I want Pedicaris alive or Raisuli dead[!]" See Woolman, *Rebels in the Rif*, 48. For more on the establishment of the protectorate, see Chapter 11 of García Figueras. For the nine main articles of the Treaty of Fez, in the original French, see Mellor, 41-43; and Victor Morales Lezcano, *España y el Norte de África—El Protectorado en Marruecos (1912-1956)*. (Madrid: U.N.E.D., 1986), 226-227.

17. al-Fasi, 92; Arraras, ed. (1913), 66-67; and Morales Lezcano, 227.

18. Payne, 116-122; Woolman, *Rebels in the Rif*, 55-67; Fleming, *Primo de Rivera*, 36-46; and Morales Lezcano, 227.

19. Mellor, 64; and Woolman, *Rebels in the Rif*, 62.

20. Payne, 114. For more on the poor state of the army circa 1909, see Fleming, "Disaster of Annual," 33-34.

21. Vaughan, 4; Carr, 521; and Blanco Escolá, 81.

22. Mellor, 66-67. For more on the army's situation in the protectorate, see Woolman, *Rebels in the Rif*, 97-100; Payne, 159-160; and Azpeitua, 107-109. For an excellent view of life in the Spanish army in Morocco from one who served as an NCO during this period, see Arturo Barea, *The Forging of a Rebel*, trans. Ilsa Barea (New York: Reynal & Hitchcock, 1946). The second part of this three-part book, *The Track*, was published in 1984 (London: Flamingo).

23. John H. Galey, "Bridegrooms of Death: A Profile Study of the Spanish Foreign Legion," *Journal of Contemporary History* 4, no. 2 (April 1969): 48.

24. Payne, 155. See Fernando Cano Velasco, ed., "Las Fuerzas Regulares Indígenas" (Zaragoza: Ediciones Palafox, 1984), vol. IV, *Historia de las fuerzas armadas,*

171-198, for a history of the *Regulares*. Also see José María Bueno Carrera, *Los Regulares: Uniformes y organización de las Tropas Regulares Indígenas de Marruecos* (Madrid: Aldaba Militaria, 1989), which contains his beautiful illustrations. For a history of native forces in the service of Spain since the 16th century, see Enrique Arques and Narciso Gibert, *Los Mogataces: Los primitivos soldados moros de España en África* (Ceuta-Tetuán: Imp. Tropas Coloniales, 1928). For even more on the indigenous forces (the *Regulares* et al.) of the old protectorate, see General of Cavalry Joaquín De Sotto y Montes, "Notas para la historia de las fuerzas indígenas del antiguo protectorado de Marruecos," *Revista de Historia Militar* 35 (n.d.): 117-154. Concerning promotions, it had been policy within the Spanish army to automatically promote to the next highest rank officers wounded in battle. This had been the case during the Cuban War, as well as the Rif campaigns of 1909 and 1911, but had been done away with after the latter campaign due to its abuse by officers who had only suffered minor flesh wounds to the arms or legs. See Ramón Garriga, *La Señora de El Pardo* (Barcelona: Editorial Planeta, 1979), 22.

    25. The system of *blocaos* will be looked at in greater detail in Chapter 3.

    26. Woolman, *Rebels in the Rif*, 67; and Payne, 156.

    27. Juan Picasso González, *Expediente Picasso: Documentos relacionados con la información instruida por el señor general de división D. Juan Picasso sobre las responsabilidades de la actuación española en Marruecos durante julio de mil novecientos veintiuno,* with a prologue by Diego Abad de Santillan (Mexico, D.F.:   Frente de Afirmación Hispanista, A.C., 1976), XVII-XVIII.

Chapter 2

Creation of the Legion, 1919–1920

"There is nothing finer than to die with honor for the glory of Spain and its army; that you will learn."[1] This was the sentiment of Lieutenant Colonel José Millán Astray y Terreros, the founder of the *Tercio de Extranjeros* (the Spanish Foreign Legion), when he welcomed the first 200 recruits to the *Cuartel del Rey* (King's Barracks) in Ceuta, Spain's *presidio* in Morocco. The nucleus of what was eventually to become eight *Banderas* (battalions) by the end of the Rif Rebellion, had set foot in the Spanish Protectorate of Morocco prepared to lay down their lives for Spain. Millán Astray was "convinced that the fierce tribesmen of the protectorate could never be successfully pacified by an army of reservists and conscripts."[2] These 200 men were the professional soldiers who would lay the foundation for his dream of creating a Spanish Foreign Legion composed of professional soldiers.

BACKGROUND TO THE LEGION'S ESTABLISHMENT

The genesis of the modern Spanish Foreign Legion can be traced back to 1919 when Millán Astray—*El Fundador*, (The Founder), as he is sometimes referred to in the Legion—then a forty-year-old army major, proposed the formation of an elite volunteer force made up of Spaniards and foreigners to become the vanguard of army operations in Africa.[3] The process of creating the Legion began on 16 August 1919 when he submitted a letter to the headquarters of the army's General Staff (Estado Mayor Central del Ejército) stating the following:

With the goal of quickly compensating for the losses suffered among our indigenous forces of Africa, and at the same time to create an effective fighting force, which can augment and collaborate for the purposes for which these forces were created, the Minister [of War, General Antonio Tovar Álvarez] has ordered that without prejudice to what in its day was agreed upon in respect to the organization of the Colonial Army by that

Center, that the methods be studied to create in those territories a foreign Legion [*Legión extranjera*]. Its members would be recruited in the Consulates of their respective Nations, concentrating them at a convenient point and sending them to Morocco in groups or nuclei of 150 to 200 men.[4]

The minister of war ordered the General Staff to study the possibility of creating a unit of foreign volunteers for the colonial campaign. The General Staff endorsed the idea.[5] With the staff report and the approval of the protectorate's High Commissioner, General Dámaso Berenguer Fusté, and General Bernardo Álvarez del Manzano y Menéndez Valdes, commanding general of Ceuta and staunch patron of the Legion, Millán Astray received a handwritten Royal Order (RO) from the minister of war dated 5 September 1919. This Royal Order gave Millán Astray the authorization to travel to Algeria and other points in Africa to study the organization of the French Foreign Legion for twenty-five days. He departed on 13 September. Making the journey by train and by ship to Tetuán, he presented himself by order of the minister of war to General Berenguer, who gave him instructions regarding the mission he was about to undertake. After spending a short time meeting with the commanding general of Ceuta, General Manuel Fernández Silvestre and the commanding general of Tetuán, General Antonio Vallejo Vila, Millán Astray took part in military operations in the region in the column led by Colonel José Sanjurjo Sacanell. Finally, on 3 October, with Millán Astray's assignment in Tetuán completed, he continued to Algeria, traveling by train and sea to Málaga. From Málaga, he embarked for Melilla. From that point, he continued by land to Oran, traversing the entire northwestern portion of Algeria and visiting the French Foreign Legion in Sidi-bel-Abbes and Tlemcen. With the authorization of the French minister of war, he studied the organization of the Legion in the Foreign Legion's *regiments de marche* (provisional regiments) in Tlemcen until 27 October, when his mission came to an end. He returned to Madrid, where he rejoined his regiment and reported on what he had observed in Algeria.[6] After having studied the French Foreign Legion, Millán Astray decided that "[he] would not make a Legion like this one [i.e., the French Foreign Legion], but would take from it, as a model, that which would not conflict with the thought which stirs in his mind."[7]

Upon his return to Spain, Millán Astray anxiously awaited a response from his superiors. One year before, he had attended a technical course in combat arms in the small town of Valdemoro (Pinto). There he met the *Wunderkind* of the Spanish army: Francisco Franco Bahamonde/Baamonde (or as his colleagues called him, "Franquito"). Franco's reputation, rightly merited for having served bravely and conspicuously with the *Regulares de Tetuán* in Morocco, was of a stern disciplinarian and an excellent tactician with nerves of steel. Millán Astray and Franco, both Galicians, quickly became friends, with the former describing his dream of forming an elite unit to fight the rebellious "natives" of the protectorate. After his return from Algeria, Millán Astray asked Franco if he would accept being his *lugarteniente* (deputy) Franco responded: "Yes, I will be the deputy."[8] The

Dioscuri of the Legion had been united. Millán Astray was promoted to the rank of lieutenant colonel with senority effective 31 December of the previous year (1919) by Circular Royal Order (ROC), dated 7 January.[9] This was a good omen for what was to happen next.

The Spanish Foreign Legion was born on 28 January 1920 when King Alfonso XIII decreed that "with the name of *Tercio de Extranjeros* [Regiment of Foreigners], an armed military unit will be created, whose troops, equipment and regulations it will abide by, shall be established by the Minister of War [José Villalba Riquelme]."[10]

Millán Astray was put in charge of organizing the newly founded *Tercio de Extranjeros* while remaining with his assigned unit, the *Regimiento de Infantería del Principe Nº 3*.[11] With this royal mandate, Millán Astray was able to create an elite fighting force that would become his own private army. Because the Legion had no roots or historical ties like other regiments of the army, it began its life without antecedents, open to shaping and molding in the image of its founder. Millán Astray's personal beliefs—fervent Catholicism, duty until death, honor above everything, love of country—became inculcated into the Legion, which would grow bigger and stronger as the Riffian War progressed. However, it would be Francisco Franco, Millán Astray's personally chosen deputy, who would reap the benefits of this private army when the time came in 1936.[12]

With a new minister of war, Luis Marichalar y Monreal (Vizconde de Eza), events progressed rapidly for the Legion. The replacement of Villalba by the Vizconde de Eza in May 1920 was the pivotal point enabling the Legion to come to fruition. On the night of 14 May, the new minister of war heard Millán Astray speak before the *Círculo Militar* (Military Circle) in Madrid (at the *Centro del Ejército y de la Armada*) about the benefits of creating a Foreign Legion and was so convinced that he authorized recruitment for the new unit.[13] The support of the king and the new minister of war allowed the Legion to overcome resistance from those in the army like General Silvestre and the *Juntas de Defensa* (Military Defense Juntas). The *Juntas de Defensa*, which existed from 1917 to 1922, supported the dissatisfaction of peninsular officers with elite units like the *Regulares* and the proposed Foreign Legion. Officers in these units (*africanistas*) would bypass promotion through seniority by taking advantage of *méritos de guerra*. Officers serving in Africa believed they deserved this privilege because they suffered the hardships of campaigning and faced possible death, whereas their counterparts in the peninsula remained in barracks throughout the major cities of Spain. This dual standard for promotion caused great animosity and divisiveness within the military.[14]

By the Royal Decree of 31 August 1920, His Majesty disposed that[15] the previous decree be put in place, dictating the appropriate standards for it.[15] There quickly followed the Royal Decree of 2 September, whereby "His Majesty was pleased to confer Command of the *Tercio de Extranjeros* to Lieutenant Colonel of Infantry José Millán Terreros [who would subsequently obtain a modification of his first surname to that of Millán Astray, his paternal surnames]."[16]

Inasmuch as the previous royal decrees began the process of creating a foreign legion, it was the Royal Decree (and ROC) of 4 September 1920 that cemented the proposal. Basically, it dictated the rules for the organization of the *Tercio*, establishing its initial formations, which would be composed of one command and administrative headquarters, with four depot and instruction companies, three *Banderas*, each one composed of two *fusileros granaderos* (rifle-grenadier) companies, and one company of *ametralladoras* (machine guns) with six machines (see Tables 1 and 2).[17]

ORGANIZATION OF THE LEGION

With recruiting centers set up in Madrid, Zaragoza, Barcelona, and Valencia, Millán Astray was dispatched to Ceuta, where on 11 September he established the Legion's central recruiting office in the King's Barracks (the ramshackle *Cuartel del Rey*) located in the Plaza de Colón.[18] At the King's Barracks, Millán Astray had put in place his headquarters staff, who were prepared to process the new recruits. The staff officers included: Captain Justo Pardo Ibáñez, Millán Astray's adjutant; Lieutenant Luis Gracía Bastarrica; and Major Adolfo Vara del Rey y Herran. After the arrival of the first Legionary on 20 September, the rest of the administrative staff arrived: Captain Pablo Arredondo Acuña and Lieutenants Ignacio Olavide Torres and Joaquín Moore de Pedro, Baron de Misena.[19]

Responding to a strong propaganda campaign of *"¡¡AL TERCIO!!"* (To the Tercio!), advanced by colorful posters plastered throughout the cities of Spain, anxious recruits began to flood in, as Millán Astray had expected. Those willing to enlist would be given a passport, 2.50 *pesetas* for the journey, as well as a signing bonus of 500 *pesetas* for four years or 700 *pesetas* for five (400 or 600 for foreigners), with half given at the time of enlistment and the other half doled out in three equal parts after completion of each year of service. Furthermore, recruits would progressively be paid 2 *pesetas* for food, 0.85 *céntimos* for uniforms and savings, and 1.25 *pesetas* in cash per day.[20]

A cablegram from the mainland to Millán Astray in the King's Barracks in Ceuta informed him that 400 men had already enlisted and were awaiting transportation, with 200 of them assembled in Barcelona. Overwhelmed with the unexpectedly large turnout and without adequate accommodations in Ceuta, Millán Astray took a bold step and responded, "Let them come!" The Barcelona contingent of 200 recruits, under the personal command of the Legion's deputy, Major Francisco Franco, was transported by rail to Algeciras, where on 10 October the group boarded the trans-Mediterranean ferry *Fernández Silvestre* for the voyage to Ceuta.[21]

Millán Astray, full of hope and enthusiasm for what was to be molded from this small nucleus of humanity, waited for the recruits to arrive at the dock. Reasons for joining the Legion were as varied as the backgrounds of those who enlisted, be they Spaniards or foreigners. Many had fought in the Great War or in

Table 1

Organization and Equipment of the *Tercio*

ORGANIZATION	Lt. Colonels	Majors	Captains	Lieutenants	Alfereces	Captain (Dr.)	Lieutenant (Dr.)	Veterinarian	OFFICERS TOTAL	Senior Sergeants	Sergeants	Corporals	Buglers	Trainees	Drummers	1st Class	2nd Class	ENLISTED TOTAL	Blacksmith	Farrier	Saddler	Armorer	Horses	Mules Draft	Mules Pack	LIVESTOCK TOTAL	Food & Equip.	Field Kitchen	Carts	Tool Boxes	Picks	Shovels	Axes	Sand bags	Machine guns	Pistols	Rifles	Short Rifles	Bayonets	Sabers	Hand grenades	First Aid Kit	Medicine Chest	Stretchers	Veterinarian's Kit	Farrier's kit	Motorcycle w/ sidecar	Bicycle
General Staff	1		1						2	2	1	2	1			2	19	27					2		3	5										6	16	1	9	1					1		1	4
Total	1		1						2	2	1	2	1			2	19	27					2		3	5										6	16	1	9	1					1		1	4
Administration		1	1	2		1			5	1	2	4					19	26					5	2		7			1							1			26	3				1		1		
Total		1	1	2		1			5	1	2	4					19	26					5	2		7			1							1			26	3				1		1		
Grand Total	1	1	2	2		1			7	3	3	6	1			2	38	53					7	2	3	12			1							7	16	1	35	4				1	1	1	1	4

Source: DO #199, Tomo III, 5 September 1920, 887.

Table 2
Organization and Equipment for a *Bandera*

	General Staff	1st Company of Riflemen	2nd Company of Riflemen	Machine Guns	Total (Combat Unit)	Administrative General Staff	Depot Company	Total (Depot)	Grand Total
OFFICERS									
Majors	1				1				1
Captains		1	1	1	3	1	1	1	4
Lieutenants or Alfereces	1	3	3	2	9		2	2	11
Doctor or Lieutenant	1				1				1
Veterinarian	1				1				1
TOTAL	4	4	4	3	15		3	3	18
SPECIALISTS									
Armorer	1				1				1
Saddler	1				1				1
Farrier	1			1	2				2
Blacksmith	1				1				1
TOTAL	4			1	5				5
ENLISTED									
Senior Sergeants	1	1	1	1	4	1		1	5
Sergeants	1	6	6	4	17	1	2	3	20
Corporals	4	16	16	4	40	2	4	6	46
Buglers	1	4	4	1	10				10
Trainees		1	1		2				2
Drummers		1	1		2				2
1st Class	3	7	7	2	19		2	2	21
2nd Class	23	134	134	45	336	9	9	18	354
TOTAL	33	170	170	57	430	13	17	30	460
LIVESTOCK									
Horses	4	4	4	3	15		3	3	18
Mules — Draft		4	4	6	14	2		2	16
Mules — Pack	14	2	2	16	34				34
TOTAL	18	10	10	25	63	2	3	5	68
VEHICLES									
Food & Equipment		1	1	1	3				3
Field Kitchen		1	1	1	3				3
Carts						1		1	1
Bicycles	1				1				1
TOOLS									
Tool Boxes	1				1				1
Picks		20	20	8	48				48
Shovels		30	30	14	74				74
Axes									
Sand bags		100	100	2100	2300				2300
WEAPONS									
Pistols	2	1	1	29	33				33
Rifles	8	134	134		276		14	14	290
Short Rifles	17	17	17	22	73				73
Sabers	2	7	7	5	21	2	2	4	25
Bayonets	11	18	18	6	53	11	3	14	67
Hand grenades		120	120	30	270		100	100	370
First Aid Kit		1	1	1	3		1	1	4
Medicine Chest	1				1				1
Stretchers		6	6	1	13				13
Farrier's kit	1			1	2				2

Combat Unit: General Staff, 1st Company of Riflemen, 2nd Company of Riflemen, Machine Guns, Total.
Depot: Administrative General Staff, Depot Company, Total.

Source: DO #199, Tomo III, 5 September 1920, 888.

Morocco and were subsequently unable to adapt to the routines of civilian life. Others were escaping poverty, hunger, the law, or women. Still others were consumed with the possibility of gaining glory in Africa, of being adventurers, or of engaging in the noble effort of serving their country. Some took advantage of the opportunity to enlist under an assumed name, something Millán Astray liked about the French Foreign Legion, which allowed a recruit to leave his past behind and be reborn within the Legion. Regardless of social class or nationality, good or bad, anarchist or Communist, the enlistees would join forces in an elite fighting unit that required only total obedience and sacrifice while promising the certainty of slaying or being slain for Spain.[22]

In *The Hotter Winds*, Patrick Turnbull concisely portrays the types of men who joined the Legion:

The Spanish foreign legion is comprised...of men who, for various reasons, have no future, nothing to live for, but who wish to take a savage revenge on life before dying. There is something akin to the Japanese in their indifference to death, though the Spanish legionnaires face it with a cold, individual contempt, as though death were something to be spat on disdainfully in its acceptance rather than the hysterical emotion born of overcharged nationalism.[23]

Death, and the possibility of dying in battle, has always been a tenet of the Legion, as evident in their motto (created by Millán Astray), *Viva la Muerte!* (Long live death!); their battle cry, *Legionarios, a luchar; legionarios, a morir!* (Legionaries, to fight; Legionaries, to die!); and their song, "El Novio de la Muerte" (The Betrothed of Death). It was expected that each Legionary would become betrothed to death and would wed her by dying a "glorious" death.[24]

When the concept for a foreign legion was being discussed in the halls of the General Staff, many of the staff officers believed that foreigners would constitute a large portion of the Legion, as in the French Foreign Legion, but contingency plans were prepared in the event that few foreigners chose to enlist. This can be seen in the General Staff's "Proyecto de creación de una legión extranjera en África, 1919."[25]

The majority of recruits who disembarked in Ceuta were, in fact, Spaniards. But there were some foreigners, including three Chinese, a Japanese, a Russian prince, a German, an Austrian, an Italian, two Frenchmen, four Portuguese, a Maltese, a Belgian (René), and an African American (William Brown) from New York. Lieutenant Olavide, whom Millán Astray called *El Organizador* (The Organizer), took a personal interest in the recruitment of foreigners to give the Legion, or as it was then known, *Tercio de Extranjeros* justification for its name. Unfortunately, these foreigners could not speak Spanish, which caused many problems between them and their officers.[26] Life in the Legion would be extremely hard, and Millán Astray held nothing back from the neophytes. "He did not flatter the recruits, but spoke to groups of newcomers about their wretched and vicious lives. Further, he offered them a path of redemption through duty. He suggested that his volunteers might purge themselves of past errors through their new vocation of military service and suffering."[27]

The commander in chief of the Legion welcomed the new recruits with the following words:

The Legion greets you with joy. You are here to form part of an honourable corps soon to become the foremost of our glorious Infantry. The life which awaits you will be hard and terrible. You may starve. You will certainly suffer the torments of thirst. A pitiless penetrating rain will beat down on you. In summer a fiery sun will burn you to the verge of madness. You will dig trenches, construct camps to the point of exhaustion never knowing when you may expect your next meal. You will receive wounds. Your bones will be broken. But your final destiny is to die that clean death which only the field of battle can offer. The Legion takes you to its heart. Welcome! *Caballeros Legionarios* attention! . . . Fall out![28]

From the previous statement, one can see Millán Astray's fervent belief that the recruits would be allowed to purge themselves of all previous wrongdoing through personal hardships. The Legion would absolve these men and give them redemption through sacrifice or possible death in battle. By dying for Spain, those who had spent their lives taking from society would be able to repay their debt with their lives.

Before being finally accepted into the Legion, each man was personally interviewed by Millán Astray whereby he reiterated the hardships he would encounter in the Legion. In a memorable meeting with one recruit, Millán Astray asked him:

"Do you know why you have come?"
The interrogee remains mute; not knowing what response he should give his superior.
"You have come to die! Yes, to die! Because from the moment you crossed the Straits [of Gibraltar] you no longer have a mother, a sweetheart, nor a family; from this day onwards the Legion will be all of these to you. Duty shall come before all else, now that you have accepted the honor of serving Spain and the Legion. You still have time to ponder if your spirit is prepared to make that sacrifice. After thinking it over, you can inform the adjutant captain [Joaqín Ortiz de Zárate] of your final decision."[29]

Those recruits not up to the task of being a Legionary were given an opportunity to return to the peninsula by simply informing the examining physician, "*Tengo dolor de garganta*" (I have a sore throat). The examining doctors themselves rejected many prospective recruits for being chronically ill or poor physical specimens.[30]

Legion officers allowed the Legionaries to select "interim corporals" ("each with the same authority as the lieutenant colonel") from among their ranks to lead them. Due to the unprecedented number of recruits, uniforms had to be borrowed from other army units (i.e., infantry, cavalry, and artillery) stationed in Ceuta. Thus, the first uniform worn by the Legion was the same as that worn by regular line units, with the exception that the national colors, red and gold horizontal stripes, were worn on the collars of their tunics. Subsequently, the

Legionaries would be issued their own particular uniforms to distinguish them from the regular army.[31]

All did not go smoothly in the first days of setting up the Legion. A false rumor that enlistment bonuses would not be paid almost led to a mutiny, which was averted when Millán Astray told Major Vara del Rey to take the 150,000 *pesetas* (30,000 *duros*) available from the cash box to the patio of the King's Barracks so that the men could see that the money was available. Those in the greatest financial need were allowed to take five or ten *duros* as an advance payment.[32]

TRAINING

The newly accepted recruits were transferred from the King's Barracks in the center of Ceuta to Position A (today known as the García Aldave Barracks), an encampment located on a hilltop three kilometers from Ceuta. There the Depot Company received its primary military instruction under the command of Major Francisco Franco Bahamonde.[33] It became the responsibility of Franco to turn these adventurers and mercenaries into an elite fighting force. The best and brightest junior officers of the army volunteered to become a part of this nascent organization, and Millán Astray personally selected those he perceived to be up to the task.[34]

At Position A, the first *Bandera* was formed on 7 October 1920 with Major Franco as its commander. His line officers included Captain Pablo Arredondo Acuña, 1st Rifle Company; Captain Luis Valcázar Crespo, 2nd Rifle Company; and Captain Eduardo Cobos Gómez, 3rd Machine Gun Company. For its battle flag, Franco selected the royal standard of the House of Burgundy, which depicts two wild boars biting an oak bough, and chose its black field.[35]

On 16 October, the Ist *Bandera* relocated from Position A to Dar Riffien, "which shall become the cradle, hearth and home of the Legion; the prime barracks."[36] It was four miles from Ceuta to Dar Riffien, and there the Legion established its depot and basic training camp. Under Franco's personal direction and supervision, within a few years, Dar Riffien possessed the finest living quarters, workshops, nurseries, and recreational facilities in the Spanish army. Fresh water was piped in from a nearby mountain stream. The Legion's own farm provided the men with fresh meat, vegetables, and fruit, thus enabling them to supplement their scant army rations.[37]

As the recruits continued to arrive in Ceuta, the IInd and IIIrd *Banderas* were forming at Position A. The command structure of the IInd *Bandera*, formed on 22 October, was as follows: Major Fernando Cirujeda Galloso, who was promptly replaced by Major Carlos Rodríguez Fontanés as the IInd *Banderas* commanding officer; Captain Alfonso Beorlegui Canet, 4th Rifle Company, who was soon to be replaced by Captain Pompilio Martínez Zaldívar; Captain Antonio Alcubilla Pérez, 5th Rifle Company; and Captain Alvaro Sueiro Villariño, 6th Machine Gun Company. Its battle flag represented the double-headed, black imperial eagle of Charles V on a red field. The IIIrd *Bandera*, formed on 23

October, was organized as follows: Major José Candeira Sestelo, the IIIrd *Bandera*'s commanding officer; Captain Miguel Pérez García, 7th Rifle Company; Captain Joaquín Ortiz de Zárate, 8th Rifle Company; and Captain Camilo Alonso Vega, 9th Machine Gun Company. Its battle flag, chosen by the IIIrd *Banderas* commander, featured a rampant tiger on a blue field. The IIIrd *Banderas* battle flag would break the brief tradition of the first two battle flags, which had honored the *Tercios* of the XVI and XVII centuries.[38]

At the same time the Ist *Bandera* was undergoing its training at Dar Riffien, the regular army with the *Regulares* was marching toward Xauen (el Raisuni's headquarters) with forty Legionaries serving as muleteers. On 14 October, the city was captured without bloodshed. This was the first time that members of the newly founded *Tercio de Extranjeros* participated in a military operation.[39]

The Legionaries underwent a rigorous training regiment that included marksmanship, military drill, and construction of elementary fortifications, all in an effort to instill an esprit de corps that was lacking in the regular army.[40] Marching songs were very popular in the Legion, as they were in the French Foreign Legion. Because of the number of foreigners who had joined the Legion from European countries, the most popular songs were "La Madelón" and its Legion version "La Madelón Legionaria," "Deutschland über Alles," and "Tipperary," all popular marching songs of the Great War. These songs united the men of the Legion no matter what their nationality and made the long marches pass more quickly. Millán Astray recognized the importance of singing on morale and wanted the Legion to have its own songs. He thus commissioned Francisco Cales to write the music and Antonio Soler to provide the words for the first hymn of the Legion, "Tercios Heroicos." This song, however, was eventually overshadowed by others that became more popular, such as "Canción del Legionario" (Official Hymn of the Legion) and "El Novio de la Muerte."[41]

On 21 October, the three *Banderas* of the Legion swore fidelity to the national flag in the Campo del Tarajal (Ceuta) before the Regiment of Ceuta *N⁰*60. However, Franco was not content with swearing fidelity to a flag that was not the Legion's: "It is not our own proper Flag, which we still have to win!"[42] The Legion would get its own flag after the end of the Rif Rebellion in 1927.

UNIFORMS AND WEAPONS OF THE LEGION

The new uniforms and field gear for the Legion arrived on 2 November. The field gear chosen for the Legion was the "Mills" type (made of woven fabric), which had been purchased from the British in Gibraltar. It was not the first time that the Spanish army had purchased military kit gear from the British, having bought sun helmets for the 1909 campaign around Melilla.[43] Distinctive uniforms would differentiate the Legion from the other units of the Spanish army:

The Legion's distinctive sidecap with red tassel (*chapiri*), the soft, broad-brimmed canvas hat—*chambergo*—popularized by Franco and perfect for the relentless sun of the protectorate, the pale greenish shirt always worn open at the neck (the original shirts had no buttons) and with the collar turned over the tunic, the cloak with hood (*capotes-mantas*), sandals (dropped after encountering the mud of Zoco el Arbaa), leather, and white canvas/rope boots (*alpargatas*) like those issued to the *Regulares*, the "Mills" field gear (this was used exclusively by the Legion), and white gauntlets for the officers.[44]

The Legion was armed with the same weapons as the regular infantry; they included the Spanish Mauser Model 1893 rifle, the Mauser Model 1916 short rifle (*mosquetón*), the Hotchkiss Model 1914 heavy machine gun, and the Hotchkiss Model 1922 (later the Model 1925) light machine gun. All the aforementioned weapons chambered 7 mm (7 x 57) ammunition. Other weapons included the Lafitte Model 1925 60 mm mortar, the Model 1905 lance used by the cavalry; and the Lafitte Model 1921 hand grenade. Legionaries had a choice of bayonets, one of their favorite weapons, either the Model 1893 ("Simson") or the longer Model 1913 sword-style. Officers, NCOs, and machine-gunners carried the Astra Model 1921 (the commercial Mod. 400) pistol, a 9 mm Largo (9 x 23) weapon that had replaced the unreliable Campo-Giro.[45]

Under the leadership of its commander, Major Francisco Franco and accompanied by Millán Astray, the Ist *Bandera* of the Legion departed for Uad Lau on 2 November. They spent the night in the Rincón del Medik. This became the first march undertaken by this new corps. While the Ist *Bandera* was on the move, the IInd and IIIrd *Banderas* were transferred to Dar Riffien from Position A, where they continued their training. The highlight of the march was when the Legion paraded before the High Commissioner, General Dámaso Berenguer Fusté, with its signature quick-step march through Tetuán, the capital of the Spanish Protectorate of Morocco. At 1600 hours on the 6th, they arrived at Uad Lau, located at the mouth of the Lau River. They proceeded to set up their encampment and carry out their mission to protect the flank of other units which were on the offensive. It was disappointing for the Legion since they wanted to serve in the vanguard like the *Regulares*.[46] For the rest of the year, the Ist *Bandera* remained at Uad Lau receiving instruction in practical military doctrine as well as theoretic instruction.[47]

On 29 December, the IInd *Bandera* left Dar Riffien by train for Tetuán, their ultimate destination Zoco el Arbaa de Beni Hassan, which is on the road between Tetuán and Xauen (see Map 2). Their mission was to guarantee safe passage and provide security in the area, as hostilities were expected. Again, this defensive assignment was not welcomed by the officers and men, who were anxious to engage the enemy in close combat. The IInd was quickly followed by the IIIrd *Bandera*, which left by train on 31 December for Tetuán. From Tetuán, the troops marched the remaining distance to their final destination, Ben Karrich. The IIIrd *Bandera* was ordered to protect the route between Tetuán and Xauen from a position behind the village of Zoco el Arbaa.[48]

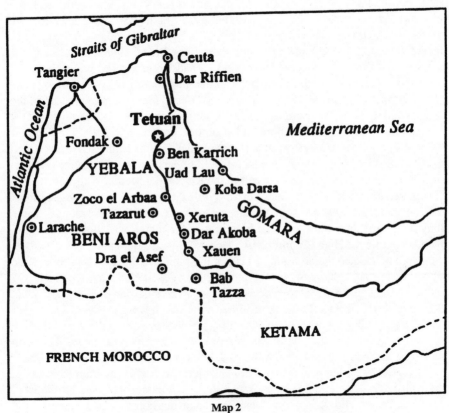

Map 2
The Western Zone; The Yebala & Gomara, 1920-1921

SUMMARY

The year 1920 saw the Legion grow from the first germ of an idea promulgated by the king in January, through the various changes that would eventually culminate in the effective formation of the Legion eight months later. With the enthusiasm and drive of Lieutenant Colonel José Millán Astray y Terreros, the Legion quickly grew as recruits from Spain and foreign lands flocked to its standard. The Legion was given its own uniform and carried battle flags that paid homage to the great captains of the victorious *Tercios* of the past. Legionaries received higher wages and an enlistment bonus, were armed with the best available weapons, ate better food than offered in the regular army, and were led by the most experienced officers in the Spanish infantry. All of this was done to instill in the Legionary the idea that he was superior to those in the regular army. and in Moroccan tribes. Furthermore, he was expected to perform the most hazardous of duties, obey all orders, and die bravely for the glory of Spain. Nonetheless, not all segments of the Spanish military were in favor of the Legion's creation. General Silvestre was adamantly opposed to the Legion on the grounds that pacification of the protectorate should be carried out with Spanish conscripts. Career officers, particularly those stationed in the peninsula, expected promotion through seniority and thus feared the formation of an elite unit within the army led by *africanistas* who would receive promotions through battlefield heroics. In addition, because of giving higher pay and enlistment bonuses rather than using draftees, the Legion would be expensive to fund. But as Millán Astray stated in his proposal to create the Legion, each Legionary would take the place of two conscripts. One Spaniard would be spared, his place in the ranks filled by a volunteer, Spaniard or foreigner, willing to fight and die for Spain.

Nevertheless, by the end of 1920, the Legion was made up of three *Banderas* performing convoy and protection duties in the area around Tetuán. However, in a short time they would become the spearhead of the Spanish army in the protectorate. Not yet "blooded" in combat, the Legion would, in the following year, be in the vanguard of attacks in the Yebala and have the distinction of saving Melilla.

NOTES

1. General Carlos De Silva, *General Millán Astray (El Legionario)* (Barcelona: Editorial AHR, 1956), 127.

2. John Scurr, *The Spanish Foreign Legion*, Osprey Men-at-Arms Series, no. 161 (London: Osprey Publishing, 1985), 4. While the term *"Tercio de Extranjeros"* was used for the newly created army unit in homage to the *Tercios* of the 16th and 17th centuries, it was called "La Legión" by Millán Astray and all those who served within its ranks, and it continues to be so called to the present day. See José Millán Astray, *La Legión* (Madrid: V. H. Sanz Calleja, 1923), 3. In "(LA LEGIÓN! 75 años de trayectoria esforzada y heroica," *Defensa: Revista internacional de ejércitos, armamento y tecnología* 18, no. 204 (april 1995), 50, Rafael García Serrano noted that when Millán Astray was asked about the *Tercio*, he would quickly cut them off by stating: "Supongo que hablas de la Legión. Yo no sé

nada del Tercio" (I suppose you are speaking about the Legion. I know nothing of the Tercio). José María Bueno Carrera, *La Legión: 75 años de uniformes legionarios* (Málaga: Gráficas Urania, 1994), 9, wrote that on 2 May 1937, the name *"La Legión"* (The Legion) was officially accepted. The word *Bandera* in Spanish signifies a flag, banner, or standard, as well as, in the case of the Legion, a battalion-size unit. A Legionary's primary loyalty, within the Legion, is always to his *Bandera*.

3. Payne, 156. It is interesting to note that the first mention of a foreign legion in Spanish history, besides the famous *Tercios de Flandes e Italia* of the 16th and 17th centuries, occurred when the marquis José Esteban Maccarrani proposed to organize a regiment of foreigners in Spain in the year 1819 (coincidentally 100 years before the proposal for the present-day Legion), but his proposal was rejected by King Ferdinand VII. *Archivo General Militar* (henceforth *AGM*), Legajo (File) #246, SECCIÓN #2, DIVISIÓN #10. Millán Astray was so certain of his mission to create a Legion that when a good friend asked him if he realized what failure would mean to his career and prestige, he coolly responded, "If I fail, I will shoot myself." De Silva, 110.

4. *AGM*, Legajo #246, SECCIÓN #2, DIVISIÓN #10. Ministerio de la Guerra #1518 Subsecretaria. See De Silva, 110-112, for details of Millán Astray's visit with General Tovar, wherein he expresses the purpose for the Legion, and the opinion of the High Commissioner for Morocco, Dámaso Berenguer, who was fervently in favor of replacing conscripts with volunteers. See also, Paul Preston, *Franco: A Biography* (New York: Basic Books, 1994), 26.

5. Subinspección de la Legión, ed., *La Legión española: Cincuenta años de historia, 1920-1936* (Madrid: Leganes, 1975), 18. The plans prepared by the General Staff (Estado Mayor Central del Ejército) and dated October 1919 are entitled: (1) Proyecto de creación de una legión extranjera en África (Plans for the creation of a foreign legion in Africa); and (2) Consideraciones generales acerca de las plantillas que se proponen (General considerations concerning the staff organization being proposed). The plans, with fifty-five articles, contain such headings as "generalities," "organization," "recruitment," "payment," and "various concepts" and are located in the *AGM*, Legajo #246, SECCIÓN #2, DIVISIÓN #10. Lieutenant Colonel Timon Calvo Escriva, Major José Domenech Vidal, and Captain Fidel De La Cuerda Fernández made up the General Staff commission assigned to study the possibility of creating a legion of foreigners. See De Silva, 111, and page 1 of *Resumen histórico de la Legión, Diario de operaciones de la Legión* (Serrallo de la Legión, Plana Mayor del Tercio, Archivo General, Ceuta), henceforth known as the *DOL*.

6. *AGM,* Legajo #M-3204, SECCIÓN #1, DIVISIÓN #1. This is Millán Astray's personnel file and lists his activities for the year 1919. Moreover, in the same file, a three-page handwritten letter dated 1 December 1919 and signed by General Antonio Vallejo Vila details Millán Astray's visit to the Tetuán sector in September. For more on Millán Astray's trip to Algeria, see De Silva, 114-119. Millán Astray, 2. For General Dámaso Berenguer's approval for creating the Legion and having Millán Astray as its head, see n. 39 in Estado Mayor Central del Ejército, *Historia de las Campañas de Marruecos*, vol. III, (Madrid: Servicio Histórico Militar, Imprenta Ideal, 1981), 108. The original can be found in Lieutenant General Dámaso Berenguer, *Campañas en el Rif y Yebala, 1919-1920: Notas y documentos de mi diario de operaciones*, vol. II (Madrid: 1925 and 1948). *DOL*, Resumen Histórico de la Legión, 1.

7. Subinspección de la Legión, ed., 19. According to Patrick Turnbull in "Spanish Foreign Legion," *War Monthly*, no. 30 (September 1976): 16, Millán Astray based his proposed Legion on the following eight principles:

(1) The Legion will represent the highest peak of the virtues of our glorious Infantry, of our invincible Army.

(2) The Legion will serve as the base of a Colonial Army.

(3) The Legion will save many Spanish lives, because the *legionarios* will be prepared to die for all Spaniards.

(4) The Legion will be constituted by volunteers of all countries, who will sign individual engagements under either their real or assumed names, thereby absolving the Spanish State of all responsibility concerning them.

(5) The spirit of rivalry created by recruits of various nationalities will enhance the spirit of the Legion.

(6) *Legionarios* signing on for four or five years, then re-engaging will become true professional soldiers tempered by the fire of combat.

(7) The mother unit will afford a haven for vagabonds, delinquents and criminals of whom the mainland has been rid.

(8) To the homeless, the wretched, those craving military glory, the hungry, the Legion will give bread, asylum, a family, a country and a Standard for which to die.

8. De Silva, 119-120. Preston, 26-27, noted that the Valdemoro meeting took place on 28 September 1918 and that "after a brief hesitation," Franco accepted Millán Astray's offer in June 1920. Brian Crozier, *Franco: A Biographical History* (London: Eyre & Spottiswoode, 1967), 51-52; J.W.D. Trythall, *Franco: A Biography* (London: Rupert Hart-Davis, 1970), 34; and George Hills, *Franco: The Man and His Nation* (New York: MacMillan Company, 1967), 106. On 144, n. 31, Franco Salgado, in a most candid and revealing interview with the author, disclosed that "Franco agreed to Millán Astray's offer of second-in-command of the Legion in the belief that he would be free to return home once the Legion was organized; but there it was, the Legion had to go into action straightaway, before its training was completed; then he had to return again at the king's command; and then Primo de Rivera wanted him there." Luis De Galinsoga, *Centinela de occidente*, with the collaboration of Lieutenant General Franco Salgado (Barcelona: Editorial AHR, 1956), 37. Ricardo De La Cierva, *Franco* (Barcelona: Editorial Planeta, 1986), 57. Woolman, *Rebels in the Rif*, 68-69. See the prologue by Millán Astray to Francisco Franco's own *Marruecos: Diario de una Bandera* (Madrid: Privately printed, 1922), where he wrote: "Franco possesses all the characteristics that a good military man should have, which are: valor, intelligence, martial spirit, enthusiasm, love of work, spirit of sacrifice and virtuous living." Franco was also known as *El comandantín* (The little major). When it came to their personal lives, Millán Astray and Franco could not be any more different. While the former never denied himself carnal pleasures, the latter abstained from smoking, drinking, and the company of wanton women.

9. *AGM*, Legajo #M-3204, SECCIÓN #1, DIVISIÓN #1.

10. *Servicio Histórico Militar* (henceforth *SHM*), DO #22, (29-I-1920), Tomo (Vol.) I, Año de 1920, Primer Trimestre (Madrid: Talleres del Deposito de la Guerra, 1920), 293, L 128. SHM, Colección Legislative del EjércitoC1920CMinisterio de la Guerra #49 (Legislative Collection of the Army [henceforth CL]) #35, (28-I-1920), (Madrid: Talleres del Depósito de la Guerra, 1920), 60. The statement from the CL read as follows:

The advantage of utilizing all the resources that can help in reducing the recruitment quotas in our zone of the Protectorate in Morocco, impels the Minister [of War] who endorses the advice of the General Staff in regards to the creation of a *Tercio de extranjeros*, to be made up of men from all countries, who voluntarily want to enlist in order to render military service, *as much in the Peninsula as in the different Commands of that territory* [my emphasis]. Based upon these considerations, the Minister, in agreement with the Council of Ministers, has the honor to submit for the approval of H. M. the following plan of decree. Madrid twenty-eighth of January of nineteen twenty. Signed—José Villalba.

Hills, 112, called the first proposal for the creation of the Legion an "Order-in-Council" and subsequent additions or amendments to the original charter "Warrants."

11. *AGM*, Legajo #M-3204, SECCIÓN #1, DIVISIÓN #1; and De Silva, 122.

12. R. Geoffrey Jensen, "José Millán-Astray and the Nationalist 'Crusade' in Spain," *Journal of Contemporary History* 27, no. 3 (July 1992): 432-441, covers Millán Astray's personal beliefs, his incorporation of the Code of Bushido into the Legion, and Catholicism.

13. Preston, 27. This period of the Legion's history is covered in Javier Martí, *La Legión extranjera y El Tercio* (Ceuta: Privately printed, 1997).

14. Carolyn P. Boyd, *Praetorian Politics in Liberal Spain*, (Chapel Hill, NC: University of North Carolina, 1979), 172, observed that the *Juntas de Defensa,* particularly junior officers stationed on the peninsula, were opposed to the creation of the Legion because they were "suspicious of elite units" and that General Silvestre "continued to believe, against all the evidence, that the war ought to be fought with Spanish conscripts led by regular officers." His opposition to the whole idea of a foreign legion was so strong that while the Legion was proving itself a success in the Yebala, "Silvestre refused to authorize the formation of comparable units" in the Rif sector. For more on the *Juntas de Defensa,* see Payne, 123-151. According to Julio Busquets, 99-100, Gabriel Cardona looked at the impact of *méritos de guerra* on promotions in the infantry branch for the class of 1910. Because of the Moroccan War (1909-1927), twenty years after they left the Academy of Toledo, *africanistas* like Franco (jumped 2,438 places) and Yagüe (jumped 1,595 places) enjoyed meteoric promotions, whereas classmates who remained in Spain languished in the lower ranks.

15. *SHM*, DO #195, Tomo III (1-IX-1920), 837. *SHM*, CL #416 (31-VIII-1920), 700. *"Disponiendo se organice el Tercio de Extranjeros"* (Disposing for the organization of the *Tercio de Extrajeros*). It contains three articles:

(1) We will proceed, of course, with the organization of the aforementioned unit, establishing through the Ministry of War the troops, salaries and regulations by which it will govern itself.
(2) All of the expenditures which the above-mentioned Tercio should incur shall be defrayed by account of chapter 1, article 2, of Section 13 of the prevailing Budget, with the exception of the rations of bread and fodder and billeting, which will be by chapter 5, article 1; hospitalities, by chapter 5, article 4; transport from the frontier or points of enlistment to their destinations, by chapter 5, article 3, and the renting of locations, if it were necessary, by chapter 5, article 5, of the same Section.
(3) The increase in spending which the creation of the aforementioned unit shall produce will be compensated by the savings which will be obtained, as a consequence of not having to cover the casualties that will occur in the mainland troops in Africa during the present exercise, by repatriation of units, and, in the meantime, by the discharging of individuals from their third year of service in the above-mentioned troops, in the proportion of two of these for each soldier enlisted in the Tercio.

Dated 31 August 1920 and signed: ALFONSO.—and the Minister of War, Luis Marichalar y Monreal. De La Cierva, 58.

16. *AGM*, Legajo #M-3204, SECCIÓN #1, DIVISIÓN #1; and Tercio Duque de Alba, 2° de la Legión, *LXXIII Aniversario, 1920-1993* (Ceuta: Privately printed, 1993), 2. Jensen, 428-429, noted that the military press in Spain had a varied response to the formation of the Legion depending on a paper's targeted readership. *Ejército y Armada*, aimed at the NCOs in the army, responded favorably, whereas *La Correspondencia Militar*, geared toward regular officers, had few words to say about the new unit. It was the other military daily, *El Ejército Español*, also aimed at regular officers, that had the most say on the subject, especially when it was announced that Millán Astray would command it. His reputation for bravery, organization, and energy was well recognized within the army and would make the Legion a success.

17. Tercio Duque de Alba, 2° de la Legión, 2. This source claims that originally the Legion had only one depot company. *SHM*, DO #199, Tomo III, 883-890 (5-IX-1920); and *SHM*, CL #423, 706 (4-IX-1920). See Appendix A for the forty-six articles; the salient points of the document are to be found in what Fernando Cano Velasco, 141, called the Magna Carta of the Legion. *SHM*, Legajo #54, Rollo 16, *Colección de Historiales* (microfilm), "Organización inicial—Características y plantillas," 16. Bueno Carrera, *La Legión*, 9. Scurr, 5-6. Both this source and Bueno state that the Legion had four depot companies, at least by 31 October. Crozier, 54, noted that "strictly, a *Bandera* was smaller than a battalion." Galey, 51, stated that each *Bandera* also included "a platoon of sappers, and a transport and supply unit." With its own administration, command, depot, and instruction capabilities, as well as uniforms and equipment, the Legion would become, in the words of Galey, "an army within an army." He went on to say, "It [the Legion] could be used separately or in conjunction with other troops when the occasion demanded." Ibid., 49. Although the Legion was officially created on 4 September, Legionaries celebrate the anniversary of the founding of the Legion on 20 September, the date on which the first Legionary joined its ranks.

As the Legion grew and expanded, minor adjustments were made to the ROC of 4 September (DO #199) that created the Legion. In an ROC dated 16 October (DO #234 of 17 October), which pertains to the progressive organization of the Legion, regulation #40 from DO #199, eight articles were added to its precursor. However, the aforementioned adjustment (article #2 [dealing with livestock] from DO #234) is further amended by an ROC dated 19 October. Finally, the ROC of 10 November deals with underage Spanish volunteers by amending regulation #29 of DO #199. These changes were made as situations unforeseen in the original plans arose. As time went on, new regulations would be added and those already on the books would be modified. See *AGM*, Legajo #246, DO #234 (17-X-1920), 179-182; *SHM*, CL #477 (ROC 16-X-1920), 787 (eight articles); *SHM*, CL #479 (ROC 19-X-1920), 795 (modification to #2 of the above-cited entry); and *SHM*, CL #510, DO #256 (ROC 10-XI-1920), 849 (regards the validity of the enlistment agreement [bounty] of underage Spanish volunteers in the Legion). The final administrative adjustment for the year to the plan that created the Legion (DO #199) was the ROC of 20 December, which broadened the organizational plan of the Legion to include a chaplain first class to come from the Ecclesiastic Corps of the army. The chaplain chosen to tend to the spiritual needs of the Legion was Alejo Fernández Ocaranza. See *SHM*, CL #573 (ROC 20-XII-1920), 935; and de Arce, 53.

18. Scurr, 4.

19. Tercio Duque de Alba, 2° de la Legión, 2. Arguably, the first man to join the Legion was Marcelo Villarreal Enitau, a thirty-year-old Ceutian who would subsequently

be killed in the occupation of Monte Malmusi following the Alhucemas Bay landings of 1925, having reached the rank of *Suboficial*, the present-day equivalent of a sergeant major (*Brigada*). He achieved this rank through battlefield promotions (*meritos de guerra*). According to *La Legión* (a small booklet put out by the Legion), "The first Legionary to join was Anibal Calero Pérez who signed-up on 25 September 1920 [five days after the Ceutian] in the recruiting center of Albacete for a period of five years. He was discharged on 6 September 1922 for having been a minor at the time of his enlistment; however, he rejoined for three years on 1 February 1926," 3. *DOL, Negociado de campaña: Diario de operaciones de la Legión desde su Organización en el mes de septiembre del Ano [sic] hasta el dia de la fecha* (1927), Año 1920, 1 October 1920, 1. Cano Velasco, ed., 142. Having Major Vara del Rey in the headquarters of the Legion would lead to future animosity between him and prospective recruits from Cuba, and especially those from the United States; see Rafael Fermoselle, *The Evolution of the Cuban Military, 1492-1986* (Miami: Ediciones Universales, 1987), 134. Upon joining the Legion, Pablo Arredondo Acuña had already been awarded Spain's highest medal for valor (*La Cruz Laureada Individual de la Real y Militar Orden de San Fernando*), one he would go on to receive a second time during the Rif Rebellion, becoming the only Legionary to achieve this great honor.

20. José Llacuna and José María Polls, *Novios de la Muerte: Historia de la Legión* (n.p.: 1987), 11-12. Azpeitua, 131, gives the per diem payment of a Legionary of 5 *pesetas*, whereas the aforementioned source, as well as Scurr, 5, puts it at a total of 4.10. Boyd, 172, noted that the reason the Legion was able to pay so well was because for every new Legionary who enlisted, two third-year regular army conscripts were discharged. Carlos Mico y España, *Los caballeros de la Legión (El libro del Tercio de Extranjeros)*, with a prologue by Tomás Borras and with various letters from Lieutenant Colonel José Millán Astray, first commander of the *Tercio de Extranjeros* (Madrid: Ucesores De Rivadeneyra, 1922), 19, shows the recruitment poster, which read as follows:

Enlist in the Legion of Foreigners! Spaniards and foreigners: Those who are fond of the Army and of its glories, those who enjoy life in the field, enlist! The Tercio de Extranjeros is an Infantry Corps which will have its own banner, and its soldiers shall be sheltered by it. It is an honorable Corps; in battles it will go in the place of honor; the uniform is attractive; the wages, sufficient; the food, healthy and abundant. Those who become good soldiers, disciplined and valiant, can make the profession of Arms an honorable career.

Concerning the enlistment bonuses for recruits of the Legion, see *SHM*, DO #199 (5-IX-20), Tomo III, Tercer Trimestre, L130, 889, Chart C (Enlistment Bonuses) in Appendix G. Bueno's book on the uniforms of the Legion contains a reproduction of the first recruiting poster on page 8. Hills, 112, has an explanation on the denomination of the Legion/*Tercio* and its historical antecedents.

21. Llacuna and Polls, 12. According to this source the word from the King's Barracks in Ceuta was "*¡Qué Vengan!*" De La Cierva, *Franco*, 59, recorded that Millán Astray's exact word was "*Mandádmelos*," which literally translates to "Send them to me." Scurr, 5. Fernando de Valdesoto, *Francisco Franco* (Madrid: Afrodisio Aguado, 1943), 23.

22. Luis Bolín, *Spain: The Vital Years*, with a foreword by Sir Arthur Bryant C.B.E. (Philadelphia and New York: J.B. Lippincott, 1967), 85-89. Scurr, 5. Barea, 170-172, described the tragic and personal story of his friend Sanchiz, who joined the Legion hoping to be killed. Ironically, he was one of the very few original members of the Ist *Bandera* to have survived (without a scratch!) the reconquest of the Melillan command after

the Annual debacle. Preston, 27; Llacuna and Polls, 13; Cano Velasco, ed., 142; Crozier, 53; Galey, 53; and Subinspección de la Legion, ed., 21. See Franco, 19, for the disadvantage to having signed up under an assumed name. When it was time to collect their per diem payment of 5 *pesetas*, many of the Legionaries had forgotten what name they had given at the time of enlistment and had to look inside their pockets for the piece of paper on which they had written their new names. According to Carlos de Arce, *Historia de la Legión española* (Barcelona: Editorial Mitre, 1984), 24, some of the more colorful *noms de guerre* included Pedro Calderón de la Barca (Spanish dramatist of the 1600s), Rodrigo Díaz de Vivar (El Cid Campeador), and Bienvenido Tortola del Campo. However, Captain Francisco Sacristán Romero, formerly of the Legion (Vth *Bandera*/2nd *Tercio*), provided the author with an eight-page document from the archives of the Legion (2nd *Tercio*, Serrallo de la Legión-Ceuta)) entitled "*la primera lista de revista (octubre de 1920)*," which lists the names of more than 500 Legionaries who enlisted in the very beginning and showing typical Spanish names.

One man who took choosing a pseudonym a bit too far was a syndicalist who wanted to call himself José Millán Astray. The sergeant responded by saying to him: "If you spend four years fighting and if you are promoted and decorated and if they have not killed you, which is most probable, maybe then you might resemble the left boot of the one who goes by the name that you have chosen to give yourself. The man selected the name Gómez, with neither a first nor a last name." Ricardo De La Cierva, *Franco: Un siglo de España* (Madrid: Editora Nacional, 1973), 162.

According to Richard Sablotny in *Legionnaire in Morocco* (Los Angeles: Wetzel Publishing Co., 1940), 43; "The Foreign Legion scorns no one. No one is asked from where they came nor what they have done before arriving in Africa." The author also explained (on page 26) that since a Legionary was given the opportunity to enlist under any name he chose, fingerprints became very important in record keeping.

23. Patrick Turnbull, *The Hotter Winds* (London: Hutchinson, 1960), 27. The author goes on to describe an encounter with ex-Legionary Captain Hernández in Tetuán several years after the end of the Rif Rebellion, who told him, "You don't join the *Tercio* to live, to retire. You join it to die."

24. Payne, 156-157; Turnbull, 16; and Woolman, *Rebels in the Rif*, 68. Galey, 55, observed the following concerning death and the Legion: "In the Spanish Legion it [death] was an obsession. The legionnaire's first death occurred when he left behind his past life in order to join the organization. His second death came on the battlefield when the Legionary achieved the apogee of his heroic transfiguration. Death was revered, coveted, beloved."

25. *AGM*, Legajo #246, SECCIÓN #2, DIVISIÓN #10, 4.

26. Turnbull, 16. Galey, 51, has more on the colorful pasts and nationalities of other volunteers. When the question of what percentage of foreigners made up the Spanish Foreign Legion, one can turn to Turnbull in the aforementioned source (page 17), where he stated "Only nine per cent of the *Novios de la Muerte* were of 'foreign' extraction." His figure is very close to that of Scurr who wrote on page 4 that "over the years the Spanish composition of the unit remained fairly consistently at 90 per cent" and Philip K. Scaramanga, "The Spanish Legion[:] professional core of Spain's rapid deployment force?," *International Defense Review* (March 1988): 274, who wrote, "... foreigners, ... have never accounted for more than 7 or 8% of the total strength." In his book, Millán Astray gives the figure of "1/5th" of the recruits being foreigners with the majority coming from Western Europe and thereafter (especially after Annual) from Cuba, 97. This estimate of 20 percent is a bit high. However, his figure is not far off the mark from Kenneth W. Estes, "New

brigade structure cements future of Spanish Legion," *International Defense Review* (May 1995): 68, who wrote, "Despite its heritage as a foreign legion, the Spanish Legion only recruited 17.5% of its ranks from foreigners in its first decade of existence, over half of these hailing from Portugal, Germany, and Cuba." On page 69, he elaborated on his aforementioned information by saying, "During the period 20 September 1920 to 31 August 1930, the legion recruited 24,521 men to its ranks, of whom 4,304 were foreigners from 48 countries. Contributors of over 100 volunteers each were: Portugal (1,086), Germany (912), Cuba (546), France (365), Italy (194), and Argentina (140)." Llacuna and Polls, 14; and Payne, 156. The information on the 800 Germans (see Sablotny entry below) who joined the Legion in 1923 also appears in this source on 217. Woolman, *Rebels in the Rif*, 68; Franco, 17; Crozier, 54; and De Silva, 126 and 132. For more on Lieutenant Olavide and his work on organizing the Legion's recruits in Ceuta, see Millán Astray, 5-6 and 121-128. Foreign recruitment depended greatly on political and economic conditions in Europe and Latin America. Sablotny (16th Company/IVth *Bandera*), 8, wrote that in 1923 and because of the massive economic inflation plaguing Germany at the time, a number of Germans (800) were recruited for the Legion in Hamburg. A Spanish agent promised the prospective volunteers that they would go to Morocco and form part of an organization that was "something like a police force." Another German who joined the Spanish Foreign Legion in June 1924 was Walter Meyer. Like many others who could not stand the brutal conditions of campaigning in Morocco and/or the harsh discipline and ill-treatment from their officers, Meyer deserted. See Walter Meyer, *Dreitausend Kilometer barfuss durch Afrika* (Stuttgart: Loewes Verlag Ferdinand Carl, 1929). In a famous painting by Portabella of Millán Astray welcoming twenty volunteers to Ceuta, William Brown, clad in a red-and-white horizontally stripped athletic shirt, is clearly visible standing amidst his nineteen companions. Captain Francisco Sacristán Romero provided the author with William Brown's enlistment file, which contains the following information: William Broun Broun (*sic*), native of the United States of America, twenty-three years of age, of the Protestant faith, previously employed as a seaman and chauffeur, enlisted for four years in the Legion on 22 September 1920 in Ceuta, and began his enlistment on 25 September, becoming the fifth man to join the Legion, saw combat and rose to the rank of Legionary, and ended his commitment to the Legion on 23 July 1921 when he deserted. It appears that William Brown took advantage of the situation following the Annual disaster and the Legion's forced march to Tetuán and Ceuta to desert, and he did not make the journey to rescue Melilla.

27. Payne, 156; and Preston, 28. De Silva, 134, states that without the spiritual foundation instilled by Millán Astray into the recruits, the Legion could never be an everlasting work. Or as Turnbull wrote in "Spanish Foreign Legion," 16, the Legionaries had a "mission" to fulfill. See Appendix C for "The Legion's Creed" which represents the ideals Legionaries are expected to live by and uphold.

28. Turnbull, 16. All Legionaries who begin their military career with the Legion continue to be addressed as *Caballero* (Gentleman) and the initials C.L. (*Caballero Legionario*) precedes all personal names. See Cano Velasco, ed., 142, for other welcoming speeches from Millán Astray, such as "You shall always fight in the vanguard, death shall become our constant companion. Many of you will die, perhaps all." Millán Astray's words become prophetic when one looks at the high number of casualties suffered by the Legion during the Rif Rebellion. Of the 960 commanding officers and other officers, 441 became casualties, or 45.94 percent; and of the 19,923 enlisted men, 7,655 became casualties, or 38.43 percent; all for a grand total of 20,883 officers and men in the Legion, with 8,096 or 38.77 percent becoming casualties. See Federico Ramas Izquierdo, *La Legión: Historial de guerra (1 septiembre 1920 al 12 octubre 1927)* (Ceuta: Imprenta África, 1933), 18-19.

For more on the number of casualties during the Rif campaign, see Appendix B.

29. De Silva, 128-129; Blanco Escolá, 86-87; and Hills, 114. Scurr, 3, gives an English translation of the event.

30. De Silva, 130-131. Crozier, 54-55, gives examples of those who came to join the Legion and says that "of the hundred [who were examined], about a score failed their medical." Of all the prospective recruits who showed up to join the Legion in Melilla after the Annual disaster, without a doubt the most attractive was a Javanese woman described as being "slender, blonde, sweet of voice, and green-eyed." Millán Astray mistook her for a foreign journalist and invited her to dine at his table, but she informed him over dessert that she was a painter and writer and wanted admittance into a front-line company. See Millán Astray, 78-79.

31. De Silva, 133; and Subinspección de la Legión, ed., 21-22. Sablotny, 33, detailed the power wielded by corporals within the Legion and how "according to the self-made law of the Legion, if a legionnaire dared to defend himself by so much as lifting a hand to a superior, then that one had the right to kill him immediately, without warning." Bueno erred on 33, Figure #1 of his recently published book on the uniforms of the Legion, when he depicted the first uniform worn by the Legion with the national colors on a ribbon worn between the second and third button of the tunic, instead of on the collar, where in regular army line units the regiment's number would be displayed.

32. Llacuna and Polls, 15; and De Silva, 134.

33. Cano Velasco, ed., 142. While at Position A, the recruits were paid a portion of their enlistment bonus, what Millán Astray called "a meager fistful of pesetas!" This money was quickly spent on wine, tobacco, and women and signified the end of civilian life as they prepared to move out to Dar Riffien the next day (16 October); see Millán Astray, 18, and Franco, 18. To avoid the aforementioned debauchery in Ceuta, future Legionaries were paid their bonuses at Dar Riffien; see Mico y España, 49.

34. *AGM*, Legajo #246, DO #234 (17-X-1920), 182; under the heading Destinos (Postings), the following officers were transferred from the regular army to the Legion: Captain Antonio Alcubilla Pérez, Lieutenant Juan San Miguel Rasilla, and *Alféreces* (2nd Lieutenants) Pedro Echevarria Esquivel and Ángel Arevalo Salamanca. For a listing of the first officers to serve with the Legion and their units, see *SHM*, Legajo #54, Rollo (Reel) 16, *Colección de Historiales* (microfilm), "La Legión: Resumen histórico," Primeros jefes y oficiales fundadores de la Legión, 15-16. Boyd, 331, (n. 37), recorded that "officers volunteering for service in the Tercio received an annual supplement of 1,500 pesetas."

35. *DOL, Negociado de campaña,* 1 October 1920, 1; and Subinspección de la Legión, ed., 22. It is interesting to note that the newly founded Legion, like the Roman legions of old, would always fortify their positions every time they set up camp, and naturally this was done at Position A; see Llacuna and Polls, 16. See De Silva, 140, for Franco's selection of black for his Ist *Bandera*'s House of Burgundy battle flag. The commander of each *Bandera* was to place his own personal stamp on the unit he commanded. For example, when the Ist *Bandera* was in Xauen in early June 1921, Franco one day sported long sideburns with a wide bottom (*boca de hacha*). Quickly copied by the men of the Ist *Bandera*, this later spread to other Legionaries. Even today, long, wide-bottomed sideburns are particular to the Legion. See Mico y España, 224, and Bueno, *La Legión*, 34.

36. Subinspección de la Legión, ed., 22; Millán Astray, 19; and Mico y España, 47-49. In *The Track*, 172-173, Barea's Legionary friend, Sanchiz, gives the following reason for the move to Riffien: "they [the officers] had to tackle the First Standard [*Bandera*]—you remember, the first thing we did in Ceuta was to bump off three or four

people, and then they had to send us posthaste to Riffien!" Preston, 28, elaborated on Barea's story: "On the night of their arrival in Ceuta, the legionaries terrorized the town. A prostitute and a corporal of the guard were murdered. In the course of chasing the culprits, there were two more deaths." However, in a telephone conversation on 16 February 1994 with Captain C.L. Alejandro Zamacola Monis (Ret.) in Ceuta, Zamacola told the author that the move to Dar Riffien was made because of the large influx of recruits and the need for a larger and secure training site, since the area around Tetuán had not been completely pacified. Until the termination of the protectorate in 1956, Dar Riffien would be the Legion's headquarters, site of its museum and archives, and command center of the 2nd *Tercio*, Duque de Alba.

37. Scurr, 5; Galey, 57; and De Galinsoga, 45. For more on the farm established by the Legion at Dar Riffien and the breeds of livestock raised there, see de Arce, 75-76. The most-detailed work on the Dar Riffien farm and barracks (*Obras, Granja, Talleres, y Biblioteca*) is La Legión, *Riffien: Memoria de las obras y mejoras realizadas* (Ceuta: Revista África, 1930). Hills, 115; on page 142, n. 8, noted that Franco's own cousin, Francisco Franco Salgado-Araujo ("Pacon"), was in charge of the farm for a while. Preston, 29, wrote that Captain Camilo Alonso Vega was entrusted with the job of setting up the farm and constructing better barracks. A different picture of Dar Riffien was painted by Sablotny, 32-33, who underwent basic training at Dar Riffien in 1924 and recorded that it lacked running water, electricity, and toilets. Trythall, 35, recounts the deplorable conditions encountered by British volunteers at Dar Riffien during the early days. The above-mentioned story ("Home from Morocco") appears in the *Times* (London), 26 November 1921, 11-12.

38. Cano Velasco, ed., 144; Ramas Izquierdo, 13; and Millán Astray, 61-62. To commemorate the ferocity they exhibited in the battle of Buharrat on 29 June 1921, Millán Astray gave them the sobriquet "Tigers of Buharrat."
The Legion's emblem of the X-crossed crossbow and arquebus, with a "truncated pike" (actually a halberd) running through the middle and in the center of it all; a crown was found in the archives of the Spanish Infantry by the Captain Adjutant of the Legion, Justo Pardo Ibañez, ibid., 63. De Silva, 140. *SHM*, Legajo #54, Rollo 16, *Colección de Historiales* (microfilm), 32, "La Legión: Resumen histórico," 21-22. *SHM*, "Campaña de Marruecos, Historial de guerra, 1ª y 2ª Banderas," 123, see 151, for information on the IIIrd. De Arce, 56 and 58. *DOL*, "Tercio Duque de Alba, 2° de la Legión" (Historia de las Banderas), (Guión de la I Bandera, Guión de la II Bandera, and Guión de la III Bandera). For a description of Majors Rodríguez Fontanes (IInd *Bandera*) and Candeira (IIIrd *Bandera*) from one who was there, see Mico y España, 224-226.

39. Franco, 18. For more on the Xauen campaign, see Estado Mayor Central del Ejército, vol. III, Chapter 4, 129-160; Preston, 28; Woolman, *Rebels in the Rif*, 69-70; Payne, 160; Morales Lezcano, 232; and Arraras, ed. (1920), 106-107.

40. De Silva, 138-139; Llacuna and Polls, 20; Scurr, 7; Barea, 173; and Galey, 57. See Sablotny, 58-59, for more on marksmanship training at Dar Riffien. Meyer, opposite page 16, contains a color drawing of Legion recruits taking target practice on the beach shooting at empty wine bottles.

41. Scurr, 7. Coronel de Infantería Ramón Moya Ruiz, *La Legión española: La música de la Legión* (Privately printed by the author, n.d.). *SHM*, Legajo #54, Rollo 16, *Colección de Historiales* (microfilm), "Los Himnos [The Hymns]," 9-14, and "La Legión: Resumen histórico," 37-47. Millán Astray, 35-37 and 53-54; and De Silva, 150. For the Cuban musical contribution ("La Chamelona"), see Luys Santa Marina, *Tras el aguila del César: Elegía del Tercio, 1921-1922* (Barcelona: Planeta, 1980), 128-129. See Appendix

D for the words to "Song of the Legionary," "The Betrothed of Death," and "Tercios Heroicos."

42. *SHM*, Legajo #54, Rollo 16, *Colección de historiales* (microfilm), "Campaña de Marruecos, Historial de guerra, 1ª y 2ª Banderas," 123-124. Franco, 20.

43. Franco, 21; Preston, 28; and Morales Lezcano, 232. Gibraltar, located on the Spanish peninsula and directly across from the protectorate, became an "army surplus store" for the Spanish army. Vaughan, 7. In *Mi responsabilidad en el desastre de Melilla como Ministro de la Guerra* (Madrid: Gráficas Reunidas, 1923), 118, the minister of war, the Vizconde de Eza (Luis Marichalar y Monreal) detailed all the shortcomings of the *salacot* (sun helmet) and recommended that it be replaced with an impermeable beret for winter wear and a wide-brimmed straw hat for summer.

44. Millán Astray, 67-69; and De Silva, 139. Galey, 55, erred when he gave Millán Astray and Franco credit for "the creation of the material symbols of the Legion which distinguished it from the rest of the army in Morocco and gave it prestige." That credit should have gone to Major Adolfo Vara del Rey for the light green shirt and, to a lesser extent, to General Álvarez del Manzano for the hooded cloak. He also went on to write that "Franco designed the distinctive garrison cap with the red tassel; he considered it more aesthetic than the customary Spanish beret." The "distinctive garrison cap with the red tassel" known as an *Isabelino,* was a traditional Spanish army headpiece. What Franco did do was to find and popularize the *chambergo* among the officers and NCOs in Morocco; and it was Millán Astray, not Franco, who considered it more aesthetic than the customary Spanish beret. *Times* (London), 26 November 1921, 11. In this article, the English interviewee, Captain W.F.R. Macartney, who had just been cashiered from the Legion, mentioned that "socks were never issued." He also referred to the uniform that Millán Astray was so proud of for its martial appearance as "grotesque gear." For the most extensive information on the uniforms, field gear, and musical instruments of the Legion from its inception to 27 January 1943), see *SHM*, Legajo #54, Rollo 16, *Colección de Historiales* (microfilm), "Vestuario: Modificaciones en la uniformidad," 109-126. Bueno's book (*La Legión*) on the uniforms of the Legion covers the organization from its inception to 1994. The reader should beware, however, since it does contain a substantial number of mistakes. Nevertheless, Bueno's drawings of uniforms and paraphernalia make his book a worthwhile reference. Captain Francisco Sacristán Romero, formerly a lieutenant in the Legion (Vth *Bandera*), told the author an amusing anecdote on 30 April 1997 about a veteran Legionary who told him that the red tassel on the *chapiri* (the Legion's sidecap) was there to serve as a fly whisk!

45. De Arce, 54-55; and Colonel Juan Mateo y Pérez de Alejo, *La Legión que vive . . . Episodios de la Legion* (Ceuta: Imprenta África, 1927), 172. Ramas Izquierdo, 4. For more information on the Hotchkiss Model 1914 machine gun, see Major F.W.A. Hobart, *Pictorial History of the Machine Gun* (New York: Drake Publishers, 1972), 94 and 128. Ian V. Hogg and John Weeks, *Military Small Arms of the 20th Century* (Northfield, IL: DBI Books, 1985), 150, 216, 218, 58-59. Pedro Hernández Pardo, ed., *Historia de las fuerzas armadas*, vol. V (Zaragoza: Ediciones Palafox, 1984), 41, 52, and 56. Jerry L. Janzen, *Bayonets* (Tulsa, OK: By the author, P.O. Box 2863, 1987), 175. Scurr, 41, wrote that the individual Legionary carried 210 rounds of ammunition in his cartridge boxes, as opposed to the 150 rounds carried by infantrymen in the regular line infantry units. Sablotny, 109, as a member of the 16/IV and one who took part in the bitter fighting against the Riffians at Sidi Mesaud (10 May 1924), recorded that "the pouches of the belts were filled with one hundred and eighty cartridges [180] for the rifle."

46. *DOL, Negociado de campaña*, November 1920, 2. *AGM*, Legajo #M-3204,

SECCIÓN #1, DIVISIÓN #1, 4-5. Franco, 21-30; and Cano Velasco, ed., 144. A major difference between the French Foreign Legion and the Spanish Foreign Legion is in their style of marching, with the French slow and dramatic, the Spanish quick (180 paces per minute) and purposeful with the arm not shouldering the weapon swung across the chest. This arm movement is known as *braceo*. G. Ward Price, *In Morocco with the Legion* (London: Jarrolds, 1934), 15, in an interesting observation, revealed that the reason for the French Foreign Legion's slow marching gait was a result of the average older age of its members. Hills, 117-118, describes the Ist *Bandera's* stay at Uad Lau.

47. *DOL*, *Negociado de campaña*, December, 1920, 3. See Franco, 31-42, for details of the six months the Ist *Bandera* spent at Uad Lau. Crozier, 56-58, lists the highlights of what transpired at Uad Lau in English, including the randy rendezvous of certain Legionaries and the local native girls. De Galinsoga, 46; and Llacuna and Polls, 22. While the Ist *Bandera* was at Uad Lau, the IInd and IIIrd *Banderas* remained at Dar Riffien continuing with their basic training.

48. Cano Velasco, ed., 144; Llacuna and Polls, 18-19; and De Silva, 158. *DOL*, *Negociado de campaña*, December 1920, 3. *AGM*, Legajo #M-3204, SECCIÓN #1, DIVISIÓN #1, 5. This file which is Millán Astray's service file, erroneously states that it was the IInd *Bandera* which was posted to Beni Karrich, and not the correct IIIrd *Bandera*. For a brief summary of the major events of the Ist, IInd, and IIIrd *Banderas* in 1920, see *SHM*, Legajo #54, Rollo 16, *Colección de Historiales* (microfilm), *La Legión*, "Acciones de guerra de las distintas Banderas de la Legión (1920-1939)," 1, 7, and 14, respectively. Subinspección de la Legión, ed., 509, has a brief summary of the actions of the Legion.

Chapter 3

First Operations of the Legion, 1921

The three *Banderas* of the Legion were stationed in the Yebala region of the protectorate when the new year began. There they guarded convoys supplying Spanish *blocaos* (blockhouses) with food, ammunition, and the most critical of all commodities, water. The Spanish military mission in the protectorate was to pacify the region by way of establishing small *blocaos* every few kilometers. As per General Berenguer's directive, the Spanish constructed between 130 and 150 *blocaos* in the sector. In principle, *blocaos* were to be erected in triangles of threes so as to afford mutual support and protection in case of enemy attack. In reality, however, they were randomly dispersed throughout the *comandancia* (command), in most cases isolated and exposed to every conceivable peril. The *blocaos* themselves were rather small, usually no more than twelve by eighteen feet, and built by stacking sandbags about chest high and finished with wooden walls and corrugated metal roofs. Windows (loopholes) were cut into the sides of the walls, and three or four strands of barbed wire surrounded the *blocao*. In a number of instances, as many as twenty-five men lived inside these buildings, spending their days eating, sleeping, and futilely delousing their uniforms while awaiting their next reconnaissance mission. Without storage facilities (or sanitation facilities, as "one oil barrel held drinking water, and another was used as a toilet"), each *blocao* had to be periodically resupplied by way of convoys from the larger outposts in the region such as Annual and Dar Drius. Usually, these supply convoys were the only contact the *blocaos* had with the other outposts, and they provided these small forts with all the supplies they needed to live and fight. Needless to say, the *blocao* system led to poor morale, and most Spanish soldiers considered being posted to a *blocao* "hardship duty." In addition, Spanish officers were rather unconcerned with the logistical implications of the system, as enemy attacks, for example, could effectively cut these *blocaos* off from essential supply convoys, thereby rendering them absolutely helpless.[1]

    This technique of setting up *blocaos* to control the countryside had been used in Cuba during the campaign against Cuban rebels.[2] But what had been acceptable in tropical Cuba did not succeed in the arid mountains of northern Morocco. What made the *blocaos* most vulnerable to the enemy was their dependence on regular deliveries of water. If the water convoys were halted, the position would be in peril. Moreover, *blocaos* were usually built on the crest of hills in order to provide the occupants with the best visibility possible and clear fields of fire against tribesmen trying to sneak up on the position. This left streams at the bottom of the hills both difficult and deadly to reach.

    On 7 January 1921, the Legion was "blooded" (*bautismo de sangre*) for the first time. A rebel war party in search of weapons encountered a squad of Legionaries belonging to the 6th Company of the IInd *Bandera* under the leadership of *Cabo* (Corporal) Baltasar Queija de la Vega. The IInd *Bandera* was operating in the Zoco el Arbaa sector. The squad of Legionaries was escorting a water convoy between their encampment and Beni-Hassan when they were set upon by tribesmen who gravely wounded the corporal and tried to finish him off in order to wrest the weapon from his hands. Although lying on the ground and near death, Queija de la Vega defended himself valiantly, receiving several stab wounds, but refusing to surrender his weapon. Rifle fire from his companions drove off the attackers, and the moribund corporal was carried from the battlefield still firmly clutching his weapon. The Legion was its first member killed in action.[3]

    On 16 January, the IIIrd *Bandera* temporarily transferred from Beni Karrich to Kudia Taimunt, which was closer to Zoco el Arbaa and on the western (right) flank of the route to Xauen.[4] By the first of February, however, the IIIrd *Bandera* would be back at its main post of Beni Karrich. Meanwhile, the Ist *Bandera* was at Uad Lau, and the IInd *Bandera* at Zoco el Arbaa.

    The first major attack against a Legion unit took place on 5 April 1921, when the 4th Rifle Company of the IInd *Bandera* under the command of its captain, Pompilio Martínez Zaldívar, deployed to cover the road between Zoco el Arbaa and Xarquia Xeruta. Hostile tribesmen attacked the 4th Rifle Company, but Legionaries of the 5th Company swiftly counterattacked, throwing themselves at the enemy's position. The machine guns of the 6th Company quickly provided supporting fire for the charging Legionaries. The enemy was surprised by the unexpected reaction of the Legionaries and broke off the engagement. The first cavalry squadron of the *Regulares de Tetuán* then covered the *Bandera*'s withdrawal to its encampment. In the firefight with the Yebala tribesmen, Captain Martínez Zaldívar was killed (becoming the first officer of the Legion to be killed in action), and Captain Antonio Alcubilla Pérez of the 5th Company, along with four Legionaries, was wounded.[5]

    The 5 April battle had several ramifications for the Legion. Not only had a commanding officer been killed, but the martial tenacity and fearlessness of the Legionaries was something that had not been seen before in the protectorate. The

High Commissioner, General Dámaso Berenguer, was so impressed with the Legion's fighting capabilities that he wrote a glowing letter of praise to the minister of war, Visconde de Eza. A new wind was blowing through the rugged mountains of the Yebala. No longer would the tribesmen be able to intimidate and harass Spanish supply columns with impunity as long as the Legion was entrusted with their protection. The Legionariess had clearly demonstrated that they could withstand an enemy attack, repel it, and quickly counterattack. In the near future, the Legion would be employed in offensive operations along with the *Regulares*, but within the main body of the columns of the regular army. This was something that they preferred not to do, but it was an important beginning in defining its more aggressive potential.[6]

Also in mid-April, General Berenguer had decided on mounting an offensive to deal with el Raisuni. In order to accomplish this, he had to use military force to obtain the submission of the tribes of the Gomara. Setting off from the pacified region of Uad Lau, a stronger column would march toward Xauen. Once this had been achieved, a link would be established through the mountains to Alcazarquivir and Larache in the west, leaving el Raisuni surrounded in his mountain fortress of Tazarut. This force, under the command of Colonel Alberto Castro Girona, with Lieutenant Colonel Millán Astray as second-in-command, was composed of the three *Banderas* of the Legion, a thousand *Regulares*, one unit each of Moroccan light cavalry, and infantry. The total force numbered 3,000 men who were spread along the length of the Gomara coast. The Legion was deployed within the body of the column despite a desire to be placed in the vanguard. The closest the Legion got to the firing line was when sappers were needed to fortify captured positions. Repeatedly requesting to be put in the vanguard, Millán Astray begged General Sanjurjo, "Even though it may be only once, my General!" However, it was not to be. The enemy's resistance was weak, and so pacification of the Gomara was accomplished in one week. The towns of Kaseras, Targa, and Tiguisa were occupied. The *Regulares* retained their place as the shock troops of the Spanish army in the protectorate.[7]

During the first few weeks of June, the three *Banderas* of the Legion continued to occupy small villages in their sector without sustaining casualties. This was about to change, though. On 29 June the three *Banderas* of the Legion, this time fighting in the vanguard, met the enemy in fierce combat.[8]

The Ist and IInd *Banderas* took part in the operation, whose objective was to seize and occupy the position known as Muñoz Crespo; the IIIrd *Bandera* was to attack Buharrat. At Buharrat, the IIIrd *Bandera*, especially the 7th and 8th Companies, distinguished itself by attacking the enemy with a ferocity that harkened back to the encounter of the IInd *Bandera* at Xeruta. As Cano Velasco wrote, "The entire bandera hurls itself at the enemy in a violent bayonet assault. The bugle blares like the buzzing of a hornet and the legionaries slay and are slain. The enemy retreats."[9]

The day-long battle resulted in one officer killed, three officers wounded, including Captains Pablo Arredondo Acuña, in command of the 1st Company, and

Joaquín Ortiz de Zárate; eleven Legionaries killed and nineteen wounded. The commanders of the column noticed the valor of the Legionaries. The *Regulares*, who until then had always been in the vanguard of all engagements, looked upon them with the admiration of fellow fighting men. Millán Astray stated that the men of the IIIrd *Bandera* had fought like tigers and that a rampant tiger would be placed on their standard to commemorate the event.[10]

Nor did the battlefield actions of the Legion on 29 June go unnoticed by the High Commissioner, General Dámaso Berenguer Fusté. In a letter to the minister of war, Viscount of Eza, the day after the battle, the High Commissioner stated:

The Tercio de Extranjeros [the Spanish Foreign Legion] is worthy of special mention. It can write the first glorious page of its history. While withdrawing from the field, the enemy tribe with its principal chieftains at its head, attempted to reach the machine guns in their emplacements. In a brilliant offensive reaction, the rest of the Bandera to which they belonged, not only prevented it, but put the enemy to hasty flight. Bewildered and with substantial losses, the enemy began a rapid escape under fire.[11]

The superior performance of the Legion on 29 June at Buharrat (Muñoz Crespo) had clearly demonstrated to the High Commissioner, the generals of the army, and the *Regulares* that they were more than up the task of being the elite unit of the Spanish army in the protectorate. However, this encounter would come to signify only the beginning of what was to come during the six years of the Rif Rebellion. Within a month, the Legion would be called upon to salvage what was left of the tattered remains of the Melillan command and save the longtime Spanish enclave itself from the Riffian threat.

A new cycle of operations was called for in early July by General Berenguer in the Beni Aros region of the Yebala. The attacking force was composed of 15,000 troops. The Legion, without time for rest and recuperation, was again chosen to participate. The goal of the operation was to seize Tazarut, the headquarters of el Raisuni, pasha of Arcila and evidently the head of the opposition to Spanish authority in the western zone. The Legion, taking its hard-earned place in the vanguard, was represented by the Ist and IIIrd *Banderas* and by the 4th Company of the IInd.[12] The column, under the command of General Marzo, advanced slowly, but with purpose. On 6 July, the troops occupied Robba el Cozal with two Legionaries receiving wounds. Robba el Cozal would serve as the base camp for the rest of the campaign. In the following two weeks, Bab el Sor (11 July), Mas Mula (16 July, and the beginning of the decisive push), and Zoco el Jemis de Beni Aros (20 July) were taken, with the wounding of one officer and four Legionaries. By 21 July, the Spaniards had el Raisuni surrounded in his stronghold of Tazarut and made all necessary preparations to wipe out the rebel seat.[13] However, in a far off outpost in the Melillan command called Annual, something had gone terribly wrong.

On 22 July at 0200 hours, Millán Astray received orders stating that one of the two *Banderas*, either the Ist or the IIIrd, had to leave immediately for el

Fondak de Ain Yedida. There the *Bandera* would receive further instructions. By the luck of the draw, the Ist was selected to go, and at 0400 hours it began its long march. The IIIrd *Bandera* went to Zoco el Arbaa. Meanwhile, the IInd *Bandera* encamped at Ben Karrich, then relocated quickly to Tetuán in order to link up with the Ist. The march for the Ist *Bandera* was difficult and exhausting. When they bivouacked in Fondak following a march of more than sixty kilometers (37+ miles), they were urged to continue on toward Tetuán by the morning of the 23rd. The men were physically exhausted; two Legionaries died of exhaustion along the way. Nevertheless, reveille was sounded at 0300 hours, and the march continued thirty minutes later. By 1000 hours, they were in Tetuán, where they learned that there had been a terrible disaster in Melilla and that General Silvestre had committed suicide at the head of his troops. Millán Astray addressed the Legionaries, impressing upon them the honorable mission that had been entrusted to them as well as the anguished situation of the army in Melilla. The Ist and IInd *Banderas* boarded a train for Ceuta. In the port city, to the stirring sounds of the Legion band and the good wishes from the commanding general of Ceuta, General Álvarez del Manzano, they boarded the steamer *Ciudad de Cádiz* at 1800 hours on 23 July. On board and steaming full speed for Melilla were General José Sanjurjo Sacanell (future Marques del Rif), who led the expedition; Lieutenant Colonel José Millán Astray, commander of the Legion; Majors Francisco Franco Bahamonde in command of the Ist *Bandera* and Carlos Rodríguez Fontanés in command of the IInd *Bandera*; and the Legion band. The Legion contingent totaled 920 men. Also embarking aboard the *Escolano* were two *tabores* (battalions) of the *Regulares de Ceuta*, under the command of Lieutenant Colonel Santiago González Tablas y García Herreros, as well as three mountain batteries.[14]

When the situation became critical in the eastern zone of the protectorate and the Riffian forces of Abd-el-Krim, after having annihilated the army of General Silvestre, were poised outside the city gates of Melilla, the only well-disciplined and effective fighting force in the Spanish army that could respond to the urgent call for succor was the Legion. Barely one year old, but battle-tested in numerous encounters with rebellious tribesmen in the western zone, the Legionaries had proved their discipline, valor, and ferocity time and time again. When the desperate and anguished call from Melilla came to the attention of the High Commissioner, he did not hesitate in turning to the Legion to save the citizens of Melilla, and preserve the honor of Spanish arms. The regular army was riddled with corruption, inefficiency, and incompetence, and it had appallingly low morale. Furthermore, the *Regulares* who had been the vanguard of the army in the protectorate were not to be trusted after elements of the *Regulares de Melilla* betrayed their comrades and joined the Riffians. In an incredibly swift march, the Ist and IInd *Banderas* of the Legion (the IIIrd remained at Zoco el Arbaa guarding the Tetuán to Xauen road), along with Millán Astray and the future *Caudillo* of Spain, Franco, boarded a ship that would race to the rescue of the Melillan command.

THE ANNUAL DISASTER

In the western zone of the protectorate, General Berenguer and his army moved slowly and cautiously against the tribes of the Yebala, Beni Aros, and Gomara. By July 1921, he was about to capture el Raisuni. Meanwhile, in the eastern zone the daring and impetuous General Silvestre was operating, trying to pacify the region that extended from Melilla to Alhucemas Bay (see Map 3). This region, dominated by the Rif Mountains and populated by the bellicose Rif tribes, offered a difficult challenge for Silvestre and his forces. Under his command, General Silvestre had an army of 25,700 men, of which 20,600 were Spaniards, and 5,100 were Moroccan *Regulares*. By early 1921, General Silvestre had crossed the Kert River and had taken Annual on 15 January and Sidi Dris on 15 March. Also in March, the High Commissioner visited the Melillan front and, after meeting with tribal chiefs on the beach at Alhucemas, came away feeling that the situation was favorable and that Silvestre was accomplishing his goal admirably. Not all the tribes of the Rif were willing to submit to Spanish control, however. Mohammed ben Abd-el-Krim el Khattabi and his younger brother, Mahammed, of the Beni Urriaguel tribe, opposed the advance of Spanish forces into the Rif, especially their ultimate goal, which was to reach Alhucemas Bay, located in their territory. The Abd-el-Krim brothers took it upon themselves to liberate their country from foreign domination. The first step toward this objective was to destroy the army of General Silvestre.

In late May, Silvestre decided to move deeper into the Rif against the expressed wishes of Berenguer, crossing the Amekran River and in early June setting up a position on Monte Abarran, located eighty miles from Annual. Militarily, Abd-el-Krim welcomed the Spaniards advancing deeply into the Rif, since this would bring them farther from Melilla and thus lengthen their supply lines, and making them more vulnerable. As Ricardo Fernández De La Ruguera and Susana March observed in *El desastre de Annual*: "The general had dug his own grave. All they [the Riffians] had to do was throw dirt on top of him."[15] Next followed a series of minor defeats that inevitably led to the Annual debacle. First, a thousand Riffian tribesmen acting in concert with a number of native *Regulares* who betrayed their Spanish officers attacked the Spanish outpost at Abarran. The Spaniards, and the *Regulares* who remained loyal, were no match for the Riffians. The position was wiped out, with nearly 200 killed; most important, an artillery battery was captured along with small arms and ammunition. Emboldened by their success at Abarran, the Abd-el-Krim brothers attracted other Riffian tribesmen to their side with the promise of rifles and loot.

The next Spanish position attacked was Igueriben on 16 July. Situated three miles from Annual, it was quickly surrounded and cut off from the larger base. General Silvestre, in Melilla at the time, quickly gathered what forces he could and rushed by car to Annual to take personal charge of the relief operations. Several attempts were made to break the siege and deliver desperately needed supplies, including two cavalry charges personally led by Silvestre, but withering

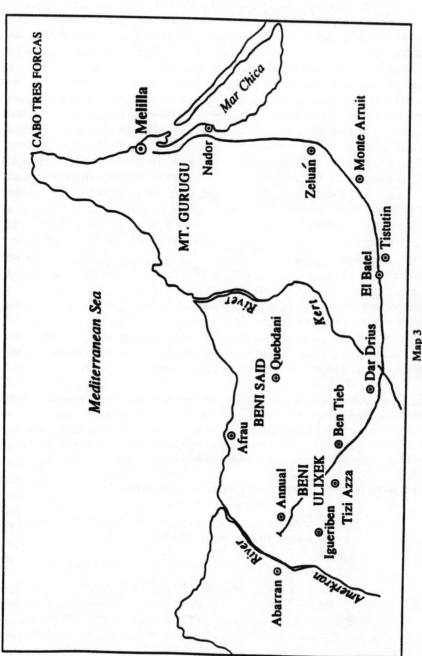

Map 3
The Melillan Command, 1921

machine gun and artillery fire from the Riffians repelled all attempts. Igueriben fell to the Abd-el-Krim's *harka* (war party) of roughly 4,000 men, thus sealing the fate of Annual, for Annual was located in a valley and Igueriben overlooked it. General Silvestre, with a force of 4,000 men, was also cut off at Annual. Silvestre fired off three radiograms in a row to General Berenguer asking for major reinforcements. With ammunition for small arms and cannons, as well as food and water running dangerously low, Silvestre, along with his officers, saw the possibility of having to abandon the major position in the Rif. After convening a council of officers to decide the fate of Annual, a vote was taken to withdraw. On the morning of 22 July, Silvestre gave the order to abandon Annual and to try to reach Ben Tieb en route to Monte Arruit. What should have been an orderly, fighting withdrawal quickly turned into a rout as panic-stricken conscripts dropped their weapons (a few had the presence of mind to keep the bolts from their rifles) and ran for their lives. The Riffians slaughtered those they caught, with soldiers and civilians (camp followers, sutlers, etc.) alike being put to the knife. In the end, Spanish casualties numbered from a conservative 8,000 to a high of 15,000, with another five hundred or so taken prisoner and held for ransom. General Silvestre perished at Annual, although whether he was killed by the enemy or died by his own hand was never conclusively established. From what we know of General Silvestre's character and military bearing, I and others in the Spanish military tend to believe that the latter was the case. What had taken twelve years of blood and treasure to conquer had now been lost in a few days. Spain's ignominious rout at the hands of Riffians tribesmen was the greatest defeat suffered by a European power in an African colonial conflict in the 20th century.[16] Carr summed up the situation of the Melillan command in late July as follows:

In a few days five thousand square kilometers had been lost. What remained of the demoralized army was either cooped up with defeatist civilians in Melilla or shortly to be slaughtered in the surrounding posts like Monte Arruit; it had lost its guns and equipment, and only the arrival of troops from the western zone and the fortunate accident that Abd el Krim could not use his captured guns saved Melilla itself.[17]

THE LEGION, MELILLA, AND THE RECONQUEST

Having left Ceuta after an all-night forced march to rush to the defense of Melilla, the Legion was about to embark on what would prove to be one of the high points in its young history.

When the *Ciudad de Cádiz* docked in the harbor of Melilla at 1400 hours on Sunday, 24 July, the populace of the threatened city gathered at the pier frantically waving their handkerchiefs. Panic-stricken and hoping to get aboard the ferry in order to sail away to Spain and safety, the citizens were pacified by the arrival of the highly respected General Sanjurjo and the Foreign Legion. The High Commissioner, General Berenguer, had arrived the previous day and taken stock of the situation. "All has been lost, including honor!"[18] Prior to the ship's docking, Berenguer had sent a message by his aide-de-camp, Juan Sánchez Delgado, saying that nothing remained of the Melillan command; the army had been defeated; the city was defenseless; nothing had been heard of General Felipe Navarro; and the people of Melilla were in a state of sheer terror and needed to have their spirits and morale lifted. The troops should therefore disembark with the greatest rapidity, with flags and standards unfurled, and parade through the town in proper military formation. This demonstration, the general hoped, would elevate the flagging morale of the people and convince them that Melilla would not fall to the Riffians. From the railing of the ship, Millán Astray addressed the anxious people at the wharf: "People of Melilla: the Legion which comes to save you, greets you. We are ready to die for you. We find ourselves under the orders of the heroic General Sanjurjo and we shall triumph. Forget fear! The chests of the Legionaries stand between you and the enemy! Long live Spain! Long live Melilla! Long live the Legion!"[19]

To rousing choruses of "La Madelón Legionaria," as played by the Legion's band, the Legionaries disembarked and assembled on the quay. Having been on the march and at sea for four days, the men were "filthy, unshaven, and smelled of war," but the *peludos de Beni Aros* (the hairy ones from the Beni Aros) filled the hearts of the Melillans with joy and reassurance that Melilla would be saved. As per Berenguer's orders, the two *Banderas* of the Legion marched past the inhabitants of the suffering city demonstrating their quick-step march. In *Marruecos: Diario de una Bandera*, Franco at the head of his Ist *Bandera*, recorded the comments he heard that day: "There goes Millán Astray, look how young he is. These are soldiers! How dark and hairy they come. Look at the officers, how careless they are, with their discolored uniforms smelling of war. These [men] will avenge us!"[20] The Legionaries were welcomed with applause, hugs, kisses, and gifts from the grateful Spanish populace. Women, men, and even Legionaries wept from the emotion that had consumed them all as they shouted, "¡Viva la Legión, Viva Millán Astray, Viva Sanjurjo, Viva González Tablas, Viva los *salvadores* [saviors]!" From the port they proceeded to their bivouacs, with the Ist *Bandera* sent to the eastern sector and the IInd *Bandera* to the western sector of the city's periphery.[21]

When González Tablas and the two *tabores* of the *Regulares de Ceuta Nº 3* arrived aboard the *Escolano* an hour after the *Ciudad de Cádiz*, which had brought the Legion, they received a less warm or friendly reception. This was a result of the desertion and treachery of some of the *Regulares de Melilla* during the Annual disaster.[22] The *Regulares de Ceuta*, in contrast, had proven themselves to be loyal and excellent soldiers during the long campaign in the western zone; they were soon to prove this to the people of Melilla during the reconquest of the lost territory.[23]

General Berenguer now had, under the command of General Sanjurjo, the two *Banderas* of the Legion, two *tabores* of the *Regulares de Ceuta*, and three infantry battalions (Borbon, Extremadura, and Granada) from the peninsula to bolster the 1,800 useless soldiers who remained in Melilla. The number of combatants now totaled 4,500. These troops were employed in securing the environs of the city and waited for more reinforcements to arrive from Spain. The day after their arrival in Melilla, the Legion, under the personal leadership of Millán Astray, took up defensive positions on the outskirts of the city, seizing and fortifying the heights of Taguel Manin (a *blocao*), Ait-Aixa, and Sidi Musa. At the same time, a *blocao* was also set up on the *barranco del infierno* (ravine of hell). On 26 July, the Legion's 5th Company/IInd *Bandera* moved out to strengthen their position on the southeastern part of the city, taking and occupying Sidi Hamed el Hach and Atalayon. From these forward positions, the Legionaries could see their besieged comrades in Nador, but they were not permitted to organize a relief column because Berenguer needed the reinforcements to hold Melilla. He also felt that the 4,500 men at his disposal were not enough to launch an offensive against the Riffians. The Spaniards holed up at Nador, Zeluán, and Monte Arruit would have to be left to their fates.[24]

Though the initial threat to Melilla had passed, the city was not out of harm's way because Mt. Gurugú, located to the southwest of the town, was bristling with Riffian guns. These guns had an excellent field of fire from the heights and could dominate the landscape with accurate and murderous cannon fire. It was obvious from the beginning that ridding Mt. Gurugú of the Riffian artillery would be an important and difficult task that would most surely fall on the shoulders of the Legion and the *Regulares de Ceuta*. However, it would be at least a month before enough forces could be assembled for an operation of this magnitude to be undertaken.

The priority of the Legion during the last days of July was the protection of the pack mule convoys to resupply with food, water, and ammunition those positions that had previously been established. Legionaries also fought off attacks to their defensive positions. On 28 July, the Legion engaged the enemy in combat while protecting a convoy to resupply Sidi Hamed el Hach. This was followed up the next day when the Legion seized and occupied the Blocaos "Intermedio" and Dar Hamech, later renowned as *el blocao de la Muerte* (the *blocao* of death). On 30 July, a Legion convoy to resupply the 4th Field Battery on Atalayon fended off rebel attacks. While the Legion and the *Regulares de Ceuta* were engaged in these assignments, fresh units were arriving from Spain that increased the Spanish force in Melilla to about 14,000 men.[25]

Although responsibilities heaped upon the Legion were enormous, the Legion carried them out superbly. Nonetheless, as casualties mounted daily from rebel snipers and close combat, the need for replacements became evident. The proposal to increase the Legion by two *Banderas* (the IVth and Vth) was forwarded on 27 July. Just days after the Ist and IInd *Banderas* of the Legion had sped to Melilla, the critical role of the Legion in the *presidio*'s survival had become obvious to all in the military. Thus, on 27 July 1921, the king ordered that the Legion be increased by two more *Banderas*. This augmentation was followed up on 9 August with modifications to the Legion's original charter.[26]

August began with the Legion continuing its assigned task of convoy protection and the manning of defensive positions. A new offensive, this one moving in a southeastern direction, aimed at recapturing what had been surrendered to the rebels. With Melilla and its outskirts secure from Riffian attacks, the focus of the military's attention fell on the Spanish posts that were still holding out against the enemy: Nador, Zeluán, and Monte Arruit (see Map 4). It was too late for Nador and Zeluán, which fell to the rebels on 2 August. The loss of Nador and Zeluán, closer to Melilla than Monte Arruit, signaled the inevitable loss of Monte Arruit, where General Felipe Navarro and his army had taken refuge after the fall of Annual. What remained of the Spanish air force tried its best to air-drop supplies, especially blocks of ice, to the defenders, but many times they missed their targets because of accurate Riffian ground fire. Following heavy bombardment, Monte Arruit, out of food, water, medicine, and ammunition and with little hope for relief, surrendered on 9 August, having first received Berenguer's permission. Though Navarro had agreed on a formal surrender, the Riffians slaughtered the majority of its defenders and took Navarro and around 600 men captive.[27]

The surrender of Monte Arruit brought to an end the final outpost of the Annual disaster, as well as the Melillan command. After Monte Arruit, the only part of the Melillan command that remained in Spanish hands was Melilla and its suburbs. Naturally, the government fell as the people of Spain looked for someone or something that would assume responsibility for such a humiliating defeat at the hands of Berbers. Antonio Maura returned as prime minister, replacing Manuel Allende-Salazar; and Juan de La Cierva replaced the Vizconde de Eza as minister of war. Who was responsible: the army, Berenguer, Silvestre, the king, the politicians, the industrialists? A commission was set up under General Juan Picasso González to investigate why the army had collapsed and who had been responsible for it. The High Commissioner, Dámaso Berenguer, offered to resign, but the king and the new minister of war refused to accept it.[28]

Nevertheless, while the politicians in Madrid wrestled with finding culpability for the Annual disaster, the reconquest of the Melillan command continued. During the first two weeks of August, the Ist and IInd *Banderas* of the Legion kept the lines open to the advanced *blocaos* (e.g., Atalayon and Sidi Hamed) while sustaining five casualties. Every three or four days, supply convoys had to run the gauntlet of Riffian snipers, who knew that the relief convoys would be moving down a certain road and would catch it in enfilading rifle fire. In *Melilla, 1921*, Arsenio Martínez de Campos detailed the experience of a typical relief convoy to Sidi Hamet El Hach under the overall command of General Miguel Cabanellas Ferrer:

At the head go the Regulares and with them their brave [L]ieutenant [C]olonel González Tablas. They are the ones that have to place themselves between the second *Caseta* and Sidi Hamet, covering the passage of the convoy. The Tercio de extranjeros will place itself between Sidi Hamet and Atalayon; but as it has its headquarters established in the third *caseta*, from there they should leave to occupy their place. Behind the Regulares and the Tercio go the corps of the regular conscripted soldiers, serving as support for the aforementioned and covering other less dangerous sectors of the combat front.[29]

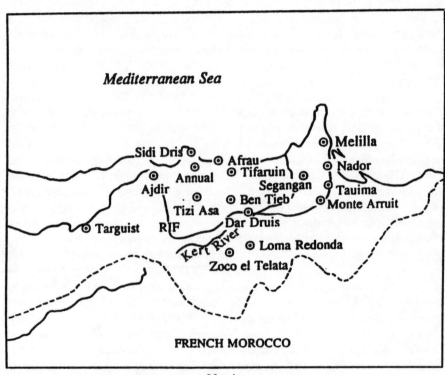

Mediterranean Sea

Sidi Dris ⊙ — ⊙ Afrau

⊙ Annual   ⊙ Tifaruin

⊙ Melilla

⊙ Nador

Ajdir   Segangan ⊙

Tizi Asa   ⊙ Ben Tieb   ⊙ Tauima

⊙ Targuist   RIF   Dar Druis   ⊙ Monte Arruit

Kert River

⊙ Loma Redonda

⊙ Zoco el Telata

FRENCH MOROCCO

Map 4
The Reconquest of the Melillan Command, 1921-1924

Meanwhile, Millán Astray had left for Madrid in order to promote the Legion and enlist soldiers for the two new *Banderas*. In his absence, his deputy, Major Francisco Franco, took over command of the Ist and IInd *Banderas*. The Annual disaster actually became a boon for Legion recruitment. New offices opened throughout Spain as well as in North and South America. Two factors accounted for this massive and rapid increase in the number of volunteers: (1) the incentive of enlistment solely for the duration of the campaign against the Riffians, instead of for four or five years, as had previously been the case; and (2) a sense of outrage and a thirst for revenge for the dishonor suffered by Spanish arms in the protectorate. Now, not only adventurers and those seeking to escape from hunger and/or justice, were flocking to join the Legion. The majority of volunteers would still come from Spain, but a large number would come from Latin America, especially from Cuba. Volunteers were recruited in the United States at the Spanish consulate in New York and Chicago, with most of the prospective volunteers having served in the American Expeditionary Force during the Great War. Not love for Spain but their impecunious situations drove many to join up, as the volunteers hoped to get three meals a day. Pay for a Legionary was 4 1/2 *pesetas* per day, or less than 60 cents. According to a newspaper account, enlistment bonuses were 400 *pesetas* for four years and 700 *pesetas* for five. Some ex-army officers applied for commissions as officers in the Legion.[30]

In Morocco, the fighting and dying continued unabated. On 15 August, without waiting for artillery support, Franco led his Legionaries in a bitter, hard-fought battle with the Riffians that resulted in the taking and occupying of Sidi Amaran on the Hidun road. The cost was one officer and two Legionaries killed, as well as eight other Legionaries wounded. However, after taking the position, and defending against a counterattack that drove the rebels away, the Legion was not quite finished. Franco, asking General Sanjurjo's permission, then led a punitive action against the villagers who had earlier attacked them. Not only were their dwellings put to the torch, but inhabitants were "put to the knife" as well. A radically different fighting unit had come from the western zone to reconquer what had been lost, and it was going to do whatever necessary to be victorious.[31]

With Millán Astray having returned from his recruitment drive in Spain, the rest of August was spent escorting supply convoys to their forward positions at Sidi Hamed, Atalayon, and Zoco el Had. On 31 August, the Legion, at the head of the column and thus the first to "see what happens" (*a ver que pasa*), took back the *blocao* of Mezquita, which had fallen to the Riffians, and recovered the bodies of Spanish soldiers who had died there. The high price paid by the Legion for keeping these posts well supplied was six Legionaries killed and forty-three wounded.[32]

The first day of September found the Ist and IInd *Banderas* of the Legion in Melilla bivouacked at the *Granja/Huerta de los niños* (Farm/Orchard of the Children), while in the western zone, the IIIrd *Bandera* relocated from Zoco el Arbaa to Dar Acobba. During the first week, the Legion continued its difficult task of supplying and protecting forward posts, with strenuous combat taking place at Zoco el Hach, Atalayon, Ait-Aixa, and the *blocao* of Dar Hamed, which left one Legionary dead and four officers and seventeen Legionaries wounded.[33]

On 8 September, the Ist and IInd *Banderas* of the Legion, along with the *Regulares de Ceuta*, engaged the enemy in the bloodiest battle since the reconquest of the Melillan command began. The strong point of Casabona, southwest of Melilla and at the base of Mt. Gurugú, needed to be supplied and a *blocao* (Peucha) established, but strong and well-entrenched Riffians were making passage to it very difficult. With the Legion and the *Regulares de Ceuta* in the vanguard of General Neila's column, the convoy to Casabona set out from Zoco-el-Had. One *tabor* under the command of Major Ferrer moved along the left flank; the other *tabor* and the Legion, under Millán Astray and Franco, proceeded along the right flank. Dug in and able to enfilade the terrain below them, the Riffians were driven off in a concerted frontal assault by the *Regulares* while the Legion took them from behind. Showing the same ferocity and disdain for life that the IIIrd *Bandera* had displayed at Buharrat, the Legion carried the day at the point of the bayonet. A vigorous Riffian counterattack was likewise repelled with the struggle many times coming down to hand-to-hand combat. Clearing the way to provision Casabona was very costly for the Legion, with one officer and twenty-one Legionaries killed and four officers and sixty-four Legionaries wounded (one-third of the attacking force). The *Regulares de Ceuta* likewise suffered around 100 casualties, including the wounding of their commander, Lieutenant Colonel Santiago González Tablas. The toll in men lost had been very steep; but unlike Silvestre's attempts to break through and relieve Igueriben in July, the Legionaries had "let their hair down" (*soltarse el pelo*, a Legion expression meaning "throwing caution to the wind") and accomplished their mission, regardless of the price. For their actions at Casabona, the Legion and *Regulares de Ceuta* were congratulated, in the highest of terms, by order of the High Commissioner and cited in army general orders (Orden General del Ejército).[34]

The week following the battle of Casabona, the Legion was back to its usual assignments, sustaining three casualties in the process. However, on 14-15 September, the Legion would again rise to the occasion, writing another entry into the Legion's *El libro de Oro* (The Golden Book) when it accepted the manning of the *blocao* at Dar Hamed, known to all as *El Malo* (The Bad One). This forward and vulnerable position was occupied by an army disciplinary battalion, which was shelled by artillery fire and surrounded by Riffians. With its officer seriously wounded and the *blocao* in perilous danger of falling, Lieutenant Eduardo Agulla Jiménez-Coronado of the Ist *Bandera* asked for volunteers to reinforce *El Malo*. Knowing full well that it was a suicide mission, all the Legionaries in his detachment stepped forward to volunteer. Lieutenant Agulla selected Legionary 1st Class Suceso Terrero López and fourteen others from the 1st Company. Under cover of darkness, the fifteen Legionaries had to fight their way into the *blocao* with two men sustaining wounds even before they could cross the barbed wire perimeter. Inside, a few soldiers lay dead. The Riffians increased their fire on the position, but the Legionaries were able to hold them off with their rifles and hand grenades. Eventually, the Riffians brought up a cannon and at point-blank range (less than 50 meters) reduced *El Malo* to ruins, burying all those inside. The gravely wounded who survived the collapse of the *blocao* fought to the death with the Riffians. They had followed to the letter the Legion's tenet of discipline, "Do your duty, obey until death." The fifteen men of *el blocao de la Muerte*, and especially Suceso Terrero, have gone down in the annals of the Legion's history as its first heroes.[35]

By 17 September, General Berenguer felt that he had enough troops in Melilla to go on the attack. The threat to Melilla had passed, and the combination of the Legion and the *Regulares de Ceuta* had fortified the outskirts of the city. The objective for this large offensive column was to seize and occupy the Spanish town of Nador, the nearby hills known as the Tetas de Nador, and Monte Argos. Nador, located just ten miles south of Melilla, had capitulated to the Riffians on 2 August. Spaniards who were able to escape told of unspeakable barbarities committed by the Riffians against the inhabitants. For this reason, the Legionaries could not wait to recover the long-suffering town and expel the Riffians. This would be the first time the Legion would be on the offensive. The overall commander of the operation was General José Cavalcanti, with General José Sanjurjo leading the vanguard (which included, among others, the spearhead of the operation, namely, the two *Banderas* of the Legion and two *tabores* of the *Regulares de Ceuta* under the command of Lieutenant Colonel Emilio Mola Vidal; 8,674 men in total), General Federico Berenguer (Dámaso's brother) led the main body (7,563 men in total), and General Tuero was in charge of the mobile reserve (3,316 men in total). The two columns would be supported by a heavy artillery barrage from the battleships *España* and *Alfonso XIII*, floating batteries, land-based artillery, a "*salchicha*" (an observation balloon shaped like a sausage), and even a squadron for air support. At 0700 hours the bugle blared and the attack began with Sanjurjo's vanguard advancing from Sidi Hamed under cannon fire from Riffian positions on Mt. Gurugú. The vanguard was held up by withering Riffian rifle and machine gun fire at the Amadi gorge. Then, while Millán Astray and Franco were deliberating in the most advanced position, a bullet struck the Legion chief in the chest and knocked him to the ground, critically wounding him. Evacuated from the field on a stretcher, he went to the Red Cross Hospital in Melilla, and then on to Spain for further treatment. Franco now took command of the Legion and under murderous fire pushed the enemy at bayonet point from the heights all the way to Monte Arbos. Legion casualties for the day were one Legionary killed plus Millán Astray, another officer, and twenty-five Legionaries wounded.[36]

The Spanish army's entry into Nador, the first Spanish town to be liberated, revealed to the world the barbarities the Riffians had committed against its inhabitants. Those fortunate enough to have escaped to Melilla circulated horrific stories. In *Tropas Regulares Indígenas*, Delfin Salas wrote:

When Nador was reconquered by Spanish troops it was possible to witness Dantesque scenes: women nailed by the hands to the walls and with their bellies open, whereby one could see fetuses still in gestation; small children with heads smashed against walls; women with stakes thrust up into their genitals, castrated soldiers with their manly attributes in their mouths; ears cut-off and many decapitated victims. All these horrors and many more, one was able to witness in Nador in 1921.[37]

The aforementioned description is one of many to be found regarding the liberation of Spanish towns and military outposts. All the military chronicles have described the incredible nauseating stench and the difficult task of burying or burning the thousands of dead. Arturo Barea, an army engineer, described this most unpleasant duty:

Those dead we were finding when they had lain for days under the African sun which turned fresh meat putrid within two hours; those mummified dead whose bodies had burst; those mutilated bodies, without eyes and tongues, their genitals defiled, violated with the stakes from the barbed wire, their hands tied up with their own bowels, beheaded, armless, legless, sawed in two—oh those dead![38]

For the next few days, the Legion set up its forward encampment outside Nador and resumed operations on 23 September when it participated, along with the *Regimiento de Caballería de Alcántara*, in taking and occupying of Tauima (aerodrome), losing one Legionary killed and thirteen wounded in the process. The Legion closed out the active month of September by providing protection for the supply convoys from Melilla and refitting and resting in Nador.[39]

Since its arrival in Melilla to halt the advance of the victorious Riffians, the Legion had been in the vanguard of all the major confrontations and had paid the price in blood. In describing the Legion, Martínez de Campos declared: "Its soldiers are audacious, and as they have the initiative and instinct of rapine, they are never at rest, and today a group is going to raze enemy dwellings, and another day attack some Moorish guard, etc. The Tercio is expensive; but as much money has been invested in it, it has resulted in fruition."[40]

As has been previously mentioned, the augmentation of the Legion by two *Banderas*, as well as the reorganization of each existing one, brought in a wave of enlistees, with many of these coming from the Americas. The first group of 300 volunteers departed for Morocco on 13 September aboard the steamer *Antonio López*. Sixty men hailed from the United States; the rest were from Canada, Cuba, and Mexico. Captain Donald McGregor, who had fought in three wars, was in command of the 300 who left New York destined for Cádiz and then Africa. A week later, the *Alfonso XII* sailed from Havana with about half of the 1,350 Cubans who had been recruited to fight the rebels. Aboard the ship, along with 200 stowaways, was the Cuban Legion Captain Santiago Espino Rodríguez had recruited. It was composed of Cubans, Puerto Ricans, and Spaniards. Besides the soldiers, they were accompanied by a priest, medical doctors, and nurses. Although the Cuban Legion did make it to Morocco, the recruits never saw combat as a group because they were not permitted to fight under their own leader. Most of them returned to Cuba, though some remained and joined the Legion.[41]

On 1 October, the Ist and IInd *Banderas* were in Nador; the IIIrd Bandera was in Dar Acobba after relocating from Zoco el Arbaa; and the newly formed IVth *Bandera*, under the command of Major Emilio Villegas Bueno, was being assembled at Riffien. The IVth *Bandera*, with the ensign of don Juan de Austria (half brother of King Felipe II) at the battle of Lepanto (*El Cristo y la Virgen*) on a red field as its standard, was constituted that day. It was made up of personnel from the other *Banderas*, and the depot company. Each *Bandera* was reorganized by adding an additional rifle company in order to increase its firepower. The new configuration was as follows: "Ist *Bandera*, 1, 2, 3, and 13; IInd *Bandera*, 4, 5, 6, and 14; IIIrd *Bandera*, 7, 8, 9, and 15; and IVth *Bandera*, 10, 11, 12, and 16; 3, 6, 9, and 12 were machine gun companies. The 13th and 14th Companies, which joined the 1st and 2nd *Banderas* in the field on 24 October, contained an influx of recruits from Central and South America."[42]

September had been an arduous and costly month in terms of casualties for the Legion; October would be no different. General Berenguer decided to clear the Riffians from Mt. Gurugú and to strike westward toward the Kert River. Once again the Legion (Ist and IInd *Banderas*) and the *Regulares de Ceuta* formed the vanguard of General Sanjurjo's column. On 2 October, the Legion attacked the southeastern heights of the mountain and in a bitter struggle was able to overwhelm, again at the point of the bayonet, the well-entrenched defenders at Sebt and Ulad-Dau. Under the command of Major Franco while Millán Astray was recuperating in Málaga, the Legion had been entrusted with the most difficult part of the operation. The Legionaries accomplished their mission. Sebt and Ulad-Dau had, however, been gained at a steep price: one officer and 26 Legionaries killed, plus seven officers and 129 Legionaries wounded.[43]

Three days later on 5 October, the Legion was on the move again, this time assisting in the seizing and occupying of Atlaten. The Legionaries, with supporting artillery fire, scaled its cliffs and dislodged its defenders from their positions with the *arma blanca* (i.e., the bayonet) or "as a certain legionary said `looking at him in the face and wounding him in the belly.' " In a final push, the Legionaries were able to reach the summit of Atlaten, occupy the main bunker, and plant the standards of the House of Burgundy (Ist *Bandera*), and Emperor Charles V (IInd *Bandera*). Atlaten had cost the life of one officer and seven Legionaries, plus four officers and forty Legionaries wounded, but the Legion now dominated the land of the bellicose Beni-bu-Ifrur tribe.[44]

On 8 October, while the Ist *Bandera* remained at Atlaten securing their gains, the IInd *Bandera*, which was in the vanguard of the assault column, entered Segangan without firing a shot. Segangan and the mines of San Juan (San Juan de las Minas), objectives of the 1909 campaign, had been populated by Spaniards who labored in the iron ore mines. The Riffians evacuated the town before the advancing column, taking doors, windows, and their frames with them. What the Moroccans didn't loot, the Legionaries appropriated to furnish their own living quarters.[45]

The final operation that would secure Melilla from Riffian artillery harassment and pave the way for the recapture of what had been lost after Annual began on 10 October. It would prove to be very dear for the Legion. The objective was Mt. Gurugú. Driving the Riffians from its base fell to the column of General Sanjurjo. With only the Legion now in the van, he attacked from Segangan in a south-to-north direction, while General F. Berenguer's column attacked from north to south. Sanjurjo's column, with Colonel Alberto Castro Girona in charge of the vanguard, served as a shield against Riffian attacks, allowing the other column to seize and occupy Mt. Gurugú. The Riffians knew the value and importance of controlling Mt. Gurugú and fought tenaciously to keep it. Caught in this viselike maneuver, the Riffians counterattacked when the *Batallón de la Princesa* abandoned their position because of heavy casualties among their officers. The Legion, with effective artillery support from the Galician batteries, succeeded in securing its objective of Taxuda Nº 1 but lost three officers and twenty-one Legionaries. The wounded included four officers and eighty-nine Legionaries.[46]

After Mt. Gurugú was made secure, the Legion directed its next operations, which commenced in mid-October, toward the flatlands to the west of Melilla. Knowing that his army would be decimated in a set battle with the more than 100,000-man army Spain had in the region, Abd-el-Krim declined to give battle and retreated to more mountainous terrain that better suited his style of warfare. On 14 October, two Legion *Banderas* assisted in recapturing Zeluán and Buguencein. In this operation, only one Legionary was wounded. In the aforementioned towns, the mummified remains of its defenders and their inoperable equipment were another testament to the brutality of the fighting that took place. However, the atrocities discovered in Zeluán would pale next to the carnage and butchery at Monte Arruit after its defenders, under the command of General Felipe Navarro, surrendered only to be slaughtered or taken captive by the Riffians. General Sanjurjo's column, which included the Legion in its van, secured Monte Arruit on the 24th without shots being fired. The men's olfactory senses were, however, overwhelmed by the incredible stench of rotting corpses. This was followed by the stomach-turning sight of hundreds of soldiers who had been murdered and then mutilated. The Legionaries immediately swore to avenge this barbarous act, and it was a promise they would uphold for the rest of the campaign.[47]

While the first two *Banderas* of the Legion were on the offensive against the Riffians in the eastern zone (Melilla), a shooting war erupted in the western zone of the protectorate on 23 October. There had been warfare with the tribes in the west following the Annual disaster, especially at the end of August (27-28), which left hundreds of Spanish soldiers dead. Riffian successes had emboldened these tribes, and by late October Mhammed Abd-el-Krim (Abd-el-Krim's younger brother) and a war party of select Riffians had gone into the Gomara to urge the tribesmen there to rise up against the Spanish. General Dámaso Berenguer, taking advantage of the vast field experience of the recently transferred Castro Girona, reacted quickly to counter the Riffian threat and again pressure Sherif el Raisuni.[48]

On 23 October, the newly created IVth *Bandera* under the leadership of its commander, Major Emilio Villegas Bueno, took part in an operation to escort a convoy to Kaseras and to relieve the siege of Monte Magan. In this *Bandera*'s first engagement with the enemy, a bloody, eight-hour battle was fought that left two officers and twenty Legionaries dead. In addition, six officers and seventy-four Legionaries were wounded. The cost was high, but the IVth *Bandera*'s objective was accomplished with Monte Magan being reinforced and resupplied. With the job done, the IVth *Bandera* left for Uad Lau.[49]

Five days later the IVth *Bandera*, which was in the van of General Marzo's column, had to return to Monte Magan to relieve the encirclement by Abd-el-Krim's elite Beni Urriaguel *harka*. General Marzo's strong column set up an artillery position at Axazar that was able to provide fire support for the besieged men at Monte Magan, who sallied forth to meet the enemy. The combination of the artillery support and the supporting attack of those inside allowed the relief column to advance. The IVth *Bandera* hurled itself at the Riffian trenches with abandonment and engaged the enemy in fierce hand-to-hand combat. The Legionaries achieved a complete victory, forcing the Riffians to leave the Gomara and return to the Rif. Abandoned by the Riffians, the indigenous tribesmen of the Gomara sought an accommodation with Spanish authorities. Again, the IVth *Bandera* had paid a heavy toll with the loss of one officer, one corporal, and twenty-six Legionaries. Six officers and forty-nine Legionaries were wounded. In less than a month after being formed, the IVth *Bandera* had 285 casualties; this was almost 50 percent of its force after just two battles.[50]

The first day of November saw the *Banderas* of the Legion established and operational in both zones of the protectorate. The Ist and IInd *Banderas* were in Segangan; the IIIrd was in Dar Acobba; and the IVth was in Uad Lau. The Vth *Bandera*, composed of members from the other *Banderas*, as well as from the depot company, became operational. The Vth was under the command of Major Juan José Pérez de Liniers y Muguiro, who would eventually rise to the rank of colonel and become commander in chief of the Legion. As its standard, the Vth *Bandera* exhibited the coat of arms of *El Gran Capitán* (Gonzalo Fernández de Córdoba), a black eagle on a yellow field.[51]

In the eastern zone, the military command thought it vital to establish fortified positions on Taxuda, so the battle for Taxuda Nº 2 began on 2 November. The operation consisted of three columns: General Sanjurjo's, with the Legion in the vanguard, would seize the rocky slopes, while General Riquelme's and General F. Berenguer's would operate to the right of Sanjurjo's. The battle began on a fog-shrouded morning with the 13th and 14th Companies, mainly made up of Hispano-Americans, in the lead. They had been given this "place of honor" (*lugar de honor*) and were eager to do battle. With artillery support from the batteries on Atlaten, the Legionaries fixed bayonets and proceeded to dislodge the enemy from the cliffs. In fierce man-to-man combat (the Riffian *gumia* [dagger] versus the Legion *machete*), the Legionaries fought the well-entrenched Riffians, who defended themselves admirably. Nevertheless, the combination of effective artillery fire support and Legion pugnacity drove the Riffians from their positions. The Legion lost one officer and seven Legionaries, plus two officers and seventy-seven Legionaries wounded. The majority of the casualties naturally came from the 13th and 14th Companies. Franco acknowledged, "The Cubans and South Americans had had a great part in this glory." For their actions at Taxuda Nº 2, the Legion was recognized and exalted in a general order from the command.[52]

On 7 November, the operation of the day called for Sanjurjo's column to occupy Sebt and Tazarut as well as the plateaus of Tlat and Beni Faklan. The plan called for Sanjurjo's column to draw the attention of the Riffians to itself while the other columns set out from Zoko el Had to conquer and fortify Yazanen and Tifasor. The two *Banderas* left their base camp of Segangan at the crack of dawn. With winter quickly approaching and the temperature dropping, the Legionaries scaled the slopes of Taxuda just as they had done days before. The Legion quickly secured the spurs, taking them by surprise. This allowed the column to pass without sustaining any casualties. Later the Legionaries reached the heights that dominated Sebt-Tazarut. There, they met strong resistance from the enemy. Meanwhile, the other column accomplished its mission and began to withdraw under cover of the Legion. It was tough going for the Legion as the Riffians persisted in sticking close to them, but the combination of Legion expertise and the accurate fire of the machine gun companies allowed the column to pull back. One Legionary was killed, and one officer, Captain Alonso of the 14th Company, and seventeen Legionaries were wounded.[53]

General Sanjurjo's column, with the Legion in the vanguard, set out for Sebt-Tazarut on 11 November. The day's operation called for the Legion to draw the enemy's attention away from the other column, whose mission was to take and occupy Zoko el Had de Yazanen and Tifasor before continuing to march on to Zoko el Had. Although the Legion's objective involved an element of risk, they were able to secure the pass between Sebt and Tazarut without alerting the enemy. The column was able to accomplish its mission without casualties, with the Legion withstanding the brunt of the enemy's fire. The Legion successfully covered the withdrawal at the cost of one officer and seven Legionaries wounded. The following day, the Legion set out for Nador. They were back in their encampment at Segangan on the 13th.[54]

The next operation for the Legion was securing the forts that topped the imposing Mt. Uisan in the realm of the Beni bu Ifrur tribe. Since Uisan was well defended and a frontal assault in daylight would have resulted in heavy casualties, Franco, with the consent of General F. Berenguer, decided on a surprise attack. Originally planned for 17 November, the operation had to be postponed because of torrential downpours that had made the roads impassable. Before dawn on 18 November the Legionaries set out without pack animals, carrying all munitions and supplies on their backs and with their shiny rifle bolts covered by their cloaks to prevent detection. The Legionaries were under strict orders against smoking or talking and had instructions not to shoot until the prescribed signal was given. Accompanied by the native police, the Legionaries rapidly and silently scaled the slopes of a ravine. When dawn broke, the signal was given to attack. Both attackers and defenders raced toward the safety of the walls of the small fort of San Enrique, but the Legionaries beat the Riffians to it. In a day-long battle, with the Riffians desperately trying to recover the fort, the Legion held as the Spanish flag waved from the highest peak in Beni-bu-Ifrur. Franco's strategy of stealth had paid off, with only nine Legionaries wounded.[55]

In the western zone (Beni Aros region), Millán Astray, at the head of the IIIrd, IVth, and Vth *Banderas*, joined the column of Colonel Serrano, which also included the *Regulares de Ceuta Nº 3*. Millán Astray returned to Ceuta on 10 November, even though treatment for his chest wound had not been completed. On 19 November, they fought a pitched battle at Ayalia and took it by assault. They remained there until the 22nd, when they again formed part of the vanguard of Serrano's column in the operation to occupy Telafta.[56]

With the weather improved on 21 November, the plan to conquer Ras-Medua was put into effect. The column under General F. Berenguer, with the *Regulares* in the vanguard, would climb the slope of Taxuda and occupy the plateau of Telat. Soldiers under General Sanjurjo, with the Ist and IInd *Banderas* in its van, would launch a frontal attack on the plateau of Ras-Medua, an old military position. Sanjurjo's column marched to the watering hole of Ras-Medua. There the two *Banderas* split up: The Ist took an old military road; the IInd followed a path that women used to fetch water. After a preliminary bombardment from the batteries, the machine guns also went into action to soften up the enemy. Meanwhile, an airplane dropped a bomb on the turret of the old redoubt. The assault began with the Legionaries rapidly charging from two directions. One company attacked straight ahead. Another threatened from the right flank of the ruins of the old fortification. An airplane dropped a message declaring that the enemy was in full retreat on the opposite side. The loss to the Legion on this day was light, with no one killed and only thirteen Legionaries wounded.[57]

The final operation of the month took place on the 30th, when the Legion in the van of General Sanjurjo's column seized "loma Negra," in the vicinity of Mt. Uisan. Artillery batteries were set up on the hill. The Legion set out early in the morning to find the enemy. With the enemy located on the heights of Tauriat Hamed/Uchen, the Legionaries waited for fire support before advancing. Having recently arrived from the peninsula, the Artillery Instruction Group with its 155 mm pieces laid down a murderous barrage on the Riffians. The Legionaries advanced toward Tauriat Hamed and the hills nearby as the enemy retreated. The Riffians harassed the flanks of the column from the many ravines, but each time the Riffians were driven off. As the sun set, the Riffians opened fire on the withdrawing column and its pack animals. Once again the Legionaries repelled them. The Legionaries found numerous Riffian bodies and weapons the following day. For the Legion, the toll was three Legionaries killed—Lieutenant Gallego Morales and *Alféreces* Díaz Criado and Díaz de Rabago—and seven Legionaries were wounded.[58]

On the first day of December, the Legion, at the head of a column, was involved in establishing a post at El Harcha.   This time it was the cold temperatures that hampered the constructive efforts of the Legionaries, not the enemy, who offered no serious resistance. Nevertheless, Captain Valcazar and one Legionary suffered minor wounds as a result of "friendly" artillery fire.[59] The following day, the three columns came together in the *kabila/kabyle* of Beni-bu-Ifrur to punish the tribesmen for the atrocities they had committed during the Annual disaster, as well as for their resistance to Spanish authority. After rounding up the villagers, their dwellings were put to the torch. Some of the villages in Tauriat Hamed submitted, along with the native chief, Kaddur-Ben-Ab-Selam.[60]

The operations proposed for December called for a westward movement, with the Kert River as its primary objective. On 11 December, the Ist and IInd *Banderas* assisted in the operation, which was to take and occupy Kadur and Tazarut, both close to the Kert River; it was accomplished without casualties.[61] The Legion's exploits shifted from the eastern zone to the western zone on 19 December, when the IIIrd and Vth *Banderas* under the command of Millán Astray participated in taking Dar Hamido. In the hard-fought encounter, the Legion suffered two Legionaries killed, plus one officer and twenty-four Legionaries wounded.[62] On 20 December, in the eastern zone, the Ist and IInd *Banderas*, forming part of General Sanjurjo's column, assisted in the same type of operation at Tauriat-Buchit and Tauriat Zag with no casualties.[63] The final operation of 1921 in the eastern zone took place on 22 December, when the columns of Colonels Saro and Fernández Pérez were ordered to seize and occupy Ras-Tikermin on the left bank of the Kert River. General F. Berenguer was given overall command of the operation. The two *Banderas* of the Legion would be in the vanguard of Fernández Pérez's column, which would coordinate closely with Saro's column. The enemy gave battle near Sidi-Salem and the ravines of Monte Mauro. All day the fighting was fierce, with the enemy attacking and retreating as the Legionaries pressed ahead. Supported by the covering fire of their machine guns, the men of the 2nd and 3rd Companies rushed out to engage the enemy in a battle of insults— "*¡perros!*" (dogs) "*¡cobardes!*" (cowards)—and cold Toledo steel. As the Legionaries were withdrawing, the Riffians attacked again but were kept at bay by aerial bombardment, a mountain battery, and Legion counterattacks. The battle of Ras-Tikermin was costly for the Legion. It resulted in the deaths of two officers and six Legionaries.   The wounded included five officers and thirty-six Legionaries.[64]

SUMMARY

In 1921, the Legion had clearly demonstrated its fighting capabilities. It was no longer second to the *Regulares de Ceuta N° 3* in the campaign against el Raisuni in the Yebala. Founded by Dámaso Berenguer in 1911, the *Regulares* had been the elite fighting force in the protectorate and the career path for ambitious army officers, including the majority of those who would later go on to serve in the Legion. Although nine years its junior, the Legion had rapidly attained equal status with the *Regulares* and then surpassed it as the most effective shock unit in the Spanish army in Africa. The emergence of the Legion was a result of its superior leadership, blind obedience to orders, and high esprit de corps enhanced by a martial reputation unmatched by that of any other unit in the Spanish army. As has been stated, Legionaries were better paid, fed, and equipped than the regular line units, and they had the further distinction of being volunteers. That they were on a mission to fight and die for the honor and glory of Spain had been inculcated in them by their superiors from Millán Astray on down. This sentiment became even stronger, even a personal issue, after the massacre at Annual was discovered. Moreover, the hierarchy of the Legion, composed as it was of avowed *africanistas*, was certain that Spain's destiny was linked to the protectorate in Morocco and that only a committed and professional corps of soldiers could hold on to it. The events that occurred after 24 July really put the Legion in a special category. The mere presence of the Legion in the panic-stricken city of Melilla was a victory. From their arrival to the last battle of 1921, the Legion would be in the vanguard of all operations to reconquer what had been lost. This was the case in both the east and the west. In *Historia de la Legión española*, Carlos de Arce summed up the Legion's impact on the protectorate: "The campaign for the reconquest of the Melillan territory led the Legion to become a necessary, useful, and nearly indispensable Corps. It also gained popularity because of its hundreds of heroic and distinguished acts. The general public gloried in its achievements. This led to Spain and the new Maura government to back the growth of the Legion."[65]

For the Legion in particular, the Rif Rebellion was a godsend. The rebellion enabled the Legion to grow from the original three *Banderas* to five by the end of 1921, but it would continue to grow in size and importance as the spearhead of Spain's army in Africa. Along with the rise of the Legion, the careers of José Millán Astray and especially Francisco Franco Bahamonde (Spain's most important historical figure of the 20th century) flourished. Furthermore, both men became household names, popularized through their own writings and the press of the time. It can be said that without the combination of the Spanish Foreign Legion and his experiences in Morocco, Franco would not have risen to become, at the age of thirty-three, the youngest general in Europe or the future *Caudillo* of Spain.[66]

NOTES

1. Fleming, "Disaster of Annual," 78-80, and 49; Woolman, *Rebels in the Rif,* 100; Barea, 67-69; and Payne, 155. Azpeitua, 107, stated that the dependence on the water convoys was "the Achilles' heel of a position." The word "*blocao(s)*" can also be found spelled "*blokau(s)*." R. Ernest Dupuy and Trevor N. Dupuy, *The Encyclopedia of Military History from 3500 B.C. to the Present* (New York: Harper & Row, 1970), 1005, called the strategy of establishing a series of *blocaos* by the Spanish and French armies in Morocco a "cordon defense."

2. Rafael Fermoselle, *The Evolution of the Cuban Military, 1492-1986* (Miami: Ediciones Universales, 1987), 64.

3. *La Legión*, a booklet printed by the Legion with a brief history of its activities, 4. In the aforementioned source, a telegram from Millán Astray to Zoco el Arbaa stated:

Telegram to Zoco [el] Arbaa. - The Chief of the Legion to Commander of the Legion. - Text: Upon hearing of the baptism of blood of the Legion with the heroic death of Corporal Baltasar Queija, I send you greetings. The Legion shall avenge its dead. Bury him with the greatest solemnity. - Millán.

Cano Velasco, ed., 144. *DOL, Negociado de campaña*, 7 January 1921, 3; and *SHM*, Legajo #54, Rollo 16, *Colección de historiales*, "La Legión: Resumen Histórico," 8-9. In death, Corporal Baltasar Queija de la Vega became the first inductee into the Legion's pantheon (*El libro de oro*,[The Golden Book]) of those who met a "glorious death" for Spain and the Legion. Moreover, he is also remembered for the stirring verses he wrote about the Legion, "full of emotion and love" and which would serve as the basis for the lyrics to "The Legionarie's Song," see Juan de Samargo, *Guía del Museo de la Legión* (Ceuta: By the museum, 1990), 12; and de Arce, 79-80 for the lyrics. Mico y España, 238-240, has the words written by Baltasar about the Legion. He also stated on 238 that the first Legionary to be wounded in battle was Teobalde Díaz Álvarez, who was wounded on 22 January 1921 defending the convoy going from Tetuán to Ben-Karrich. In contrast, de Arce, on 79, wrote that the first Legionary wounded in action was a member of the Ist *Bandera* at Uad Lau in early January, he was wounded in the leg while taking coffee to a forward position.

4. Cano Velasco, ed., 144. *SHM*, Legajo #54, Rollo 16, *Colección de historiales*, "Campañas de Marruecos, Historial de guerra, 1ª y 2ª Banderas," 151. This source deals with the IIIrd *Bandera*.

5. *DOL, Negociado de campaña*, 5 April 1921, 4; and *SHM*, Legajo #54, Rollo 16, *Colección de historiales*, "Campañas de Marruecos, Historial de guerra, 1ª y 2ª Banderas," 125. Ramas Izquierdo, 25, has more on the death of Captain Pompilio Martínez Zaldívar. Mico España, 36. Cano Velasco, ed., 144. This source erroneously gives the date of the engagement as 16 April, instead of 5 April. The author, accompanied by retired Legion Captain Alejandro Zamacola Monis, had the opportunity of visiting the grave site of Captain Pompilio Martínez Zaldívar at the Spanish military cemetery in Tetuán, capital of the former protectorate, on 7 November 1993. The gravestone read as follows: "Legión Extranjer, Capitán D. Pompilio Martínez Zaldívar, Muerto Gloriosamente en el Combate del Zoco del Arbaa el Dia 5 de Abril 1921, D.E.P [R.I.P]." The death of Captain Martínez Zaldívar and the wounding of Captain Alcubilla Pérez set a precedent in the Legion, where the commanding officers always led their units from the front. It was expected that an officer of the Legion would lead his men into battle, thus instilling courage in his troops by personal example. This tradition had also been part of the *Regulares*. Millán Astray's successor, Lieutenant Colonel Rafael Valenzuela Urzaiz, was killed at Tizzi-Azza leading his men in an attack. Casualties among officers of the Legion during the Rif Rebellion was

46 percent compared to 38 percent for the troops. For the casualty figures, see Ramas Izquierdo, 18-19. The Spanish military cemetery in Tetuán, where Captain Pompilio Martínez Zaldívar is buried, is also the final resting place for the first Spanish High Commissioner, General Felipe Alfau Mendoza, as well as for the third, General Francisco Gómez Jordana.

6. Cano Velasco, ed., 144-145, wrote the following on the impact that the Legionaries had in the skirmish: "On the Xauen road, between Xarquia Xeruta and Zoco el Arbaa the Legion's bugle call of 'legionaries to fight, legionaries to die,' had resounded like the crow of a fighting rooster, and there they were with their captain at the forefront of the company; the first one killed. It was a new style, it was the road of honor." General Dámaso Berenguer Fusté, *Campañas en el Rif y Yebala, 1921-1922: Notas y documentos de mi diario de operaciones* (Madrid: Sucesores de R. Velasco, 1923), 29. The High Commissioner mentioned the Legion in his diary report: "The success of the operation, in which the recently created Foreign Legion took part, was due in greater part to the successful political negotiations which preceded them, by which the enemy's resistance was reduced to its minimum expression. Spanish forces suffered no setbacks whatsoever." For more on the Yebala campaign in 1921 up to the Annual disaster, see Estado Mayor Central del Ejército, vol. 3, Chapter 5, 161-192.

7. de Arce, 80. *DOL, Negociado de campaña*, 18-19 April 1921, 5. *SHM*, Legajo #54, Rollo 16, *Colección de historiales*, "Campañas de Marruecos, Historial de guerra, 1ª y 2ª Banderas," 125-127. Cano Velasco, ed., 145. *AGM*, Legajo #M-3204, SECCIÓN #1, DIVISIÓN #1 (April 1921), 6. Berenguer, 26-27. For the role of the Ist *Bandera* in the operations in the Gomara, see Franco, 40-48. C. Richard Pennell, *A Country with a Government and a Flag: The Rif War in Morocco, 1921-1926* (Wisbech, Cambridgeshire, England: Menas Press, 1986), 88. See Barea, 77, for colorful descriptions of Generals Berenguer, Marzo, Serrano, and Colonels Castro Girona and González Tablas. Crozier, 58; Hills, 118; Trythall, 36; and De Galinsoga, 46-47.

8. *DOL, Negociado de campaña*, June 1921, 5-6. For an insight on the campaign in the Yebala during June 1921 from a Legionary who was present, see Mico y España, 69-87. For more on the Legion and a vivid portrayal of Millán Astray during this time, see Chapter 7 in Barea, 84-92.

9. Cano Velasco, ed., 145. *DOL, Negociado de campaña*, June 1921, 6. *AGM*, Legajo #M-3204, SECCIÓN #1, DIVISIÓN #1 (June 1921), 7. Scurr, 8, erroneously gives the date of the battle as 27 June, instead of 29 June. Llacuna and Polls, 23. In this book, the authors state that the IIIrd *Bandera*'s actions at Buharrat constituted the Legion's true baptism by fire as an elite unit. This sentiment is seconded in Subinspección de la Legión, ed., 22. Millán Astray, 177. *SHM*, Legajo #54, Rollo 16, *Colección de historiales*, "Campañas de Marruecos, Historial de guerra, 1ª y 2ª Banderas," 127. See 152, for more on the IIIrd. Preston, 31. According to the wishes of General Sanjurjo, the position was named Muñoz Crespo in honor of an *Alférez* of the *Regulares de Tetuán* killed there.

10. Cano Velasco, ed., 145; de Arce, 85-86; and Franco, 63. For more on the death of Lieutenant Manuel Torres Méndez, see Ramas Izquierdo, 31. Mico y España, 245-247, gives a descriptive, first-person account of Arredondo Acuña and Ortiz de Zárate in the

battle. De Silva, 160-161. The rivalry between the *Regulares*, the established spearhead of the army in the protectorate, and the newly created Legion who wanted that honor, was evident. This was illustrated by a satirical verse circulated among the officers of the *Regulares* at the time which said:

¿Quiénes son esos soldados	Who are those soldiers
de tan bonitos sombreros?	with such pretty hats?
El Tercio de legionarios	The Tercio of legionaries
que llena sacos terreros.	which fills sandbags.

See De La Cierva, 174; and Crozier, 58. However, Crozier wrote that it was the Legionaries themselves, not the *Regulares*, who came up with the self-deprecating couplet. Later it was changed to

¿Qué soldados son aquéllos	What soldiers are those
que llevan tantos galones?	who wear so many stripes?
El Tercio de Legionarios	The Tercio of Legionaries
que luchan como Leones.	who fight like lions.

The above couplet comes from Felipe Guillen, El primer Legionario fue . . . ???" letter to the Legion's webpage (www.lalegion.com—La Tertulia del Mesón de los Tercios), 1 January 1998, 1. For their achievement at Buharrat, the IIIrd *Bandera* was permitted to place the name of the battle on a ribbon that became part of its standard. Bueno, *La Legión*, 9. The author had the opportunity to view the now-tattered, original battle flag of the IIIrd *Bandera* from 1920 in the Legion's museum (Ceuta) in November 1993.

      11. Estado Mayor Central del Ejército, vol. III, Chapter 5, 180 (n. 34). See Berenguer, 58, for "the brilliant comportment of the Tercio Extranjero [i.e., the Spanish Foreign Legion], which that day inaugurated its first formal combat." Accurate battlefield casualties for the Moroccan rebels during the Rif War are, to the best of my knowledge, nonexistent. Official Spanish records consulted sometimes recorded exact "body counts," especially after a particularly fierce battle. Usually, they mention information such as "numerous cadavers" or "many dead enemies" found after a battle. For the rebels, there was no government or military organization (e.g., Graves Registration) to compile such figures. In an e-mail correspondence dated 15 July 1998, Professor C. Richard Pennell of the University of Melbourne told the author, "My impression is that the Rifi administration was much more concerned with the practical question of husbanding resources of money[,] food[,] and weapons taking care of dead people who were the responsibility of their kin." While Pennell's response focused on the Riffians in the east, it also applied to the tribes of the Yebala and Gomara in the west.

      12. Cano Velasco, ed., 145; *DOL*, *Negociado de campaña*, July, 1921, 6; Llacuna and Polls, 24; and *SHM*, Legajo #54, Rollo 16, *Colección de historiales*, "Campañas de Marruecos, Historial de guerra, 1ª y 2ª Banderas," 153. This page deals with the actions of the IIIrd.

13. *DOL*, *Negociado de campaña*, July, 1921, 6; *AGM*, Legajo #M-3204, SECCIÓN #1, DIVISIÓN #1 (July 1921), 7-8; *SHM*, Legajo #54, Rollo 16, *Colección de historiales*, "Campañas de Marruecos, Historial de guerra, 1ª y 2ª Banderas," 127-128; García Figueras, 177-178; Cano Velasco, ed., 145; Llacuna and Polls, 24; Scurr, 8; De Silva, 161-162; de Arce, 86-87; Mico y España, 87-88; Pennell, 88-89; Millán Astray, 178; and Morales Lezcano, 232.

14. *DOL*, *Negociado de campaña*, July 1921, 7; and *AGM*, Legajo #M-3204, SECCIÓN #1, DIVISIÓN #1 (July 1921), 8. See Berenguer, 242, for a transcript of the official coded radiogram sent to the commanding general of Melilla on 22 July 1921 at 1545 hours, which in part read, "I [Berenguer] shall send Your Excellency [Silvestre] two banderas of the Tercio and its two companies of machine guns with its lieutenant colonel, two tabores [battalions] [of the] Regulares [de] Ceuta with its machine gun company and its lieutenant colonel, a mountain battery and one ambulance; these forces will take individual tents, and General Sanjurjo will probably go with them." Estado Mayor Central del Ejército, 195. Berenguer left for Melilla aboard the gunboat *Bonifaz* on 23 July and was in the Spanish town the next day to welcome the others. For a detailed account of the forced march, see Franco, 71-74. Preston, 31; Hills, 120; Crozier, 59-60; and Trythall, 38. Cano Velasco, ed., 145-146; Llacuna and Polls, 24 and 26; Scurr, 8; de Arce, 89-91; Mico y España, 89-91; Subinspección de la Legión, ed., 110; and Millán Astray, 178-181. See Barea, 101, for a realistic look at what life was like aboard the ship headed for Melilla.

15. Ricardo Fernández de la Ruguera and Susana March, *El desastre de Annual* (Barcelona: Editorial Planeta, 1968), 37.

16. Annual was the greatest colonial defeat for a European power since the Italian defeat at Adowa at the hands of the Ethiopians on 1 March 1896. Spanish losses vary depending on the source. Official Spanish reports claimed 13,192 dead, but figures range from as low as 8,000 to as high as 19,000. For more on the life of Abd-el-Krim, the Rif Rebellion, and the Annual disaster, see Woolman, *Rebels in the Rif*; Fleming, "Disaster of Annual" and *Primo de Rivera*; Rupert Furneaux, *Abdel Krim—Emir of the Rif* (London: Secker & Warburg, 1967); Payne; Vincent Sheean, *An American among the Riffi* (New York: The Century Co., 1926) and *Personal History* (Garden City: Country Life Press, 1934-35); J. Roger-Mathieu, ed., *Memoires d' Abd-el-Krim* (Paris: Librairie des Champs-Elysees, 1927); Germain Ayache, *Les origines de la Guerre du Rif* (Rabat, Maroc: SEMER, 1981); Pennell; Pessah Shinar, "Abd al Qadir and Abd el Krim: Religious Influences on their Thought and Action," *Asian and African Studies*, vol I, Annual of the Israeli Oriental Society (Jerusalem, 1965); Ramón Salas Larrazábal, *El Protectorado de España en Marruecos* (Madrid: Editorial MAPFRE, S.A., 1992); García Figueras; Robert B. Asprey, *War in the Shadows: The Guerrilla in History*, vol. I (New York: Doubleday & Co., 1975); De La Cierva; Emilio Ayensa, *Del desastre de Annual a la Presidencia del Consejo* (Madrid: Rafael Caro Raggio, 1930); Hills; Sir Charles Petrie, *King Alfonso XIII and His Age* (London: Chapman & Hall, 1963); Indalecio Prieto, *Con El Rey o contra El Rey: Guerra de Marruecos*, vol. I (Barcelona: Editorial Planeta, 1990); Basil Davidson, *The People's Cause: A History of Guerrillas in Africa* (n.p.: Longman Studies in African History, 1981); al-Fasi; and Abdallah Laroui, *The History of the Maghrib: An Interpretive*

Essay, trans. by Ralph Manheim (Princeton, NJ: Princeton University Press, 1977). A recently published book that contains excellent photographs, maps of battle sites, troop deployment, and informative text is Antonio Carrasco García, *Las imágenes del desastre: Annual, 1921* (Madrid: Almena Ediciones, 1999).

17. Carr, 521.

18. Azpeitua, 83.

19. de Arce, 96; Millán Astray, 182-185; and Scurr, 9. *AGM*, Legajo #M-3204, SECCIÓN #1, DIVISIÓN #1, 8-9; Arraras, ed. (1921), 115; Subinspección de la Legión, ed., 111; De La Cierva, 182, and in *Franco*, 66; and García Figueras, 181. For a vivid description of the arrival of the Legion in Melilla, see Franco, 77-80. It should be noted that on 24 July, the first unit to arrive in Melilla after the Annual disaster was the Regiment of the Crown (*Regimiento de La Corona*), followed very shortly thereafter by the Legion.

20. Franco, 80; Hills, 123-124; Crozier, 62; Cano Velasco, ed., 146; and Subinspección de la Legión, ed., 111. This source states that the only things that the Legionaries had that was clean were their weapons.

21. Mico y España, 96; Llacuna and Polls, 27; Cano Velasco, ed., 147; *SHM*, Legajo #54, Rollo 16, *Colección de historiales*, "Campañas de Marruecos, Historial de guerra, 1ª y 2ª Banderas," 128-129; and Preston, 31. De La Cierva, 115, commenting on the calming effect that the Legion had on the terrorized Spaniards of Melilla when they arrived on 24 July wrote, "The Legion had won a great battle." However, a different view of the Legion's arrival in Melilla was given by Barea, 102, when he wrote:

Into besieged Melilla a big steamer poured those thousands of sick, drunken, over-tired men who were to be its liberators. We set up camp, I don't know where. We heard guns, machine guns, and rifles firing somewhere outside the town. We invaded the cafes and taverns, we got drunk and rioted in the brothels. We challenged the frightened inhabitants: "Now you'll see! Now we're here and that's that. Tomorrow not a Moor will be left alive." The Moors had disappeared from the streets of Melilla; after the ship had anchored alongside the jetty, a legionary had cut off the ears of one of them and the authorities had ordered all Moors to stay indoors. On the following morning we marched to the outskirts of the town; we were to break through the encirclement and to begin the re-conquest of the zone.

22. Boyd, 180-181, noted that almost all the 5,000 Moroccans in the service of Spain defected to the rebels, except for a few *Regulares de Melilla* who remained loyal. Distrusted by Spanish officials, they were disarmed and had no choice but to join the Riffians.

23. Mico y España, 96; Franco, 80; and Subinspección de la Legión, ed., 124. When the High Commissioner queried González Tablas about the loyalty of his *Regulares de Ceuta*, after the Annual disaster and the betrayal of some the *Regulares de Melilla*, he responded by saying, "I am so sure of them, that after half of them have died for Spain, the other half would, if I ordered them to, be disposed to die fighting against Spain." The aforementioned quote also appears in Juan Farragut (pseud.), *Memorias de un legionario* (Madrid: Imprenta Artística, 1925), 45.

24. Arraras, ed., 115, quoted General Berenguer, describing the poor fighting qualities of the units in Melilla, except for the Legion and a few others, as saying: "It is a really extraordinary case, because it does not involve reinforcing an army with new personnel, but of creating an army to fight the next day." Berenguer, 91; *AGM*, Legajo #M-3204, SECCIÓN #1, DIVISIÓN #1, 9; Cano Velasco, ed., 147; Franco, 82-83; and Llacuna and Polls, 28; Subinspección de la Legión, ed., 114. De La Cierva, 182, wrote that Generals Berenguer and Sanjurjo rejected a relief mission to Nador by volunteers of the Legion because they felt it could not be carried out without the support of friendly and loyal *harkas*. Preston, 31-32. Hills, 125, noted Franco's recording, in his book, of Sanjurjo's statement regarding his rejection of the Legion's willingness to rescue those trapped in Nador when he said: "In war the heart must be sacrificed" (*"En la guerra hay que sacrificar el corazón"*). Ortega y Gasset, 136-137, writing for *La Libertad* (a Madrid newspaper), went to Melilla in late July 1921. There, on many occasions, he was able to visit the front lines and observe the reconquest firsthand. On pages 136-137, he described his meeting with Millán Astray and members of the Legion (Ist *Bandera*) in their barracks of San Fernando on the outskirts of Melilla. This meeting took place a few days after all the Legionaries present before Millán Astray and Franco volunteered to go to the aid of those trapped in Nador. *SHM*, Legajo #54, Rollo 16, *Colección de historiales*, "Campañas de Marruecos, Historial de guerra, 1ª y 2ª Banderas," 129. On page 180 of his book on Franco, Preston mentions that perhaps the inability of Spanish troops rescuing those trapped in Nador in July 1921 had such a strong impact on Franco that it led him to divert the Army of Africa from moving on Madrid (a strategic error which LTC Juan Yagüe Blanco pointed out at the time) to relieve those besieged in the Alcázar at Toledo in September 1936.

25. *AGM*, Legajo #M-3204, SECCIÓN #1, DIVISIÓN #1, 9. Payne, 169 and 173, gives the figure of 14,000 by 1 August and 30,000 by 12 September. Berenguer, 109-111, gives the order of battle for all the units that could be assembled on paper (36,000) in Melilla consisting of infantry, cavalry, artillery, engineers, quartermaster, etc. Arraras, ed., 116, goes on to say that by the end of August more than 36,000 men have been assembled, but they lacked munitions. Along with the increase in men, General José Cavalcanti de Alburquerque y Padierna, chosen to replace General Silvestre and General Navarro as commanding general of Melilla, was sent to assist General José Sanjurjo Sacanell, who would in a few months replace General Cavalcanti as commanding general of Melilla. Estado Mayor Central del Ejército, 479-480. For a day-to-day account of the Legion's activities during the last days of July, see *DOL, Negociado de campaña*, July 1921, 7. Before the *blocao* at Dar Hamed became famous as the *"blocao* of death," it was known to the Legionaries as *El Malo* (The Bad One).

26. *SHM*, CL #304, 462, (ROC: 26-VII-1921), DO #163, 462. This document states that following the precedent set up by the ROC of 16 October 1920, DO #234, the king has ordered that the Legion be increased by two *Banderas*. *SHM*, CL #403, 593, (ROC: 8-IX-1921), DO #174, 521. In an ROC, the High Commissioner in Morocco wants a reorganization of the Legion to include the following stipulations:

1. Allow regular army officers to transfer to the Legion.

2. Authorize the enlistment of Spaniards and foreigners for the duration of the campaign and give the amount of signing bonuses.

3. Increase each bandera by one rifle company.

4. Retain eight machines per each machine gun company, but increase each company in size of personnel and mules.

5. Assign rifle companies eight light machine guns each.

6. Proceed to implement the aforementioned changes "with the greatest urgency."

For more on CL #403, see *SHM*, Legajo #54, Rollo 16, *Colección de historiales*, "Historial de guerra del Tercio Gran Capitán," "*Cambios y organizaciones hasta el presente*," 17.

27. Payne, 169, writes that the siege of Monte Arruit was described in the Spanish press as a "second Numantia." Estado Mayor Central del Ejército, 481, says that the press called the siege of Monte Arruit "Modern Numantia" (*Moderna Numancia*). Woolman, *Rebels in the Rif*, 94. "Spaniards Holding Out," *Times* (London), 3 August 1921, 7; "General Navarro Safe," *Times* (London), 8 August 1921, 7; "The Mystery of Abd-el-Krim," *New York Times*, 8 August 1921, 10:5; and "General Surrenders," *Times* (London), 15 August 1921, 7. Morales Lezcano, 233. For all the details of the twelve-day siege of Monte Arruit, see Chapter 5 of Luis Rodríguez de Viguri y Seoane, *La retirada de Annual y el asedio de Monte Arruit* (Madrid: Sucesores de Rivadeneyra, 1924). For more on the role of the Spanish air force before and after the Annual disaster, see Chapters 4 and 5 of Beatriz Pecker and Carlos Pérez Grange, *Crónica de la aviación española* (Madrid: Silex, 1983); and *Crónica de la aviación* (Esplugues de Llobregat: Plaza & Janes, 1992), 180, 189, 212, and 219 has information and photos on the Spanish air force during the Rif Rebellion.

28. For more on the political after shocks of the Annual disaster, see Payne, 169-172; Fleming, *Primo de Rivera*, 70-73; Boyd, 183-208; Woolman, *Rebels in the Rif*, 97; and Morales Lezcano, 233. "New Spanish Cabinet," *Times* (London), 15 August 1921, 7. Rafael Bañon Martínez and Thomas M. Barker, eds., *Armed Forces and Society in Spain Past and Present* (New York: Columbia University Press, 1988), 233; in this book, the authors wrote: "The Annual disaster did serve to put an end, once and for all, to the problem of the Defense Juntas, whose nemesis was in fact their own pettiness. They succeeded in completely discrediting themselves and were finally abolished by Sánchez Guerra's government in November of 1922."

For more on the demise of the *Juntas de Defensa*, see Arraras, ed., 121. García Figueras, 182-183. The High Commissioner, General Dámaso Berenguer, was given a vote of confidence for the time being. While in Madrid, the plan for the future of the protectorate began to develop. It had three phases: "the first, to recover all the territory that was lost after Annual in the east; and in the western zone, to expel or contain el Raisuli, conquering Beni Aros and el Ajmas; the second, the landing at Alhucemas; and the third, the establishing, through political action or by force of arms, coastal positions in the tribal lands of the Beni Said, Tensaman, Bocoya, Peñón de Vélez y Metiua. The occupation of Alhucemas was considered, justifiably so, as paramount."

29. Arsenio Martínez de Campos, *Melilla, 1921* (Ciudad Real, 1922), 192. De Arce, 100, described what life was like in the forward positions thus: "They live with a

shortage of water and with a convoy every three days. Only Manolo, the valiant sutler, visits the position daily and takes the mail and fresh watermelons that alleviate thirst." Subinspección de la Legión, ed., 116, has more on Manolo the sutler.

30. Subinspección de la Legión, ed., 117. "250 Recruited Here for Moroccan War," *New York Times*, 23 August 1921, 3:6. In an accompanying article, the question of whether U.S. neutrality laws are being violated by allowing the Spanish government to recruit soldiers to fight in Morocco is brought up. Eventually, the government would halt recruitment for the Spanish Foreign Legion on U.S. soil. "Ex-Service Men Here [Chicago] Offer to Enlist," *New York Times*, 25 August 1921, 28:2. The 700 *pesetas* for a five-year enlistment is a tad high, since according to DO #199, *Cuadro C* (Primas de Enganche) of the Legion's charter, a five-year enlist bonus for a foreigner was 600 *pesetas*. Ortega y Gasset, 169, wrote of his visit to the Ist *Bandera*'s encampment, where on 14 August he met and interviewed two foreigners, one an Italian, José Humberto, and the other an Englishman, Robert Cockburn. Furthermore, he spoke with Legionary Jaime Santonja (aka Pichel the Clown). Another Legionary, Gamoneda, had performed with the circus back in Spain under the name of Kuku the Clown. See Crozier, 57.

31. *AGM*, Legajo #M-3204, SECCIÓN #1, DIVISIÓN #1, 9; Subinspección de la Legión, ed., 116-117; Llacuna and Polls, 29 and 31; Franco, 88-90; and de Arce, 100. *DOL, Negociado de campaña*, 15 August 1921, 7. This source gives the number of dead as seven; the others give the number as eight. Estado Mayor Central del Ejército, 484-485. For more on the death of Lieutenant Miguel Valero Marzo, see Ramas Izquierdo, 31. "Spanish Rout Moors in Morocco Offensive," *New York Times*, 17 August 1921, 11:2.

32. *DOL, Negociado de campaña*, 16-31 August 1921, 7-8; and *AGM*, Legajo #M-3204, SECCIÓN #1, DIVISIÓN #1, 9-10. Subinspección de la Legión, ed., 117-119, details two incidents in which the Legionaries stubbornly defended their *blocaos* against nocturnal attacks by the Riffians. Previously, when the *blocaos* had been garrisoned by conscripts, they were easy to overrun; but with the pugnacity of the Legionaries, the situation was now quite different. For other examples of the Legion's fighting spirit, see Mico y España, 113-116 and 119-121. The aforementioned source (118) mentions the first appearance in the campaign of the armored train on 28 August. The well fortified and heavily defended armored train was employed in bringing supplies to the major forward posts to which track had been reopened. The Achilles' heel of the train was its tracks, which the Riffians tore up whenever they could. For more on Riffian sabotage and defensive techniques against Spanish targets, see Martínez de Campos, 202; de Arce, 101; and Berenguer, 112.

33. *DOL, Negociado de campaña*, 1 September 1921, 8; Subinspección de la Legión, ed., 120; *AGM*, Legajo #M-3204, SECCIÓN #1, DIVISIÓN #1, 10; Llacuna and Polls, 32; and *SHM*, Legajo #54, Rollo 16, *Colección de historiales*, "Campañas de Marruecos, Historial de guerra, 1ª y 2ª Banderas" (3ª Bandera), 156.

34. *DOL, Negociado de campaña*, 8 September 1921, 8; and *AGM*, Legajo #M-3204, SECCIÓN #1, DIVISIÓN #1, 10. This source contains the congratulatory letter from the High Commissioner, signed by Colonel Jordana. This letter, as well as the events that took place at Casabona, also appears in Subinspección de la Legión, ed., 120-124. Estado

Mayor Central del Ejército, 490-492. For a good description of the battle of Casabona, see Franco, 101-107; and De La Cierva, *Franco*, 67. Preston, 37-38, contains details of an interview conducted by Juan Farragut in early 1923, in which Franco described the valor of his Legionaries during the battle of Casabona ("perhaps the hardest day of the war"). Hills, 125-126, wrote that at Casabona, "Abdel Krim had suffered his first serious reverse." Ramas Izquierdo, 77-86, has an excellent analysis of the battle, as well as recognition for those who distinguished themselves, and see 31 for more information on the "glorious death" of Lieutenant Martín Penche Martínez. Also see Millán Astray, 191-194; de Arce, 109-114; Berenguer, 112; and Cano Velasco, ed., 147. *SHM*, Legajo #54, Rollo 16, *Colección de historiales*, "Campañas de Marruecos, Historial de guerra, 1ª y 2ª Banderas," 130-131. Prieto, 49, quoted a survivor of the battle of Casabona as having said: "I have belonged to the *Tercio* since it was created and since then we have never had an expedition as difficult as the one we had today." Ferragut (pseud.), 28-30; this novel gives a wonderful insight into the Legion from one who came to the rescue from Ceuta after the Annual disaster and took part in the reconquest of the Melillan command from August 1921 to January 1922. For their achievements at Casabona, the Ist and IInd *Banderas* were permitted to place the name of the battle on a *corbata* (ribbon) and attach it to their standards. It would be the first of five battle ribbons that these two *Banderas* would earn for the same battles (Casabona, Nador, Sebt & Ulad Dau, Taxuda Nº 1, and Taxuda Nº 2) during the campaign. The IIIrd *Bandera* had two ribbons (for Buharrat and Draa Hachin), the IVth had one ribbon (for Monte Magan), and the Vth had one ribbon (for Tazarut). See RamasIzquierdo, 13-14.

35. *DOL*, *Negociado de campaña*, 9-15 September 1921, 8; and *AGM*, Legajo #M-3204, SECCIÓN #1, DIVISIÓN #1, 10. Ramas Izquierdo, 87-88. This source contains the names and rank of those who perished in the *blocao de la Muerte*. Estado Mayor Central del Ejército, 494. *SHM*, Legajo #54, Rollo 16, *Colección de historiales*, "Campañas de Marruecos, Historial de guerra, 1ª y 2ª Banderas," 129-130; and *SHM*, "La Legión: Resumen histórico," 11-12. *Subinspección de la Legión*, ed., 127-129. Millán Astray, 110-111; Cano Velasco, ed., 147; Llacuna and Polls, 33-35; Scurr, 9-10; de Arce, 120-123; Mateo y Pérez de Alejo, 11-14; and Mico y España, 177-181. Bonifacio Varea, "El Pueblo de Hormilla con la Legión," *Hermandad Legionaria* no. 7 (June 1991): 13-14, wrote that the loss of Dar Hamed was the first time the enemy had taken a position the Legion had occupied. This statement can also be found in De La Cierva, *Franco*, 67. The enemy took the position because all its defenders were *hors de combat*. To this day, Suceso Terrero (posthumously promoted to the rank of corporal) is revered by the Legion with his hometown of Hormilla being the site of a monument and yearly commemorations to his valor and sacrifice. His picture appears in all displays that feature the titans of the Legion such as Millán Astray, Franco, and Valenzuela, and even a *Bandera*, the XIIth, was named after him. In October 1993 the author had the opportunity to speak about Legion hero Suceso Terrero with Colonel of Infantry Ramón Moya Ruiz in the bar of the *Hermandad de Antiguos Caballeros Legionarios* in Madrid. It is his contention, and that of Lieutenant C.L. Gabriel Díaz Sánchez, *Redactor Jefe de la Legión*, that Suceso Terrero, although subsequently lionized for his actions in the *blocao de la Muerte*, was not decorated

posthumously because Millán Astray wanted to impress upon the rest of the Legion that Suceso Terrero's and the others' sacrifice was to be seen as typical for all Legionaries.

36. *DOL, Negociado de campaña*, 17 September 1921, 8. This source gives the number of casualties as twenty-eight, while all the others put the number at thirty-three. Franco, 108-110. Crozier, 63, noted that when Franco took command of the Legion for the first time, as a result of Millán Astray's wounding, he was only twenty-eight years old. Cano Velasco, ed., 147-148, gives the casualty figures as eight dead and twenty-five wounded. He described the battle as a "deluxe" combat—relatively few casualties for so much gained. Scurr, 10, concurred with the figures given by Cano Velasco at thirty-three casualties. Describing Millán Astray's wounding, Scurr wrote: "After exclaiming, 'They have killed me!' Millán Astray exposed the profusely bleeding wound above his heart, then jumped to his feet, shouting 'Long live Spain! Long live the King! Long live the Legion!' *AGM*, Legajo #M-3204, SECCIÓN #1, DIVISIÓN #1, 10. De Silva, 38, contains the congratulatory telegram from Alfonso XIII to Millán Astray. Mico y España, 183-194. *SHM*, Legajo #54, Rollo 16, *Colección de historiales*, "Campañas de Marruecos, Historial de guerra, 1ª y 2ª Banderas," 131-132. For a list of all the units that took part in the recapture of Nador and a summary of the battle, see Estado Mayor Central del Ejército, 496-498. Along with the *Alfonso XIII* and *España*, came the armored cruiser *Princesa de Asturias* and the gunboats *Bonifaz, Recalde*, and *Laya* (655). For more on the battleships *Alfonso XIII* and *España*, including dimensions and armaments, see Bernard Fitzsimons, ed., *The Illustrated Encyclopedia of 20th Century Weapons and Warfare*, vol. VIII (New York: Columbia House, n.d.), s.v. "España," by Antony Preston, ed.; as well as *Jane's Fighting Ships*, ed., (London, 1923), 323 (*España* and *Alfonso III*), 324 (*Princesa de Asturias*), and 330 (*Bonifaz, Recalde*, and *Laya*). Also see de Arce, 125-132; Ramas Izquierdo, 88-92; *Subinspección de la Legión*, ed., 129-131; Ortega y Gasset, 238-245; Prieto, 71-75; Llacuna and Polls, 36-37; Millán Astray, 195; Hills, 126-127; and Preston, 32.

37. Delfin Salas, *Tropas Regulares Indígenas*, vol. II (Madrid: Aldaba Militaria, 1989), 7-8; and Preston, 32.

38. Barea, 103-104. For more on what was discovered at Nador, see the sources listed in n. 29.

39. *DOL, Negociado de campaña*, 23-30 September 1921, 8-9; and *SHM*, Legajo #54, Rollo 16, *Colección de historiales*, "Campañas de Marruecos, Historial de guerra, 1ª y 2ª Banderas," 132-133. Tauima would later serve as the headquarters of the Legion (1st *Tercio, Gran Capitán*) in the Melillan zone until the end of the protectorate. Also see, Franco, 111-114; Llacuna and Polls, 38; Subinspección de la Legión, ed., 131-132; de Arce, 132-133; and Berenguer, 119.

40. Martínez de Campos, 233. A different opinion was given by Azpeitu, 131, when he stated that "each soldier of the Tercio costs, at least, six times more than a conscripted soldier. Apart from the enlistment bonus [700 *pesetas*], each legionary is paid five pesetas a day."

41. "300 to fight for Spain," *New York Times*, 14 September 1921, 21:4; and "Cuban Legion Sails to Fight the Moors," *New York Times*, 21 September 1921, 20:1.

Fermoselle, 133-134, is the source for the Cuban Legion. For more on Cubans in the Legion, see Farragut, (pseud.), 12-19; Santa Marina, 128-129; Millán Astray, 35-36; Mateo, 79-81; and Mico y España, 283-285. By the middle of October, the volunteers who had left the United States to join the Legion had painfully realized that the Spanish army was very different from the U.S. army. Many were rejected for medical reasons; others simply could not live on the meager wages paid (60 cents a day) and were destitute. Others who made it to Morocco found the Spanish officers, particularly Major Vara del Rey at Legion headquarters in Ceuta, vindictive toward them because of Spain's defeat in the Spanish-American War. The language barrier, unpalatable food (beans cooked in olive oil and garlic), freely dispensed corporal punishment, and the bellicosity of the Moroccans led almost all the volunteers to escape from the Legion any way they could. For a running commentary on the trials and tribulations of the Anglo-Saxon (American, British, and Canadian) volunteers to the Legion, see "American Recruits Suffer," *New York Times*, 15 October 1921, 15:5; "83 Turn Back on Spain," *New York Times*, 16 November 1921, 7:1; "13 Americans Quit Fighting for Spain," *New York Times*, 25 November 1921, 22:1; "Home from Morocco," *Times* (London), 26 November 1921, 11-12; "20 Americans Ill in Spanish Camp," *New York Times*, 27 November 1921, 14:1; and "Spain Releases Americans," *New York Times*, 21 December 1921, 8:4. See Mico y España, 279-282, for details on the odyssey of Englishmen (*"Los Famosos Ingleses"*) in the Legion, and 228 for kind words about Major Vara del Rey. The article on the English was written by Mico y España as a response to their allegations of brutality and ill-treatment, which had been published in the *Times* (London) 26 November 1921 article. For an amusing anecdote on the safe way to wear the Legion cap at the front from veterans to a neophyte (i.e., off to the side as the red tassel made an excellent aiming point for enemy snipers), see Santa Marina, 123. In Morocco, those soldiers who quickly learned what the natives called *saber manera* (know-how) were the ones who survived the campaign.

42. Scurr, 10. Subinspección de la Legión, ed., 144-145; *SHM*, Legajo #54, Rollo 16, *Colección de historiales*, "Historial de guerra del Tercio Gran Capitán," 6; Millán Astray, 99; and *DOL*, *Negociado de campaña*, 1 October 1921, 9. Santa Marina, 153, features an encomium dedicated to the Spaniards of America.

43. *DOL*, *Negociado de campaña*, 2 October 1921, 9; and *SHM*, Legajo #54, Rollo 16, *Colección de historiales*, "Campañas de Marruecos, Historial de guerra, 1ª y 2ª Banderas," 133. Scurr, 10. Cano Velasco, ed., 148. Franco, 115-119, wrote that among those who took part in the battle were two ex-German army officers who had joined the Legion and were serving as liaisons for the captain of the 2nd Company/Ist *Bandera*. Subinspección de la Legión, ed., 132-135; de Arce, 135-138; Estado Mayor Central del Ejército, 504-506; and Ramas Izquierdo, 92-97. The officer killed, Lieutenant Eduardo Agulla Jiménez, was the same one who two weeks earlier had sent Suceso Terrero and the other fourteen Legionaries to their deaths at *El Malo*. For more on Agulla Jiménez, see ibid., 32. Furthermore, one of the seven wounded officers was Franco's own cousin, Captain Francisco Franco Salgado-Araujo, commander of the Ist *Bandera*.

44. *DOL*, *Negociado de campaña*, 5 October 1921, 9; *SHM*, Legajo #54, Rollo 16, *Colección de historiales*, "Campañas de Marruecos, Historial de guerra, 1ª y 2ª

Banderas," 133-134; Subinspección de la Legión, ed., 136-137; and Estado Mayor Central del Ejército, 507-508. Cano Velasco, ed., 148. This source contains the direct quote on the bayonet. Why the bayonet was so important in the assault tactics, as well as the ethos of the Legion, can be found in Hills, 127, where he recorded: "He [Franco] was a fervent disciple of the bayonet school. No weapon in his opinion could break the enemy's morale more quickly." Santa Marina, 164, contains a moving tribute to the bayonet, and de Arce, 138-139, and on 142, provides a very informative quote on the use of the bayonet and the taking of Riffian heads by some Legionaries. According to Prieto, 173, it is vital for Muslims to be buried with their heads in order to reincarnate their souls on the day of resurrection. For this reason the Socialist deputy from Bilbao called for head-hunting to cease. Prieto was reacting to the case of Legionaries having sent two Riffian heads to the director of the Spanish Red Cross. See Galey, 58 (n. 20). Mico y España, 175-176, wrote about the two heads sent as a present to the duquesa de la Victoria and reacted to Prieto's statement of how Muslims must be buried with their heads in order to enter paradise as "big rumors" (*grandes rumores*). Ramón Garriga, 40, has all the details on the story of the two Riffian heads sent by the Legion to the duquesa de la Victoria, which appeared in the daily *El Sol*. Preston, 29. Sablotny, 117, wrote of how his fellow Legionaries circa 1924 continued to collect Riffian heads and ears as war trophies. Ramas Izquierdo, 32, has more on the death of Lieutenant Juan Ochoa Olalla. Franco, 120-123, also noted that after the battle for Atlaten, the *Regulares de Ceuta Nº 3* were rotated back to Ceuta having lost in two months most of their soldiers as well as both their commanders, González Tablas and Mola, having been wounded in action. On 14 October, the regiment returned to Ceuta to deal with an uprising in the Yebala and Gomara by el Raisuni supported by Abd-el-Krim. An article that appeared in the *New York Times* stated that the regiment "returned from Melilla yesterday with only 140 soldiers left from the original strength of 800." See *New York Times*, 15 October 1921, 15:5.

    45. *DOL, Negociado de campaña*, 8 October 1921, 9; *SHM*, Legajo #54, Rollo 16, *Colección de historiales*, "Campañas de Marruecos, Historial de guerra, 1ª y 2ª Banderas," 134; Subinspección de la Legión, ed., 137; Cano Velasco, ed., 148; De La Cierva, 184; and de Arce, 139.

    46. *DOL, Negociado de campaña*, 10 October 1921, 9. This source lists the total casualty count as 117, four less than the following two sources. *SHM*, Legajo #54, Rollo 16, *Colección de historiales*, "Campañas de Marruecos, Historial de guerra, 1ª y 2ª Banderas," 134-135; and Estado Mayor Central del Ejército, 511-512. Cano Velasco, ed., 148-149. Scurr, 10. Franco, 124-130, gave the total casualty figure as 116. General Sanjurjo, on horseback and wearing his customary striped pajamas, saw the column off. Subinspección de la Legión, ed., 139-143, and de Arce, 141-147. According to de Arce, it was Franco's idea to have the Spanish air force support the attack on Taxuda by dropping messages detailing Riffian concentrations, as well as by bombing and strafing them. Franco's brother Ramón, who would later become a world-famous aviator, had transferred from the *Regulares* to the air force (*Ejército del Aire*). He would fly his brother in a hydroplane (most probably a Dornier *Wal*) on reconnaissance missions around Melilla. Prieto, 114-116. Ramas Izquierdo, 97-105, has more information on those killed; see 25 for

Captain Eduardo Cobo Gómez, and 32 for Lieutenants Antonio Rodrigo Cifuentes and Joaquín Moore de Pedro, baron de Misena (Franco's adjutant).

47. *DOL, Negociado de campaña*, 14 October 1921, 10; *SHM*, Legajo #54, Rollo 16, *Colección de historiales*, "Campañas de Marruecos, Historial de guerra, 1ª y 2ª Banderas," 135-136; and Estado Mayor Central del Ejército, 512-513. Cano Velasco, ed., 149. De La Cierva, 184, noted that in a letter highly critical of the Defense Juntas written by General Cabanellas and countersigned by Franco and Mola, Cabanellas gave the number of dead at Zeluán at 500. Scurr, 10, gives the number of dead at Monte Arruit that had to be buried as "at least 800." Trythall, 40, also gives 800 as the number killed per official account. Franco, 131-135. Franco described an encounter he had at Monte Arruit with a newly arrived Legionary who had come from Cuba to avenge his fatherland (Spain) and his brother who had been at Monte Arruit. Subinspección de la Legión, ed., 143-145. de Arce, 147-150. This source described the road from Zeluán to Monte Arruit as the "Via Dolorosa" and Monte Arruit as "Calvary." Farragut, (pseud.), 54-56 and 59-60. Arraras, ed., 116, also writes that the road from Zeluán to Monte Arruit was the "Via Dolorosa of Spain." Also see Martínez de Campos, 257-259; Prieto, 133-136; Llacuna and Polls, 38; and Crozier, 64. The author was able to view black-and-white photographs taken at Monte Arruit of the military victims of the Riffians at the Museum of the Legion in Ceuta. These photos and others can also be seen in Carrasco García, 166-179.

48. Woolman, *Rebels in the Rif*, 104; Payne, 177; and de Arce, 150.

49. *DOL, Negociado de campaña*, 23 October 1921, 10. Cano Velasco, ed., 149. de Arce, 149. For more on the death of Captain Miguel Gascón Aquilue, and 42 for *Alférez* Julio Argueldo Braje, see Ramas Izquierdo, 25-26. See Berenguer, 136-138, for his special recognition of the valor of the Legion in the battle. Mico y España, 226-227, related two amusing anecdotes about Major Villegas the commanding officer of the IVth *Bandera*: He described the major going into battle with his pockets full of grenades and hurling them at the enemy as if he were a young boy throwing rocks, and he recounted the time he had his ever-present cigar shot from his mouth. The major's reaction was to declare: "Shit! They have left me with nothing to smoke, because I don't have another."

50. *DOL, Negociado de campaña*, 28 October 1921, 10. Cano Velasco, ed., 149-150; and Scurr, 11. See Ramas Izquierdo, 42 for more on the death of *Alférez* Carlos García Fernández. Berenguer, 140. The High Commissioner described the intensity of the battle and the high number of casualties involving the "recently organized Cuban companies" of the IVth *Bandera*. On 12 June 1922, at Uad Lau, Millán Astray personally presented the IVth *Bandera* with the battle ribbon "Magan" to be attached to their standard in recognition for their actions at the battle of Monte Magan. This battle ribbon had been bestowed upon the IVth by the reigning monarch, Alfonso XIII.

51. *DOL, Negociado de campaña*, 1 November 1921, 10. Cano Velasco, ed., 150. Millán Astray, 62. For more on Major de Liniers y Muguiro, see Mico y España, 227-228.

52. *DOL, Negociado de campaña*, 2 November 1921, 11. The first surname of Enrique Agudo López is listed in this document as Duro, instead of Agudo. *SHM*, Legajo #54, Rollo 16, *Colección de historiales*, "Campañas de Marruecos, Historial de guerra, 1ª y

2ª Banderas," 136-137. This source, as well as a few of the others, contains the aforementioned letter. Estado Mayor Central del Ejército, 518. Franco, 136-139. Franco wrote that Enrique Agudo López was leading his platoon into action for the first time when he was killed. Subinspección de la Legión, ed., 146-148. This source erroneously gives the date of the congratulatory letter as 3 October 1921, instead of the correct 3 November 1921. Ramas Izquierdo, 42, has more on the death of *Alférez* Enrique Agudo López, who in the aforementioned sources was given the rank of lieutenant. De Arce, 150-153.

53. *DOL*, *Negociado de campaña*, 7 November 1921, 11; *SHM*, Legajo #54, Rollo 16, *Colección de historiales*, "Campañas de Marruecos, Historial de guerra, 1ª y 2ª Banderas," 137; and Estado Mayor Central del Ejército, 518-519. Franco, 140-142. Subinspección de la Legión, ed., 148-150. Also among the wounded was a Franciscan chaplain, Father Revilla, who though attached to General Sanjurjo's column became the Legion's padre. Farragut (pseud.), 72 and 76-78, has more on Father Revilla who along with his vestment wore the Legion's *chambergo*.

54. *AGM*, Legajo #M-3204, SECCIÓN #1, DIVISIÓN #1, 11; *DOL*, *Negociado de campaña*, 11 November 1921, 11; and *SHM*, Legajo #54, Rollo 16, *Colección de historiales*, "Campañas de Marruecos, Historial de guerra, 1ª y 2ª Banderas," 137-138. Franco, 142-144. Subinspección de la Legión, ed., 150. Estado Mayor Central del Ejército, 519-520.

55. *DOL*, *Negociado de campaña*, 18 November 1921, 11; *SHM*, Legajo #54, Rollo 16, *Colección de historiales*, "Campañas de Marruecos, Historial de guerra, 1ª y 2ª Banderas," 133-134; Franco, 148-152; and Subinspección de la Legión, ed., 150-154. Estado Mayor Central del Ejército, 523. Cano Velasco, ed., 150. Scurr, 10-11.

56. *AGM*, Legajo #M-3204, SECCIÓN #1, DIVISIÓN #1, 11; de Arce, 156-157; and Scurr, 11.

57. *DOL*, *Negociado de campaña*, 21 November 1921, 11; *SHM*, Legajo #54, Rollo 16, *Colección de historiales*, "Campañas de Marruecos, Historial de guerra, 1ª y 2ª Banderas," 139; Franco, 152-154; Subinspección de la Legión, ed., 154-155; Estado Mayor Central del Ejército, 524. With the stones of the old fortifications, the Legionaries rebuilt the position of Ras-Medua and duly manned it.

58. *DOL*, *Negociado de campaña*, 30 November 1921, 11. This source claims seven Legionaries wounded, whereas Franco and Subinspección de la Legión, ed., claimed twelve. *SHM*, Legajo #54, Rollo 16, *Colección de historiales*, "Campañas de Marruecos, Historial de guerra, 1ª y 2ª Banderas," 140. Franco, 155-157; Subinspección de la Legión, ed., 155-156; and Estado Mayor Central del Ejército, 524-525.

59. *DOL*, *Negociado de campaña*, 1 December 1921, 12. *SHM*, Legajo #54, Rollo 16, *Colección de historiales*, "Campañas de Marruecos, Historial de guerra, 1ª y 2ª Banderas," 140; Franco, 157; Subinspección de la Legión, ed., 156; and Estado Mayor Central del Ejército, 525. On 1 December, the Legion was deployed as follows: the Ist and IInd were at Segangan, the IIIrd was at Dar Acobba, the IVth at Uad Lau, and the Vth at Riffien.

60. *SHM*, Legajo #54, Rollo 16, *Colección de historiales*, "Campañas de Marruecos, Historial de guerra, 1ª y 2ª Banderas," 140. Franco, 157-158; Subinspección de

la Legión, ed., 156; and Crozier, 65.

    61. *DOL, Negociado de campaña*, 11 December 1921, 12; and Franco, 159.

    62. *DOL, Negociado de campaña*, 19 December 1921, 12; De Silva, 165; and García Figueras, 183.

    63. *DOL, Negociado de campaña*, 20 December 1921, 12. *SHM*, Legajo #54, Rollo 16, *Colección de historiales*, "Campañas de Marruecos, Historial de guerra, 1ª y 2ª Banderas," 140; Franco, 160; and Subinspección de la Legión, ed., 157-158.

    64. *DOL, Negociado de campaña*, 22 December 1921, 12. Franco, 161-165. One of the Legionaries killed in the battle of Ras-Tikermin was the standard-bearer of the 13th Company. Subinspección de la Legión, ed., 158-160. On 509-511, there is a brief summary of the actions of the Legion during 1921. Ramas Izquierdo, 32 has more on the death of Lieutenant Emilio Infantes Rodríguez, and 42-43 has more on *Alférez* Francisco Marquina Liquero/Siguero. Estado Mayor Central del Ejército, 528-529; Cano Velasco, ed., 150; Farragut (pseud.), 94-95; *AGM*, Legajo #M-3204, SECCIÓN #1, DIVISIÓN #1, 11; de Arce, 157; and De Silva, 165-166. While the Ist and IInd *Banderas* were in action in the eastern zone, Millán Astray was operating in the western zone with the IIIrd and Vth *Banderas*. They participated in an operation to take and occupy Teletza Hadru (Telafta). There were no casualties. For a brief summary of the events of the Ist, IInd, IIIrd, and IVth *Banderas* in 1921, see *SHM*, Legajo #54, Rollo 16, *Colección de historiales* (microfilm), La Legión, "Acciones de guerra de las distintas Banderas de la Legión (1920-1939)," 1-3, 7-9, 14-15, and 20, respectively.

    65. de Arce, 155.

    66. Sheelagh Ellwood, *Franco* (London and New York: Longman, 1994), 22-24; and Preston, 48-49.

Early Legion recruiting poster.

Studio photo of Francisco Franco Bahamonde (with the rank of major).

José Millán Astray, founder of the Legion (early photo).

José Millán Astray (photo circa Spanish Civil War).

Colonel José Millán Astray addressing his Legionaries at Ben Tieb. Note three wound chevrons on left sleeve.

Lieutenant Colonel Rafael Valenzuela Urzaiz, second commander-in-chief of the Legion. This photo was taken November 1922. Lt. Col. Valenzuela is wearing the uniform of the *Regulares*.

Lt. Col. Rafael Valenzuela Urzaiz (left), with Captain Joaqúin Ortiz de Zárate, outside the Royal Palace in Madrid.

Sección del Tercio cargando a la bayoneta.

Staged publicity photo of the Legion. Caption reads, "Platoon of the Tercio [Legion] charging at the bayonet."

Los del Tercio haciendo una «razzia» en el avance.

Staged publicity photo of the Legion. Captain reads, "Those of the Tercio [Legion] carrying out a 'raid' in the advance."

King's Barracks, Ceuta. First headquarters of the Legion.

Officers and Legionaries after the capture of Ras Medua (November 21, 1921).

Major Carlos Rodríguez Fontanés, commanding officer of the IInd Bandera along with Legionaries of the Ist and IInd Banderas following the capture of Tauriat Hamed (November 30, 1921).

Off-duty Legionaries outside their barracks. Most are wearing the *chambergo* slouch hat. Note the bugler (center, sitting) with the loop insignia on the cuff of his tunic.

Spanish troops disembark and wade ashore during the Alhucemas landing.

Mules and supplies are unloaded at La Cebadilla / Ixdain.

Tomb of Captain Pompilio Martínez Zaldívar, first Legion officer to be killed in action in 1921, located in Spanish Military Cemetery in Tetuán, Morocco.

Chapter 4

Legion Operations, 1922–1923

The army in the protectorate swelled to 150,000 by 1922 as patriotic volunteers, and even greater numbers of conscripts, joined the ranks.[1] However, the High Commissioner, General Dámaso Berenguer Fusté, was well aware that these raw recruits would be worthless if placed in the front lines, since they were incapable of engaging the enemy in their style of guerrilla warfare. They were therefore assigned to garrison duty in the principal Spanish towns of Melilla, Ceuta, Tetuán, and Larache. Naturally, this meant that the Legion and the *Regulares* would carry the fight to the enemy and would thus incur the greatest number of casualties.[2]

Stanley Payne detailed the government's plan of action for 1922 when he wrote that Prime Minister Antonio Maura attempted not to interpose in the conduct of the war in Morocco, though he had little confidence that the military could carry out a full-scale offensive against the enemy. Cognizant of the difficulties in carrying out such a campaign, as well as the political troubles it would give rise to, Maura would have liked the army to simply defend the principal coastal cities and abandon most of the interior to the tribesmen, as had previously been the case. General Berenguer, however, supported by Juan de La Cierva (minister of war), planned to keep up the counteroffensive in the Melillan zone during 1922, prosecute the Yebala campaign against el Raisuni to a conclusive end and then occupy the Rif itself, thus shattering Abd-el-Krim's revolt and bringing to a close the occupation of the protectorate. The last phase of these operations would be the most arduous, as it would almost certainly require an amphibious invasion near Alhucemas Bay, close to Abd-el-Krim's capital of Ajdir, in order to capture the rebels from behind.[3]

The start of the new year found the five *Banderas* of the Legion in four locations: the Ist and IInd at San Juan de las Minas (Segangan), the IIIrd at Dar Acobba, the IVth at Uad Lau, and the Vth at Ayalia. The Ist and IInd *Banderas*, under the command of Major Francisco Franco, were in the eastern zone preparing for continued operations against the Riffians. The IIIrd, IVth, and Vth *Banderas* were under the command of the recuperating Millán Astray in the western zone, prepared to deal decisively with el Raisuni.[4]

Millán Astray set out from Ceuta on 3 January for Xauen by way of Tetuán in order to head up the three *Banderas* that would spearhead the operations that were to commence against el Raisuni. The operation had three goals: (1) to expel el Raisuni from his headquarters in Tazarut; (2) to conquer the tribe of the Beni Aros region; and (3) to establish a fortified line from Uad Lau to the Lukus River (the boundary with the French protectorate), including Xauen. In addition, the plan for achieving the aforementioned goals was made up of three phases. The first phase consisted of occupying the zone between the *comandancias* of Ceuta and Larache. This had taken place between 19 and 22 December 1921. The second phase required the establishment of fortified positions along the northern bank of the Lukus River (6-10 January 1922). The third phase was to reach Tazarut.[5]

With the first phase of the operation accomplished in December of the previous year, the second phase of the plan was put into effect on 6 January. Millán Astray led the IIIrd and Vth *Banderas*, forming part of General Marzo's column in seizing and occupying Hauma Beni Bara. The fighting was fierce, with the Legion having one officer and eighteen Legionaries killed. The wounded consisted of three officers and forty-seven Legionaries.[6]

While the Legion was engaged in operations in the Beni Aros region, the Ist and IInd *Banderas* were beginning operations for the year in the Rif with the immediate goal of capturing Dar Drius. On 9 January, both *Banderas* under the leadership of Franco and forming part of General F. Berenguer's column assisted in taking and occupying Dar Busada while suffering only one Legionary dead and one wounded.[7] On the following day, the Ist and IInd *Banderas* easily took the key position of Dar Drius. The enemy was so overwhelmed by the cavalry of General Cabanellas and armored cars and trucks that they fled, leaving behind several cannons.[8]

At the same time the Legion was engaged in the reconquest of Dar Drius on January 10, the other three *Banderas* were engaged in the western zone. The IIIrd, IVth, and Vth *Banderas* charged the enemy's lines at Dra/Draa el Asef. Millán Astray was subsequently sent from General Marzo's column, along with the Vth *Bandera* and other needed units, to establish a *blocao* (Gómez Arteche) and to reinforce the rear guard flank of the column Colonel Castro Girona commanded. Upon Millán Astray's arrival, the 8th Company of the Vth *Bandera* was able to reinforce one of the *tabores* of the *Regulares de Tetuán*, which was then engaged in bitter hand-to-hand combat with the enemy, who outnumbered them ten to one. The Legionaries successfully covered the withdrawal of Castro Girona's column, with Millán Astray personally relieved by Lieutenant Colonel Santiago González Tablas. A few minutes later, Millán Astray, still not fully recovered from the chest wound he had received at Nador, was lightly wounded in the right leg. The toll in casualties for the Legion was heavy that day, with three officers and twenty-four Legionaries killed. The wounded included the commander of the Legion (Millán Astray), one officer, and twenty-eight Legionaries.[9] The rest of the month of January was relatively quiet for the Legion with each *Bandera* posted to different parts of the protectorate in order to provide protection to convoys resupplying forward positions.[10]

February was a quiet month for the Legion with no major engagements, except for a nocturnal Riffian surprise attack on Dar Drius on the 28th that was successfully repelled with bullets, hand grenades, and insults hurled by its underwear-clad defenders. The mission for all the *Banderas* was to continue to escort supply units in both theaters of operations.[11]

Whereas the military situation in the protectorate was uneventful, the political and diplomatic one was quite active. In Spain, there were serious strains within the government with regards to future military actions in the protectorate. The minister of war (La Cierva), and the foreign minister (González Hontoria) were at odds over what plan of action to follow in Africa. This conflict led to the *Conferencia de Pizarra*, held from 4 to 6 February 1922. The conference took place in the province of Málaga in order to get away from the political climate of Madrid, as well as to keep the High Commissioner close to the protectorate. With this reunion of governmental and military leaders, the main topic of discussion was, as Morales Lezcano succinctly put it, "the final solution to the Moroccan problem." The military was in total agreement that Abd-el-Krim and el Raisuni must be defeated decisively, and that the best way to accomplish the former was by disembarking at Alhucemas Bay.[12]

By March the weather had improved and operations were resumed, mainly in the eastern zone against the Beni Said and Beni Ulixech tribes in order to rectify the front line north of the Kert River, which stretched from Dar Drius to the Mediterranean Sea. With the increase in the number of troops in the protectorate, the number of weapons increased as well. For the first time in the Spanish Protectorate of Morocco, tanks arrived in Melilla. The tanks used by the Spanish army in Morocco were the 6.5 ton Renault *FT-17* light tank, armed with a single 7 mm Hotchkiss machine gun. The army originally acquired nine tanks in January, but a few weeks later two more were obtained, with one of them a command tank (*FT-17TSF*). In Morocco, the tanks were organized into two sections of five tanks each. They would soon be employed against the Riffian trenches and fortifications in the zone around Dar Drius (the Tisingar-Sbu Sbaa line).[13]

The reconquest continued in the east when the weather improved. On 7 March, and under the personal leadership of Millán Astray, the first two *Banderas* formed the vanguard of General F. Berenguer's column to cover the installation of a position at Zauia de la Abada, situated some three kilometers from Dar Drius. The site was taken, as was reported, *sin novedad* (without incident).[14] The next day's mission was to assist F. Berenguer's column in taking and occupying Sepsa, and was accomplished at the cost of three Legionaries killed and seven wounded.

The same two *Banderas* assisted on 14 March in taking Istiguen numbers 1 and 2, located on the Arkab plateau. In the battle with the rebels, one officer and a Legionary were killed, plus one officer and six Legionaries were wounded. With the post constructed, the column returned to its encampment at Dar Drius with the Legionaries guarding the withdrawal.[15]

For the first time in the long history of the Spanish army, and almost certainly of Africa, tanks were employed in a major battle. The tanks, which had arrived from Melilla, were to take part in the capture of Ambar, which was situated on a plateau. On 18 March, the tanks set out on their mission, closely followed by the two *Banderas* of the Legion under the command of Millán Astray. The Ist *Bandera* was led by Major Francisco Franco Bahamonde, and the IInd by Major Carlos Rodríguez Fontanés, both experienced commanders of their respective battalions. In a hard-fought battle with Beni Said and Beni Ulixech tribesmen, the Legionaries advanced over the difficult terrain. The tanks provided covering fire for the Legionaries with their machine guns, but the going was slow. The deeper into enemy territory they went, the more resistance they encountered from the Riffian defenders until the major goal of taking Tuguntz was postponed and Ambar became the point of maximum advance. Ambar would later be fortified by military engineers and mountain guns and serve as the foremost outpost area for the Legion. In the assault, the light tanks had traveled nearly one kilometer and had become separated from their infantry support. Unable to cover their return to the Spanish lines, the Riffians quickly took advantage of the situation, converging on the tanks and hurling rocks at them. When the tanks' machine guns could no longer fire and the tanks had run out of gas, their wounded crews, including their captain, abandoned them. Those who could save themselves retreated to the Legion's fortified line. One tank crewman, the machine gunner, was slightly wounded in the face when a Riffian thrust his dagger through the vision slit of his tank. The Legionaries withdrew in an orderly and methodical manner that eventually ended with the Riffian war parties chasing them back to their own wire entanglements. In the end, the Riffians resorted to blowing up the abandoned tanks with dynamite taken from Spanish mining operations in the Rif. Thus the first collaboration of tanks and infantry in Spanish Morocco had been a disaster. Casualties for the Legion were heavy, and for the first time, but certainly not the last, a battalion commander was killed in combat: Major Carlos Rodríguez Fontanés, commander of the IInd *Bandera*, had been shot in the abdomen while withdrawing his forces and died early the next day. A volunteer chaplain of the Legion, Antonio Vidal y Pons, was also mortally wounded. Ten Legionaries were also killed, along with three officers (among them were Fontanés adjutant, a future Laureate Cross of St. Ferdinand recipient Lieutenant Fernando Lizcano de la Rosa and Lieutenant Francisco Compaired Iriarte of the 13/I) and sixty-two Legionaries wounded.[16]

The two *Banderas* remained at Ambar until 29 March, when they set out for Tuguntz as the vanguard of the attacking column. They rapidly advanced with the Legion on the right flank and the *Regulares* on the left. The column was also composed of the native police, as well as General Cabanellas' cavalry. After having secured their objective of Tuguntz and Cala, they pressed on toward the very difficult terrain of the Bas River. Suddenly, taking full advantage of the numerous ravines, the Riffians opened withering fire from both cannons and rifles on the cavalry of the *Regulares*. The column was, however, able to extricate itself from the Riffian onslaught, returning to prepared fortifications. Once again the Legion suffered heavy casualties, including the death of one officer, and six Legionaries. The wounded consisted of two officers and fifty-six Legionaries. According to Spanish sources, the Riffians suffered 170 killed and more than 350 wounded.[17]

The Legion's ability to fight the rebels using their own style and methods of warfare made them invaluable to the reconquest of the lost territory. In his diary, Franco wrote about the peninsular troops' lack of experience in fighting a guerrilla war with the Riffians. He described the situation of a company from the Battalion of Galicia that came to the rescue of the *Regulares* only to find themselves getting shot to pieces. Although they defended themselves bravely, they could not pick out their targets and were thus unable to be effective. Of the peninsular forces, the natives serving with the Spanish forces said, "*Todavia no saber manera*" ("Still they don't know how").[18]

By the end of March, the situation regarding large-scale offensive operations slowly began to change. With the threat to Melilla long gone and with a new government in power, the repatriation of peninsular forces (the short-term recruits) was about to begin. To satisfy politicians and the Spanish public's general opposition to sending conscripts to die fighting Moroccan tribesmen in a war that seemed endless, while at the same time keeping the war against the rebels going while reducing the financial cost, Berenguer agreed to repatriate no fewer than 20,000 men by 1 June. Furthermore, he agreed to suspend the Alhucemas Bay operation and what would have been a new front. For the Legion, this meant that the bulk of the advancing columns that had permitted the Legion to be its spearhead would noticeably diminish. Thus the Legion would lose power by having less support. As Cano Velasco put it, "The war in Africa, and with it the Legion, enters into a new phase."[19]

March had seen the Legion, as always, leading the way in successful operations against the Beni Said, although the toll had been high. In April the focus of Berenguer's objectives in the protectorate shifted to the western zone with the capture of Sherif el Raisuni in his *nido de Aguilas* (Eagle's nest) in Tazarut the major objective. For this reason, Berenguer transferred his most able senior general, José Sanjurjo Sacanell, from Melilla to Larache along with some of his best units. Millán Astray also returned to the western zone, and Franco once again took command of the Ist and IInd *Banderas*, which on 1 April were at Dar Drius. Both the IIIrd and Vth *Banderas* were in Riffien, while the IVth was in Uad Lau.[20]

In the eastern zone of operations, April was a successful and productive month with significant gains made with relatively few casualties. The plan was to continue with the move into the area north of the Kert River and drive toward the sea. On 6 April, Franco's two *Banderas* assisted in taking and occupying Chemorra and Lauria Immedian without incident. This was followed on the 8th with a similarly successful operation in which the Legion "took the point" for Cabanellas cavalry against Dar Quebdani, but this time having to lament the wounding of two Legionaries. Timayats was taken and occupied on the 11th; Tamasusin on the 14th; and La Chaif on the 17th, all three without any casualties. After the aforementioned operation, the two *Banderas* consolidated their gains the rest of the month.[21]

Following the success of securing Dar Quebdani on 8 April, the Legion had to secure the Peñón (crag) de Vélez de la Gomera from the possible invasion by the Riffians. The Peñón, which was Spanish property, was only 80 meters from the Moroccan coast and could be easily reached by foot during low tides. Regular army units garrisoned the crag, but as they were undermanned and under constant hostile fire from cannons and rifles, they would be unable to thwart a sustained rebel attack. When a call for volunteers went out to save the Peñón, all those present at Dar Drius from the most senior Legionary to the newest recruits volunteered to go. The contingent was composed of Lieutenant José Martínez Esparza, *Alférez* Díaz de Rabago, one sergeant, six corporals, and forty-four Legionaries. They returned to Melilla and from there traveled to the Peñón aboard the destroyer *Bustamante*. Under cover of night, the Legionaries scaled the sharp rocks and took up defensive positions in the most vulnerable locations. On the same night the Legionaries arrived, the rebels on the opposite shore, who were well aware of the fighting capabilities of the Legion, asked "if those of the Tresio [*sic*] had arrived." Though the food was less than could be desired, the Legionaries spirit and enthusiasm never waned as they traded lead and insults with their adversaries. Shortly after the arrival of the Legionaries, the enemy's ardor diminished. Eventually, the possibility of the Peñón falling into the hands of the enemy faded and the number of Legionaries was reduced to thirty men. Once again the Legion had been called upon to prevent the capture of a Spanish position, just as they had done the previous year in Melilla. The Legion's reputation as the "firemen" of the Army continued to grow.[22]

While the Ist and IInd *Banderas* were pacifying the Beni Said region, the other three *Banderas* in the western zone were proceeding with their goal of capturing Tazarut and forcing el Raisuni to submit. On 13 April, approximately 1,500 enemy tribesmen besieged Corporal Isidro Gallego Cuesta and fifteen Legionaries of the 18th Company/Vth *Bandera* while they defended the *blocao* of Miskrela Nº 1 (Xauen). Thrice the enemy attacked and thrice they were repelled, each time incurring greater losses, leaving the bodies of some eighty rebels strewn about the wire entanglements and the perimeter of the position. The Legionaries stubbornly resisted until the following day when a relief column was able to evacuate the two dead and the fourteen wounded. For their bravery and conduct in the face of overwhelming numbers, they were awarded the Military Medal (*Medalla Militar*) and were congratulated in an army general order by the general in chief. Unlike *El Malo* the year before, this time the enemy had been the loser and the Legion had gained more recognition and laurels.[23]

On 28 April, the IIIrd and Vth *Banderas* took part in an operation aimed at taking and occupying Takun, Selaca, and Besiar. In hard-fought battles with the enemy, the Legion lost five men killed and twenty-six wounded. On the same day, but on the other side of the protectorate, one Legionary died when rebels attacked the Peñón de Vélez de la Gomera.[24]

Although the Melillan campaign had officially ended, unofficially men continued to die fighting against the Riffian rebels in the eastern zone of the protectorate. Abd-el-Krim continued with his campaign to rid the Rif of Spanish forces and to have the European powers recognize his Riffian Republic. Spain's military attention shifted to the western zone of the protectorate in the hopes of dealing el Raisuni a crushing blow that would knock him out of the war. As they had done so many times before, the Legionaries once again assumed the greatest burden in the fighting that was to come.[25]

The first of May saw the Ist and IInd *Banderas* carrying out routine operations from their encampment of Dar Drius. The IIIrd was in Takun in the Beni Aros region. The IVth was in Uad Lau. The Vth was in Zoco el Jemis, also in the Beni Aros.[26] The first operation that would eventually lead to the capture of Tazarut began on 2 May, when the IIIrd and Vth *Banderas* under the leadership of Lieutenant Colonel Millán Astray and in the vanguard of General Marzo's column, assisted in the successful acquisition and occupation of Tahar Varda (Tahar-Berda).[27] Five days later the same two *Banderas* repeated a similar operation at Gran Peña and Selalen as they moved ever closer to Tazarut. The 15th Company/III *Bandera* took and garrisoned both positions. Twelve Legionaries were wounded in the assault.[28]

The main goal of the campaign was achieved on 12 May when the IIIrd and Vth *Banderas* conquered Tazarut and Aingrana after a bitter fight with the enemy. The IIIrd *Bandera* covered the right flank of the battle line, with the 15th Company reinforcing a *tabor* of *Regulares*, which was engaged in intense combat with the enemy before Selalen. The Vth *Bandera*, in the vanguard of General Serrano's column, followed the *Regulares de Ceuta Nº 3*. The Legionaries of the Vth *Bandera* set out from the *blocao* of Tacuun, until they had reached their designated objective, where they remained to protect the artillery for a short time. But when the *Regulares de Ceuta Nº 3* were being severely punished by the rebels (which included the death of their beloved commander, Lieutenant Colonel Santiago González Tablas), the *Bandera* was ordered to reinforce them. The 18th Rifle Company and the machine gun company both went into action. When the fighting grew more intense, the two remaining rifle companies hurled themselves upon the left side of the firing line, dispersing the enemy. With both objectives secured, the Vth *Bandera* remained in the newly captured positions. The toll for the Legion had been three Legionaries killed, as well as three officers and eighteen Legionaries wounded.[29]

The Vth *Bandera* continued with its operations in the same zone after capturing Tazarut. On 21 May, it assisted in the occupation of Ras Muturaka, without sustaining casualties, and around the 24th seized Rokoba Adia, establishing a *blocao*, "Mers Mesla," again with no casualties.[30]

Beginning in June, the level of fighting in both the eastern and western zones diminished with el Raisuni on the run and Abd-el-Krim scaling back his operations. Nevertheless, the Legion continued to provide its services of guarding convoys or serving in the van of assault columns. An example of the former occurred on 16 June when rebels attacked a unit of the Vth *Bandera* in Tazarut gravely wounding Lieutenant Joaquín Beorlegui Canet, who died of his wounds a week later in hospital.[31] On 18 June, both the IIIrd and IVth *Banderas* were in action, with the former taking part in the occupation of Mensora. The latter was engaged in one of the bitterest battles of the war. The men of the Legion composed the vanguard of Colonel Saliquet's column, which had as its daily mission the capture, fortification, and manning of Baba and Sugna. The vanguard of the column was composed of the IVth *Bandera* and the depot rifle companies from Riffien, the cavalry of the *Mehal-la*, and two cavalry squadrons of *Regulares* (Tetuán and Ceuta) who formed the left flank of the column. The 12/IV Machine Gun Company along with the 2nd Depot Rifle Company were in the center of the column to provide fire support. After an artillery barrage, the column advanced, capturing the villages of Marabtech and Helalech. The enemy fought back pugnaciously engaging the Legionaries in hand-to-hand combat. The rebels had the worst of it, leaving many of their own on the battlefield. With Baba and Sugna occupied, the column once again had to fend off the determined enemy while they withdrew to Draa-el-Asef, which they attacked for four hours. In the hard-fought battle, the Legion had one officer and twelve Legionaries killed; the wounded included one officer and seventy-six Legionaries. The enemy's losses were calculated at more than one hundred killed and three hundred wounded.[32]

The IIIrd and Vth *Banderas*, on 19 June, participated in taking and occupying Zauia del Tilili. These *Banderas* on 26 June later occupied Soldevila without casualties.[33]

From July to the end of the year, Legion operations were reduced to consolidating previous gains and escorting supply convoys. The Ist *Bandera* operated from Dar Drius; the IInd rested and relaxed in Melilla; the IIIrd was in Mexerach; the IVth was at Draa-el-Asef; and the Vth was in Tazarut. On 3 July, the IIIrd and Vth *Banderas* assisted in an operation that aimed at seizing and occupying Kala and Sidi Abderrahaman. Only one Legionary was wounded. The following day, these *Banderas* repeated a similar operation against Tenacot and Bab el Haman. Once again, only one Legionary was wounded. For the remainder of the month, the five *Banderas* remained in their aforementioned locales carrying out routine operations.[34]

In August, the focus of Legion activity shifted from the western zone to the eastern zone. The Ist *Bandera* was rotated to Melilla for rest and relaxation; the IInd was at Dar Drius (with Major José Candeira Sestelo having replaced the late Major Fontanés); the IIIrd in Uad Lau; the IVth in Xauen; and the Vth in Tazarut. From 2 to 25 August, the Legion performed its usual campaign duties, but on 26, 28, and 29 August, the Ist and IInd *Banderas* took part in the capture and fortification of Azib de Midar, Tauriat Uchan, and Issen Lassen, respectively. In each of the three engagements, only one Legionary received wounds.[35]

The political and military situation heated up during the summer with the High Commissioner, Dámaso Berenguer Fusté, as the major target. He received criticism in the Spanish press from Spain's most senior general, Valeriano Weyler Nicolau, for doing nothing to retrieve the prisoners from the Annual disaster. Furthermore, the Picasso Commission recommended that Berenguer, General Silvestre (if he were to be found), and General Navarro (if he were rescued or ransomed) be prosecuted for what happened at Annual. On 9 July, Berenguer submitted his resignation for the fourth and final time. It was accepted. The former captain general of Madrid, General Ricardo Burguete y Lana, replaced him on 16 July. Burguete had been an able field commander in previous Moroccan campaigns and, like Berenguer, was a politician as well as a soldier. His appointment as the new High Commissioner came as quite a shock to many in the military. In the past, he had written in favor of militarism, but now, for political reasons, he changed his stance. Both Sánchez Guerra and Burguete responded to popular opinion to terminate offensive operations in Morocco. Burguete sought a peaceful or nonmilitary solution to the situation in the protectorate. This new policy was totally impractical and went against the wishes of the *africanistas*. However, by mid-August, Burguete's policy had once again changed in favor of aggressive action in the protectorate, even being in favor of a major offensive aimed at Ajdir, Abd-el-Krim's Riffian capital.[36]

On 1 September, personnel taken from the other *Banderas* and the depot company formed the VIth *Bandera* of the Legion. Major Enrique Lucas Mercader became its first commander; its standard was the coat of arms of the Grand Duke of Alba (Fernando Álvarez de Toledo) on a red field. While the VIth *Bandera* began its training at Dar Riffien, the other five *Banderas* of the Legion were dispersed as follows: Ist and IInd at Dar Drius, the IIIrd at Uad Lau, the IVth in Xauen, and the Vth in Tazarut, all performing their usual campaign duties with no major incidents reported for the month.[37]

The new High Commissioner, Burguete, pursued an aggressive military policy toward Abd-el-Krim in the eastern zone of the protectorate until reaching his headquarters in Ajdir. Naturally, the Legion would play a pivotal role in his plans of conquest. On the first day of October, the Ist *Bandera* was in Melilla; the IInd at Dar Drius; the IIIrd at Uad Lau; the IVth in Xauen but would be transferred to the eastern zone on the 18th; the Vth in Ain Grana (Larache); and the newly created VIth remained in Riffien.[38]

The IIIrd *Bandera*, on 7 October, took part in an operation whose goal was the taking and occupying of Meter in the Gomara region. This was accomplished with no casualties. The fighting shifted to the eastern zone on 26 October when the Ist, IInd, and recently arrived IVth *Banderas* under the personal leadership of Millán Astray formed the vanguard of General Leopoldo Ruiz-Trillo's column. Colonel Alfredo Coronel Cubria led the vanguard and assisted in the capture of Hamuda, Tafersit, Buhafora, and Tayudai. For the Legion, the toll for the day was one officer and four Legionaries wounded. This was followed up two days later on the 28th when the same column, accompanied by the *Regulares de Melilla* in the vanguard, occupied and fortified Viernes and Tizzi-Azza, before establishing a *blocao* in the latter village. Two Legionaries died and seven were wounded. Tizzi-Azza would be a focal point for the Legion, resulting in suffering and death, until the Alhucemas Bay landing in late 1925.[39]

Spanish forces tried to rectify and fortify their front lines in the newly conquered area around Tizzi-Azza and on 1 November suffered a strong Riffian attack that was beaten off by the Legionaries, who nevertheless suffered over one hundred Spanish casualties (including Lieutenant Pérez Mercader of the Legion). When the Spanish press obtained the battle reports and saw the high number of casualties, the government instructed the High Commissioner, General Burguete, to cease all further offensive operations.[40] The government was sensitive to public opinion, especially after the public had been led to believe that operations in the protectorate were basically over after Melilla and its environs were secured.

On 6 November, the IVth *Bandera* assisted in taking and occupying Sidi Mesaud, a mission successfully accomplished without casualties.[41] The following day Lieutenant Colonel José Millán Astray announced his retirement as a result of his objection to the influence of the *junteros* (members of the Defense Juntas) within the Spanish army. The rivalry and animosity between the *junteros* and the *africanistas* had come to a head. Millán Astray wrote in an open letter to the king that he could not serve in an army where "two authorities operate" (the *junteros* and the government). Franco, along with the other officers of the Legion, stood behind their leader. Millán Astray's resignation was not accepted at first, but pressure from the *junteros*, objections from Liberals in the government, and the insubordinate nature of Millán Astray's action (i.e., the publication of the letter) led to the Royal Order of 13 November (DO #256), which separated him from the Legion he had founded just two years earlier. For public consumption, it was reported that his many battle wounds had left him unfit for such a strenuous command; he was posted to the 1st Military Region in Cádiz.[42]

Franco, as Millán Astray's hand-picked deputy, had expected to be named his successor, but *junteros* who resented his *africanista* sentiments delayed his promotion to lieutenant colonel, the rank necessary to command a unit the size of the Legion. Command of the Legion was instead given to a forty-one-year-old lieutenant colonel of infantry, Rafael Valenzuela Urzaiz, Knight of the Order of Santiago. Valenzuela was a courageous and highly respected officer who had founded and commanded the *Regulares de Alhucemas Nº 5* the past year. Valenzuela's short-lived command of the Legion officially began on 1 December. Franco remained with the Ist *Bandera* until 17 January 1923. The snubbed Major Franco asked to be posted back to his previous regiment, the 1st Battalion of the *Regimiento del Príncipe*, in Oviedo.[43]

The six *Banderas* of the Legion, on 1 December, were posted in the following locales: the Ist in Tafersit; the IInd in the Legion-built camp at Ben

Tieb; the IIIrd at Uad Lau; the IVth at Dar Quebdani; the Vth at Ain Grana; and the VIth in Xauen. From the first day until the 17th, all the *Banderas* performed their typical campaign services.[44] The Ist *Bandera*, on 18 December, assisted in bringing reinforcements and supplies to the forward position of Tizzi-Azza. The Legionaries had to fight their way in and then fight their way out as the Riffians put up stiff resistance to the convoy. The human cost for *Los Jabalies* (The Wild Boars) was one officer and six Legionaries killed; fourteen Legionaries were wounded.[45]

In the protectorate, 1923 began routinely enough for the Legion. As a result of the political turmoil in the peninsula, which among other developments included a new government (Sánchez Guerra's cabinet changed on 7 December 1922 to one headed by the Liberal García Prieto), the resignation of Millán Astray, and a new policy to go slow in the eastern zone, the Legion's revised mission was to provide campaign services (e.g., escorting supply convoys and protecting vulnerable outposts) for the army. On 1 January, the six *Banderas* of the Legion were stationed in the following locations: the Ist in Tizzi-Azza; the IInd in Dar Drius; the IIIrd at Meter; the IVth at Dar Quebdani; the Vth in Riffien; and the VIth in Ain Grana. This arrangement lasted until May, with the exception of the Ist *Bandera*, which moved from Tizzi-Azza to Tafersit in February.[46]

Through difficult negotiations begun by García Prieto's government in late 1922, Spanish prisoners from the Annual disaster were finally ransomed on 27 January 1923 for 4,270,000 *pesetas*. Whereas previous administrations had followed the advice of the military not to pay Abd-el-Krim one cent for the release of the prisoners, the new government thought otherwise, and with the help of millionaire banker and Abd-el-Krim's friend Horacio Echevarrieta, the prisoners were sold back to their countrymen. They arrived in Melilla aboard the *Antonio López*. Of the 570 who had gone into captivity, 45 officers, including Silvestre's executive officer, General Felipe Navarro, 245 soldiers, and 40 civilians, which included women and children, survived typhus, cholera, and ill-treatment.[47]

Not only did the García Prieto government move to ransom the prisoners against the wishes of the military, especially the *africanistas*, but it also installed a civilian High Commissioner for the protectorate. Miguel Villanueva replaced General Burguete on 2 January 1923. However, Villanueva was never able to assume his new post because of a long illness. On 17 February, Villanueva was officially replaced by another civilian, Luis Silvela. The military officers in Morocco viewed a civilian High Commissioner with suspicion, since administration of the protectorate had always gone to a general as a plum appointment. Moreover, they questioned whether a civilian commissioner would prosecute the war against Abd-el-Krim with the same fervor as would a career officer.[48]

Meanwhile, in the eastern zone, Abd-el-Krim officially declared the creation of the "Emirate of the Rif" with himself as *Amir* (prince) on the first day of February. In the territory under his control, Abd-el-Krim's strength and popularity were increasing daily. His original *harka* was now an army made up of a few thousand well-equipped men.[49]

Silvela, the new High Commissioner, found two problems on his hands regarding the two zones. In the west, el Raisuni, who had signed a pact with the Spanish in late 1922, continued to cause trouble and impede Spain's designs in the Yebala. His influence in the region had not diminished. In the east, Abd-el-Krim and his followers had the advantage in the struggle, since they were familiar with the terrain, could give battle when it suited them, and could fade away to fight another day when they appeared to be overmatched. As in any colonial struggle, they would win by not losing.[50]

In May, the war in the eastern zone began to heat up once again, and the Legion was in the forefront of it all. On the first day of May, the Ist *Bandera* was at Sidi Guariach; the IInd at Hamuda; the IIIrd in Meter; the IVth at Tafersit; the Vth in Xauen; and the VIth at Ain Grana. The first battle of many to come in the Rif took place on 16 May, when the IVth *Bandera* assisted in taking and then fortifying Peña Tahuarda in the face of minimal enemy resistance. Major Felipe Figueras Figueras, commander of the IVth *Bandera*, was gravely wounded in the assault.[51] On 20 May, the IVth *Bandera* left its base of Ben Behasa to form part of Colonel Coronel's column, whose mission was to establish a position at Tifaruin and an outpost on Farha peak (aka Izummar Nº 2) between Izummar and Afrau. There were no casualties, but in August, these positions would undergo violent enemy attacks.[52]

Emboldened by his political and financial victory over the Spanish with regards to the ransoming of the prisoners, Abd-el-Krim's next move was to wipe out the advanced position of Tizzi-Azza. As noted previously, Tizzi-Azza was like a dagger pointed toward the heart of the Rif. By the end of May, the Riffians had Tizzi-Azza surrounded. The men stationed there faced great peril because of the shortage of munitions and provisions. On 28 May, the Ist and IVth *Banderas* set out to break the Riffian siege of Tizzi-Azza. Legionaries received the mission of providing protection for the much-needed supplies. After engaging the enemy near the Tizzi-Azza-Tabuarda line, the Legion suffered losses of two officers and twenty Legionaries dead, and of one officer and thirty-two Legionaries wounded.[53]

The battle to break the siege of Tizzi-Azza continued for the next three days (29, 30, and 31 May). Setting out at dawn on the 29th from Bu-Hafora, the Ist and IVth *Banderas* served in the vanguard of Colonel Gómez Morato's column, whose mission was once again to protect the supply convoy to Tizzi-Azza and other outposts (Viernes, Peña Tauarda, and Benitez) in that sector. The 1st and 2nd Companies of the Ist *Bandera* split up with the former advancing on the left to occupy Loma Roja by force; the latter, with the support of the 3rd Machine Gun Company, secured the heights of Sidi-Ali-Musa. The IVth *Bandera*, simultaneously, proceeded rapidly toward Benitez without meeting great resistance. From Benitez, they fanned out toward the many ravines in order to expand the area of protection for the convoy. These ravines were, however, filled with well-entrenched Riffians who greeted the advancing Legionaries with a hail of lead. The only way to expel the Riffians from these gullies was at the point of the bayonet, and this the Legionaries did. One of the companies of the IVth reached the *blocao* of Teruel; from there it continued to punish the Riffians. The convoy was able to enter Tizzi-Azza, and the two *Banderas* withdrew to Tafersit. But as soon as they had withdrawn, the Riffians reoccupied their lost positions and again surrounded Tizzi-Azza. The day's toll for the Legion had been one Legionary killed and nine wounded, all from the Ist *Bandera*.[54] On the 30th, the Riffians attacked Benitez, but the Legionaries repelled them in a bitter defense. In this encounter, the Legionaries suffered eleven killed and seven wounded.[55]

The Ist *Bandera*, along with the 11th and 12th (MG) Companies of the IVth, left Tafersit on 31 May to provide protection to another convoy headed to Tizzi-Azza. They advanced past Buhafora toward Loma Gris accompanied by the forces of the native *Mehal-la de Tafersit* (pro-Spanish government soldiers). While the 1st Company of the Ist covered the Buhafora River, the 11/IV occupied Loma Gris and one platoon from the aforementioned company prepared to seize Loma Roja. Under effective machine gun fire, the 13th Company of the Ist was able to climb the ridge of Peña Tahuarda to strike at the flank of the enemy lying in ambush in the ravine of Iguermisen. This bold move by the Legionaries allowed the convoy to pass. Unfortunately, the price paid in blood by the Legion had been high with one officer and ten Legionaries killed, along with five officers and seventy-four Legionaries wounded.[56]

Prior to the precarious situation in the Tizzi-Azza sector in late May, the Legion had been preparing to receive its very own national colors (the Spanish national flag) from the queen. The ceremony was to have taken place in Madrid and the new commander in chief of the Legion, Lieutenant Colonel Rafael Valenzuela Urzaiz, along with representatives of the various *Banderas*, was to parade before the Spanish monarchs. Regrettably, the worsening situation at Tizzi-Azza led to the ceremony being postponed. Valenzuela and all Legionaries rushed back to their respective *Banderas*.[57]

On 1 June, the six *Banderas* of the Legion were positioned to provide the most effective service and support: The Ist and IVth *Banderas* were in Tafersit; the IInd at Hamuda; the IIIrd at Uad Lau; the Vth in Xauen; and the VIth in Zoco el Jemis de Beni Aros. Also on the 1st, the IInd *Bandera* from its encampment at Hamud-Beveasa cooperated in the conquest and fortification of Afarnum, located in the Dar-Quebdani sector.[58]

A strong Riffian war party surrounded Tizzi-Azza on 4 June, the day before the post was scheduled for provisioning. For such a dangerous operation as provisioning a besieged post, three *Banderas* of the Legion (Ist, IInd, and IVth), were ordered to proceed to the area of Tafersit-Bu Hafora. The Legion's orders for the day were to lift the siege of Tizzi-Azza and to protect the supply convoy. Addressing the three *Banderas* at Tafersit, Lieutenant Colonel Valenzuela told the Legionaries: "Tomorrow the convoy will enter Tizzi-Asa or we shall all die, because our race [*raza*] has not died yet!" The relief and supply convoy was composed of two columns: Colonel Coronel's column, with the Ist and IInd *Banderas* in its van, took the right flank toward Benitez; Colonel Gómez Morato's column, with the IVth *Bandera* in its van, left from Bu Hafora toward Tizzi-Azza. Two other columns covered the left flank, with the *Regulares de Melilla* in the center. The IInd *Bandera* succeeded in reaching its objective of Turhani, but the *Regulares* encountered stiff resistance from the Riffians, who were well entrenched in camouflaged foxholes at Iguermisen. With the *Regulares* held up by the Riffians' withering fire, the Ist and IInd *Banderas'* right flank attack was made difficult. The IVth, advancing on the left flank, however, made good progress. Valenzuela ordered the IInd to open space on its right for the Ist in order to reinforce the attack. The fight became more intense as the first Legionaries began to fall. Machine guns swept the ravine of Iguermisen as the Legionaries hurled hand grenades to flush out the dug-in enemy. Not seeing what had happened to the *Regulares*, the colonel of the column called for a general attack.

Valenzuela told the men of the IInd *Bandera*, "Legionaries, the moment has come to die for Spain!" and ordered his bugler to sound the Legion's call for the attack ("Legionaries, to fight; legionaries, to die"). In typical Legion fashion, Valenzuela, accompanied by his adjutant, Captain Ortiz de Zárate, took his place in front of the IInd *Bandera* as they charged up the slope with fixed bayonets. The fighting was brutal with hand-to-hand combat the order of the day, and with the Legionaries having to force the Riffians from their entrenchments at the point of the bayonet. Clutching his *chapiri* (Legion sidecap) in his left hand and firing his pistol, Valenzuela rallied his men onward with shouts of "Long live Spain," "Long live the king," and "Long live the Legion," until he was felled by a bullet through the head and another in the chest. Those around him were also cut down, as well as stretcher bearers who were dispatched to retrieve his corpse. The officers organized those Legionaries still standing and were able to drive the Riffians from their positions and put them to flight in a final charge.

Casualties for the Legion were staggering with the toll reaching 197. Besides their chief, the dead included Captain Pedro Casado Obcola/Casaux Beola (killed trying to recover Valenzuela's body), Lieutenant Justo Sanz Perea, *Alféreces* Fermín Alarcón de la Lastra and Pablo Cendra/Sendra Font, as well as fifty-three Legionaries; the wounded numbered one *Bandera* commander (a major), ten officers, and 129 Legionaries. The death of Valenzuela, the first and only commander in chief of the Legion to be killed in battle, would go down in the annals of the Legion, and his name would be included with the other heroes of the Legion in its *Libro de oro*.[59]

Valenzuela's personal display of courage under fire by leading his men from the front in the attack on Tizzi-Azza was typical of Legion officers and NCOs. Many Legion officers, like Valenzuela, had served in the *Regulares* prior to joining the Legion. These Spanish officers earned the respect, trust, and admiration of their Moroccan troops through personal courage in the face of the enemy. This practice or tradition was transplanted into the Legion. In addition, Millán Astray's personal ethos or ideology concerning death and dying a "glorious death" greatly contributed to this attitude among the leadership of the Legion. How could a Legion officer order his men into battle knowing they could be killed or grievously wounded when he himself wasn't willing to face the same fate?

With Valenzuela dead, only one man could effectively replace him as commander in chief of the Legion—Major Francisco Franco Bahamonde. Franco's appointment came quickly with the backing of the king, who sent the Legion a congratulatory telegram on 6 June. In the telegram, the king, besides lamenting the death of "one of my best soldiers" (Valenzuela), conferred command of the *Banderas* to Lieutenant Colonel Franco. Having to postpone his marriage once again, Franco returned to Ceuta to take command of the Legion on 18 June.[60]

The government prohibited the commanding general of Melilla, General Pedro Vives Vich, from pressing on with operations in the area of Tizzi-Azza to eliminate the Riffian threat to this vulnerable position. Tizzi-Azza would thus remain in great peril for months to come. For the Legion, the rest of the month was spent performing the usual campaign duties. Franco visited and reviewed the *Banderas* in both zones of the protectorate. Abd-el-Krim, in contrast, approached the Spaniards in Melilla about reviving the peace negotiations, believing that their losses at Tizzi-Azza on 5 June would make them more receptive to his demands.[61]

In July, the six *Banderas* of the Legion were dispersed as follows: the Ist at Dar Quebdani; the IInd and IVth in Tafersit; the IIIrd at Uad Lau; the Vth in Dar Akobba; and the VIth in Zoco el Jemis de Beni Aros. That month, in the eastern zone, the Legion reconnoitered the area around Tizzi-Azza, provided protection to the convoys supplying the aforementioned sector, and rotated troops back to Ben Tieb for rest and recuperation. Meanwhile on 2 July, in the western zone of the protectorate, the IIIrd and Vth *Banderas* under the leadership of their respective commanders took part in the capture and occupation of Terinos and Talambo, with no casualties reported. On 7 July, these *Banderas* assisted in seizing and fortifying Yebel Ejizyan, with one officer and one Legionary killed; the wounded included two officers and six Legionaries.[62]

Reinvigorated after their setback at Tizzi-Azza, the Riffians once again began to harass Spanish supply convoys and outposts in August. The focus area was the triangle formed by Sidi Mesaud-Tifaruin-Afrau, with Farha in the middle. While the enemy continued to concentrate on Tizzi-Azza, its major effort was now against Tifaruin. On 17 August, the Ist *Bandera*, in the vanguard of a column led by the lieutenant colonel of the Battalion of Toledo, escorted a convoy to Tifaruin and protected workers repairing the telephone line (which the Riffians had cut) from Dar Quebdani. After reconnoitering the area around Farha, they proceeded toward Tifaruin. The well-entrenched Riffians met the convoy with a hail of bullets, which held up the Legion's advance. Heavily outnumbered, the Legionaries of the 1/I tried to deploy in order to protect the primary target of the rebels, which were the machine guns of the 3/I. The bitter fighting many times involved hand-to-hand combat. Without the possibility of advancement and with the sun close to setting, the supply convoy, the Ist *Bandera*, and its wounded withdrew to Dar Quebdani. Losses for the Ist that day included one officer and nineteen Legionaries killed, and two officers (one of them Captain Jesús Teijeiro

Pérez, who was in command of the *Bandera* that day) and forty-nine Legionaries wounded.[63]

Emboldened by their success in having prevented the column from supplying Tifaurin, the Riffians proceeded to encircle Sidi Mesaud, Farha, and Afrau as well. The Spanish command responded to this threat by concentrating all available forces in Dar Quebdani so as not only to break the sieges but also to deal the Riffians a heavy blow. The IInd *Bandera*, which had been resting and recuperating in Melilla, was recalled to the front and reunited with the Ist. At 0400 hours, the Ist and IInd *Banderas* (both led by Major Enrique Lucas, commander of the Ist), formed the vanguard of Colonel Salcedo's column, which was under the direct command of Lieutenant Colonel Pintado. The force marched out to relieve the closest position, Sidi Mesaud. As soon as the advance had begun, the Riffians attacked the IInd *Bandera*, who defended themselves. As the day went by, the Riffian attacks grew stronger and more determined. The Legionaries fought back with mortars and with hand and rifle grenades. The Legionaries of the IInd had to deal not only with the fierce and stubborn resistance of the Riffians but also with the blazing sun and the lack of water. With their canteens empty and their water casks on the mules, the situation became precarious not only for the men but also for the overheated machine gun barrels, which needed to be cooled. Overcoming the aforementioned adversities, the Ist *Bandera* was able to liberate Sidi Mesaud, but Tifaurin and Afrau continued to be surrounded. Both *Banderas* returned to Dar-Quebdani, with the IInd having suffered the greatest number of casualties. The total for the day was three officers and forty Legionaries killed, plus eight officers and ninety-one Legionaries wounded.[64] Lieutenant Colonel Franco arrived in Melilla from Ceuta aboard a hydroplane on 19 August. The following day, he took personal command of the Ist and IInd *Banderas* at Dar Quebdani.

Not all the action in the protectorate was taking place in the eastern zone. The western zone also had its share of military action. On 19 August, the IIIrd *Bandera* assisted in the operations against rebel elements in the area of Peñas Acayat. It engaged the enemy and suffered six Legionaries killed and fourteen wounded. On the 21st, the Vth *Bandera* went into action when it provided protection to a convoy going to provision *blocao* Solano. The casualties for the Legion were three Legionaries killed, plus one officer and five Legionaries wounded.[65]

The Riffian siege of Tifaruin continued through the hot days of 19, 20, and 21 August with those encircled exchanging gunfire with attackers while surviving on reduced rations. Meanwhile the number of sick and wounded rose. On the 19th, with their fighting spirit unbroken, officers at Tifaruin sent the following message by heliograph to their superiors: "We shall resist until the last moment; prefer death to surrender. If it is necessary, we shall blow up the position before giving it up."[66]

Hoping to knock it out before help could arrive, the Riffians increased their attacks against Tifaruin. For those inside the town, the situation was growing more desperate by the day. Deliverance came on 22 August, when the army, navy, and air force combined for a massive show of force hoping to break the Riffian siege of Tifaruin. Of the various columns that took part that day, the Ist and IInd *Banderas* formed the vanguard of Colonel Salcedo's column, the first column. In overall command of the operation was the battle-experienced General Fernández Pérez. The original plan for the relief of Tifaruin called for the *Regulares de Alhucemas* to advance to Sidi Mesaud, while the *Regulares de Melilla* would attack from Farha, and the Ist and IInd would attack Tifaruin head-on from the center. Franco changed this plan and executed a daring stratagem whereby the *Regulares* would maintain their battle positions while the two *Banderas*, in conjunction with a naval landing of the *infantería de marina* (marines) at Afrau, swung around the entrenched Riffians in an enveloping maneuver. Franco's end run caught the stunned Riffians from the flank and rear, which decimated them in a murderous crossfire. With hand grenades and bayonets, the Legionaries routed the enemy, which left behind countless dead as well as weapons and equipment. The siege of Tifaruin was effectively broken. The Legion had lost nine Legionaries, plus two officers and twenty-one Legionaries were wounded.[67]

Abd-el-Krim clearly suffered a setback in his hopes for gaining independence from Spain. He lost not only militarily but politically and diplomatically as well. He had envisioned a propaganda coup by repeating the monumental success he had achieved at Annual in July 1921, but it was not to be. Another Annual would have been a mortal wound to Spain, for the *abandonistas* (those who favored abandoning the Moroccan protectorate) would have forced the government to wash its hands of the protectorate. Events at Tifaruin in August 1923 foiled this plan, and he was taken aback by results. A certain critical element had been absent at Annual, but was very much in evidence at Tifaruin: the Spanish Foreign Legion.

PRIMO DE RIVERA'S *PRONUNCIAMENTO*

The political situation in Spain vis-à-vis the Protectorate in Morocco, which had steadily gone from bad to worse, finally came to a head in 1923.[68] On 13 September 1923, Lieutenant General Miguel Primo de Rivera y Orbaneja (*marqués de Estella*), the captain general of Barcelona, successfully brought about a bloodless coup d'état. Taking control of the government with the consent of the king, he installed the Military Directorate, composed of eight brigadiers and one admiral. Although considered to be an *abandonista* by many in the army,[69] Primo de Rivera received the support of the military to bring an end to the Rif Rebellion with honor and dignity.[70]

Primo de Rivera's *pronunciamiento* (military rising) had a minimal effect on the situation in the protectorate, however. His intentions regarding his earlier sentiments to abandon Morocco were yet to be seen. Nonetheless, on the same day that the constitutional government in Madrid changed, there was also a change in Tetuán. General Luis Aizpuru y Mondéjar (ex-commanding general of Melilla and ex-minister of war), a well-respected Moroccan Wars veteran, replaced Luis

Silvela (the only civilian High Commissioner), becoming the seventh High Commissioner since 1912.[71]

After the battle of Tifaruin, the Legion spent the entire month of September performing usual campaign duties. On the 19th, the commander in chief of the Legion, Lieutenant Colonel Francisco Franco, inspected and reviewed the Ist, IInd, and IVth *Banderas* at Dar Drius.[72]

The first of October found the Ist, IInd, and IVth *Banderas* stationed at Dar Drius, the IIIrd and Vth at Argos/Adgoz, and the VIth at Ain Grana.[73] The Legion's first engagement of the month came on 12 October, when Riffians attacked the IVth *Bandera* at Dar Drius while providing security for the encampment; one officer was wounded.[74] For the Legion, the protection and provisioning of the vulnerable position of Tizzi-Azza continued to be of great importance. At 1500 hours on 18 October, the IVth *Bandera*, which had been assigned to its defense, sent out a platoon of thirty volunteers under Lieutenant Eyaralar to deliver a preemptive strike against the Riffians, who were preparing to blow up the position with a subterranean mine. While the rest of the *Bandera* distracted the rebels, the platoon was able to reach the Riffian work site undetected. The Legionaries attacked the Riffian guards, putting them to flight, and then proceeded to destroy their work before carrying away their weapons and equipment. They returned safely to their starting position but were quickly counterattacked by the Riffians. In the ensuing fighting, the enemy hurled a hand grenade, which gravely wounded Captain Joaquín/Jacinto Pérez Tajueco and killed three Legionaries; the wounded included one officer and seven Legionaries.[75]

Two days later, on 22 October, the same IVth *Bandera* at Tizzi-Azza prepared a punitive ambush for the rebellious tribesmen. The ruse involved sending five Legionaries under the command of *Alférez* Cortéz to the rim of the crater left by the earlier mine explosion as bait. When the Riffians saw the Legionaries, they came after them in large numbers, only to be cut down mercilessly by the well-prepared firepower of the Legionaries from the IVth. Having suffered substantial casualties, the Riffians fled after learning a costly lesson. The IVth suffered six casualties that day, but the *Bandera* had once again demonstrated to the enemy that it too knew how to conduct a guerrilla campaign.[76]

THE DICTATOR AND THE PROTECTORATE

Soon after becoming dictator, Primo de Rivera reacted quickly to the situation in the protectorate. With the approval of the Directorate, the new High Commissioner met el Raisuni on 12 October at Sidi Musa in the Beni Aros region. In what became known as the Conference of Sidi Musa, el Raisuni actively sought the position of khalif of the Spanish Protectorate of Morocco. The former khalif, Mulay el Mehdi, had just died, and so el Raisuni advanced his credentials for the job: his Sherifian bloodline and his power and influence in the Yebala. He asserted that if Spain left him to administer the Yebala, the Spaniards could instead concentrate their wealth and military power on wiping out Abd-el-Krim's rebellion in the eastern zone. Primo de Rivera knew of the previous machinations of the wily sherif and made no promises, but he did realize the need to strengthen his forces in Morocco.[77]

October was also a busy month for Franco, who returned to Spain on the 16th. While on forty days' leave, Franco met with the king, as well as with Primo de Rivera. Well aware of Primo de Rivera's reputation as an *abandonista*, Franco revealed to him his own plan for putting an end to Abd-el-Krim's uprising, a plan Franco had first revealed to the king. He proposed that instead of slowly advancing from the flanks of the eastern zone and traversing its difficult terrain, implementing an amphibious landing at Alhucemas Bay, the old Spanish plan, and then driving inland to strike at the heart of Abd-el-Krim's very own headquarters, Ajdir, would be the quickest way to end the war.[78]

After coming to power, Primo de Rivera's intentions regarding the protectorate had begun to change. Having been supported by *africanista* officers in his successful bid for power, he now devoted great energy to securing the military's position there, although not as fervently as some of the officers in Morocco would have liked. On 1 November, to counterbalance the large numbers of troops being repatriated from Morocco, he gave the necessary authorization for the formation of two reserve brigades that were to be permanently stationed in the ports of Alicante and Almeria. The brigades' were to be a reserve force for the Spanish army in Morocco, ready to embark men and matériel in case of military difficulties in the protectorate.[79]

In both zones of the protectorate, inclement weather controlled the Legion's activities. Operations were small scale, and no major offensives were carried out. Throughout November and into December, the six *Banderas* were deployed as follows: the Ist in Dar Drius; the IInd in Ben Tieb; the "Tigers" of the IIIrd in Argos/Adgoz, but relocated to the eastern zone on 19 December; the IVth at Tizzi-Azza; the Vth at Uad Lau, and the VIth at Ain Grana.[80] The first action of the month took place on 3 November when a rebel war party attacked elements of the IVth *Bandera* based at Tizzi Alma. One officer died repelling the attack.[81]

Once again the Riffians tried to blow up a Legion outpost, this time Tizzi Alma, by employing an underground mine. Alerted to the excavation work, the post's commander, *Alférez* Molins, led ten Legionaries on a preemptive strike (*golpe de mano*) on 19 November. The Legionaries killed the Riffians guarding the work, destroyed it, and then returned with Riffian weapons and work implements. Again Riffians attacked Tizzi Alma, on 28 November, and once again they were repelled, at the cost of two dead Legionaries.[82]

In December, the Ist, IInd, and IVth *Banderas* were based in the Legion's main camp in the region at Ben Tieb. There, along with the IIIrd *Bandera*, which arrived on 24 December from the western zone, they performed their typical campaign services, the most important being the protection of the Tizzi-Azza sector.[83]

SUMMARY

The Legion finished out 1922 by continuing to perform their usual duties of defense and escort. It had been a very eventful year that brought great recognition and prestige for the Legion. In the western zone of the protectorate, the Legion had paved the way for the capture of el Raisuni's mountain stronghold at Tazarut, which eventually led to his pact with Spanish authorities; in the eastern zone, the capture of Tizzi-Azza would later serve as the launching point for further penetration into the Rif, with the taking of Abd-el-Krim's headquarters at Ajdir the final objective.[84] When the Peñón de Vélez de la Gomera was threatened, it was the Legion that was called upon to deliver its inhabitants from the Riffians; and as proof of the Legion's effectiveness in battle and bravery under fire, the force was increased by another *Bandera*, the VIth, and was awarded the Military Medal. Unfortunately, all was not glory and accolades for the Legion. Major Fontanés, commander of the IInd *Bandera*, died at the battle of Ambar. Political and military conflict within the army led to Millán Astray's being squeezed out of the Legion he had founded and to his expected successor's, Major Franco, asking for and receiving reassignment to the peninsula.[85] Though 1922 had been a busy year for the Legion, 1923 proved to be just as hectic. Besides the change in High Commissioners (Villanueva replaced General Burguete, who was in turn replaced by Silvela), the Annual prisoners were finally ransomed from Abd-el-Krim. In addition, General Primo de Rivera carried out a bloodless coup d'état. With Primo de Rivera in power, the war in Morocco would take a different direction. For the Legion, 1923 was the year of Tizzi-Azza, as well as the year Franco took command of the organization he had cofounded in 1920. Lieutenant Colonel Valenzuela's heroic actions during the battle of Tizzi-Azza on 5 June have gone down in the annals of the Legion. As the new commander in chief of the Legion, Franco's reputation in Morocco and in Spain would continue to grow. As for the Legion, it would become invaluable to Primo de Rivera in his plans for ending the war in Morocco.

NOTES

1. The conscripts included many middle-class *soldados de cuota* (conscripts). For more on the *soldados de cuota*, see Boyd, 200-201. Many were eager to go to Morocco to avenge those who died at Annual, as well as to defend Spanish honor.

2. Vaughan, 6; and Woolman, *Rebels in the Rif*, 105.

3. Payne, 177. Within the government, however, all its members were not in agreement. Manuel González Hontoria, the foreign minister, was more strongly opposed to this plan of action than was Maura. He seriously doubted whether the Spanish army was capable of carrying out such a complicated operation as an amphibious landing on a hostile shore.

4. *DOL, Negociado de campaña*, 1 January 1922, 12-13; and Subinspección de la Legión, ed., 161.

5. *AGM*, Legajo #M-3204, SECCIÓN #1, DIVISIÓN #1, 11. Cano Velasco, ed., 150. Berenguer, 158-159.

6. *DOL*, *Negociado de campaña*, 6 January 1922, 13. This source also noted that the IVth *Bandera* took part in the operation, although all other sources consulted did not mention it. *AGM*, Legajo #M-3204, SECCIÓN #1, DIVISIÓN #1, 11. A *blocao* (Ureña) was named in honor of the fallen officer. Estado Mayor Central del Ejército, 236-239; Subinspección de la Legión, ed., 178; De Silva, 166; and de Arce, 157. Ramas Izquierdo, 43, gives more details on the death of *Alférez* José Ureña Selles, who in the *DOL* was given the rank of lieutenant.

7. *DOL*, *Negociado de campaña*, 9 January 1922, 13; Franco, 167-169; Subinspección de la Legión, ed., 162; *SHM*, Legajo #54, Rollo 16, *Colección de historiales*, La Legión, "Acciones de Guerra de las Distintas Banderas de la Legión (1920-1939)," 2-3; *SHM*, Legajo #54, Rollo 16, *Colección de historiales*, "Campañas de Marruecos, Historial de guerra, 1ª y 2ª Banderas," 142; and Estado Mayor Central del Ejército, 530-531. Preston, 32.

8. *DOL*, *Negociado de campaña*, 10 January 1922, 13; Franco, 169-170; Subinspección de la Legión, ed., 162; *SHM*, Legajo #54, Rollo 16, *Colección de historiales*, "Campañas de Marruecos, Historial de guerra, 1ª y 2ª Banderas," 142; Estado Mayor Central del Ejército, 531-532; and Berenguer, 167. See also, Cano Velasco, ed., 150; Llacuna and Polls, 39; Arraras, ed., 118; Crozier, 65; and Trythall, 41. Hills, 130, wrote that Franco believed that Silvestre could have stopped Abd-el-Krim's onslaught at Dar Drius if he had kept his wits about him.

9. *DOL*, *Negociado de campaña*, 10 January 1922, 13; *AGM*, Legajo #M-3204, SECCIÓN #1, DIVISIÓN #1, 11-12; Subinspección de la Legión, ed., 178-179; and Estado Mayor Central del Ejército, 239-240. Scurr, 11. Berenguer, 165-167, contains a detailed description of the High Commissioner's plan of operation in the western zone during January 1922. Also see de Arce, 157, and De Silva, 166. Ramas Izquierdo has more information on the deaths of Lieutenant Horacio Pascual Las Cuevas on 33, and for *Alféreces* Manuel Salvador Claverías and Abelardo Villar Álvarez see 43. Mico y España, 231-234, contains two letters of condolence personally written by Millán Astray to the mothers of Lieutenant Horacio Pascual Lascuevas and *Alférez* Manuel Salvador Claverías.

10. *DOL*, *Negociado de campaña*, 11-31 January 1922, 13; and Subinspección de la Legión, ed., 179. One of the chores or duties typically assigned to Legionaries was called *La Aguada* (The watering). The process consisted of daily seizing the water source (e.g., a spring or stream) nearest the camp early in the morning, appropriating from the Riffians what they controlled once the sun went down. A section of Legionaries would clear the enemy from the watering hole, then protect the water-gathering detail, who would arrive with mules bringing empty wooden casks and barrels. The water casks and barrels would be filled and carried back to the camp by the mules. Then, the Legionaries would cover the withdrawal, and the Riffians would regain the watering hole for the night. Early the next morning, the process would start anew. Eventually, if a position was to be made a permanent base camp, the water source would be continuously guarded. See Sablotny, 87-88 and 146, for a first-person account of what this duty was like.

11. *DOL, Negociado de campaña*, February 1922, 13. During February, the five *Banderas* of the Legion were posted as follows: Ist and IInd at Dar Drius, the IIIrd at Ayalia, and the IVth and Vth at Xauen. For more on the relatively minor events that transpired during the month of February at Dar Drius, see Franco, 171-173; Llacuna and Polls, 40; de Arce, 157; *SHM*, Legajo #54, Rollo 16, *Colección de historiales*, "Campañas de Marruecos, Historial de guerra, 1ª y 2ª Banderas," 142; Estado Mayor Central del Ejército, 532; and Subinspección de la Legión, ed., 162-164, which gives an excellent insight into the setup of the Legion's camp at Dar Drius from the positioning of the machine gun nests at each corner, to the proposed location for the two tents that would house the "sellers of mercenary love." On 14 February, Millán Astray arrived in Dar Drius and temporarily assumed command of the Legion in the east; Franco returned to commanding the Ist *Bandera*. For information on the Spanish army's intelligence on Abd-el-Krim and the status of his army up to early February 1922, see *AGM*, Legajo #B-3 (Ilustres). This is the personnel file of the High Commissioner, Dámaso Berenguer Fusté. In this file there exists a thorough four-page typewritten report regarding, among other things, the organization of Abd-el-Krim's forces, the treatment of Spanish prisoners of war, the availability of weapons in the Rif, and the possibility of the Abd-el-Krim brothers seeking refuge in the French zone if they should fail. It was prepared by Berenguer's General Staff and though dated 27 August 1922, was prepared during the "first fortnight of February." The title of the document is "*Documento Núm. Dos.—Relato de la situación actual en el Rif bajo el punto de vista psicológico-material, durante la primera quincena de febrero.*"

12. The *Conferencia de Pizarra* had many ramifications that caused differences between the attendants. One point of contention, which was rightly given serious consideration by the government and the military, was the prisoner of war question. Should the prisoners of war be ransomed for the amount asked for by Abd-el-Krim or, as the army wanted, should they be liberated by their brothers-in-arms? Whereas the government wanted what was politically expedient, particularly since Spanish lives were at stake, the army felt that it needed to vindicate itself after the drubbing it received at Annual. Army officers were certain that ransom money would be used to buy weapons and mercenaries, which would extend the course of the war and lead to more Spanish losses (which it did). Needless to say, what was agreed upon at the Conference of Pizarra came to naught as the Maura government was replaced on 7 March by one headed by Sánchez Guerra. Subsequently, the staid Sánchez Guerra moved quickly to cancel all arrangements for a landing at Alhucemas Bay. Nonetheless, an important step was taken by the minister of war (La Cierva) following the Conference of Pizarra in preparation for the proposed Alhucemas Bay landing when he purchased six large K-type landing craft from the British. See Fleming, 204. For more on the various aspects of the *Conferencia de Pizarra*, see Arraras, ed., 118-119; García Figueras, 183-184; Berenguer, 175-177 and 252-253; Estado Mayor Central del Ejército, 533-534; De La Cierva, 191; Fleming, 73-75; and Morales Lezcano, 234.

13. Cano Velasco, ed., 150; and Scurr, 11. Berenguer, 185. The High Commissioner also detailed the steps taken to fortify the Peñón de Alhucemas, located in Alhucemas Bay, with two batteries of four modern 155 mm howitzers. These pieces

engaged the Riffians, with their captured cannons emplaced on the heights overlooking the bay, as well as on the shore, in artillery duels. In addition, the Peñón de Vélez was also reinforced with men, munitions, and food. Alhucemas Bay was a dangerous place for Spanish vessels who came too close to shore. On 19 March, the mail steamer *Juan de Juanes* did just that and was sunk by Riffian cannon fire. For more on the sinking of the *Juan de Juanes*, see García Figueras, 184; Berenguer, 190; and Woolman, *Rebels in the Rif,* 105. Additional information on the *FT-17* light tank, including specifications, can be found in Kenneth Macksey and John H. Batchelor, *Tank: A History of the Armoured Fighting Vehicle* (New York: Charles Scribner's Sons, 1970), 38-39; and Javier de Mazarrasa, *Blindados en España, 1ª Parte: La Guerra Civil, 1936-1939, 2* (Valladolid: Quiron Ediciones, 1991), 18.

14. *DOL*, 7 March 1922, 14; Subinspección de la Legión, ed,. 16; Franco, 173; *SHM*, Legajo #54, Rollo 16, *Colección de historiales*, "Campañas de Marruecos, Historial de guerra, 1ª y 2ª Banderas," 142; *AGM*, Legajo #M-3204, SECCIÓN #1, DIVISIÓN #1, 12; and Berenguer, 185. De Silva, 168; and de Arce, 156.

15. *DOL*, *Negociado de campaña*, 8 and 14 March 1922, 14; *SHM*, Legajo #54, Rollo 16, *Colección de historiales*, "Campañas de Marruecos, Historial de guerra, 1ª y 2ª Banderas," 142; *AGM*, Legajo #M-3204, SECCIÓN #1, DIVISIÓN #1, 12; Subinspección de la Legión, ed., 164-165; and Franco, 173-174. De Silva, 168. See Ramas Izquierdo, 43, for more on the death of *Alférez* Manuel Ojeda Gamón of the 2nd Company/Ist *Bandera*.

16. *DOL*, *Negociado de campaña*, 18 March 1922, 14; and *AGM*, Legajo #M-3204, SECCIÓN #1, DIVISIÓN #1, 12-13. For his actions and those of the Legion, Millán Astray was congratulated by the commanding general of Melilla, General Sanjurjo, the commander of the column, General F. Berenguer, and by the colonel commanding the vanguard. Millán Astray, 201-202. *SHM*, Legajo #54, Rollo 16, *Colección de historiales*, "Campañas de Marruecos, Historial de guerra, 1ª y 2ª Banderas," 143. Estado Mayor Central del Ejército, 537-541. Franco, 175-177, provides an excellent description of what transpired during the battle of Ambar. In addition, on 177-179, Franco detailed his personal opinions on the employment of tanks in the Moroccan campaign, as well as his numerous recommendations for improvement. Whereas others in the military declared that "The tanks have failed," or "Tanks are useless in Morocco, [that] they are inappropriate in this terrain," he, along with Dámaso Berenguer, believed otherwise. He boldly stated, "*Los carros de asalto y tanques son de gran aplicación en esta guerra. Veremos si el tiempo me da la razón*" ("Armored cars and tanks are greatly suitable for this war. We shall see if time proves me right"). For General Manuel Goded Llopis' opinion on the use of tanks in the Moroccan campaign, see General Goded, *Marruecos: Las etapas de la pacificación* (Madrid: Compañía Ibero-Americana de Publicaciones, 1932), 68. Subinspección de la Legión, ed., 165-169. Cano Velasco, ed., 150. His figure for the number of wounded is twenty-two, which is way off what was reported in the *DOL* (sixty-two). Llacuna and Polls, 40-41. Scurr, 11-12. Woolman, *Rebels in the Rif,* 105, has more details on the Riffian attack upon the tanks. De Silva, 168. Crozier, 66. For more on the death of Major Carlos Rodríguez Fontanés and the battle of Ambar, see Ramas Izquierdo, 24 and 108-117. De Arce, 158, contains the following poem dedicated to Millán Astray after the battle of Ambar

when he reviewed his troops:

> Whoever once saw him, would never forget him
> trembling like a flexible bow
> about to launch an arrow, or such Toledan steel;
> eyes blazing beneath his chambergo, his noble crown;
> and that virile face, and his arm raised
> signaling toward the Moorish mountains:
> "There are the stars for Legionary tunics, my sons."
> And his white gauntlet against the blue
> was the talon of a white gyrfalcon.

17. *DOL, Negociado de campaña*, 29 March 1922, 14; *SHM*, Legajo #54, Rollo 16, *Colección de historiales*, "Campañas de Marruecos, Historial de Guerra, 1ª y 2ª Banderas," 143-144; *AGM*, Legajo #M-3204, SECCIÓN #1, DIVISIÓN #1, 13; Subinspección de la Legión, ed., 169-170; and Franco, 179-181. Estado Mayor Central del Ejército, 543-545, contains the casualty figures for the Riffians. For more on the death of *Alférez* Claudio Álvarez Llaneza Bango (13/I) and the occupation of Tuguntz, see Ramas Izquierdo, 44 and 117-121.

18. Franco, 181.

19. Cano Velasco, ed., 150; Berenguer, 193 and 206; Payne, 178; and Trythall, 41.

20. *DOL, Negociado de campaña*, 1 April 1922, 14-15; Millán Astray, 203; *AGM*, Legajo #M-3204, SECCIÓN #1, DIVISÓN #1, 13; de Arce, 158; Morales Lezcano, 234; Subinspección de la Legión, ed., 179; Cano Velasco, ed., 152; and Payne, 179. García Figueras, 184, recorded that in the final days of April, General Barrera, the commanding general of Larache, was named sub-secretary of war; General Sanjurjo (who had been commanding general of Melilla since December) replaced him at his former post, and General Ardanaz was named the new commanding general of Melilla.

21. *DOL, Negociado de campaña*, 6, 8, 11, 14, 17, 28 April 1922, 15; *SHM*, Legajo #54, Rollo 16, *Colección de historiales*, "Campañas de Marruecos, Historial de guerra, 1ª y 2ª Banderas," 144-145; Subinspección de la Legión, ed., 170 and 172; and Estado Mayor Central del Ejército, 546-548. Franco, 182 and 186-187. Franco wrote that after the occupation of La Chaif, tanks were operating along the banks of the Kert River keeping the enemy at bay.

22. *SHM*, Legajo #54, Rollo 16, *Colección de historiales*, "Campañas de Marruecos, Historial de guerra, 1ª y 2ª Banderas," 145; Subinspección de la Legión, ed., 171-172; and Franco, 182-185. Franco recounted how the food on the Peñón lacked sufficient meat, which led the Legionaries to hunt down the forty or fifty feral cats that roamed the crag and prepare them as if they were rabbits. The only cat exempt from this fate was the commander's pet, but when a supply ship was late in provisioning the garrison, it too was consumed by the carnivorous Legionaries. According to the Legionaries, the commander's cat was not hunted down, but "committed suicide." Llacuna and Polls, 42.

Berenguer, 194, gave the number of Legionaries sent on the rescue mission as sixty; while Franco gave the number as fifty; and Millán Astray, 207, gave the number as forty Legionaries, with two officers. *Jane's Fighting Ships* (1923), ed., 328, has the specs and a photo of the destroyer *Bustamante*. The officer chosen to lead the operation to secure the Peñón de Vélez, Lieutenant José Martínez Esparza, would, as a colonel, go on to command the 269th Infantry Regiment (*Regimiento Esparza*) of the 250th Infantry Division of the German army (the Spanish "Blue Division") on the Russian front during World War II. For more on his World War II exploits, see José Martínez Esparza, *Con la División Azul en Rusia* (Madrid: Ediciones Ejército, 1943).

23. *DOL*, *Negociado de campaña*, 13 April 1922, 15; Estado Mayor Central del Ejército, 250-252; Cano Velasco, ed., 150; and García Figueras, 184. For more details on the attack on the *blocao* of Miskrela Nº 1, see Ramas Izquierdo, 105-108. Berenguer, 197; and Subinspección de la Legión, ed., 179-181. Page 172 (ibid.) contains the telegram sent by the king to the commander of the Legion, which said: "The King to Lieutenant Colonel Millán Astray. Chief of the Tercio. I congratulate the Tercio for its splendid defense of the blocao Miskrela and for the spirit found in all those of the Banderas of Melilla who volunteered to go to the Peñón, and you, as creator of that force, receive the thanks of your King and a strong embrace. Alfonso King."

24. *DOL*, *Negociado de campaña*, 28 April 1922, 15; *AGM*, Legajo #M-3204, SECCIÓN #1, DIVISIÓN #1, 13; de Arce, 158; and Estado Mayor Central del Ejército, 253-256.

25. Llacuna and Polls, 43. The "termination" of the reconquest of Melilla meant that those who had enlisted solely for the duration of it could leave the service. This also applied to the Legion. On 11 September 1922 in Ceuta, Millán Astray reviewed the troops and spoke to those who would be leaving the Legion. "He asks them not to forget the Legion and when they speak of it to stick out their chests with pride and say: 'I was a Legionary!' " See Subinspección de la Legión, ed., 173. The Picasso Commission, which had been established after the Annual disaster to find out the reasons for it, finished its investigation on the military aspects (but not the political) of it on 18 April 1922. "The main conclusion drawn was that the officers of the Spanish army had simply not been capable of meeting the challenges presented by the Moroccan campaign." The findings of the commission were not made public, but disclosed solely to the government. No one found culpable by the commission was ever brought up on charges before military judicial authorities. See Payne, 178-179, and Picasso González, 294-296, for the original in Spanish.

26. *DOL*, *Negociado de campaña*, 1 May 1922, 16. From the first of May until the final days of August, the Ist and IInd *Banderas* at Dar Drius and Ben Tieb in the eastern zone, respectively, had it relatively easy. See *SHM*, Legajo #54, Rollo 16, *Colección de historiales*, "Campañas de Marruecos, Historical de guerra, 1ª y 2ª Banderas," 145-146. Subinspección de la Legión, ed., 172.

27. *DOL*, *Negociado de campaña*, 2 May 1922, 16. One officer and two Legionaries were killed, and eight Legionaries were wounded in the operation. *AGM*, Legajo #M-3204, SECCIÓN #1, DIVISIÓN #1, 13; Subinspección de la Legión, ed., 181;

Millán Astray, 205; and Estado Mayor Central del Ejército, 256-257. Ramas Izquierdo, 44, has more on the death of *Alférez* Carlos España Gutiérrez of the Vth *Bandera*, who served as Major de Liniers y Muguiro's adjutant.

      28. *DOL, Negociado de campaña*, 7 May 1922, 16; *AGM*, Legajo #M-3204, SECCIÓN #1, DIVISIÓN #1, 13; and Subinspección de la Legión, ed., 181.

      29. *DOL, Negociado de campaña*, 12 May 1922, 16; *AGM*, Legajo #M-3204, SECCIÓN #1, DIVISIÓN #1, 13-14; Millán Astray, 205-206; Estado Mayor Central del Ejército, 259-262; and Subinspección de la Legión, ed., 181-182. This source gives the number of officers wounded as four (among them Captain Daniel Regalado Rodríguez, Lieutenant Juan de Cisneros Carranza, and Lieutenant Pedro Ciria del Castillo) and the number of Legionaries wounded as seventeen. Also see Berenguer, 200-202; García Figueras, 185; and Ramas Izquierdo, 121-122. Although el Raisuni's mountain stronghold in Tazarut fell to Spanish forces, el Raisuni had already fled to Buhaxen after Selalem fell on 7 May. Payne, 179, recorded that although el Raisuni had escaped, his situation was nevertheless becoming quite precarious. He was faced with either fleeing to Abd el-Krim (whom he loathed) or surrendering to the Spaniards. Arraras, ed., 119, noted that "[el Raisuni] was hoping for a life saving event: the fall of Berenguer." For their actions in the capture of Tazarut, the Vth *Bandera* was permitted to attach a battle ribbon (*corbata*) bearing its name to their standard. Woolman, *Rebels in the Rif*, 105-106. Crozier, 70. *SHM*, Legajo #54, Rollo 16, *Colección de historiales*, "Campañas de Marruecos, Historial de guerra, 1ª y 2ª Banderas" (3ª Bandera), 161-162. On 8 June 1999, the author, along with four ex-Legionaries from Ceuta, had the unique opportunity to visit the site where LTC Santiago González Tablas was mortally wounded. On the side of a massive boulder situated above the village of Tazarut is an inscription, chiseled by a Legionary, recording the event.

      30. *DOL, Negociado de campaña*, 21 and 24 May, 16; and Estado Mayor Central del Ejército, 263-264.

      31. *DOL, Negociado de campaña*, 16 June 1922, 16-17. Estado Mayor Central del Ejército, 265. De La Cierva, 192. Ramas Izquierdo, 33, has more on the death of Lieutenant Joaquín Beorlegui Canet. *DOL, Negociado de campaña*, 1 June 1922, 16, recorded the posting of the Legion on the first day of June as follows: The Ist and IInd *Banderas* were in Dar Drius; the IIIrd was in Tazarut; the IVth was at Uad Lau, and the Vth was in Zoco el Jemis de Beni Aros. Also see Cano Velasco, ed., 152.

      32. *DOL, Negociado de campaña*, 18 June 1922, 17; and Subinspección de la Legión, ed. (182-183). This source gives the Legion's casualties as one officer and ten Legionaries killed, and one officer and eighty-two Legionaries wounded. *AGM*, Legajo #M-3204, SECCIÓN #1, DIVISIÓN #1, 14. Millán Astray, 209-211, erred when he gave the day of the battle as 18 July, instead of 18 June. He did pay tribute to many of the officers who took part in the battle including Major Juan Yagüe Blanco of the *Regulares de Tetuán*, who would command units of the Legion during the Asturian uprising of October 1934, and the entire Legion during the Spanish Civil War. Estado Mayor Central del Ejército, 267-268. See Ramas Izquierdo, 122-130, for an excellent account of the seven phases of the battle, and 44 for more on the death of *Alférez* Ángel Arévalo Salamanca. Captain Pedro Pimentel Zayas, of the depot company, who distinguished himself in the

battle, would nineteen years later, as a colonel, go on to command a regiment (*Regimiento Pimentel*/262nd Infantry Regiment) of the 250th Infantry Division (the Spanish "Blue Division") on the Russian front during World War II.

33. *DOL*, *Negociado de campaña*, 19 and 26 June 1922, 17; and Estado Mayor Central del Ejército, 268-269. Administratively, the Legion on 22 June (by a ROC), established guidelines in its constitution for the cancellation of enlistment for Spaniards found to be under twenty-three years of age, unmarried, and from the civilian sector. The guidelines were instituted as a result of "numerous petitions received by this Ministry [of War], [and] brought forth by parents or guardians of minors who serve in the Tercio de Extranjeros [the Legion]" See *SHM*, DO #138 ("*Rescisión de Compromisos*"), Tomo II, 949-950, (23-VI-1922); ROC (22-VI-1922); CL #221, 313-315, (22 junio). This amendment contains eight articles on how those deemed to be affected by this order would be processed.

34. *DOL*, *Negociado de campaña*, 1, 3, and 4 July 1922, 17; and Subinspección de la Legión, ed., 207.

35. *DOL*, *Negociado de campaña*, 1, 26, 28, and 29 August 1922, 18; and *SHM*, Legajo #54, Rollo 16, *Colección de historiales*, "Campañas de Marruecos, Historial de guerra, 1ª y 2ª Banderas," 146. Major José Candeira Sestelo, the new commander of the IInd *Bandera*, had been the first commander of the IIIrd *Bandera*. For its actions in the Melillan territory following the Annual disaster, the Legion was collectively awarded the Military Medal on 14 August 1922 by Royal Order of his Majesty. See *SHM*, DO #181 (*Medalla Militar*), Tomo III, 527-528, (15-VIII-1922); ROC (14-VIII-1922); CL #311. The Legion's companion in the reconquest of the Melillan territory, the *Regulares de Ceuta Nº 3*, was also awarded the same decoration as a unit. Millán Astray and Franco were both awarded the Individual Military Medal (*Medalla Militar Individual*) for their valor during the reconquest. In addition, Franco was recommended for promotion to the rank of lieutenant colonel. See *AGM*, Legajo #M-3204, SECCIÓN #1, DIVISIÓN #1, 15; and De La Cierva, 192.

36. The most complete treatment of this is to be found in Boyd, 221-222. See also, Fleming, *Primo de Rivera*, 75-77; Payne, 179-181; Woolman, *Rebels in the Rif*, 106-107; Cano Velasco, ed., 152; and Estado Mayor Central del Ejército, 270. For Berenguer's version of all the behind-the-scene activities during summer 1922, see Berenguer, 211-224. De La Cierva, 192. On 189, the author wrote that upon hearing the news that Burguete had been named the new High Commissioner, Franco thought there was nothing left for him to do but to request a transfer back to Spain, believing that Burguete was an *abandonista*, as well as pro-*junteros*. To Franco's gratification, he proved to be otherwise. Arraras, ed., 120; de Arce, 159. Barea, 177-179, gives a vivid description of General Burguete, as well as the political and military situation in Morocco at the time.

37. *DOL*, *Negociado de campaña*, 1 September 1922, 18; Millán Astray, 62; Cano Velasco, ed., 152; and Bueno, *La Legión*, 10.

38. *DOL*, *Negociado de campaña*, 1 October 1922, 18; and Subinspección de la Legión, ed., 185. In order to free his hands for his proposed offensives in the eastern zone against Abd-el-Krim, Burguete came to an agreement with el Raisuni by way of the Pact of

Buhaxen. According to Woolman, *Rebels in the Rif*, 106-107, the terms of the treaty called for el Raisuni to submit himself and the Yebala to the *Blad l-Makhzen* (the land controlled by the government). In return, he was allowed to keep his power in the Yebala, along with his personal bodyguard and his small palace at Tazarut (on 8 June 1999, the author and four ex-Legionaries visited el Raisuni's palace in Tazarut, which today serves the villagers as a community center), which Spanish soldiers promptly began to rebuild for him. General Burguete also gave el Raisuni a large monetary settlement. For the time being both sides had achieved their immediate goals, for Spaniards the fighting in the Yebala ended abruptly, and for the crafty el Raisuni, once again escape from a possibly life-threatening predicament was achieved. Woolman also observed that the Spanish authorities committed grievous mistakes when they transferred many of their military units from the Yebala, neglected to relieve the tribesmen of their weapons—the same fateful mistake they had committed in their drive toward Alhucemas two years earlier and a factor in the Annual disaster—and failed to strengthen and secure the Beni Aros hills. When the retreat from Xauen began in 1924, thousands of men would lose their lives because of these mistakes. Also see Payne, 180-181; Fleming, *Primo de Rivera*, 77; and Arraras, ed., 120-121.

39. *DOL, Negociado de campaña*, 7, 26, and 28 October 1922, 19; *SHM*, Legajo #54, Rollo 16, *Colección de historiales*, "Campañas de Marruecos, Historial de guerra, 1ª y 2ª Banderas (3ª Bandera), 146; Estado Mayor Central del Ejército, 564-568; *AGM*, Legajo #M-3204, SECCIÓN #1, DIVISIÓN #1, 15; Subinspección de la Legión, ed., 186 and 207-208; and Cano Velasco, ed., 152. Millán Astray, 213-214. Taking part in the battle alongside the IInd *Bandera* was Lieutenant Colonel Rafael Valenzuela Urzaiz, founder of the newly formed *Regulares de Alhucemas*. In a little over a month's time, he would be named commander in chief of the Legion replacing Millán Astray. De Silva, 169. de Arce, 159. Woolman, *Rebels in the Rif*, 107, observed that like other Spanish outposts in Morocco, Tizzi-Azza was located on a mountain peak surrounded by rugged terrain. Ignoring the painful lesson learnt from the Annual disaster, Spanish officials sited Tizzi-Azza in such a location that it produced a logistical nightmare for the army. Provisions had to be brought into Tizzi-Azza by way of a deep, unprotected gorge. Tizzi-Azza was located roughly on the line General Silvestre had occupied, and it was along this line that the Riffians had decided to make their stand. Cognizant of the fact that they could not successfully engage Spanish forces in a set-piece battle in open terrain, where their overwhelming firepower could be brought to bear, the Riffians opted to fall back to more defensible positions. The hills, boulders, and ravines around Tizzi-Azza gave Riffian guerrillas the advantage as they fired down on Spanish positions and supply columns from the crests above. Spain's plan to advance beyond Tizzi-Azza was thus checked. De La Cierva, 192, observed that Tizzi-Azza was a "mortal threat" (*reto mortal*) to Abd-el-Krim, and he "would try desperately to turn the Legionary redoubt into a second Igueriben; but Franco's first order after occupying the position had been to assure a permanent supply of water by means of a system of wells and sluices."

40. Estado Mayor Central del Ejército, 568 and 570; Subinspección de la Legión, ed., 187; Payne, 181-182; Woolman, *Rebels in the Rif*, 107; Arraras, ed., 121; and de Arce, 159-160. García Figueras, 187, noted that Burguete had occupied Tizzi-Azza with the

intention of continuing on toward Ajdir, but the government's halt to further advancement not only would leave the position vulnerable to constant Riffian attack but also would be a serious military concern for High Commissioners to come. *DOL, Negociado de campaña*, 1 November 1922, 19, recorded the desposition of the Legion as follows: The Ist *Bandera* was guarding the critical position of Tizzi-Azza; the IInd at Dar Drius; the IIIrd at Uad Lau; the IVth at Dar Quebdani (Melillan zone); the Vth in Ain Grana; and the VIth in Xauen.

41. *DOL, Negociado de campaña*, 6 November 1922, 19; and Estado Mayor Central del Ejército, 568-569.

42. For more on the events that led to Millán Astray's resignation and the event itself, see Subinspección de la Legión, ed., 186-187; *AGM*, Legajo #M-3204, SECCIÓN #1, DIVISIÓN #1, 16; Preston, 35; Woolman, *Rebels in the Rif*, 109; Boyd, 228; Cano Velasco, 152; Payne, 182-183; Arraras, ed., 121; De Silva, 169-170; de Arce, 160; Hugh Thomas, *The Spanish Civil War* (New York: Simon & Schuster, 1961), 415; De La Cierva, 192; and Barea, 175. Furneaux, 93, noted that Millán Astray was also opposed to the ransoming of the prisoners. Scurr, 12.

43. *AGM*, Legajo #B (*sic*)-284, SECCIÓN #1, DIVISIÓN #1. This is Rafael Valenzuela Urzaiz's personnel file. For 1922, it noted that on 15 November, by a Royal Order of the same day (DO #257), he was posted to command the *Tercio de Extranjeros* (the Legion). He arrived in Ceuta on 1 December, taking charge the same day. Subinspección de la Legión, ed., 187 and 188-189, features a copy of an order, dated 2 December, from the new commander in chief (Valenzuela) to the men of the Legion. Cano Velasco, ed., 152, wrote that Valenzuela took charge of the Legion on 10 December. See also Preston, 35; Boyd, 229; Bueno, *Los Regulares*, 8; De La Cierva, 192; and Barea, 175-176. Trythall, 41-43, covers Franco's Oviedo period, as does de Arce, 160; and Scurr, 12. Franco returned to Oviedo not only to rejoin his old regiment but to marry his longtime sweetheart, Carmen Polo Martínez.

44. *DOL, Negociado de campaña*, 1-17 December 1922, 19. Subinspección de la Legión, ed., 187-188, contains a description of the Legion's camp at Ben Tieb which was built by the Legionaries of the IInd *Bandera*.

45. *DOL, Negociado de campaña*, 18 December 1922, 20; Subinspección de la Legión, ed., 188; Estado Mayor Central del Ejército, 572; and Cano Velasco, ed., 152. Ramas Izquierdo, 44, has more on the death of *Alférez* Armando de la Aldea Ruiz.

46. *DOL, Negociado de campaña*, January-April, 1923, 20; Subinspección de la Legión, ed., 188-189 and 208; and Cano Velasco, ed., 152. On 11 January 1923, Major Francisco Franco Bahamonde was awarded the Individual Military Medal for valor. It was pinned on his chest by the commanding general of Melilla and was witnessed by the Legionaries of the Ist, IInd, and IVth *Banderas*, as well as by the new commander in chief of the Legion, Lieutenant Colonel Rafael Valenzuela Urzaiz. See also De La Cerva, 195; Preston, 37; and *AGM*, Legajo #B (*sic*)-284, entry for 11 January 1923.

47. Estado Mayor Central del Ejército, 575-581, contains an extensive list of all those who were ransomed. Fleming, *Primo de Rivera*, 82. Woolman, *Rebels in the Rif*, 110-111. Payne, 184, gives the amount of the ransom paid by Spain to Abd-el-Krim as 3 million *pesetas*. However, Fleming's 4,270,000 *pesetas* is a more accurate figure.

Furneaux, 90-92, has more information on the women who were captured (Isabella, "La Rubia," and Cipriania), as well as the equipment (an airplane, three cars, and a field telephone) and weapons bought by Abd-el-Krim with the ransom money. García Figueras, 188-189. De La Cierva, 195. Arraras, ed., 123, claims that along with the money paid to Abd-el-Krim were diamond rings and other jewels for his relatives. The Spanish prisoners were kept in chains by the Riffians, and these same chains were seen by the author in the Spanish Army Museum, at the African exhibit (*Sala de Tropas Especiales de África*) then being exhibited in the Alcázar of Toledo during fall 1993.

    48. García Figueras, 189; Arraras, ed., 123; Woolman, *Rebels in the Rif*, 112; Fleming, *Primo de Rivera*, 82; Payne, 184-185; and Eduardo Benzo, *Al servicio del ejército: Tres ensayos sobre el problema militar de España*, with a prologue by G. Marañón (Madrid: Javier Morata, 1931), 121.

    49. Payne, 185, has more on Abd-el-Krim's futile attempt to create his own "Air Force of the Riff" and the state of his army. Woolman, *Rebels in the Rif*, 111-112, recorded that Abd-el-Krim proclaimed the emirate on 1 February 1923, not 1922. Roger-Mathieu gave the wrong date in his book (106-107). Woolman used the date revealed to him by David Hart in a private letter, which gave the date as "14 Jumada II on the Arabic calendar, or 1 February 1923" (238, Ch. 8, n. 2). Furneaux, 85, noted that Abd-el-Krim called himself "Emir of the Rif" (ca. 1923), but "he rejected the title of 'Sultan,' which some of his followers and the French Foreign Legion deserter, Joseph Klems, wished to call him, and he forbade his people to pray for him in their mosques on Fridays." See also, Pennell, 114-116; Barea, 176.

    50. García Figueras, 190; Woolman, *Rebels in the Rif*, 112; and Payne, 185. Fleming, *Primo de Rivera*, 83, has details on peace talks between Abd-el-Krim and General Alberto Castro Girona (head of the Office of Native Affairs in Melilla) that took place aboard a boat in Alhucemas Bay on 10 April. Nothing came of the talks, since Abd-el-Krim wanted "total sovereignty" and the Spanish were unwilling to agree to it. For more on the peace talks with Abd-el-Krim, see Estado Mayor Central del Ejército, 587-589. Subinspección de la Legión, ed., 208, covers IIIrd *Bandera* operations in the west during the month of March.

    51. *DOL*, *Negociado de campaña*, 16 May 1923, 21; and Estado Mayor Central del Ejército, 589.

    52. Estado Mayor Central del Ejército, 589-590; and Cano Velasco, ed., 152.

    53. *DOL*, *Negociado de campaña*, 28 May 1923, 21. Estado Mayor Central del Ejército, 590-592, has a detailed description of the battle starting with the building of Riffian trenches and fortifications on the 27th, to all the Spanish units (infantry, cavalry, artillery, etc.) which took part in the action, and the names of all the officers wounded or killed. Subinspección de la Legión, ed., 189-190, gives a detailed account of the battle and the battlefield but concentrates solely on the deeds of the Ist, IInd, and IVth *Banderas*. It also noted that this furious attack on a supply convoy had been the first since 22 December 1922. *SHM*, Legajo #54, Rollo 16, *Colección de historiales*, "Campañas de Marruecos, Historial de guerra, 1ª y 2ª Banderas," 147. Cano Velasco, ed., 152, gave the Legion's casualty count for the day as follows: Ist *Bandera*: 1 captain, 1 *alférez*, and eight

Legionaries dead, and one *alférez* and eight Legionaries wounded. The IVth *Bandera*, which supported the Ist on its right flank, had eight dead and nine wounded. Ramas Izquierdo, 26, has more on the death of Captain Isidro Quiroga Jordá and, 44-45, has more on the death of *Alférez* Carlos García Junco.

54. *DOL, Negociado de campaña*, 29 May 1923, 21; Subinspección de la Legión, ed., 190; and Estado Mayor Central del Ejército, 592-593.

55. Subinspección de la Legión, ed., 190; Estado Mayor Central del Ejército, 593; and Cano Velasco, ed., 152. This source states that the attack on Benitez was on the 29th, instead of on the 30th.

56. *DOL, Negociado de campaña*, 31 May 1923, 21; Subinspección de la Legión, ed., 190-191; and Estado Mayor Central del Ejército, 593-594. This source gives the name of the Legion officer killed as *Alférez* Yancia Indart. *SHM*, Legajo #54, Rollo 16, *Colección de historiales*, "Campañas de Marruecos, Historial de guerra, 1ª y 2ª Banderas," 147. Ramas Izquierdo, 45, has more on the death of *Alférez* Pedro Yanci Yudart, and 130-133 gives more details on the battle.

57. Subinspección de la Legión, ed., 191; Scurr, 18; and De La Cierva, 201. The standard the Legion so richly deserved, one "stained by the blood" of its members, would finally be presented, after the pacification of the protectorate, by Queen Victoria Eugenia, proclaimed "Godmother of the Legion," on 5 October 1927 at Dar Riffien.

58. *DOL, Negociado de campaña*, 1 June 1923, 21; and Subinspección de la Legión, ed., 191. Cano Velasco, ed., 152, detailed that with the capture of Afarnum, which was in the middle of the front line, a line connected by way of Afrau on the coast, Tifaruin, Farha, Afarnum, and Tizzi-Azza. These places were isolated and needed to be supplied with everything.

59. *DOL, Negociado de campaña*, 5 June 1923, 21-22. For their heroic acts during the battle of Tizzi-Azza, Lieutenant Colonel Valenzuela, as well as the Ist, IInd, and IVth *Banderas*, were awarded the Military Medal; the former individually, and the latter collectively. Subinspección de la Legión, ed., 192-194, gives details on the actions of the Legion exclusively, while Estado Mayor Central del Ejército, 595-600, gives information on all the units which took part in the battle. It also states that according to reports received, the number of enemy dead exceeded 600. In addition, it contains the contents of a battle report written by General Echagüe, and telegraphed to the Ministry of War on 9 June. Among other things it stated: "The deed achieved by the Forces of the Tercio and its Lieutenant Colonel can be considered as a heroic sacrifice [and] unanimously classified as the most brilliant to have taken place in this territory since the beginning of our rule in 1909." (Comandancia General de Melilla. Año 1923. Legajo 25, carpeta 3-5).

AGM, Legajo #B (*sic*)-284, SECCIÓN #1, DIVISIÓN #1, entry for 5 June 1923. This source noted that Valenzuela had been shot a total of five times. Valenzuela's body was recovered two days later (his gold wristwatch later turned up in a local native market, where it was purchased and turned over to his widow), along with the body of *Alférez* Sanz Perea and those of other Legionaries. On 14 April 1926, by RO #14 (DO #84), he was promoted to colonel of infantry, retroactive to 5 June 1923. *SHM*, Legajo #54, Rollo 16, *Colección de Historiales*, "Campañas de Marruecos, Historial de guerra, 1ª y 2ª Banderas,"

147-150. Garriga, 42-43. De Arce, 177-178, gave Valenzuela's pre-battle speech as follows: "Tomorrow we shall save our companions of Tizzi-Azza; tomorrow the convoy shall enter or I shall perish. Tomorrow we shall execute this feat, because our race has not yet died." The author also mentioned that besides carrying his Legion sidecap in his left hand, Valenzuela also carried his officer's baton. The "glorious death" of Valenzuela was captured by the artist Bertuchi in a painting entitled *Tizzi-Azza*. This painting hangs proudly in the Military Medals Room (*Sala de Medallas Militares*) of the Museum of the Legion in Ceuta. Arraras, ed., 127-128. De La Cierva, 199, wrote that the attack on Tizzi-Azza by Abd-el-Krim proved that he was being disingenuous with Castro Girona and the Spanish government about ending the rebellion. García Figueras, 190, noted that after Tizzi-Azza, the government mistakenly failed to continue the drive toward Alhucemas as the High Commissioner, Silvela, had recommended and sought nonmilitary means. Woolman, *Rebels in the Rif*, 113-114, recorded that both sides knew that Tizzi-Azza was the linchpin to the entire Spanish position in the Melillan zone, and that if the rebels were able to break through and wipe out the Spanish outposts from this crucial position, another Annual could easily follow. The army was not about to let this occur. Also see Mateo, 21-24; Scurr, 12-13; Preston, 38; Payne, 185; and Barea, 176-177. Cano Velasco, ed., 152-154, gives the number of Legion casualties as 187. Ramas Izquierdo, 133-144, describes the battle and the deeds of those officers who distinguished themselves. Among the many were the much-wounded and decorated Lieutenant Fernando Lizcano de la Rosa of the 14/II and Lieutenant Federico de la Cruz Lacaci of the 4/II. The former was awarded Spain's highest decoration for valor, the Laureate Cross of St. Ferdinand (RO of 10 August 1926 [DO #177]). For more on the deaths of Lieutenant Colonel Rafael Valenzuela Urzaiz, Captain Pedro Casaux Beola, Lieutenant Justo Sanz Perea, *Alféreces* Fermín Alarcón de la Lastra and Pablo Sendra Font, see 20-24, 26, 33, and 45, respectively.

60. Franco's promotion (RO 8 June 1923, [DO #125]), retroactive to 22 January 1922, was based on *méritos de guerra*. His promotion in this fashion was hailed as a victory by the *africanistas*. De La Cierva, 199-201, contains the telegram from the king to the Legion appointing Franco as its new chief. Cano Velasco, 154, states that Franco took command of the Legion on 19 June, not on the 18th. Subinspección de la Legión, ed., 194-195, contains a copy of the king's telegram, and see 195-196 for Franco's installment as Legion chief, including his introductory speech to the corps. Furneaux, 93, recorded that "when the King was asked to appoint a new commander he exclaimed: 'It has to be Franco. There is no one who surpasses him.' " Preston, 38, wrote, "An emergency cabinet meeting three days later, on 8 June 1923, decided that the most suitable replacement for Valenzuela was Franco." *SHM*, DO #125, (9-VI-1923), Tomo II, 901, on Franco's promotion. *SHM*, Legajo #54, Rollo 16, *Colección de historiales*, "Campañas de Marruecos, Historial de guerra, 1ª y 2ª Banderas," 165. Woolman, *Rebels in the Rif*, 114. Boyd, 250. Trythall, 43, noted that Franco was only thirty years old when he was promoted to lieutenant colonel. Hills, 132 (in English), and Crozier, 53 (in Spanish), contain an amusing ditty, sung to the tune of "La Madelón," regarding Franco's postponement of marriage to rejoin the Legion:

Colonel Franco is a military toff,
To come out and fight he put his bride off.
El commandante [sic] Franco
es un gran militar
que aplazo su boda [para] ir a luchar.

See de Arce, 178; Scurr, 13; and Crozier, 71-72. Payne, 186, noted that the Legion "within two years, had become the combat elite of the Spanish Army." Barea, 180-181, wrote the following about Franco, his *africanista* sentiments, and the hauteur of the Legion:

Among the "warrior" party was the new Chief of the Foreign Legion. And the Legion grew quickly into a state within a State, a cancer within the army. Franco was not content with his promotion and his brilliant career. He needed war. Now he held the *Tercio* in his hands, as an instrument for war.

Even the last soldiers in the ranks of the *Tercio* had their share in it and felt independent from the remainder of the Spanish Army, as though set apart. They would draw themselves up, recall their deeds and express their contempt of the others.

"We saved Melilla," they said. And it was true.

61. Payne, 186. The author also recorded on 489 (n. 55) that General Vives Vich, as an officer in the Engineers, had been the "principal creator" of the Spanish air force. *DOL, Negociado de campaña,* 6-30 June 1923, 22. For more on the negotiations between Abd-el-Krim and the Spanish government, including the text of the letters exchanged between them, see Woolman, *Rebels in the Rif,* 115-118. Fleming, *Primo de Rivera,* 83-84, has more on the political and military goings-on in Spain and the protectorate (*abandonistas* versus *africanistas*). Estado Mayor Central del Ejército, 601, recorded that General Vives resigned as commanding general of Melilla and was replaced by General Severiano Martínez Anido. He, too, would soon be replaced by General Enrique Marzo Balaguer. According to Pennell, 156-157, Martínez Anido resigned "when the Spanish government rejected his plans for a landing at Alhucemas. Martínez Anido himself estimated the landing would cost 6,000 casualties." García Figueras, 190.

62. *DOL, Negociado de campaña,* 1, 2, and 7 July 1923, 22; Subinspección de la Legión, ed., 196 and 208; and de Arce, 178. Ramas Izquierdo, 45-46, has more on the death of *Alférez* Francisco Solano Álvarez, but he erred on the date of death, 7 June, instead of the correct 7 July.

63. *DOL, Negociado de campaña,* 17 August 1923, 23. Subinspección de la Legión, ed., 196-197. Estado Mayor Central del Ejército, 605-607, gives more background and details on all the army units that took part in the battle that day. *SHM,* Legajo #54, Rollo 16, *Colección de historiales,* "Campañas de Marruecos, Historial de guerra, 1ª y 2ª Banderas," 165. Cano Velasco, ed., 154. De La Cierva, 202-203, and 206, wrote that Tifarauin was attacked by the greatest number of Riffians ever assembled up to that time, a division of nearly 9,000 men. Equipped with mostly captured Spanish cannons and advised by Germans, and possibly Soviets as well, Abd-el-Krim hoped to repeat the events of Annual. As De La Cierva noted, however, Abd-el-Krim made two mistakes: (1) the areas

under siege were within range of the 12 inch guns of the Spanish battleships *España* (on 26 August 1923, she ran aground at Cabo Tres Forcas and was lost) and *Alfonso XIII* and (2) those besieged maintained their discipline and there was no panic. It also heralded the first instance of combined operations by the Spanish military with the army, navy, and air force all working together, not to mention the first operation of its kind by any nation in Africa. Of major importance were the thirty-three planes of the Spanish air force, which effectively bombed and strafed Riffian troop concentrations. *Jane's Fighting Ships*, ed. (1923), 323, has photos of both ships. Scurr, 13. Ramas Izquierdo, 144-146, gives more details on the battle that took place on 17 August and, 33, has more on the death of Lieutenant Alfredo Sánchez Ferreiro.

64. *DOL*, *Negociado de campaña*, 18 August 1923, 23. Subinspección de la Legión, ed., 197-198. This source also recorded that the besieged position of Tifaurin, under the command of *Alférez* Topete, was supplied by air with food and blocks of ice on the fourth day of the siege. The observer, Captain Boy, also dropped Topete a communique that among other things said, "You can rest assured because Franco is coming tomorrow." De Galinsoga, 49-50, recorded the exchange noted above as follows: (army communique) "*Resistid unas horas más. Franco va en vuestro socorro.*" (Topete's heliographed reply) "*Si viene Franco resistiremos. ¡Viva España!*" ("Resist a few more hours. Franco is coming to your rescue." "If Franco is coming we will resist. Long live Spain!") Crozier, 73. Cano Velasco, ed., 154. *SHM*, Legajo #54, Rollo 16, *Colección de historiales*, "Campañas de Marruecos, Historial de guerra, 1ª y 2ª Banderas," 165-166. Estado Mayor Central del Ejército, 607-609. Ramas Izquierdo, 146-152, provides more details on the officers who distinguished themselves that day. For more on the deaths of Captain Sebastián Vila Olaria of the 14/II (who was posthumously awarded the Laureate Cross of St. Ferdinand for his actions in the battle), Lieutenant Julián Santamaría Zunda, and *Alférez* Alfredo Martínez Mateu, see 26, 33-34, and 46, respectively.

65. *DOL*, *Negociado de campaña*, 19 and 21 August 1923, 23; and Subinspección de la Legión, ed., 209-210. Cano Velasco, ed., 154, recorded that previously on 9 August, the IIIrd *Bandera* under the leadership of Major José Valdés Martel had harshly punished the rebels when they attacked the position of Ad Gos, situated in the Lau River basin.

66. Estado Mayor Central del Ejército, 609-610.

67. *DOL*, *Negociado de campaña*, 22 August 1923, 23. While the Ist and IInd *Banderas* were involved in lifting the siege of Tifaruin, the IVth *Bandera* was protecting a convoy to the Tizzi-Azza area, having one officer killed, Captain Pedro Jareño Hernández (16/IV), and two officers and eight Legionaries wounded. Subinspección de la Legión, ed., 198-199, noted that the Legion's casualties for the day were "insignificant" as a result of Franco's "brilliant maneuver which has saved hundreds of lives." Estado Mayor Central del Ejército, 610-615. *SHM*, Legajo #54, Rollo 16, *Colección de historiales*, "Campañas de Marruecos, Historial de guerra, 1ª y 2ª Banderas," 166-167. General Fernández Pérez, the overall commander of the operation, praised the Legion when he said, "Although it had to traverse a great distance, it added to its tradition, gallantry, [and] impetuousness, a technique, an ability, and a perfect understanding of warfare, which may not be surpassable

by anyone." Cano Velasco, ed., 154. Scurr, 13. De La Cierva, 207-208, has interesting photos of Tifaruin, the coastline of Afrau, and the misidentified *Alfonso XIII*. See also de Arce, 178; Hills, 132; Crozier, 73; Trythall, 44; and Preston, 39-40. Ramas Izquierdo, 27, has more on the death of Captain Pedro Jareño Hernández, who was posthumously awarded the Individual Military Medal for bravery. Arraras, ed., 130, features a photograph taken of the joyous defenders of Tifaruin after being relieved on 22 August 1923. García Figueras, 190, observed that the government committed an egregious mistake by not exploiting the military's overwhelming success at Tifaruin and wiping out Abd-el-Krim and his rebellion for good.

68. For more on the conditions that led to Primo de Rivera's bloodless coup d'état and the establishment of a military directorate on 13 September 1923, see Boyd, 236-261; Payne, 187-189; Woolman, *Rebels in the Rif*, 120-121; Fleming, *Primo de Rivera*, 85-87; Preston, 40; García Figueras, 191-195; Arraras, ed., 128-132; and De La Cierva, 208-212.

69. Alonso Baquer, 278, wrote that on two occasions, once in Cádiz in 1917, and the other in Madrid in 1922, Primo de Rivera had recommended that Morocco be abandoned.

70. For more on Primo de Rivera and his coup d'état, see Fleming, *Primo de Rivera*, 87-108; and Boyd, 262-273. Also see, Woolman, *Rebels in the Rif*, 121-124; Payne, 189-193; Preston, 40-41; Furneaux, 95; Arraras, ed., 142-145; Hills, 133; and Crozier, 73-74. De La Cierva, 216, wrote that on 15 November, Primo de Rivera accompanied the king and queen to Italy, where Alfonso XIII introduced Primo de Rivera to Italo Balbo by saying, "This is my Mussolini." García Figueras, 198, recorded that Primo de Rivera promised that his solution to the Moroccan problem would be "*pronta, digna y sensata*" ("quick, honorable and sensible").

71. For more on the new High Commissioner, General Aizpuru, see García Figueras, 198; Payne, 208; Fleming, *Primo de Rivera*, 108-111; Woolman, *Rebels in the Rif*, 124; Subinspección de la Legión, ed., 199; De La Cierva, 213; and Cano Velasco, ed., 154.

72. *DOL, Negociado de campaña*, September 1923, 23; and Subinspección de la Legión, ed., 199.

73. *DOL, Negociado de campaña*, 1 October 1923, 23-24; and Subinspección de la Legión, ed., 210.

74. *DOL, Negociado de campaña*, 12 October 1923, 24.

75. *DOL*, 18 October 1923, 24; and Subinspección de la Legión, ed., 199-200. Ramas Izquierdo, 27, has more on the death of Captain Joaquín Pérez Tajueco of the 11/IV. For his courageous behavior during the battle of Tizzi-Azza on 5 June 1923, he was posthumously awarded the Individual Military Medal.

76. *DOL, Negociado de campaña*, 20 October 1923, 24; and Subinspección de la Legión, ed., 200.

77. Woolman, *Rebels in the Rif*, 124-125. Morales Lezcano, 235. Fleming, *Primo de Rivera*, 112-114, gives plenty of details on the negotiations with el Raisuni; he also noted that the khalif died on 24 October, not on 12 October as Morales Lezcano stated. On 117-118, he also details the peace negotiations between Spain and Abd-el-Krim,

including Spain's attempts to establish a gun buy-back program whereby the Riffians would be paid 250 *pesetas* for a rifle and 100 *pesetas* for every 1,000 rounds of ammunition. Payne, 208-209; and García Figueras, 198-199.

78. Scurr, 13. While in Spain, all was not strictly business for Franco, who after two previous attempts was finally able to wed his longtime fiancée, Carmen Polo Martínez-Valdés, on 22 October in Oviedo, after having received the king's permission and blessing. They were wed in the Church of San Juan el Real in Oviedo, with the king (General Losada, the military governor of Oviedo, acting as proxy) serving as his *padrino* (bestman). See De La Cierva, 214-216, for more on the meetings with the king and Primo de Rivera, plus details of the wedding, and 204-205 for the pictures. Preston, 41-43, covers the wedding and Franco's conversation with the king regarding the Alhucemas Bay landing. De Arce, 179, erroneously recorded the date of Franco's wedding as 16 October.

79. Payne, 209; García Figueras, 200; Woolman, *Rebels in the Rif*, 125; and Fleming, *Primo de Rivera*, 119-120.

80. *DOL, Negociado de campaña*, 1 November 1923, 24; and Cano Velasco, ed., 154.

81. *DOL, Negociado de campaña*, 3 November 1923, 24. Ramas Izquierdo, 34, has more on the death of Lieutenant Julio Compagny Fernández.

82. Subinspección de la Legión, ed., 200.

83. Subinspección de la Legión, 200. *SHM*, Legajo #54, Rollo 16, *Colección de historiales*, "Campañas de Marruecos, Historial de guerra, 1ª y 2ª Banderas," 167, and 164 for the 3ª Bandera. Subinspección de la Legión, ed., 210, recorded that the IIIrd *Bandera* was transported to Melilla aboard the *España número 5*. This source also contains on 511-513 a brief summary of the actions of the Legion for the years 1922-1923. For a brief summary of the events of the Ist, IInd, IIIrd, IVth, and Vth *Banderas*, see *SHM*, Legajo #54, Rollo 16, *Colección de historiales*, La Legión, "Acciones de guerra de las distintas Banderas de la Legión (1920-1939)," 3, 10, 15-16, 21, and 26, respectively.

At the same time the Legion was engaged with the enemy in the protectorate, new regulations and amendments were added to its original charter. These changes or additions covered a variety of subjects ranging from awards and decorations, to payments for those leaving the organization. *SHM*, Legajo #54, Rollo 16, *Colección de historiales*, "Legislación relativa a la Legión," Año 1923. The following indicates what each of the items of legislation dealt with: ROC (26-II-1923), CL #78 (95), resolves the question of who is to substitute for the senior major [Major Vara del Rey in Ceuta] when he is absent or sick, and that the Office of Assistant of the Corps be a lieutenant; ROC (16-IV-1923), CL #170 (205), DO #85 (204), modifies the previous legislation of 21-I-1921 regarding how much Legionaries discharged for being minors have to repay for the enlistment bonus (usually half of it) and wages they received while in the Legion; ROC (30-IV-1923), CL #198, regulates the use of the Military Medal [collectively] awarded to the Legion; ROC (8-VI-1923), CL #261 (320-321), sets forth the manner of paying salaries and bread rations of those who join or stay in the Legion; ROC (30-X-1923), CL #485 (564-565), determines the rules to be followed with those individuals in the Legion when liquidating their food allowance; ROC (14-XI-1923), CL #513 (591), decides how to deal with deserters from the

Legion; ROC (15-XII-1923), CL #574 (648-649), DO #278 (882), grants amnesty to all the individuals of the Legion, according to the three conditions expressed, including cases of simple first desertion; ROC (26-XII-1923), CL #532, creates an emblem for the Legion, for generals, commanders of *Banderas*, and officers who have served or are serving in the Legion, with conditions indicated. For more information on the Legion's new emblem and the conditions and regulations governing its wear, see Bueno, *La Legión*, 27. *AGM*, Legajo #264, SECCIÓN #2, DIVISIÓN #10. On 19 July 1923, Lieutenant Colonel Franco, as commander in chief of the Legion, wrote a letter to the Ministry of War (#RO. 27717) detailing (with four reasons) the need to keep the anonymity of its members (in the Legion) from the inquiry of family members.

84. *Africanistas* welcomed the capture of Tizzi-Azza, which made further advancement possible in the Rif. However, *peninsulares* (army officers serving in Spain) and other critics of the government's policy in Morocco were not as sanguine.

85. For a brief summary of the major events of the Ist, IInd, IIIrd, IVth, and Vth *Banderas* in 1922, see *SHM*, Legajo #54, Rollo 16, *Colección de historiales* (microfilm), La Legión, "Acciones de guerra de las distintas Banderas de la Legión (1920-1939)," 2-3, 9, 15, 21, and 26, respectively. For more on the political situation during the last days of 1922, see Fleming, *Primo de Rivera*, 78-81; Payne, 184; and García Figueras, 187.

Chapter 5

Xauen, 1924

Nineteen twenty-four began with a tenuous stalemate in both zones of the protectorate. In the west, the pact with el Raisuni remained in effect but was about to unravel when one of his major underlings, Ahmed Heriro, defected to Abd-el-Krim's side. This situation would lead to Abd-el-Krim's expansion into the Gomara and Yebala. For Spain, the military campaign in the western zone reached a critical point, leading to the evacuation of large areas of land and to the death of thousands of its soldiers. In the east, the Riffians had been pushed deeper into their own territory, where the mountainous terrain afforded them excellent grounds for defense. With their advance positions continually harassed by the rebels, the Spanish advance was both slow and costly. The conflict would become a war of attrition between the Riffians and the Spanish army, with the Legion doing most of the fighting and suffering the lion's share of the casualties.[1] Primo de Rivera paid major attention to the Melillan sector in early January. In this sector, he proposed that to prevent another Annual disaster, where one position fell after another like dominoes, a "defense-in-depth" system needed to be instituted. This system employed two geographic zones: The first was a "vanguard zone" (*zona de vanguardia*); and the second was a "rear guard zone" (*zona de retaguardia*). The vanguard zone, named the Silvestre line, was in the front lines of the campaign against the Riffians. Under the command of General Fernández Pérez, it established military columns at the three most important positions: Dar Quebdani, Dar Drius, and Tafersit. The Legionaries, now with four *Banderas*, the Ist, IInd, IIIrd, and IVth, based in the eastern zone and under the personal command of Franco, were to be stationed at their main outpost of Ben Tieb. They were to serve as the shock troops of the zone. In the rear guard zone, large stockpiles of supplies and troops were to be kept at the major posts of Tistutin, Nador, Segangan, and Melilla. Primo de Rivera felt that this deployment provided flexibility for Spanish forces to regroup and counterattack in the event of a major Riffian attack.[2] Spain's new posture in the eastern zone was clearly defensive, not offensive.

Militarily, the situation in the protectorate was at a near standstill in early 1924. Poor weather conditions, brought on by the harsh winter climate, had hampered large-scale operations for both the Riffians and the Spanish army. However, Abd-el-Krim was not inactive during this time, as he consolidated his position in the central part of the Rif and prepared to go on the offensive in the western zone of the protectorate. Abd-el-Krim moved quickly to fill a critical power vacuum in the Gomara left by the decline of el Raisuni's power and influence in late 1923. By early January 1924, Riffian *harkas* had entered the Gomara and in some cases were wringing from each house a tax of fifteen *pesetas* (or its equivalent in material goods) to provide for their occupation.[3]

As noted previously, Primo de Rivera did not take the necessary measures in the western zone that he did in the east. The difficult natural terrain of the western zone, with its many craggy hills and deep, verdant valleys, was dotted with Spanish *blocaos* that had been erected during the pacification campaigns of General Dámaso Berenguer from 1919 to 1922. The most important road connected the protectorate's capital of Tetuán with Xauen. This dirt road, which had recently been completed, covered the forty-plus miles between the two towns. The other avenue for Spanish movement was the Lau River, which reached the Mediterranean Sea and the Spanish fortified outpost of Uad Lau at its mouth. These exposed and vulnerable Spanish positions were ripe for Abd-el-Krim's proven strategy of winning the local tribesmen of the region to his side, severing Spanish supply lines, and then engaging in persistent attacks until the besieged were compelled to abandon the outpost to the rebels. This technique had worked at Annual and would no doubt be once again successful in the west. Primo de Rivera knew this, but he was slow to respond to the looming threat.[4]

The first of January found the Legion deployed as follows: the Ist, IInd, IIIrd, and IVth *Banderas* were at their principal encampment in the eastern zone, Ben Tieb; the Vth was at Argos; and the VIth was at Ain Grana (Larache). This deployment would carry over through February, with the Legion carrying out its usual operations of escorting convoys, providing protection to assailable outposts in their sector, and instructing new replacements during the month of January.[5] The only significant clash with the enemy during the month took place on the 13th, when elements of the Vth *Bandera* and other military forces were violently attacked at Argos/Adgoz in the western zone. This attack cost the life of an officer, along with that of one Legionary; one officer was also wounded.[6]

On 16 February, Abd-el-Krim initiated the first major offensive of 1924 when he sent a Riffian war party under the command of Ahmed Heriro to attack the Spanish base at M'Ter/Meter. This riparian position, the army's most advanced position in the Gomara region (Beni Buzra territory), was besieged for a month. To keep the outpost viable, supplies were dropped by air from Ceuta. The air force also bombed the rebel-held area around M'Ter. In addition, because the post was situated on the coast, the Spanish navy provided fire support. The cruiser *Cataluña* arrived on 3 March, employing its two 9.4 inch main battery and its eight

5.5 inch secondary guns. However, the Riffians, using a pair of field guns captured in 1921, were able to hit the *Cataluña* from their emplacements in the hills above the coastline. Suffering serious damage and loss of life among its sailors, the ship was forced to steam for Cádiz to undergo repairs.[7]

From early March, the Riffians began to fight the Spaniards with a vengeance.[8] As usual, the targets were the vulnerable supply convoys and outposts. The first sanguinary encounter took place on 3 March when the Ist *Bandera* under Major Luis Valcazar assisted in the protection of a convoy to Benitez. In the firefight that ensued, the Legion, which was in the vanguard, successfully broke through the Riffian resistance to deliver the supplies. The 2nd Company of the Ist *Bandera* remained at Benitez to reinforce it. On that day, the Ist suffered eight Legionaries killed, plus one officer and three Legionaries wounded.[9]

Two days later, on 5 March, the IIIrd *Bandera* went into the field. Commanded by Major Villalba, the IIIrd took part in protecting the safe passage of several tanks through the Heli/Hal'il gorge. This operation, whose goal was to clear the rebels from the road between Tafersit and Tizzi-Azza, cost the life of a junior officer and resulted in the wounding of eight Legionaries.[10]

The stiff Riffian resistance to the supply convoys alerted Spanish authorities to the fact that reinforcements would be needed to prevent a repetition of the events that had occurred at Tizzi-Azza in June 1923. The government quickly reacted by transferring one of the two reserve brigades that had been stationed in Alicante to Melilla. The Legion's response to this mobilization in the eastern zone was for Franco to assume field command of the Ist, IInd, IIIrd, and IVth *Banderas*, which would be based in the forward position of Tafersit.[11]

On 7 March, in preparation for an important relief convoy to the Tizzi-Azza area, the High Commissioner, General Aizpuru, relocated from Tetuán to Melilla to oversee this operation personally. Franco commanded the column on the left, which departed from Tafersit and was made up of Legionaries, the *Regulares de Alhucemas*, and other native units. The mountain batteries of the regular army provided artillery support for the vanguard's advance. As they advanced through the ravine and reached a bend, strong enemy resistance held them up and inflicted punishment at short range. The enemy's numbers grew, forcing Franco to call upon the 16th/IV *Bandera* to deal with this impasse. The grenadiers of the 16th counterattacked, driving the enemy from their entrenched positions and opening a passage for the native forces. The rest of the IVth *Bandera*, as well as a mortar platoon from the IIIrd, supported these advancing forces. Franco pressed the advance with the artillery having to wait for the sappers to prepare the road for the advance. The IVth's machine gun company, which had been emplaced in the heights commanding the advance, along with the mountain batteries, laid down effective covering fire for the column. Franco called upon the IIIrd *Bandera* to attack the ruins of a small settlement, which they did at the point of the bayonet, while the *Regulares* advanced to the right of them. Fighting until their objective was reached, the column withdrew in an orderly fashion.

Simultaneously, the Ist and IInd *Banderas* fought in the vanguard of another column and likewise engaged the enemy in hard-fought combat. The casualties for the Legion were 9 Legionaries killed; seven officers and 105 Legionaries wounded.[12]

The next day, 8 March, the IInd *Bandera* led by its commander, Major Canellas, assisted in escorting a supply convoy to Benitez. This endeavor cost the lives of eight Legionaries, along with the wounding of one officer and eighteen Legionaries.[13]

The advanced position of Tizzi-Azza and its surrounding outposts continued to cause high casualties for the Legion, which was called upon time and time again to open the way for the vital supply convoys. As noted, Tizzi-Azza intended to be a permanent outpost in the Rif; its purpose as a springboard for further penetration into the rebel's domain remained clear. Military planners in the eastern zone were well aware of the vulnerable location of Tizzi-Azza, but orders had come from above prohibiting advance beyond this point. In a valley flanked by hills and mountains, Tizzi-Azza afforded the enemy an excellent vantage for attacks on the critical relief convoys. Had Spanish forces advanced beyond Tizzi-Azza and established a more secure front line, one that took the surrounding terrain into consideration, the Spanish army could have used its superior artillery and air power to keep the Riffians at bay. This was not the case, and so Tizzi-Azza would have to be resupplied at the cost of men's lives. The other alternative would have been to abandon these advanced outposts and withdraw to a more defensible position. This issue caused a rift between the leaders of the Legion, the *Regulares*, and other *africanistas* who wanted to proceed into the interior and those high-ranking officers in the military (e.g., General Valeriano Weyler Nicolau) who favored a strategic withdrawal to defensible positions.[14]

The Ist *Bandera* protected a convoy to Benitez on 10 March. In the operation, the "Wild Boars" of the Ist, along with Legionaries of the 14/II and the 7/III who seized key positions along the road, engaged the enemy and suffered ten dead and thirty-five wounded. On the 12th, the IIIrd *Bandera* took part in covering the passage of tanks through the Tizzi-Azza gorge. At 0800 hours on the morning of 14 March, the IInd *Bandera*, minus its 4th Company, also protected a convoy to the Tizzi-Azza sector. When they reached *blocao* Valenzuela, they were met with a hail of Riffian bullets that rained on the Legionaries and the Tizzi-Azza road. As a result, the 5th and 14th Companies went over to the attack, with the former taking possession of the road and the latter assaulting the heights between Benitez and Tizzi-Azza. In the furious fight with the rebels, the convoy reached its destination and then withdrew to its base camp at Tafersit. The "Eagles" of the IInd paid the price with the death of five Legionaries and the wounding of sixteen, including Lieutenant Navarrete who was gravely injured. Lieutenant Colonel Franco personally led the four *Banderas* from their base camp at Tafersit on 17 March in yet another convoy to the Tizzi-Azza sector. Through Franco's deft deployment of this overwhelming force, the objective was accomplished with only one Legionary killed and four wounded. The last operation of the month took place on 25 March when the IIIrd *Bandera* suffered casualties when it escorted a convoy to Tizzi-Azza.[15]

The difficult situation in the eastern zone continued with the Legion escorting convoys to their destinations or manning threatened outposts.[16] They would fight their way in, then fight their way out while inflicting casualties on the enemy and receiving casualties themselves. A major encounter between the Legion and the Riffians happened on 18 April when Franco led the Ist, IInd, and IIIrd *Banderas* from Tafersit toward Azib-de-Midar, which had been attacked by the rebels. In addition, the Legionaries escorted a convoy to Issen-Lassen. The enemy's plan was to hinder and/or prevent the passage of the convoy. Well entrenched in their defensive positions, the Riffians opened fire on the convoy as soon as it neared Issen-Lassen. The Ist *Bandera* deployed its rifle companies near Tauriat-Azzus, while its machine gun company (3/I) laid down effective covering fire that allowed the IInd *Bandera* to advance. Instantly, their own machine gun company (6/II) joined the Ist's in raking the heights overlooking Tauriat-Azzus with withering machine gun fire. Having taken control of the battle, the convoy entered Issen-Lassen. The *Banderas* then returned to their principal encampment at Ben Tieb, where they performed their usual duties for the duration of the month.[17]

By 1 May, the six *Banderas* of the Legion had been shuffled to new postings within their sector of operations. The Ist, IInd, and IVth *Banderas* were back at Ben Tieb; the IIIrd was at the forward post of Benitez; the Vth was at García Uria; and the VIth was in Tagusut.[18] The Riffians had recovered from the losses incurred during the siege of Tizzi-Azza the previous March and were preparing for a new offensive. Having been rebuffed in and around the Tizzi-Azza sector, they shifted their focus to the Spanish position of Sidi Mesaud in the Dar Quebdani sector. The Spaniards dug trenches and prepared fortifications, taking into account the vulnerable location of Sidi Mesaud, which was surrounded by dominating hills. During the day those in Sidi Mesaud fired on the laboring rebels, who continued working under the cover of night with the obvious intention of laying siege to the Spanish outpost. With Sidi Mesaud in peril of falling to the Riffians, the IIIrd *Bandera* was ordered on 7 May to escort a supply convoy to the outpost. Having reached the proximity of Sidi Mesaud, the enemy opened fire on the convoy from prepared positions. The Legionaries of the IIIrd deployed with the machine guns of the 15th Company, setting up on the hill situated between Morabo, Sidi Mesaud, and Farha. The *Bandera*'s commander ordered the 8th Company to drive the rebels from their positions. The Legionaries left behind a trail of casualties fallen to murderous enemy fire. What remained of the 8th, along with reinforcements of the 7th Company, fixed bayonets and flung hand grenades at the dug-in enemy. Finding themselves overmatched for this operation, the Legionaries were ordered to disengage and withdraw from battle. The IVth *Bandera*, sent on a forced march from its base at Dar Quebdani, arrived just in time to assist in the withdrawal. Though successful in turning back the convoy, the Riffians had suffered numerous casualties. For the Legion, the losses had been reasonable for such a bitterly fought contest: two officers and thirteen Legionaries killed; one officer (Lieutenant Manuel Sánchez Suárez) and fifty-eight Legionaries wounded.[19]

Having failed in its primary attempt to break the Riffian encirclement of Sidi Mesaud and deliver the needed supplies, the army made another effort on 10-11 May. General Fernández Pérez led a strong column that he divided into two groups. The left, under the command of Lieutenant Colonel Franco, consisted of a *tabor* of the *Regulares de Alhucemas*, three batteries of mountain artillery, and three *Banderas* (the IInd, IIIrd, and IVth) of the Legion. Lieutenant Colonel Pozas Perea led the group on the right, composed of three *tabores* of the *Regulares de Melilla*, the Battalions of Toledo and Andalucia, and auxiliary units. The group on the right engaged the enemy first, absorbing the enemy's initial thrust; but it was the group on the left, the one with the three *Banderas*, that went on the offensive against the entrenched rebels and drove them from their positions in a brutal and bloody bayonet assault. Forced from their defensive positions, the rebels tried to retreat but were once again set upon by the Legionaries. In the first phase of the operation to liberate Sidi Mesaud, the Legion had three officers and eighteen Legionaries killed; the wounded numbered six officers and sixty-two Legionaries.[20]

After breaking the siege of Sidi Mesaud, the three *Banderas* bivouacked on site and, on the following day, continued with their punitive measures against the rebels and the surrounding villages. The IInd *Bandera* took part in these mopping-up operations and established a position named Valverde in honor of an officer slain the day before. Not to be outdone, the 7/III also hit the enemy hard when it stormed a trench, inflicting a great number of casualties. For the Legion, the losses for 11-12 May were two Legionaries killed and twenty-two wounded.[21]

The Riffians remained quiet in the eastern zone until August following their recent defeat by the Spanish army. For the remainder of May, the Legion continued with its campaign services.[22]

The convoy to Sidi Mesaud had proved once again that without the Legion, the Riffians could prevent the regular forces of the army from maintaining control over conquered terrain. The winning combination of Franco's military acumen and the fighting spirit of the Legion was essential to Spain's plan for domination and pacification of the protectorate. The sword hand of the Spanish army was without doubt the Legion, and with it remarkable things could be accomplished.

Franco reviewed the Ist, IIIrd, and IVth *Banderas* at Ben Tieb on 1 June. He also awarded decorations and promotions to those Legionaries who had distinguished themselves in the battles in and around Sidi Mesaud.[23] From 2 June to 29 June, the Legion engaged the enemy solely in minor skirmishes while performing typical duties. During this time, only eight Legionaries were wounded.[24]

Whereas the eastern zone had quieted down after Sidi Mesaud, the reverse was the case in the western zone, where the rebels increased their activities beginning in May. Tribes operating in the area of the Lau River, as well as in Magan, M'Ter, Ben Karrich, and Buharrat, interfered daily with supply convoys. These problems were most severely felt in the territories of the Beni Hozmar (Ben Karrich), Beni Said (Uad Lau), and other parts of the Gomara (Beni Buzra territory). These aforementioned tribes, along with the Beni Hassan, were uneasy about the increase of Spanish forces along the Wad Lau sector. Ahmed Heriro, along with other Riffian representatives, incited the three tribes to join Abd-el-Krim's rebellion in June 1924.[25]

On 30 June, the Vth and VIth *Banderas* of the Legion under the command of Franco took part in an operation that had as its objective the supplying of Tazza and Solano. Providing the vanguard for the column, the two *Banderas* engaged the enemy, leaving the Legion with nine Legionaries killed and one officer and twenty-five Legionaries wounded.[26]

The situation in the western zone grew progressively worse for Spain by 1 July as el Raisuni, suffering from acute dropsy, was unable to exert control over the Yebala tribes. Thus the agreement he and the High Commissioner had signed could not be implemented. Having fought the Spanish army to a standstill, Abd-el-Krim was nearly at his zenith of power. The Legion had blunted his thrusts in the eastern zone (e.g., Tizzi-Azza, Sidi Mesaud, and Tifaruin), so he shifted his focus to the vulnerable region of the Yebala and Gomara, hoping to deal the Spaniards another crushing defeat, one that would equal Annual. To counter this rising threat, the Ist *Bandera* of the Legion moved from the eastern zone to the west. Sablotny, a member of the IVth *Bandera*, wrote that the officers of the four *Banderas* present at Ben Tieb "built a lottery pot and drew lots" to see which *Bandera* would go westward.[27] Once again, it was the Ist *Bandera* that won, just as they had when Melilla was in danger of falling to the Riffians in July 1921.[28]

From the moment the Ist *Bandera* waded ashore at Uad Lau beach, they were called upon to rescue a convoy trapped at Coba/Kobba-Darsa. They accomplished their mission but suffered three Legionaries wounded.[29] The following day, 2 July, the Vth and VIth *Banderas*, who were under the personal command of Lieutenant Colonel Franco, assisted in the day's operation to escort a convoy to Tazza. The cost for the Legion that day: three Legionaries killed, plus two officers and seventeen Legionaries wounded.[30]

On 4 July, the army launched a major attempt to break the rebels' siege of Cobba Darsa. Two columns set out from Uad Lau. The first column under Colonel García Fuentes took the right flank of the advance; the second, under Colonel Nieto, took the left. Nieto's task force included Major Luis Valcazar Crespo's Ist *Bandera*. Colonel García Fuentes and his troops proceeded along the right from Uad Lau to Tisgarin, where both columns united under the overall command of General Julián Serrano Orive. Following a heavy artillery barrage upon the foothills of Cobba Darsa, the Ist *Bandera* advanced under the cover of its machine gun company, which had set up at the foot of Tisgarin. In a tough fight with well-armed rebels, the Legionaries assaulted the crests, inflicting casualties on the enemy as well as incurring them. With nightfall descending, the Legionaries fortified their positions, staying the night while the rest of the forces withdrew to Tisgarin. The Ist *Bandera*'s casualties for the day were two officers and twenty-one Legionaries killed, with seven officers and 189 Legionaries wounded.[31]

While the Ist *Bandera* was in action, another column, with the Vth *Bandera* and two companies of the VIth under the leadership of Franco, left García Uria. Its mission was to divert enemy forces and/or reinforcements away from the other column. The Legionaries carried out a reconnaissance-in-force in and around the Ibuhasen/Ibujaren gorge. The enemy did not seriously impede the advance of the column, which occupied the small hamlet of Tirines. In the operation, the Legion suffered only five Legionaries wounded.[32] The Ist *Bandera* was on 5 July, once again in the vanguard of another operation hoping to break the siege of Cobba Darsa. In the hand-to-hand fight that ensued, the Ist had ten Legionaries wounded.[33] By 6 July, the situation had grown so critical that an effort was made to lift the enemy's siege of Cobba Darsa at all cost. With reinforcements having arrived from the eastern zone, General Serrano organized an assault column in Tisgarin, which included the Ist and Vth *Banderas* under Franco. After a long and efficacious artillery bombardment of the crests and foothills of the hill before Cobba Darsa, the assault began with the column battling, against stiff resistance, their way into the position. The rebels had been driven from Cobba Darsa and the siege broken. A company of sappers fortified the hilltop adjacent to the outpost, and most of the column remained there for the night. The human toll for the Legion had been two officers and three Legionaries killed; two officers and thirty-seven Legionaries were wounded.[34]

It is important to mention here that after Cobba Darsa, the Legion went on the defensive in both zones. Instead of seizing the initiative in pressing the attack against the rebels, the Legion was now reacting to the enemy's attacks, plugging up holes in the line, covering withdrawals, and "putting out fires."[35]

From 7 July through to 27 July, all the units of the Legion performed their usual campaign tasks of escorting supply convoys and manning forward outposts. Casualties for this period were light, with only two Legionaries killed and nine wounded.[36] The final operation of the month for the Legion took place on 29 July when the Ist *Bandera* took part in a combat in Zoco el Arbaa. In this difficult operation where the Ist provided protection, the casualties numbered eight Legionaries killed and fourteen wounded.[37]

THE BEN TIEB INCIDENT

In July 1924, General Primo de Rivera decided to visit the protectorate to gain a firsthand account of the military situation and meet the troops in the forward positions. His fact-finding mission began on 18 July when Primo de Rivera and his staff sailed from Ceuta to Melilla aboard the light cruiser *Reina Victoria*

Eugenia. On the following day, Primo de Rivera visited Ben Tieb, the Legion's main encampment in the eastern zone. Here, the IInd, IIIrd, and IVth *Banderas*, as well as the *Regulares de Melilla*, were present for the event. At this gathering of junior officers (both Legion and *Regulares*) who were fervent *africanistas*, Primo de Rivera's plan to decrease the intensity of the war would be poorly received. In an interview in 1972, Franco told De La Cierva that General Sanjurjo had ordered him to host a luncheon for Primo de Rivera at Ben Tieb. A barracks was accordingly transformed into a dining hall, where Primo de Rivera sat at the head of the table with Sanjurjo on his right. Since the dining hall had been a barracks for Legionaries, the walls had been plastered with the slogans of the Legion (see Appendix C), which were all removed except for one that was difficult to take down. In his speech at the luncheon, Franco broached the subject of the possible abandonment of the protectorate, saying they were in Morocco not because of some whim, but because they had been ordered there by the government and their superiors. He had hoped that Primo de Rivera would have put their minds at ease by saying that the protectorate would not be abandoned. Franco ended his speech by thrice shouting, "¡Viva España!" Primo de Rivera stood up to thank the officers for their candid opinions on the situation in Morocco; he then recommended that the sole remaining Legion slogan be changed from "the spirit of fierce and blind aggressiveness of the Legion before the enemy" to one that would allude to "iron discipline." With this statement it was to be understood by all present that the Legion (and the *Regulares*) would faithfully obey any orders issued to them, even orders to abandon the protectorate. An officer from Primo de Rivera's entourage of colonels and lieutenant colonels, who were seated at a connecting table, responded by saying, "Good, very good."

Major José Enrique Varela of the *Regulares* reached across the table, grabbed him, and yelled, "Bad, very bad." Primo de Rivera retorted, "That gentleman, be quiet." He finished his speech and sat down to a total absence of applause. Incensed by the lack of respect shown him by the officers of the Legion and *Regulares*, he sprung to his feet, spilling his coffee, and said to Franco, "For that you should not have invited me." Franco replied, "I have not invited you; my commanding general [Sanjurjo] has ordered me to. If it is not agreeable to you [,] it is less so for me." Assuming all the blame for what had just transpired Franco said, "My general, I have received a good [officer corps]. If the officer corps is now bad, I have made it bad." The situation was tense as Primo de Rivera and his entourage filed out of the barracks. Franco, who had submitted his resignation, was ordered to report to Primo de Rivera shortly thereafter. When Franco did so, they spoke for two hours, during which time Primo de Rivera told Franco that he had learned many things during his visit.

It was clear to Primo de Rivera, who refused to accept Franco's resignation, what the Legion thought of the possibility of abandoning or scaling back operations ("semiabandonment") in Morocco. Too many brave officers and Legionaries had fought and given their lives for Spain, for him to surrender the protectorate. During its brief existence, the Legion had never refused an order and had always begged to be in the position of greatest danger. It had "saved" Melilla from the Riffians and proved invaluable to the success of the reconquest of the Melillan command. However, the Legionaries let it be known that they would not be a party to leaving their dead comrades behind in Morocco. Franco and the Legion were able to get away with this blatant act of insubordination because both Primo de Rivera and Franco knew that the Spanish army needed the Legion and the *Regulares* to continue serving as the vanguard of the army in Morocco. Franco's and the Legion's popularity and reputation were so great, both at home and in Morocco, that for Primo de Rivera to have cashiered Franco would have been difficult. Furthermore, Primo de Rivera was well aware of the Legion's accomplishments and knew that he desperately needed the Legion in order to carry out his upcoming plans of withdrawing all military forces in the western zone (the Yebala region) to more defendable positions while maintaining the status quo in the eastern zone.[38]

The Ben Tieb incident had the effect of modifying Primo de Rivera's original plan to abandon the protectorate. The new plan called for the Spanish army to "pull in its skirt" in the western zone. All the isolated and vulnerable outposts would be abandoned in favor of concentrating large numbers of troops in the major towns. The garrisons of those posts in the interior (e.g., Xauen), which had perpetually been in danger of being cut off, would be withdrawn to safer positions such as Tetuán, Larache, and Ceuta. This retreat was meant to avoid another Annual catastrophe. With the so-called Primo line or Estella line in place, forces could be concentrated so that the army would have shorter lines of communication and supply. The final phase of his strategy would be to carry out an amphibious landing at Alhucemas Bay to strike at the heart of Abd-el-Krim's rebellion. For these plans to succeed, the participation of the Legion and the *Regulares* would be crucial.[39]

In late July and continuing into early August, alarming news began filtering back to Tetuán via the native police that the Riffians were infiltrating into the Gomara and Yebala in increasing numbers.[40] General Castro Girona was able to convince High Commissioner Aizpuru that he should transfer the three remaining *Banderas* (the IInd, IIIrd, and IVth) from the Melillan sector, since the situation was relatively quiet. Franco spent the first two weeks of August reconnoitering the principal lines of communication and defense between Ceuta, Tetuán, and Xauen, while Aizpuru prepared to reinforce the three most threatened sectors: (1) the valley of the Lau River, (2) the all-important Tetuán-Xauen road via Zoco el Arbaa and Dar Akoba, and (3) the gorges of the Beni Aros.[41] The Legion's first engagement took place on 8 August when the VIth *Bandera* assisted in an operation around Tagasut. In the ensuing battle, an officer and a Legionary were killed, and another officer and three Legionaries were wounded.[42]

In a military briefing of 12 August attended by top generals in the western zone as well as by Lieutenant Colonels Franco (Legion) and Mola (*Regulares*), it was decided that the most imminent threat was in the Lau valley. That afternoon, Franco left for Uad Lau aboard the cruiser *Extremadura* to take command of the Ist and Vth *Banderas*.[43]

By mid-August the situation became more precarious as rebels struck in both zones. On 13 August the IIIrd and IVth *Banderas*, rushed from Ben Tieb to the coastal outpost of Afrau, which the Riffians surrounded. They were to form the vanguard of the middle of three columns under the overall command of General Sanjurjo. On 14 August, they reached Dar Quebdani, and Farha the 15th. The Legion's attack began on 16 August at 0600 hours when the IVth stormed up the hills before Afrau and in a bitterly fought contest took possession of them by 0800 hours. The Legionaries drove the rebels from the ravines and then from their dwellings in Arrach-Bel-Hach. The IIIrd supported the attack of the IVth and captured houses in Bel-Hayy. Both *Banderas* continued their advance the following day. Losses for the Legion in the two-day battle involved two officers and four Legionaries killed, along with two officers and forty Legionaries wounded.[44]

While the IIIrd and IVth *Banderas* were battling their way into Afrau, Franco's Ist and Vth *Banderas* were engaged in a reconnaissance mission that took them from Uad Lau to Ensat/Emsath. The operation took place on 17 August with the column, which also included a *tabor* of *Regulares*, encountering strong resistance from rebels who tried to impede their advance. Under artillery cover from Spanish field pieces, the Legionaries threw themselves at their obstinate foe, at times resorting to the use of cold steel to dislodge them. On that day the Legion lost two officers and eighteen Legionaries. The wounded consisted of two officers and seventeen Legionaries.[45] The VIth *Bandera* under its commander, Major Rada, likewise saw action on 17 August, escorting a convoy to Talambo/Talambot. In a firefight, the VIth suffered four Legionaries killed plus two officers and seventeen Legionaries wounded.[46]

As the situation worsened in the western zone, Primo de Rivera saw himself as having to amend his earlier plans for semiabandonment. By mid-August he decided to retire from all three (i.e., the Lau River valley, Xauen, and the Beni Aros). The army would withdraw to the more defensible coastal areas while at the same time continuing to protect the city of Tetuán and its lines of communication with Larache, Tangier, and Ceuta. Troops were to be pulled back to the new defensive line from over 400 forward outposts.[47]

Relinquishing control of Xauen proved most difficult for Spanish authorities. Its capture in 1920 by Dámaso Berenguer and Castro Girona had been greeted with great fanfare, and Spanish building projects had been undertaken. Now all would be surrendered as Spanish forces fought their way out of the city and back to Tetuán.[48] The first phase of the withdrawal began on 20 August in the Lau sector with the full knowledge of the enemy. General Julián Serrano Orive, arguably one of the top five generals in the Spanish army, was in charge of the operation. His two subordinates, Lieutenant Colonels Franco and Mola, at the time serving as a member of General Serrano's General Staff, were the cream of the crop in the Spanish army in Africa.[49]

Franco, along with the Ist and Vth *Banderas*, took and occupied Yebel Combo/Cobba on 21 August. The brutal fight lasted all day and was continued the next day, with the Legion losing twenty-two Legionaries, plus four officers and fifty-four Legionaries wounded.[50]

The Ist and Vth *Banderas* were in action again on 23 August when they were involved in an attack at Peñas Carbonell. In the action against the rebels, the Legion suffered four Legionaries killed, in addition to one officer and twenty-eight Legionaries wounded.[51] Concurrently, the VIth *Bandera* successfully fought off an enemy attack to its encampment at Tagasut. This bold rebel attack on a Legion camp clearly demonstrated that the situation was going downhill. Typical rebel tactics involved the classic ones of guerrilla warfare: Strike where and when your opponent is weakest; cut off vulnerable outposts; use your knowledge of the terrain to the best advantage; and when confronted by superior forces, melt away to fight another day. Now, here at Tagasut, the rebels were going after the watchdog (i.e., the Legionaries), instead of the sheep. The rebels were turned back at Tagasut, but at the cost of the life of one officer and the wounding of six Legionaries.[52]

The Legion's last operation for the month took place on 30 August when Franco led the Ist and Vth *Banderas* from Hoj to Loma Verde, where a column would be formed to take a supply convoy to Solano, which had been encircled for several days. Two *tabores* of the *Regulares* were entrusted to secure the crests surrounding Tirines. When effective enemy gunfire held up the *Regulares*, the Ist *Bandera* fought all the way to the summit of Tirines by midmorning. A *tabor* relieved the Ist and allowed it to remove its wounded. However, the battle was not over, as the rebels poured down murderous fire on the left flank, stopping its advance cold. Well-entrenched in caves and behind rocks and redoubts, the rebels were difficult to "neutralize" with Spanish mountain guns. Spanish casualties mounted, and carrying the wounded off the battlefield became more and more difficult. Supply mules were also hit and tumbled down the slopes. Furnishing ammunition to the combatants was becoming problematic. The order for a mass assault along the entire line by the two *Banderas*, the *Regulares de Ceuta*, and the *Mehal-la* was given, but by 1045 hours, and with casualties mounting, the attack was canceled. Once all the wounded had been gathered, the withdrawal began. Those besieged at Solano held out as long as they could, but the rebels eventually overran the position and killed the majority of the troops defending their posts. Casualties for the Legion: six Legionaries killed, with one officer and forty-six Legionaries wounded.[53]

The inability of the Legion to break the siege of Solano was the first military failure, one Franco took personally. Moreover, he and the Legion had failed in carrying out their mission and had to withdraw in order to avoid being surrounded by the rebels. General Serrano was likewise shaken up by the turn of events in the Lau sector (the capture of Solano and Tazza by the rebels), especially since the premier unit of the Spanish army had been frustrated in its attempt to rescue those entrapped. Franco began to see the parallel between what had happened to Silvestre after Abarran in 1921 and what was happening to Serrano at Solano in 1924.[54]

On 31 August, the IInd, IIIrd, and IVth *Banderas* came from the eastern zone to the more active western zone. The IInd and IIIrd *Banderas* sailed from Melilla for Ceuta aboard the *Vicente Puchol*; the IVth *Bandera* arrived in Ceuta aboard the venerable *Almirante Lobo*.[55]

With the arrival of the three *Banderas* from Melilla, the protection of the eastern zone had been left to the *Regulares*, regular Spanish army regiments, and other native forces. All six *Banderas* of the Legion were now concentrated in the western zone and were dispersed as follows: the Ist and Vth at Hoj; the IInd, IIIrd, and IVth just arrived in Ceuta; and the VIth at Tagasut.[56]

Abd-el-Krim's *harkas*, emboldened by their military successes and their ability to interfere with supply convoys at will, hoped for another Annual in the western zone. The Gorgues massif, southeast of Tetuán, provided excellent cover for the rebels, who used its ravines and bluffs to harass convoys trying to bring essential supplies to the *blocaos* that dotted the landscape. On several occasions the enemy was able to site an artillery piece and lob shells into Tetuán, the capital of the protectorate, itself.[57]

Abd-el-Krim's battlefield victories, as well as dissatisfaction with Spanish colonial policies, converted many Moroccans to his cause. M'hamed Abd-el-Krim commanded a Riffian army comprised of 3,000 to 4,000 well-trained guerrillas called *Regulares* (the nucleus of their army), as well as a much larger, ever-changing number of tribesmen who, at their peak strength, possibly totaled 80,000 men.[58]

The IIIrd *Bandera*, which had just been brought over from the eastern zone to Ceuta, arrived by train in Tetuán on 1 September. The following day Major Villalba's command formed the vanguard of a relief column to Gorgues, encircled by rebels who were prepared for the arrival of the Legionaries. The 7th Company entered the fray first with the 15th Company supporting its advance. In vicious combat with the well-entrenched enemy, Legionaries were caught by a hail of murderous rifle fire from the crests above. The number of wounded began to rise. The 8th Company advanced along the left flank, supporting the progress of the column, and was able to seize control of the nearby peaks, driving the enemy out. The situation quickly turned sour, however, as they were cut off from the rest of the *Bandera* and the commander of the column. With their position worsening by the minute, they decided to withdraw. The 8th Company remained behind to save the rest of the column, fighting on until all ammunition was spent, then resorted to hurling hand grenades and rocks at the enemy, before finally defending themselves with bayonets. Eventually, they were overrun by superior numbers of rebels, and those left alive were taken into captivity. The convoy had been ignominiously turned back. The 7th and 15th Companies of the IIIrd *Bandera* returned to their point of origin having been badly mauled; the 8th Company never came back. The casualty list had been high for the Legion, with five officers and ninety-five Legionaries killed, plus five officers and fifty-eight Legionaries wounded.[59]

Far from where the IIIrd *Bandera* was being punished, but on the same day, the Ist *Bandera* energetically fought off an attack on its encampment at Kudia Kobbo in the Lau sector, sustaining one Legionary killed and three wounded.[60]

Not to be left out of the day's actions, the IVth and IInd *Banderas* also engaged the enemy on 2 September. The IVth left Riffien and was rapidly moved from the train station in Tetuán to the front, hoping to back up the IIIrd. Forming the vanguard of the column, the IVth headed for the Gorgues massif via the Beni Salah zone, which was on the left. They engaged the enemy while advancing toward Kudia Nich, where they believed the 8th Company of the IIIrd would be resisting. Both the IVth and IInd gave their utmost to try to reach their beleaguered comrades. Made aware that nothing remained of the 8th, they then withdrew to Tetuán after fortifying the positions they had reached. In all, the IInd *Bandera* suffered ten Legionaries wounded in the enterprise.[61] Riffian occupation of the Gorgues massif enabled them to shell the city of Tetuán, much to the dread of its inhabitants. This was not unlike what the populace of Melilla had felt prior to the arrival of the Legion in July 1921. The alarming situation in the western zone brought Primo de Rivera back to the protectorate on 5 September, this time with Generals Gómez Souza, Rodríguez Pedre, and Muslera (all members of his Military Directorate).[62]

RETREAT FROM XAUEN

Primo de Rivera's arrival in Tetuán, along with that of his closest advisors, signaled the start of the most critical operation in his plan for semiabandonment of the western zone: the retreat from Xauen (see Map 5). Fresh battalions (e.g., the Battalions of Asturias, Saboya, Granada, and de la Reina) arrived in Morocco under the command of the veteran campaigner General Alberto Castro Girona. Although these regular army units would provide the bulk of the Spanish forces, whether the operations to evacuate Xauen would be a success or a great failure would be up to the Legion and the *Regulares*.[63]

On 6 September, the IInd, IIIrd, and IVth *Banderas* of the Legion escorted a convoy to Zinat, south of the Gorgues. The column, under the command of General Gonzalo Queipo de Llano, left from Ben Karrich with the IInd leading the way and with the other two *Banderas* following close behind. The 12/IV set up its machine guns on a hill, protected by the 10/IV, and provided fire support for the rest of the units in the column. The two rifle companies from the IInd advanced along the left flank until they reached a hill that overlooked Zinat. When the Spanish forces were halfway up the hillside, the enemy opened fire on the attackers, stopping them completely. The High Command ordered the Legionaries to hold their position in order to protect General José Riquelme's column. The IInd, especially the 6/II Machine Gun Company, covered the withdrawal of the troops. The IIIrd, despite lacking its 8th Company and suffering heavy casualties among its other companies, contributed to the success of the troop

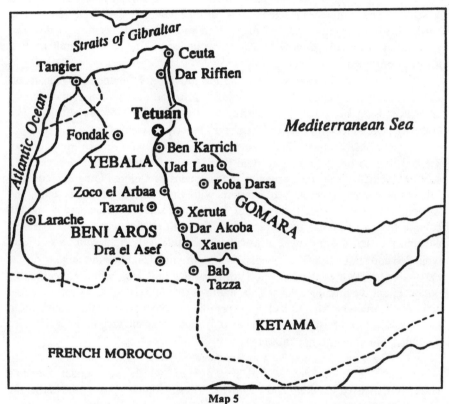

Map 5
The Retreat from Xauen

withdrawal. The Legion had two officers and twenty Legionaries killed, as well as one *Bandera* commander (Major José Candeira Sestelo of the IIIrd), one officer (Captain Rafael Corales Romero of the II), and 112 Legionaries wounded.[64]

The VIth *Bandera* was also in action on 6 September when it evacuated its encampment at Tagasut/Taguesut. In hard-fought combat with the enemy, the VIth suffered seven Legionaries dead, plus three officers and forty-three Legionaries wounded.[65]

The bloodied but unbroken IIIrd *Bandera* was on its way back to Ben Karrich on 7 September to join Castro Girona's column when rebels ambushed it at Semsa. The companies reacted to this surprise attack by deploying rapidly and turning back the enemy, who left many dead and wounded. Losses for the IIIrd were light, with only three Legionaries wounded. The return march to Ben Karrich continued.[66]

The IVth *Bandera* was also on the move on 7 September when it left Xauen, protecting a convoy to Kala Bajo. It also had the mission of blowing up cliffs near Kala Bajo, where the enemy used to hide itself before attacks. The objectives were met with only one Legionary receiving wounds.[67]

On 8 September, the IInd and IVth *Banderas*, with Franco in command, assisted in escorting a convoy to Beni Salah in the foothills of the Gorgues, just south of Tetuán. The IInd served as the vanguard of Colonel Oregon's column. When the enemy attempted to interfere with the passage of the column, the Legionaries of the IInd deployed for battle and smashed them, allowing the column to proceed. The timely arrival of the IVth on the scene of the skirmish covered the IInd's withdrawal. Casualties were relatively light with two officers wounded and six Legionaries killed, plus nine wounded and one missing.[68]

Also on 8 September, the IVth *Bandera,* operating with its column, set out on a punitive mission against Kala, a village that had served as a center of rebel activity. These rebel attacks had been spreading to other parts of the sector. With the mission accomplished and having only one sergeant and four Legionaries wounded, the VIth returned to Xauen.[69]

The Legion continued moving from one hot spot to another. On 10 September, the IInd, IIIrd, and IVth *Banderas*, which were under Franco's leadership, assisted in taking and occupying Monte Conico. During the battle, the Legion suffered one Legionary killed and thirty wounded, but the mission was a complete success.[70]

The next day, 11 September, the same three *Banderas* were in action with the IIIrd forming the vanguard of Castro Girona's column. They advanced along the southeastern zone of Monte Conico toward Alalex/Alalax. The 9/III Machine Gun Company provided withering machine gun fire that allowed the other companies to advance. The 7/III also performed admirably in the assault, and the *Bandera* bivouacked in the vicinity after having evacuated its casualties, which were one Legionary killed and seven wounded. Simultaneously, the IVth *Bandera* was operating in and around Alalex, where it established a *blocao* and quickly advanced toward Kudia Hedia, having accomplished all its objectives. Casualties for the IVth were two Legionaries killed and thirteen wounded.[71]

On 12 September, the IInd and IVth *Banderas* assisted in taking and occupying El Fondak de Ain Yedida. This was accomplished with no enemy resistance and without casualties. At the same time, the VIth *Bandera* escorted a convoy to Kala and encountered rebel opposition. The VIth had one Legionary killed and the commander of the *Bandera*, one officer, and five Legionaries wounded.[72]

The Ist and Vth *Banderas* left from Uad Lau on 14 September to evacuate Tisgarin, an outpost on the banks of the Lau River. Enemy opposition was absent and the operation went off *sin novedad*. On the same date, the VIth *Bandera*, now under the command of Captain Cerdeño, took part in escorting a convoy to Kala, where they engaged the enemy, leaving one officer and eleven Legionaries dead and thirty-eight Legionaries wounded. The IVth *Bandera* would once again return to Kala, on 17 September, on a similar mission, this time suffering twelve Legionaries wounded.[73]

On 15 September the IInd *Bandera*, after having spent the previous night at Laucien (west of Tetuán), was on the march as part of Lieutenant Colonel Adalid's column, which was to operate in the Larache territory.[74]

The enemy's occupation of the Gourges massif continued to interfere with Spanish operations in the region as the rebels continuously besieged the small outposts. Furthermore, in Tetuán there was the threat of artillery bombardment from Riffian guns emplaced on the peaks. The decision was made to drive the enemy from this position. The operation began on 18 September and lasted for three days. General Castro Girona led this important mission, and Franco personally commanded the IVth and Vth *Banderas*.[75] At 0230 hours on 18 September, the 10/IV began its difficult mission to climb stealthily up the massif in order to "take out" the enemy sentries. Without firing a shot and employing only their bayonets, the Legionaries fell upon the sentries and took possession of the crests to the left of the Mers. The rest of the IVth *Bandera* quickly reinforced the 10th Company. As the remainder of the Spanish forces crawled up the mountain, the enemy eventually spotted them and opened fire. The Legionaries flung themselves at the enemy with fixed bayonets and killed fourteen without firing a single shot. Luys Santa Marina once wrote of the Legion's use of the bayonet against the rebels, "The knives [bayonets] were thirsty, and it took a long time to quench them."[76]

The rest of the IVth reached the advance company before sunrise. The column, which included the Battalion of the Queen and the Battalion of Barbastro, arrived at Beni Salah at daybreak. The column's artillery batteries were set up to provide support for the rest of the advance. For the final push, the combination of artillery and machine guns permitted the Legionaries to assault the enemy's defenses from both the front and the left flank. With the day's objectives reached, the Legionaries and engineers fortified their defenses for the night. Thus 19

September was spent fortifying and provisioning the units, which were to carry out the second phase of the assault the following day. The second phase of the operation began on 20 September with the objective being the crests to the right of the Mers. The IVth, backed up by the Vth, launched an attack that secured Loma Negra and Peñón Rocoso. The troops spent the night at these lightly fortified positions. The following day, 21 September, the bulk of Castro Girona's column left the way open to the Gorgues. The Battalion of Barbastro occupied the terrain just taken, while the *Banderas* of the Legion returned to Tetuán. Total Legion casualties for the operation were four officers and 101 men either dead or wounded.[77]

POLITICAL CONTENTION IN THE PROTECTORATE

The political situation vis-à-vis the protectorate was anything but tranquil. *Africanista* officers remained dissatisfied with Primo de Rivera's policy of giving up all the small outposts Spanish blood and treasure had purchased. This dissatisfaction reached its climax when three lieutenant colonels approached General Queipo de Llano about plotting to kidnap the dictator and the generals who had accompanied him to Tetuán. One of the three aforementioned officers was Francisco Franco Bahamonde, commander in chief of the Foreign Legion. Queipo de Llano wrote that on 21 September 1924 he spoke with the officers and Franco told him that disgust with the government's Moroccan policy was rampant among the officer corps and that the officers of the shock troops (i.e., the Legion and *Regulares*), as well as some from the peninsular battalions stationed in Tetuán, had resolved to incarcerate Primo de Rivera along with his accompanying generals in El Hacho (the fortress prison in Ceuta). They needed an officer of high standing (e.g., Queipo de Llano), however, to bring this plot to fruition. Franco declared that he had arranged for one *Bandera* to carry out the operation and that he would move against the generals when Queipo de Llano gave the order. But nothing came of this conspiracy because Queipo de Llano thought it imprudent to act at such a perilous juncture in the Moroccan campaign. Furthermore, support for the move was lacking among the officer corps in the peninsula, and failure would have meant a firing squad for all involved. Franco later attributed this episode more to dissatisfied officers venting their frustrations than to a serious, treasonous scheme.[78]

If Primo de Rivera was ever aware of the plot against him, he did not let on. The only officer to suffer punishment at this time (a result of unrelated previous disagreements he had had with Primo de Rivera) was Queipo de Llano, who was removed from his post on 22 September, taken out of the protectorate, and sent back to the peninsula, where he was sentenced to a month's imprisonment. Franco and the other officers escaped punishment because Primo de Rivera either did not know of the plot or if he did know, believed they were critical to the success of his plans for the protectorate and could ill-afford to have the officers court-martialed. What is important to note is that Franco had put himself and the military power of the Foreign Legion in a position to strike a blow against the dictator personally and the Spanish government as a whole barely two months after what had transpired at Ben Tieb. The Foreign Legion's potency was becoming undeniable. The force would continue to grow and develop as battlefield successes added to their reputation.[79]

While the plot against the dictator was being hatched and aborted, the war in the western zone continued its daily grind. On 22 September, the IInd *Bandera* assisted in the occupation of Arrof, which cost the lives of one officer and one Legionary and the wounding of four Legionaries.[80]

On 23 September, Franco led the Ist and IIIrd *Banderas* on a reconnaissance-in-force to the south of the Gorgues to study the terrain over which the column would be traveling the following day. The 1/I and the 13/I set out to occupy the heights to the left of the villages, thus facilitating the passage of the column on this side. With its own machine guns, as well as those of the IIIrd *Bandera* (9/III), the 3/I departed from Gorgues before dawn, joining up with the rest of its units and a *tabor* of the *Regulares de Alhucemas,* which had orders to occupy the crests of the hills on the right. There they waited in a gully for the rest of the column to arrive. The 1/I and the 13/I caught the enemy by surprise and were able to achieve their objective. The rebel's strong resistance from their well-defended positions halted the advance of the *Regulares*. The IIIrd *Bandera* had to move along the left flank to take the heights of Dar Raid. With the *Regulares* in trouble, the "Tigers" of the IIIrd faced Riffian gunfire in order to assist them advancing along their extreme right. The 7/III reinforced the *Regulares*, while the newly reconstituted 8/III suffered so many casualties in the fight that they had to withdraw. Combat on the left flank was just as rough, with the right wing of the 1/I needing reinforcements. With the casualties mounting and little or no progress being made, the decision was made to withdraw from the most advanced positions, with the 13/I covering the withdrawal. The columns bivouacked in the central gully, the Legion providing protection on both the front and left flanks. The casualties were one officer killed and five wounded, eleven Legionaries killed and 110 wounded, plus eight missing.[81] The IVth and Vth *Banderas* were also in action on 23 September when they assisted in taking and occupying Hensura. Fifteen Legionaries were wounded.[82]

The following day, 24 September, the IVth and Vth *Banderas* again escorted a column. The IVth, forming the left flank of the column, headed toward Zinat and the hillock of Keri Kera, marching parallel to the railroad tracks. Nothing occurred until the column was some two kilometers from its destination: Rebels violently attacked it from Zinat and its immediate crests. The shooting lasted all day as the IVth covered the passage of the column. Breaking off the encounter was difficult, however, because the rebels tried to separate the *Bandera* from the rest of the column. The Legionaries counterattacked with their old dependable friend, the bayonet, and opened the way to the column. The IVth returned to Keri Kera with its casualties as well as captured enemy weapons. Meanwhile, the Vth *Bandera* was on the right flank of the column, and it too provided protection for the column. Casualties for both *Banderas* were two officers wounded, six Legionaries killed, and twenty-nine wounded.[83]

Casualties for the Legion continued to mount as it faced combat every day escorting convoys, protecting columns, or performing its two most important missions: (1) to protect the city of Tetuán from rebel attacks and (2) keeping the lines of communication open between Tetuán and Xauen.

The Ist and IIIrd *Banderas* under Franco's command took part in the operation scheduled for 25 September, which was to operate in the area of Taranes, on the road between Tetuán and Zoco el Arbaa. In a firefight with the enemy, the two *Banderas* suffered two Legionaries dead and fourteen wounded.[84]

The Legion had a very busy day on 26 September when all six *Banderas* went into action. Franco led the Ist and IIIrd, while their respective commanders led the IVth and Vth in an operation in the area of Zoco el Arbaa. Zoco el Arbaa, situated halfway between Tetuán and Xauen, was a strategic juncture in that vital roadway. In a hard-fought action with the enemy, the Legion suffered five Legionaries killed, plus one officer and twenty-three Legionaries wounded. While the aforementioned *Banderas* were in Zoco el Arbaa, the IInd *Bandera* assisted in evacuating Tahar Varda, having one officer missing in action, twenty-five Legionaries killed, and twenty-two wounded. The VIth *Bandera* also helped escorted a convoy to Mula Tahar. In a firefight with the enemy, it suffered one Legionary killed, as well as one officer and fourteen Legionaries wounded.[85] On 27 September, Franco led the Ist and IIIrd *Banderas*, which took part in escorting a convoy to Timisal; in the combat that ensued with the enemy, the Legion had eight Legionaries wounded.[86]

EVACUATION OF XAUEN

Preparations for the evacuation of Xauen began on 28 September when the Ist and IIIrd *Banderas* under Franco's leadership assisted General Castro Girona's column in opening of the road to Xauen, which Abd-el-Krim's men had cut. In the inevitable combat with the Riffians, the casualties for the Legion were five Legionaries killed, plus two officers and eighteen Legionaries wounded.[87]

The final operation for the Legion in September took place on the 30th. Once again, the Ist and IIIrd *Banderas*, after having bivouacked on the way to Xauen, continued with their operations in the sector. The *Banderas* set up two *blocaos* at Abbada and, in the process, engaged the Riffians in brutal hand-to-hand combat. Resorting to cold steel, the Legionaries got the job done, leaving eighty-seven of their opponents dead. The Legion suffered relatively light casualties with one officer and seven Legionaries killed, plus two officers and twenty-eight Legionaries wounded.[88]

Knowing that Primo de Rivera planned to evacuate Xauen because it was difficult to supply and defend, Abd-el-Krim had moved his troops there hoping for another Annual. The VIth *Bandera* had been doing all the fighting for the Legion in the Xauen zone, but now most of the other *Banderas* would be concentrated in and around Xauen in preparation for the evacuation.[89] Having reached Xauen, the next phase of the operation was to gather the garrisons of all the small outposts (*blocaos*) in the Gomara region and concentrate them in Xauen. Once there, they would be escorted back to Tetuán, traveling approximately forty-five miles on the dirt road the Spanish had recently completed. It would be a long and costly forty-five miles back to Tetuán—a journey that would leave a thousand Spanish troops dead along the roadside.[90]

The Legion (less the IInd *Bandera*) would have a dual role to play in the evacuation of Xauen: (1) to neutralize the activities of the enemy, who dedicated itself to besieging positions, impeding the passage of convoys, and carrying out attacks on Spanish forces; and (2) to pave the way for the general withdrawal by establishing defensive and support positions that would provide protection once the evacuation had begun, thus helping to reduce the number of casualties.[91] On 1 October, the Ist and IIIrd *Banderas* under Franco's personal command fortified the village of Abbada and especially the nearby heights of Morabo.[92] The Ist *Bandera* bore the brunt of the fighting and needed to be reinforced by the IIIrd. In the ensuing hand-to-hand combat with the enemy, one officer and four Legionaries were killed, and two officers and five Legionaries were wounded. The 1/I was left behind to defend Abbada and Morabo.[93]

Two days later, on 3 October, these *Banderas* left Dar Akobba to provide protection on the Tetuán-Xauen road that ran between Hamara and Xeruta. Harassed by the rebels, the Legionaries aggressively fought back, causing a number of casualties among the enemy. For the Legion, the losses were negligible, with one officer and four Legionaries wounded.[94]

The Ist and IIIrd *Banderas* left their Dar Akobba encampment at dawn on 8 October to regain *blocao* Peire, which the enemy had seized after killing the garrison. The Legionaries regained and rebuilt the *blocao*, leaving on station a sergeant and seventeen Legionaries from the 1/I. Only one Legionary was wounded during this operation.[95]

On 13 October, the IIIrd *Bandera* marched from Dar Akobba to Xauen to join with Castro Girona's column. Three days later the Ist *Bandera* also relocated to Xauen. Now all the *Banderas*, with the exception of the IInd, operating in the Larache territory, were in Xauen.[96]

Before the actual evacuation of Xauen, the area around it had to be secured to keep the road open. In addition, the troops manning *blocaos* around Xauen had to be evacuated to Xauen, and from there evacuated back to Tetuán. The Legion and the *Regulares* would be assigned the task of rounding up the defenders of these isolated outposts and escorting them back to Xauen. The Ist, IVth, and VIth *Banderas*, under the leadership of Franco, assisted in the operation scheduled for 16 October, which had as its goal the capture of Garusin. The assault column also included cavalry from the *Regulares*, a *tabor* of infantry, and a battery of mountain guns. The column departed Xauen and formed for battle at a post called Muñiz. With the cannons and machine guns emplaced to provide fire support for the advance, the infantry moved toward the well-entrenched enemy. Both the Legion and the *Regulares* possessed plenty of know-how when it came to the tactics of the Riffians, and they prepared accordingly. The *tabor* of infantry advanced along the right, while the Ist *Bandera* moved along the left to capture the cliffs that overlooked the riverbank below. The VIth *Bandera*, with its two rifle companies, advanced in a different direction hoping to seal off the only possible escape route for the enemy; the IVth *Bandera* and the Battalion of Segorbe constituted the reserve and prepared to relieve the primary attackers. As soon as enemy forces began to feel the force of the attack, they fled along the riverbed, expecting to escape. To their surprise they encountered withering gunfire from every direction. They left twenty dead, along with their weapons. Legion losses were two officers and fifty Legionaries wounded.[97]

In the political arena, as it related to the protectorate, the leadership changed once again on 16 October when Primo de Rivera personally assumed the position of High Commissioner of the protectorate following General Aizpuru's resignation.[98]

On 18 October, Franco led the Ist, IVth, and VIth *Banderas*, while the IIIrd and Vth *Banderas* under their respective commanders joined forces to occupy Miskrela. In the battle with the rebels, fourteen Legionaries were wounded.[99] Three days later, on 21 October, the same units began the evacuation of the outpost at Kala, located north of Xauen. In a bitter engagement, the Legion had seven Legionaries killed, plus two officers and fifteen Legionaries wounded. Harris observed that in trying to evacuate these small outposts, the rescuers suffered more casualties than the number of men being rescued.[100]

The IInd *Bandera*, which was operating in the Larache territory, took part in the occupation of Taixera on 22 October with no interference from the enemy and no casualties sustained. Concurrent with the IInd *Bandera*'s operation, the IIIrd, Vth, and VIth *Banderas* sustained a rebel attack in Xauen, having five Legionaries wounded in the fray.[101]

On 23 October, the *Banderas*, with the exception of the IInd, operated in the area of Dacarrat and performed their typical responsibility of keeping the lines of communication open and countering snipers. The Ist, IVth, and VIth *Banderas* faced stiff enemy resistance, which caused the death of two Legionaries as well as the wounding of one officer and eight Legionaries. The IIIrd and Vth *Banderas*, in contrast, encountered no resistance in their sector and had no casualties.[102]

The following day, the Ist, IVth, and Vth *Banderas* formed part of Franco's column. Also taking part in the operation was a *tabor* of *Regulares* who had its objectives assigned. The IVth *Bandera* was to follow closely behind them and secure what had been covered by the *Mehal-la* and friendly *harkas*, which was the front and the right flank of the column. The woods of Tenafe were such an important position in the success of the operation that a company from the IVth occupied them to assault the rocky heights that dominated access to Uta-Lecha.

The rest of the column reached Uta-Lecha and set up its battery of guns to provide support for the advance. The Ist and VIth (minus its 21st Company) advanced on the village and took up positions there, along with the Battalion of Segorbe, whose troops established themselves in the ruins of a *blocao* at the entrance of the village and on the right flank. It was then that the enemy, well concealed in the thick coppice, aggressively attacked the 11/IV, which responded with a bayonet charge. The 16/IV reinforced the 11/IV, and together they inflicted numerous casualties on the enemy. In the woods closer to Tenafe, the enemy also unleashed an attack, but the 18th and 19th Companies of the Vth *Bandera* reinforced the position, surrounded the enemy, and annihilated them with hand grenades and the *arma blanca*. Having taken control of this part of the woods, the Vth was able to prevent the enemy from cutting off the convoy or its means of withdrawal. The column continued to Tenafe with minimal harassment from the enemy and established a *blocao* at Gars. The convoy moved to Draa-el-Asef, where it set up another *blocao*. Two officers and sixty-nine Legionaries were either dead or wounded.[103]

On 25 October, Franco led his *Banderas* to evacuate Bab el Haman. This was accomplished without resistance or casualties.[104]

One of the bloodiest battles in this campaign to consolidate all the troops in the Xauen sector took place on the 26th when Franco led the Ist, IVth, and VIth *Banderas* to evacuate Draa-el-Asef. Franco's column left before dawn for Uta-Lecha, clearing the way to Akarrat and covering the march of Núñez de Prado's column and convoy until they had reached the outpost. Right from the start, they encountered intense enemy resistance on the left flank, with the enemy running along the slopes of Sugna. The Ist *Bandera* covered the southern front, which faced the village. The IVth was at the *blocao* of Gars covering the right part of the line; they joined the *Regulares* and secured the high peak of the woods near the village. The VIth *Bandera* remained at Draa-el-Asef, entrusted with forming the last echelon of the column, and joining with a *tabor* of *Regulares*. The movement of the column went according to plan, but with ever-increasing hostility from the rebels. The supply convoy, carrying food and munitions, along with the wounded, was slow and long. Once the column had passed, the withdrawal of the protecting units began with one *Bandera* covering the other in echelons (i.e., the IVth covering the VIth and the *Regulares*). The 17/V reinforced the passage of the other units through the village, taking the point in the withdrawal and received the brunt of the Riffian assault. The 17/V reacted to the enemy's attack under the leadership of its adjutant Captain Alfonso de los Reyes González. The withdrawal slowed to remove the wounded and to prevent gaps from forming in the line. The final withdrawal back to Uta-Lecha went off without incident. However, the Spaniards still needed to fight their way back to Akarrat. The Legion and the Battalion of Segorbe covered this final phase. The IVth *Bandera* had to send one of its companies to cover the left flank, near the Tanafe woods, which was crawling with rebels who harassed the retreat. The Legionaries and army regulars bivouacked at Akarrat for the night. Legion losses for the day were six officers and 119 Legionaries either dead or wounded.[105]

After the hard-fought battle to evacuate Draa-el-Asef the previous day, the Legion once again faced action, on 27 October escorting a convoy of wounded soldiers from Mura Tahar to Xauen. One Legionary died and eight were wounded on the trip.[106]

On 28 October, the Ist, IIIrd, IVth, Vth, and VIth *Banderas* assisted in evacuation of Dacarrak. Franco, who usually led the Ist, IIIrd, and Vth *Banderas*, this day led the IVth and VIth. The Ist, IIIrd, and Vth *Banderas*, led by their respective commanders, accomplished their mission without encountering resistance. Franco's two *Banderas* had one Legionary killed in the operation. The IInd *Bandera* evacuated Zoco el Jemis de Beni Aros without rebel interference.[107]

The final operations for the Legion during the month of October took place on the 30th and 31st when the IInd *Bandera* evacuated Bab el Sor and Robba el Gozal. It accomplished both evacuations without incident.[108]

On the first day of November, the Ist, IIIrd, IVth, Vth, and VIth *Banderas* were all in Xauen; the IInd was now at Zoco T'Zenin (Larache). On this day, the IVth *Bandera* distinguished itself when early in the morning it carried out an assault on the heights of el Mago, on which the enemy had emplaced a cannon. This cannon had been hurling shells into Xauen, and the time had come to put an end to the bombardment. When the fight was over and the rebel guards had been neutralized, the Legionaries of the IVth wheeled the captured field piece back to their encampment.[109]

On 2 November, the Ist, IVth, and VIth *Banderas*, back under Franco's command, as well as the IIIrd and Vth *Banderas*, under their respective commanders, assisted in protecting a supply convoy to Miskrela, suffering one officer and nine Legionaries wounded.[110] From 3 to 8 November, all the *Banderas* performed their usual campaign duties with no combat reported during these five days—a welcomed breather from what the Legion had suffered.[111] While not involved in providing protection for the evacuation of Xauen, the "Eagles" of the IInd *Bandera* were admirably performing their invaluable duty in the Larache territory. On 9 November, the IInd relieved Dar Telata. The battle that ensued cost the lives of five Legionaries and the wounding of nine others.[112]

By mid-November all the outposts of the Xauen sector were evacuated. The next step was the evacuation of Xauen, which would commence in earnest on 15 November when General Castro Girona led the majority of the troops silently out of Xauen without interference from the Riffians or Yebalis. By 18 November the advance guard of Castro Girona's column had reached Zoco el Arbaa. Now more than 40,000 men were spread between the two positions (i.e., Xauen and Zoco el Arbaa). The Legion, under Franco's personal command, which had remained behind to serve as the rear guard for the evacuation, left Xauen at midnight on 17 November.[113] Prior to departing that evening, Franco deceived the Riffians by having his troops position straw-filled dummies wearing Legion tunics and sidecaps in front of the loopholes on the walls. From the surrounding heights and peaks they occupied, Abd-el-Krim's men could see the counterfeit "Legionaries" and believed that the five *Banderas* had remained in Xauen. Once the sun had risen, the enemy realized that they had been duped and quickly reacted to cut off the retreating Legionaries, who by this time had reached Dar Akobaa. Having control of both flanks of the heights that dominated the road, the Legionaries exchanged gunfire with the rebels. The Legion suffered one officer and seven Legionaries wounded, but Franco and the Legion succeeded in allowing the principal evacuation columns to gain a head start on the enemy pursuit.[114]

The second phase of the evacuation from Xauen, which began on 18 November, involved moving from Dar Akobba to Xeruta and then to Zoco el Arbaa. The five *Banderas* that took part in this rear guard action (Ist, IIIrd, IVth, Vth, and VIth) all fought a phased withdrawal; that is to say, they attacked the enemy before it had the time to group its forces or seize advantageous terrain. The Legion took the initiative away from them.[115]   Each *Bandera* maneuvered independently in the operation as they filled in gaps in the lines, seized important defensive positions along the Xauen-Tetuán road, manned *blocaos*, and protected the rear of the column. On 18 November, the Ist and VIth *Banderas* joined together for their day's assignment while the IVth, Vth, and IIIrd operated independently. In the battles that took place that day, many of them settled at the point of the bayonet, the Legion saw one officer and twelve Legionaries killed, plus Major Figueras of the IVth *Bandera*; in addition, an officer and forty-nine Legionaries were wounded. Also on the same date, the IInd *Bandera* relieved Ain Razta/Rapta, having five Legionaries wounded.[116]

The persistent harassment of the 7,000 Riffians and Yebali in Abd-el-Krim's army, along with the inclement weather, hampered the evacuation. The weather was cold, and the incessant rains turned the dirt road into a quagmire, making the going miserably slow and treacherous. The soldiers' uniforms were soaked and tattered, their weapons dirty. Food for the men and feed for the beasts of burden did not reach the columns. Cannons, horses, pack mules, and men sank in the mud, making the evacuation even more arduous.[117] A famous comment, uttered by an unknown Spanish officer during the evacuation, summed up the whole situation: "We were fighting shadows and we lost thirty men to their one." Having evacuated Dar Akobba the previous day, the Legion assisted in the operation scheduled for 19 November—the evacuation of Xeruta.   All the *Banderas*, except for the IInd, took part in the evacuation, each under the leadership of its respective commander. Franco was already in Zoco el Arbaa making preparations for the arrival of the Spaniards. With the Legionaries protecting the columns, the enemy attacked them right from the start. The fighting involved vicious hand-to-hand combat with no quarter asked for and none given. In one particular encounter, Captain Pablo Arredondo Acuña led the 1/I in protecting other units withdrawing from the battle. Although wounded, he stoically remained with four other officers and Legionaries from his company, all sacrificing themselves for the good of Colonel Gómez Morato's column. Overwhelmed by superior numbers, they perished fighting to the end. The human toll for the Legion was steep that day with the deaths of five officers, including Captain Pablo Arredondo Acuña and eighty-six Legionaries. The wounded included five officers and 100 Legionaries.[118]

The retreat from Xauen had taken its toll on the column; so after the battle of Xeruta, the High Command in Tetuán decided to halt at Zoco el Arbaa to rest and recover. It became a time for casualties to be substituted, weapons replaced or repaired, and ammunition stocks replenished. The enemy surrounded Zoco el Arbaa for nearly three weeks waiting for the Spanish to make their next move. The Spaniards, meanwhile, were hoping for better weather while making the final leg of their retreat to Tetuán.[119]

The Legion's final operation for the bloody month of November took place on 29 November when the Ist, IIIrd, IVth, and Vth Banderas under Franco's command assisted in the evacuation of el Llano and the blocaos of Meyahedi in the Zoco el Arbaa sector. Engaging the enemy in combat, one officer and twenty-three Legionaries were wounded.[120]

While the rest of the evacuation column refitted before embarking on the next leg of the journey to Tetuán, the Legion continued carrying out its duties.[121] On 2 December, three volunteer detachments from the IInd Bandera left their encampment (Mexerah) at 2000 hours to evacuate the forward outpost of Kala. The Legionaries used cover of night and stealth to carry out their operation. The men of the IInd Bandera gathered those stationed at Kala and were preparing to return to Mexerah when the enemy became aware of what had happened and attacked them. Only a counterattack at bayonet point allowed the Legionaries to return to their base with those evacuated from Kala, and their own wounded.[122] On 5 December, the IInd Bandera was once again in action, charged with removing artillery emplaced at Quesil, as well as relieving the garrisons of Guerben, Fafersa, Quesil, and their advanced positions. This was all done while exchanging fire with the rebels. The very next day, 6 December, while marching toward the blocao of Valle, the Legionaries secured the heights in preparation for the withdrawal and then returned to Mexerah.[123] Also on 5 December, Franco's IIIrd and IVth Banderas took part in the recovery of the blocao of Sidi Musa, fighting the enemy continuously from the start of the operation. Losses for the Legion were nine Legionaries killed, plus one officer and thirty-three Legionaries wounded.[124] The IInd Bandera was back in action on 7-8 December when it evacuated the positions of Fendak Yebel and the blocao of Magot/ "Amargot." In bitter fighting with the enemy, especially by Sergeant Antonio Sangiorgio and a squad from the 14th Rifle Company, the IInd suffered eleven Legionaries killed and four wounded.[125]

FINAL STAGES OF XAUEN'S EVACUATION

The last phase of the evacuation of Xauen began on 10 December with the abandonment of Zoco el Arbaa. The Spanish army intended the column to move toward the next stop on the Xauen-Tetuán road, which was Taranes. As usual, it was up to the Legion, under Franco's personal command, to protect the column by securing the heights that dominated the road. The Ist *Bandera* would be the last to leave Zoco el Arbaa, so it spent the previous day making all the necessary preparations for the retreat. Like a well-oiled machine, one *Bandera* supported the withdrawal of another in echelon. This was a maneuver the Legionaries had mastered. The Vth *Bandera*, from its fortified post at Taimutz, provided the evacuation with fire support from its twelve machine guns and its mortars. As soon as the operation began, the enemy began to harass the column. The Legionaries counterattacked on numerous occasions. The fighting was bloody, in many cases hand-to-hand combat. Because of the fighting acumen and discipline of the five *Banderas*, the bulk of the column was able to reach its destination of Taranes, where it bivouacked. For the Legion, the casualties had been high with six officers, including one *Bandera* commander, Major Ricardo de Rada Peral, and 115 Legionaries killed. Seven officers and eighty-seven Legionaries received wounds.[126]

The IInd *Bandera* had also participated in an operation that day. In the vanguard of Colonel González Carrasco's column, it protected a convoy to Serilla/Seriya/Sevilla, encountering no resistance. This was followed by a withdrawal and evacuation to the camp at Teffer.[127]

On 12 December, the Ist, IIIrd, IVth, Vth, and VIth *Banderas* were once again on the move, evacuating Taranes and withdrawing to Zinat, the next stop on the way to Tetuán. The afternoon before, all the matériel, pack mules, and horses had been sent ahead, so that the column could travel faster. The march began at night, with the first stop at Keri Kera. At 0300 hours, with the *Regulares* covering the road, Afroit, Ramla, and all the *blocaos* evacuated, the Legion set out on the high road. By daybreak, the Legion reached Keri Kera and provided protection for the retreating men and their equine companions until they reached Zinat. The Legionaries once again employed their successful withdrawal by echelons, with effective fire support from their machine guns. Harassed by the enemy as they neared Zinat, a company of Legionaries successfully rebuffed them. Legion losses were one Legionary killed and one *Bandera* commander and twenty-two Legionaries wounded.[128]

On 13 December, the Legion evacuated Zinat and headed for Ben Karrich, the last stop on the road to Tetuán. In a fighting withdrawal with the rebels, the Legionaries were able to reach Ben Karrich with only one Legionary killed and six wounded. On the same day, the Ist and IVth *Banderas* marched triumphantly through the streets of Tetuán to the enthusiastic cheers of the crowd.[129]

It had taken nearly a month for the more than 40,000 men to cover the forty-plus miles from Xauen to Tetuán, and the number of casualties suffered by Spain ranges from a little less than 2,000 to an incredible 18,000. Despite the casualties incurred, the Spanish army was now behind the Estella line, in most part because of the discipline and martial spirit of the Legion.[130]

General Primo de Rivera welcomed the survivors of the retreat to Tetuán with the following address:

You enter Tetuán in triumph, having carried out the most difficult operation, after having raised the sieges and assured the evacuation of outlying Posts. You have retired through a long valley, the hills on both sides of which were held by the enemy. This was necessary in the interests and for the honour of Spain. In realizing this operation, far more arduous than any offensive, you have given an example of sacrifice and of discipline. Bravo! Generals, commanding officers, officers, and men.[131]

The final operations for the IInd *Bandera* began on 14 December when it broke out of Teffer and headed toward the "Sacred Forrest," where it took up combat positions to provide protection for cavalry units sallying from there. The IInd suffered only a handful of wounded in this operation. Having completed that operation, it relocated to Taatof, from where it departed early on 17 December to evacuate Dar-el-Ata. The Legionaries engaged the enemy in battle but were able to keep them at bay while the evacuation went on. The IInd *Bandera* later established itself in Alcazarquivir. From there, it assisted in the evacuation of Yuma-el-Tolba and Hayera Tuila.[132]

Although the evacuation column had arrived in Tetuán, the Spaniards still had to deal with rebellious tribes behind the Estella line. Another important mission for Spanish forces behind the line was to keep the lines of communication open between Ceuta, Tangier, and Larache. On 15 December, the Ist *Bandera* assisted in establishing a defensive position in Rio Martín, having two Legionaries killed and three wounded.[133] On 17 December, the IIIrd and VIth *Banderas*, under Franco, stormed and occupied the fortified position of Ainyir. In a bitter fight with the rebels, the Legionaries suffered thirteen dead and twenty-eight wounded.[134] On 18 December, the Ist, IVth, and Vth *Banderas* took part in the advance against Zoco el Jemis de Anyera with the goal of enlarging the position. Encountering effective resistance from the enemy, the Legionaries had one man dead and fourteen wounded.[135] These *Banderas* were in the field the next day, 19 December, as they helped evacuate Yarda, with six men wounded.[136] On 20-21 December, the *Banderas* took part in their last operation for the year as they evacuated Zoco el Jemis de Anyera and Zinac/Zinat. During this two-day operation, the Legionaries fought the enemy and suffered one Legionary killed, plus one officer and six Legionaries wounded.[137]

The IIIrd *Bandera* and Legionaries of the VIth participated in the last operation for the Legion in 1924, when under Franco's leadership they took part in the fortification of outposts in Ain Sixo on 30 December. In brutal combat with the rebels in that sector, the Legion suffered seven Legionaries killed, as well as one officer and twenty-two Legionaries wounded.[138] On 31 December, all the *Banderas* of the Legion were in various locations behind the Estella line, engaged in carrying out their typical campaign duties as the year came to a close.[139]

SUMMARY

In 1924 the Legion once again demonstrated its value and importance to Spain's control of the protectorate. It fought the Riffians to a standstill in the eastern zone after having pushed them back to the fringes of Annual. With Tizzi-Azza as their most forward outpost in the region, the Legion was not allowed to proceed any farther; it was expected to hold the line in this sector against all enemy incursions. As the focus of the rebellion shifted from the eastern zone to the western zone during the middle of the year, the Legion redeployed to deal with these new flareups. When the rebels besieged Kobba Darsa in early July, Franco with the Ist and Vth *Banderas* rescued those trapped when other units had repeatedly failed.

In mid-July, Primo de Rivera visited the troops in Morocco to prepare the groundwork for scaling back Spain's military actions in the protectorate. As we saw at the Legion's principal basecamp at Ben Tieb, the junior officers of the Legion and the *Regulares* would have no part of it and told him so. The Legion forced Primo de Rivera to modify his plans in the eastern zone by maintaining the status quo. It was doable, since the forward lines were secure and the tribesmen in that region had been disarmed and "pacified." This led to a tactical withdrawal to better defensive positions that were closer to the coastal enclaves in the western zone. Knowing full well that his plans for semiabandonment depended on the participation of the Legion, the evacuation of Xauen and other smaller outposts began in September and were completed by early December. The pivotal role the Legion played in the evacuation of Xauen is best summed up by Arturo Barea's friend Sergeant Córcoles when he declared: "I can't stomach those fellows in the *Tercio*. Every one of them has either killed his own father or something like it, or else he's fit for the madhouse. But the truth is that without them the rest of us would never have got out alive."[140]

Franco was unhappy with the Xauen withdrawal, but he carried out his orders as Primo de Rivera had told him he would do when the time came. For his actions during the evacuation of Xauen, Franco was promoted to the rank of colonel. At thirty-one, he was now the youngest colonel in the Spanish army. Moreover, Primo de Rivera and the High Command would now give consideration to his plans for an amphibious landing at Alhucemas Bay.[141]

NOTES

1. Woolman, *Rebels in the Rif*, 128-129, wrote that Ahmed Heriro had at one time served with the *Regulares de Tetuán* and was an effective leader of men.

2. Fleming, *Primo de Rivera*, 120-121. Fleming also noted that the extensive military preparations Primo de Rivera planned for the eastern zone were not reproduced in the western zone. Estado Mayor Central del Ejército, (vol. IV, part 9), 6. Scurr, 14. Vaughan, 6.

3. Fleming, *Primo de Rivera*, 133.

4. Fleming, *Primo de Rivera*, 134.

5. *DOL*, *Negociado de campaña*, 1 January 1924, 24-25. Subinspección de la Legión, ed., 200 and 210. This source recorded that Franco joined the four *Banderas* at Ben Tieb on 25 February.

6. *DOL*, *Negociado de campaña*, 13 January 1924, 25; Subinspección de la Legión, ed., 200; and *SHM*, Legajo #54, Rollo 16, *Colección de historiales*, "Campañas de Marruecos, Historial de guerra, 1ª y 2ª Banderas," 167. Ramas Izquierdo, 27-28, provides more information on Captain José García Uria, who lost his life trying to aid the wounded Lieutenant Armando Ocon Urzaiz.

7. Fleming, *Primo de Rivera*, 135-136. Woolman, *Rebels in the Rif*, 128. Estado Mayor Central del Ejército, 6. Among the casualties was Corvette Captain (Lieutenant Commander) Jaime Janer Robinson. For more on the *Cataluña*, see Fitzsimons, ed., vol. V, 532, and *Jane's Fighting Ships*, ed. (1923), 324. de Arce, 179, noted that Abd-el-Krim put the captured war booty to good use. In the case of the field pieces, Abd-el-Krim needed skilled artillerists to service them. These he found among the deserters who joined his ranks. Not all had been deserters or mercenaries, however. According to the author, "The Russians sent him [Abd-el-Krim] a colonel of Artillery, Serge Kugushev, to train his men in the use of the 75 and 105 millimeter Schneider cannons." Hills, 135. According to Woolman, *Rebels in the Rif*, 129, Baron Peter Wrangel, the former general of the White Russian army in the Crimea, had offered Primo de Rivera his services, along with that of more than 100,000 of his men. This army had escaped from the victorious Bolsheviks and was in need of employment. Primo de Rivera declined this offer of a Russian expeditionary force to fight against the Riffians, claiming employing the force would violate the Spanish Constitution, which forbade foreign troops on Spanish territory. Whereas the White Russians as a group were precluded from joining the Legion, individuals were not. One was Nikolai Vsevolodovich Shinkarenko (1890-1968), a Russian cavalry officer who began his military career in the imperial army of Tsar Nicholas II during World War I. During the Russian Civil War, as a brigadier general of cavalry, he fought on the side of the Whites. Following their defeat, he enlisted in the Spanish Foreign Legion and served as an officer during the Rif campaign and throughout the Spanish Civil War. Shinkarenko's memoirs, in Russian, can be found in the World War I holdings, File #CSUZ68020-A, Hoover Institute, Stanford University.

8. *DOL*, *Negociado de campaña*, 1 March 1924, 25. The Ist and IIIrd *Banderas* were at Tafersit; the IInd and IVth were at Ben Tieb; the Vth remained at Argos; and the VIth was now at García Uria, named in honor of the late captain José García Uria.

9. *DOL*, 3 March 1924, 25. Subinspección de la Legión, ed., 201, gave the number of Legionaries wounded as fourteen, instead of three.

10. *DOL*, *Negociado de campaña*, 5 March 1924, 25. Ramas Izquierdo, 46, has more on the death of *Alférez* José Bonet Pérez.

11. Estado Mayor Central del Ejército, 6. Subinspección de la Legión, ed., 201, noted the "necessity of taking steps to destroy or punish the enemy and clearing the way to the Sector [Tizzi-Azza]."

12. Subinspección de la Legión, ed., 201-202. *DOL*, *Negociado de campaña*, 6 March (*sic*) 1924, 25. This source gives different casualty figures: twenty-three

Legionaries killed; six officers and ninety-eight Legionaries wounded. Estado Mayor Central del Ejército, 6-7. *SHM*, Legajo #54, Rollo 16, *Colección de historiales*, "Campañas de Marruecos, Historial de guerra, 1ª y 2ª Banderas," 168. García Figueras, 200. Ramas Izquierdo, 153-158, gives an excellent description of the engagement and the officers who distinguished themselves in it.

13. *DOL*, *Negociado de campaña*, 8 March 1924, 25.

14. Estado Mayor Central del Ejército, 7 (n. 7). In the footnote, General Primo de Rivera himself acknowledged that these advanced positions "were bad due to the orographic configuration."

15. *DOL*, *Negociado de campaña*, 10-31 March 1924, 25-26; Subinspección de la Legión, ed., 202-203; and *SHM*, Legajo #54, Rollo 16, *Colección de historiales*, "Campañas de Marruecos, Historial de guerra, 1ª y 2ª Banderas," 168.

16. *DOL*, *Negociado de campaña*, 1 April 1924, 26. By the first of April, three of the four *Banderas* in the eastern zone had been moved up closer to the line of fire, which was the Tizzi-Azza sector. The Ist was in Tizzi-Azza itself; the IInd, IIIrd, and IVth were at Tafersit; the Vth remained at Argos; and the VIth remained at García Uria. Primo de Rivera's earlier statements on what his policy would be in pursuing the war against Abd-el-Krim disturbed the *africanistas* in the army. In the April issue of *La Revista de Tropas Coloniales*, a journal founded by Brigadier General Gonzalo Quipo de Llano and other officers in Ceuta, Franco wrote an article entitled "Passivity and Inaction" in which "he had complained of the inveterate habit successive governments had of reducing supplies or numbers as soon as the Spaniards had recovered lost ground. This, he argued, created a vicious circle, for as soon as Spanish pressure eased, the Moors regrouped and attacked. That way, victory was always just out of reach and the war never ended." See Crozier, 75; De La Cierva, 226, has the complete text of Franco's article. Needless to say, the dictatorship did not take too kindly to this criticism of its Moroccan policy and responded by shutting down the journal. For more, see Preston, 43; García Figueras, 201, Payne, 210, De La Cierva, *Franco*, 78.

17. Subinspección de la Legión, ed., 203-204. See 210 for information on the combat that took place on 17 April and involved a unit of the 17/V (under the command of *Alférez* Casquero) in the area around M'Ter in the Gomara. *DOL*, *Negociado de campaña*, 2-30 April 1924, 26. Total casualties for the month were four Legionaries killed, two officers and thirty-one Legionaries wounded. Furneaux, 98, noted an interview conducted in April by the journalist Ward Price of the London *Daily Mail* with Primo de Rivera, who stated the following about the military situation in the eastern zone: "There [at Tizzi-Azza] we have an outpost in a difficult strategic position held by about three companies and a battery of guns. Together with subsidiary posts and protecting flanks the whole garrison of Tizzi[-]Azza amounts to about 1,500 men. The recent Moorish attack on a convoy proceeding thither cost them forty dead, while our column lost only eight lives in dispersing the enemy and supplying the post." Primo de Rivera also told the newspaperman that in the near future "it might be possible to concentrate Spanish troops in coastal towns and dominate the interior by means of aeroplanes, as the British army had done in parts of the Middle East. For this purpose he proposed to increase the number of Spanish aeroplanes in

Morocco from fifty to one hundred and fifty" (99).

18. *DOL*, *Negociado de campaña*, 1 May 1924, 26.

19. *DOL*, 7 May 1924, 26; Subinspección de la Legión, ed., 204-205; Estado Mayor Central del Ejército, 7-8; and *SHM*, Legajo #54, Rollo 16, *Colección de historiales*, "Campañas de Marruecos, Historial de guerra, 1ª y 2ª Banderas," 169. Fleming, *Primo de Rivera*, 139-140. Ramas Izquierdo, 158-161, gives a concise yet detailed description of the battle and those officers who distinguished themselves. For more on the deaths of *Alféreces* Ignacio Gerber/Germert de la Concha and Ignacio Imaz Echevarri, see 46. Cano Velasco, ed., 154. Preston, 44. Sablotny, 102-109. As a German volunteer with the rank of corporal in the 16/IV of the Legion, Sablotny was in Ben Tieb, the Legion's principal base camp in the eastern zone, when the IIIrd *Bandera* was turned back by the Riffians on 7 May. He described the situation at Ben Tieb and the preparations made for another attempt to supply Sidi Mesaud and to punish the rebels as well.

20. *DOL*, *Negociado de campaña*, 10 May 1924, 26-27. Estado Mayor Central del Ejército, 8. This source gave the final casualty toll for the operation as 208. This included Europeans as well as Moroccans serving in the *Regulares*. Subinspección de la Legión, ed., 205-206. *SHM*, Legajo #54, Rollo 16, *Colección de historiales*, "Campañas de Marruecos, Historial de guerra, 1ª y 2ª Banderas," 169-170. Cano Velasco, ed., 154-155, recorded that this confrontation between the Legion and the Riffians was "savage" and comparable to the battle of Casabona back in 1921. García Figueras, 201. Sablotny, 110-126, gives an excellent first-person account of the battle for Sidi Mesaud. Unfortunately, on 110, he confused the future aeronautical exploits of Ramón Franco Baamonde and his brother Francisco, who was Commander in Chief of the Legion. In an observation which pertains to the subject matter of the subsequent footnotes, the author (246) encountered an old, blind "Moor" in the Rif who said he had lost his sight as a result of poisonous gas bombs dropped by Spanish aviators. (Blindness is indicative of having been exposed to mustard gas). Fleming, *Primo de Rivera*, 140-141. The author described the number of bombs dropped by the Spanish air force on the Riffians. The bombs dropped by the air force included "a combination of incendiary, fragment, and poison gas bombs." Poison gas bombs (blistering agents/gases [vesicants] such as nitrogen mustard [dichlorethyl sulphide] or "Yperite," as it was also known because the Germans used it against the French during the third battle of Ypres in 1917) proved most efficacious against the rebels and were increasingly used by the end of May. For more on poison gas aerial bombs and their use during the Rif Rebellion (to the best of my knowledge the first time in history), see Rudibert Kunz and Rolf-Dieter Müller, *Giftgas gegen Abd el Krim: Deutschland, Spanien und der Gaskrieg in Spanisch-Marokko, 1922-1927* (Freiburg: Verlag Rombach, 1990). Woolman, *Rebels in the Rif*, 129, observed that armored cars were being used in the campaign against Abd-el-Krim and noted that the Riffians "had long ago learned that they could halt and destroy them by trapping them in wide trenches, then attacking them with grenades from above." Because of the difficult terrain and the traps built by the Riffians to ensnare them, the tanks were not used in the battle of Sidi Mesaud. See Subinspección de la Legión, ed., 205. Ramas Izquierdo, 161-166. For more on the deaths of Lieutenants Feliciano Rojas Rojas, Clemente Valverde Villareal, and Antonio de Leone Molina, see 34-35. Lieutenant

Fernando Lizcano de la Rosa, commander of the 14/II, led his men in a valiant bayonet attack that routed the enemy before him. For his heroism, he was awarded Spain's highest medal for valor, the Laureate Cross of St. Ferdinand. In a conversation at the *Servicio Histórico Militar* in Madrid in October 1993, Colonel of Infantry Ramón Moya Ruiz told the author that Lizcano de la Rosa was executed by Republicans in Barcelona (Montjuich Fortress) during the first days of the "uprising" (*Alzamiento*) along with General Manuel Goded Llopis.

21. *DOL, Negociado de campaña*, 11-12 May 1924, 27. Subinspección de la Legión, ed., 206, gave the number of Legion casualties as fourteen. *SHM*, Legajo #54, Rollo 16, *Colección de historiales*, "Campañas de Marruecos, Historial de guerra, 1ª y 2ª Banderas," 170-171. Ramas Izquierdo, 167-171.

22. *DOL, Negociado de campaña*, 13-31 May 1924, 27.

23. *DOL, Negociado de campaña*, 1 June 1924, 27; and Subinspección de la Legión, ed., 206.

24. *DOL, Negociado de campaña*, 2-29 June 1924, 27.

25. Woolman, *Rebels in the Rif*, 129. In retaliation for joining Abd-el-Krim, the Spanish struck back at them by bombing their villages (e.g., Beni Hozmar) from the air, killing old men, women, and children and dealing them a propaganda setback that Abd-el-Krim exploited internationally.

26. *DOL, Negociado de campaña*, 30 June 1924, 27; and Estado Mayor Central del Ejército, 8-9.

27. Sablotny, 196.

28. Estado Mayor Central del Ejército, 9. Payne, 210-211. Subinspección de la Legión, ed., 210. This source erred on 206 when it noted that on 1 July 1924, the IIIrd *Bandera*, not the correct Ist *Bandera*, was transferred to Uad Lau. *DOL, Negociado de campaña*, 1 July 1924, 27. The Ist *Bandera* was transferred from Melilla to Uad Lau aboard the steamer *Barcelo*. The IInd and IVth were in Ben Tieb; the IIIrd was at Benitez; the Vth was at García Uria; and the VIth was at Tagasut. See also Fleming, *Primo de Rivera*, 142; Trythall, 45; Crozier, 75; and de Arce, 179. Scurr, 14, noted that Abd-el-Krim's army of roughly 80,000 men was well equipped with both captured and purchased weapons from Britain, France, and Czechoslovakia, including approximately 200 artillery pieces. Hills, 135.

29. *DOL, Negociado de campaña*, 1 July 1924, 27-28; and Subinspección de la Legión, ed., 211. Estado Mayor Central del Ejército, 9, lists all the units that made up the column escorting the convoy to Cobba Darsa. García Figueras, 201.

30. *DOL, Negociado de campaña*, 2 July 1924, 28.

31. *DOL, Negociado de campaña*, 4 July 1924, 28. Estado Mayor Central del Ejército, 9-10, contains the names of all the units that took part in the battle. *SHM*, Legajo #54, Rollo 16, *Colección de historiales*, "Campañas de Marruecos, Historial de guerra, 1ª y 2ª Banderas," 172. Ramas Izquierdo, 171-175, has more information on the officers who distinguished themselves in the battle and, 34-35, on the deaths of Lieutenants Manuel Carrasco Grajera and Julián Fournier Carranza.

32. *DOL, Negociado de campaña*, 4 July 1924, 28. Estado Mayor Central del

Ejército, 10, claims that nine Legionaries were wounded. De Arce, 179.

33. *DOL*, *Negociado de campaña*, 5 July 1924, 28. Subinspección de la Legión, ed., 211. The casualties were one officer and seventeen Legionaries dead, eight officers and ninety-eight Legionaries wounded. In my opinion, the body count sounds way too high for such an insignificant engagement. Sablotny, 196-197, recorded that his friends, Alfred Hochhaus and Curt Behn of the Ist *Bandera*, took part in the 5 July battle and that the latter "had remained on the battlefield with a bullet in his breast."

34. *DOL*, *Negociado de campaña*, 6 July 1924, 28. Subinspección de la Legión, ed., 211 and 214-215. Once again the casualty toll for the Legion in this source (eight Legionaries wounded) does not correspond with the one noted in the *DOL*. This time it is much lower than the other. Estado Mayor Central del Ejército, 10-11. *SHM*, Legajo #54, Rollo 16, *Colección de historiales*, "Campañas de Marruecos, Historial de guerra, 1ª y 2ª Banderas," 173. Cano Velasco, ed., 155. Arraras, ed., 152 and 189. Because of the serious turn of events in the protectorate, Primo de Rivera left for Morocco on 10 July for an inspection tour. Ramas Izquierdo, 35, has more on the death of Lieutenant Francisco Agusti y Valls and, on 47, on that of *Alférez* Luis Teresa Pomares. Crozier, 76, wrote of how Cobba Darsa had not been supplied in four attempts and how the High Command in Tetuán was opposed to a fifth, thinking it too would be turned back. When the fate of those besieged hung in the balance, one of those present blurted out, "Why not call in Franco?" Franco was brought in from García Uria, arriving in Tetuán by mid-morning to meet with the other officers. Franco put forth his demands that he be given full control of the rescue operation and that a boat be furnished to deliver him to Uad Lau. He reached Uad Lau at 1300 hours and told the officers there, "We're going to save Koba Darsa." When he informed them that they would attack at 1500 hours, they were stunned, since it was almost 1500 hours, the sun's rays were merciless, and it was *siesta* time. Exactly, said Franco, they'll be napping and we'll catch them totally by surprise. And so it came to pass that by 1630 hours, the enemy had been driven off, the siege finally broken, and the garrison relieved. De Galinsoga, 87-88. De La Cierva, 224, has a photo of the "heroes of Koba Darsa," featuring Franco and General Serrano.

35. Subinspección de la Legión, ed., 211.

36. *DOL*, *Negociado de campaña*, 7-27 July 1924, 28; Estado Mayor Central del Ejército, 11-12; and *SHM*, Legajo #54 Rollo 16, *Colección de historiales*, "Campañas de Marruecos, Historial de guerra, 1ª y 2ª Banderas," 173-174.

37. *DOL*, *Negociado de campaña*, 29 July 1924, 28.

38. This footnote covers the entire Ben Tieb episode. De La Cierva, *Franco*, 79-80, gives all the details of the event as Franco remembered them. Also refer to De La Cierva, *Franco: Un siglo de España*, 224-227, for more information (and photos) on the Ben Tieb incident. Payne, 211-212, also has more on the visit of Primo de Rivera to Ben Tieb. He translated the offending Legion slogan as "The Legion's spirit is blindly and fiercely aggressive." De Galinsoga, 88-91, wrote that the *Regulares* present were of Alhucemas, not of Melilla, and that Primo de Rivera wanted the slogan to read: "The spirit of the Legion is of *blind obedience* [my emphasis] and fierce aggressiveness before the enemy." Woolman, *Rebels in the Rif*, 131-133, has more on Primo de Rivera's visit to

Morocco and his future strategy. Before it was all over, Primo de Rivera told Franco: "Now I talk to you in an informal way, but on the day when your orders are given to you, you will have no choice but to obey them, whatever they may be." Crozier, 77-79. Garriga, 46-49. The "eggs" episode was a story circulated by Arturo Barea and Rafael García Serrano about what was served at the luncheon for Primo de Rivera. As eggs are a Spanish euphemism for "balls" or testicles, it was said that the entire menu was based on eggs prepared in various ways. The gist of the story was that when Primo de Rivera asked why so many eggs, he was told that those who wanted to stay in Morocco needed "eggs," whereas those who wanted to get out had no need for them. For more on the "eggs" story, see Barea, 234-235; Bolín, 77; Woolman, *Rebels in the Rif*, 132; and Payne, 211. Fleming, *Primo de Rivera*, 144-166, thoroughly covers Primo de Rivera's actions and its ramifications from late May through to late August. However fanciful or amusing the "eggs" story was, Franco denied it ever took place. In an interview conducted by historian Ricardo De La Cierva (q.v.) on Saturday, 1 July 1972, the Generalissimo said: "It is not true. There was no such menu based on eggs." (*"No es verdad. No hubo tal menú a base de huevos."*) See Rogelio Baon, *La cara humana de un caudillo—401 Anecdotas* (Madrid: Editorial San Martín, 1975), 137. Cano Velasco, ed., 155. Subinspección de la Legión, ed., 213. de Arce, 179-180. *Jane's Fighting Ships*, ed. (1923), 326, has more information and a photo of the *Reina Victoria Eugenia*. Major José Enrique Varela Iglesias would go on to become one of the greatest and most decorated soldiers in the history of Spain. He was twice awarded the Laureate Cross of St. Ferdinand for gallantry (almost receiving it for an unprecedented third time), commanded the *Regulares* during the Rif Rebellion, led Nationalist armies during the Civil War, and after 1939, was named minister of the army. Sablotny, 194-195. At Ben Tieb when Primo de Rivera came to visit, Sablotny wrote of what he saw and heard. For the Legionaries stationed there, one of the good things that came out of the visit was that on that day, they were given lots of good food, cognac, and two cigars per man. Preston, 44-45, wrote that "Sanjurjo, who accompanied him [Primo de Rivera], later told José Calvo Sotelo, the Dictator's Minister of Finance [whose retaliatory murder on 13 July 1936 would touch off the Spanish Civil War four days later], that he had kept his hand on the butt of his pistol throughout the speeches, fearing a tragic incident." Preston translated the concurring colonel's `*Bien, muy bien*," as "Hear, hear." Also see, Hills, 135-136; Trythall, 46; Arraras, ed., 189-190; and Benzo, 130-131.

39. Woolman, *Rebels in the Rif*, 133, recorded that the Estella line "was to extend from the sea at Rio Martín, on the Mediterranean just outside Tetuán, continue west through Fondak Ain Jedida, and loop south, passing slightly east of Alcazar all the way to the French zonal border." Vaughan, 6, observed that the Primo line consisted of "a series of blockhouses about a quarter of a mile apart, each built on dominating ground where possible and equipped with searchlights. The spaces between the blockhouses, especially around Tangier, were mined." Payne, 212-213. Subinspección de la Legión, ed., 213. García Figueras, 201-202, referred to this new policy in the protectorate as "*semiabandono*" (semiabandonment). Furneaux, 124. Benzo, 130, noted that among the professional officer class, Primo de Rivera's policy of abandoning the interior outposts and concentrating them in the coastal *presidios* was derisively known as the Plan of Hebrews (*Plan de hebreos*). In

addition, on 136 the author noted that the Estella/Primo line was badly named because it should have been christened the Abd-el-Krim Line, since Abd-el-Krim was the enemy that had compelled the dictator to establish it.

40. *DOL, Negociado de campaña*, 1 August 1924, 28-29; and Subinspección de la Legión, ed., 215. On the first day of August, the six *Banderas* of the Legion were split into two equal parts with three of them in the western zone and three in the east. They were stationed as follows: the Ist was in Zoco el Arbaa; the IInd, IIIrd, and IVth were at Ben Tieb; the Vth was at Tisgarin; and the VIth was at Tagasut/Taguesut.

41. De La Cierva, 227 and 230; and Scurr, 14.

42. *DOL, Negociado de campaña*, 8 August 1924, 29. Ramas Izquierdo, 28, has more on the death of Captain Adalberto de Hevia Maura.

43. De La Cierva, 230. *Jane's Fighting Ships*, ed. (1923), 327, has the specs and a photo of the 3rd Class Cruiser *Extremadura*.

44. *DOL, Negociado de campaña*, 16-17 August 1924, 29. Subinspección de la Legión, ed., 216-217, gives the Legion's casualty list as follows: two officers wounded, one Legionary killed, and fourteen wounded. Estado Mayor Central del Ejército, 12, gives the total casualty count for all units of the army as follows: 113, with 15 of those killed in action. *SHM*, Legajo #54, Rollo 16, *Colección de historiales*, "Campañas de Marruecos, Historial de guerra, 1ª y 2ª Banderas" (3ª Bandera), 171. Sablotny, 199-217, described his personal participation in the battle to break the siege of Afrau as a light machine gunner with the 16/IV. He also noted the effective gunfire a Spanish cruiser was able to provide the operation because Afrau was situated on the Mediterranean coast. Ramas Izquierdo, 175-178, has all the details on the battle written by the two commanders. For more on the deaths of Captain Juan San Miguel Rasilla of the 11/IV and Lieutenant José Nogueras Márquez, see 28 and 35, respectively.

45. *DOL, Negociado de campaña*, 17 August 1924, 29. Subinspección de la Legión, ed., 215, noted that twelve Legionaries of *Alférez* Patón Medina's platoon were also missing in action. *SHM*, Legajo #54, Rollo 16, *Colección de historiales*, "Campañas de Marruecos, Historial de guerra, 1ª y 2ª Banderas," 173-174, has more detailed information on the battle. Ramas Izquierdo, 179-181, has more information as well. For more on the deaths of *Alféreces* José Martínez Molins and Julián Patón Medina, see 47. According to this source, *Alférez* Patón Medina was captured and died in captivity as a result of brutal treatment. For his bravery at Tizzi-Azza on 5 June 1923 (the day LTC Valenzuela was killed at Tizzi-Azza), he was awarded the Individual Military Medal.

46. *DOL, Negociado de campaña*, 17 August 1924, 29. Subinspección de la Legión, ed., 217. Both sources cited give the same number of Legionaries killed (4), and officers wounded (2), but differ on the number of wounded Legionaries (1 sergeant). It also gives the name of the battle as "Taura."

47. Scurr, 14. See also, De La Cierva, 231; and Payne, 212-213.

48. Woolman, *Rebels in the Rif*, 138, detailed the military and civilian reaction to the ignominious retreat from Xauen. De La Cierva, 230. On three successive days, 18-20 August, the three *Banderas* in the west performed their typical operations in the most advanced positions, suffering two Legionaries killed and twelve wounded. See *DOL*,

Negociado de campaña, 18-20 August 1924, 29.

49. De La Cierva, 231-232. A then unknown Spanish officer serving with *Harcas Amigas* (pro-Spanish Moroccans/irregular levies), Major Agustín Muñoz Grandes, participated in the evacuation of the Lau sector. He would make a name for himself during the Alhucemas Bay landings, and serve Franco as a corps commander during the Spanish Civil War, as well as captain general of the army and minister of war. During World War II, General Muñoz Grandes was chosen to command the Spanish "Blue Division" in Russia, where he was awarded Germany's highest decoration for bravery, the Knight's Cross of the Iron Cross. His service to Spain and General Franco continued into the 1960s, when as vice president of the Spanish government he represented both at the funeral of U.S. president John F. Kennedy in 1963. According to the author, Muñoz Grandes was the only soldier Franco feared. On pages 79-82 of his book, Luis Bolín gives an excellent detailed eyewitness account of the Wad-Lau operation.

50. *DOL, Negociado de Campaña*, 21-22 August 1924, 29. Subinspección de la Legión, ed., 216, gives different names for the battle fought. It stated that the Ist *Bandera*, in the vanguard of Franco's column, left Tisgarin on 20 August to break the siege the enemy had placed around Hoj. While the Ist engaged the enemy first, the Vth *Bandera* joined in to bolster the former's assault. After clearing the way to Hoj, they returned to Tisgarin. *SHM*, Legajo #54, Rollo 16, *Colección de historiales*, "Campañas de Marruecos, Historial de guerra, 1ª y 2ª Banderas," 174. Ramas Izquierdo, 300-302, has more on the battle by way of the citation for the Laureate Cross of St. Ferdinand that was awarded to Captain Félix Angosto Gómez-Castrillón for his valorous deeds during the battle of Kudia-Cobba (22 August 1924). The citation for the award can also be found in the DO #49, 28 February 1927.

51. *DOL, Negociado de campaña*, 23 August 1924, 29.

52. *DOL, Negociado de campaña*, 23 August 1924, 29. Ramas Izquierdo, 35, has more on Lieutenant Ángel Puig García, killed when a mortar he was setting up exploded.

53. Subinspección de la Legión, ed., 216; and *SHM*, Legajo #54, Rollo 16, *Colección de historiales*, "Campañas de Marruecos, Historial de guerra, 1ª y 2ª Banderas," 174-175. Arraras, ed., 190. Ramas Izquierdo, 181-184, has more details on the battle.

54. De La Cierva, 232.

55. *DOL, Negociado de campaña*, 31 August 1924, 30. Subinspección de la Legión, ed., 217-218. *SHM*, Legajo #54, Rollo 16, *Colección de historiales*, "Campañas de Marruecos, Historial de guerra, 1ª y 2ª Banderas," 182. *Jane's Fighting Ships*, ed. (1923), 332, has the specs and a photo of the *Almirante Lobo*.

56. *DOL, Negociado de campaña*, 1 September 1924, 30. Subinspección de la Legión, ed., 218, locates the Ist at Kuddia-Kobbo.

57. Subinspección de la Legión, ed., 218. De Galinsoga, 93, observed that "Gorgues was for Tetuán what Gurugú had been for Melilla." Arraras, ed., 190.

58. Woolman, "In Spanish Morocco," 16. Sablotny, 280, wrote the following of the *Regulares* in Abd-el-Krim's army: "Riffian soldiers with green turbans, decorated at the right side with a red angle, any one with a turban with such a symbol was considered to be a professional soldier in the Riffian army." Pennell, 166.

59. *DOL*, *Negociado de campaña*, 2 September 1924, 30. Subinspección de la Legión, ed., 218-220, has more on the battle including the personal account of Captain Francisco López de Roda, who was taken prisoner. *SHM*, Legajo #54, Rollo 16, *Colección de historiales*, "Campañas de Marruecos, Historial de guerra, 1ª y 2ª Banderas" (3ª Bandera), 175-176, noted that after the battle, the IIIrd *Bandera* was brought back to Tetuán to be reconstructed with Legionaries from Dar Riffien. Ramas Izquierdo, 184-188. For more on the death of Captain José Lobato Sánchez, see 28-29; for Lieutenant Luis Oset Fajardo, see 36; for Captain Francisco López de Roda, who was subsequently awarded the Individual Military Medal for heroism during the battle, see 29; for Lieutenants Francisco Revuelta Franco and Manuel Sánchez Suárez, see 35-36. As a prisoner, Lieutenant Sánchez Suárez was unbowed as he adamantly refused to perform any and all tasks he deemed beneath his station as an officer and a gentleman of the Legion.

60. Subinspección de la Legión, ed., 220.

61. Subinspección de la Legión, ed., 220-221. *DOL*, *Negociado de campaña*, 3 September 1924, 30. This operation is listed in this source as having taken place on 3 September, instead of 2 September, as in the previous source. *SHM*, Legajo #54, Rollo 16, *Colección de historiales*, "Campañas de Marruecos, Historial de guerra, 1ª y 2ª Banderas," 182. On 3 September, the IInd and IVth *Banderas* escorted a supply convoy to Beni Salah resulting in two Legionaries killed, and eight wounded. See, *DOL*, *Negociado de campaña*, 3 September 1924, 30.

62. García Figueras, 202. Lieutenant General Francisco Gómez Souza (General Staff) was also known as Gómez-Jordana and was the son of the much-beloved former High Commissioner of the protectorate. During World War II, the Anglophile General Jordana replaced Franco's brother-in-law, Ramón Serrano Suñer, as foreign minister in October 1942 as the tide of battle was turning against the Germans. Francisco Gómez-Jordana y Souza, *La tramoya de nuestra actuación en Marruecos* (Madrid: Editora Nacional, 1976), 68. Estado Mayor Central del Ejército, 13. See also, De La Cierva, 233; Payne, 212; De Galinsoga, 93; and Scurr, 14. Also on 5 September, the Ist and Vth *Banderas* under Franco's command participated in the day's operation to withdraw the front line from the defile of the Lau River. The casualties were one Legionary killed plus one officer and three Legionaries wounded. See, *DOL*, *Negociado de campaña*, 5 September 1924, 30; and *SHM*, Legajo #54 Rollo 16, *Colección de historiales*, "Campañas de Marruecos, Historial de guerra, 1ª y 2ª Banderas," 175.

63. Estado Mayor Central del Ejército, 13. Cano Velasco, ed., 155. Payne, 212-213. Harris, 136-137, gave the operational plans for the four columns that were to evacuate Xauen. The four column commanders were Colonel Ovilo, General Castro Girona, General Serrano, and General Federico Berenguer (reserve column). Woolman, *Rebels in the Rif*, 137. Salas Larrazábal, 159, wrote that Primo de Rivera's plan for withdrawal from the Gomara region and parts of the Yebala had four major points to consider for the defense of what was to be kept: (1) defense of Rio Martín, Tetuán's port, connected to the city by way of a railway; (2) control and domination of the Gorgues massif, of extraordinary importance for the defense of Tetuán; (3) maintenance of the lines of communication of Tetuán, with Larache and Tangier open; and (4) defense of the Tangier-Fez railway.

64. *DOL, Negociado de campaña*, 6 September 1924, 30. Subinspección de la Legión, ed., 221-222. *SHM*, Legajo #54, Rollo 16, *Colección de historiales*, "Campañas de Marruecos, Historial de guerra, 1ª y 2ª Banderas" (3ª Bandera), 176-177 and 182-183. Ramas Izquierdo, 188-194. It appears that the author erred when he wrote that this operation took place on 8 September, instead of the correct date of 6 September. See 36 for details on the death of Lieutenant Joaquín Hermida Fernández, and 48 for *Alférez* Agustín Cortés Farres.

65. *DOL, Negociado de campaña*, 6 September 1924, 30. Subinspección de la Legión, ed., 226-227. Estado Mayor Central del Ejército, 14. Cano Velasco, ed., 155, noted that Tagasut was evacuated on 7 September, along with Ad Gos, and that M'Ter, situated on the Gomara coast, was abandoned the next day. Harris, 135, wrote that "twenty-nine officers and 740 men, with six pieces of artillery, were withdrawn by sea from Mter, near the mouth of the Wad [river] Lau." Sablotny, 280, wrote that after deserting from the Legion and being captured by the Riffians, he passed through M'Ter (or "Meta" as he called it) after the Legion had abandoned it, and that M'Ter became M'hamed Abd-el-Krim's general headquarters.

66. Subinspección de la Legión, ed., 222.

67. Subinspección de la Legión, ed., 227.

68. *DOL, Negociado de campaña*, 8 September 1924, 30-31, recorded the number of casualties as two officers wounded and seven Legionaries killed and ten wounded. Subinspección de la Legión, ed., 222.

69. Subinspección de la Legión, ed., 227. While the Spanish army was busy with its plan to withdraw to more secure and defendable positions closer to Tetuán, the problem of el Raisuni's personal protection was also considered. Furneaux wrote on 125 that "as well as evacuating Shauen [Xauen], the Spaniards needed to ensure Raisuni's safety. It was undesirable that he should be captured when the Rifi swarmed over the evacuated territory. He refused to abandon his fortress at Tazrut, where he had great stores of grain, arms, and wealth. The Rifi, he boasted, would be unable to dislodge him from his impregnable stronghold."

70. *DOL, Negociado de campaña*, 10 September 1924, 31; Subinspección de la Legión, ed., 222; and *SHM*, Legajo #54, Rollo 16, *Colección de historiales*, "Campañas de Marruecos, Historial de guerra, 1ª y 2ª Banderas" (3ª Bandera), 177 and 183.

71. *DOL, Negociado de campaña*, 11 September 1924, 31; Subinspección de la Legión, ed., 222; and *SHM*, Legajo #54, Rollo 16, *Colección de historiales*, "Campañas de Marruecos, Historial de guerra, 1ª y 2ª Banderas" (3ª Bandera), 17 and 183.

72. *DOL, Negociado de campaña*, 12 September 1924, 31. Fleming, *Primo de Rivera*, 179. Subinspección de la Legión, ed., 227.

73. *DOL, Negociado de campaña*, 14 September 1924, 31; and Subinspección de la Legión, ed., 222. Sablotny, 286-287, described the Spanish camp at Uad Lau and the battles fought in and around it. Ramas Izquierdo, 36-37, has details on the death of Lieutenant José Ollero Morente.

74. Subinspección de la Legión, ed., 222. *SHM*, Legajo #54, Rollo 16, *Colección de historiales*, "Campañas de Marruecos, Historial de guerra, 1ª y 2ª Banderas," 249, has

more on the operations undertaken by the IInd *Bandera* on 16 (Zoco el Telata), 17 (Megart), and 18 September (Zoco el Jemis de Beni Aros).

75. De La Cierva, *Franco*, 82, wrote that the people of Tetuán referred to the Riffian artillery piece emplaced in the Gorgues massif by Abd-el-Krim's advisor, ex-French Foreign Legion deserter Joseph Klemms, and only seven kilometers (just over four miles) from the capital, as "the cannon of the Gorgues."

76. Santa Marina, 34.

77. Subinspección de la Legión, ed., 223-224. *DOL, Negociado de campaña*, 18 September 1924, 31, recorded that the IVth and Vth *Banderas* had one officer (Lieutenant Ángel González García, who died on 9 October from his wounds) and one Legionary killed, plus three officers and thirty-nine Legionaries wounded. The IIIrd *Bandera* had eight Legionaries killed, plus one officer and fifty-five Legionaries wounded. *DOL, Negociado de campaña*, 19 September 1924, 31, had the Ist and IIIrd *Banderas* fighting in Kudia Tahar and having Lieutenant (*sic*) Francisco Carvajal Mendicuti and six Legionaries killed, as well as one officer and thirty-one Legionaries wounded. The IInd *Bandera* took and occupied Loma de Tercio at the cost of two Legionaries dead and fifteen wounded. In addition, the VIth *Bandera* assisted in the protection of a *blocao* in the immediate area around Xauen, suffering five Legionaries dead and thirteen wounded. *DOL*, Negociado de campaña, 20 September 1924, 31-32, noted that the Ist and IIIrd *Banderas* took part in the operations in the Gorgues and in combat with the enemy, suffering one Legionary killed plus one officer and three Legionaries wounded. *SHM*, Legajo #54, Rollo 16, *Colección de historiales*, "Campañas de Marruecos, Historial de guerra, 1ª y 2ª Banderas" (3ª Bandera), 177-178. De Galinsoga, 94. Fleming, *Primo de Rivera*, 183-184. Scurr, 14, observed that clearing the enemy from the Gorgues "both thwarted Abd el Krim's designs on Tetuán and was a first stage towards opening the road to Xaüen." De La Cierva, *Franco*, 82. Crozier, 80. Ramas Izquierdo, 194-199. See 39 for more on the death of Lieutenant Ángel González García, and 47-48 for details on the death of *Alférez* Francisco Carvajal Mendicuti.

78. De La Cierva, *Franco*, 81-82. Fleming, *Primo de Rivera*, 182-183, noted that the High Commissioner, Aizpuru, was also to be arrested and imprisoned, and that Franco "never publicly disputed Queipo's story and it is plausible, given the situation in the Protectorate, that he could have shared in a plot against the Dictator." See also Trythall, 46-47; Payne, 213-214; and Preston, 45-46. Gonzalo Queipo de Llano, *El General Queipo de Llano perseguido por la dictadura* (Madrid: Javier Morata, 1930), 104-107. On 104-105, Queipo de Llano identified the three lieutenant colonels as the commanding officer of the Battalion of Segovia (an old acquaintance from the Cuban War, but Queipo de Llano did not know his name), (Eliseo) Álvarez Arenas (Romero) of the *Regulares*, and Franco Baamonde of the Legion.

79. Fleming, *Primo de Rivera*, 183. De La Cierva, *Franco*, 82. Payne, 214, wrote that "Queipo sent a letter to the dictator asking to be relieved of command in Morocco if his services were not to be utilized in a combat post or in a position of responsibility. On September 24, Primo acceded to this request but at the same time sentenced Queipo to a month's imprisonment in Spain for 'creating obstacles for the command.' If the dictator was aware of Franco's plotting, he gave no public notice of it." General Gonzalo Queipo de

Llano, a longtime Moroccan Wars veteran, would go on to play a pivotal role in the early and critical days of the Spanish Civil War when as the military commander of Seville he secured the city for the rebels, thereby enabling the first "airlift" that brought the elite Army of Africa from the protectorate to Spain. Without the use of this professional army, the uprising would most probably have fizzled in the first few days.

80. *DOL*, *Negociado de campaña*, 22 September 1924, 32; *SHM*, Legajo #54, Rollo 16, *Colección de historiales*, "Campañas de Marruecos, Historial de guerra, 1ª y 2ª Banderas" (3ª Bandera), 178-179, and 183; and Subinspección de la Legión, ed., 249. Ramas Izquierdo, 48, gives the date of this operation as 23 September, instead of 22 September, and has more on the death of *Alférez* Joaquín Calles Zuluaga.

81. Subinspección de la Legión, ed., 224-225, contains a congratulatory report written by Franco in recognition of Captain Pablo Arredondo Acuña of the 1/I. In this message, Franco wrote of his bravery in withdrawing all the men ("man by man") from his company, which was under enemy fire, and being the last man back to Spanish lines. *DOL*, *Negociado de campaña*, 23 September 1924, 32, had one officer and twenty-one Legionaries killed, plus five officers and eighty-nine Legionaries wounded. *SHM*, Legajo #54, Rollo 16, *Colección de historiales*, "Campañas de Marruecos, Historial de guerra, 1ª y 2ª Banderas" (3ª Bandera), 178-179. Preston, 46. Ramas Izquierdo, 199-201. For more on the death of Lieutenant Francisco Vela Estela, see 37.

82. *DOL*, *Negociado de campaña*, 23 September 1924, 32.

83. Subinspección de la Legión, ed., 226. *DOL*, *Negociado de campaña*, 24 September 1924, 32, noted eleven Legionaries killed, plus one officer and thirty-six Legionaries wounded. Ramas Izquierdo, 201-204.

84. *DOL*, *Negociado de campaña*, 25 September 1924, 32. *SHM*, Legajo #54, Rollo 16, *Colección de historiales*, "Campañas de Marruecos, Historial de guerra, 1ª y 2ª Banderas," 249, has information on the actions of the IInd *Bandera* on 25 September when it reached the vicinity of Ain Grana.

85. *DOL*, *Negociado de campaña*, 26 September 1924, 32; *SHM*, Legajo #54, Rollo 16, *Colección de historiales*, "Campañas de Marruecos, Historial de guerra, 1ª y 2ª Banderas" (3ª Bandera), 183-184; and Subinspección de la Legión, ed., 249. De La Cierva, 236, wrote that both Dar Akobba (Mola commanding) and Xeruta (Rosaleny commanding) between Tetuán and Xauen had been encircled by the Riffians for a few weeks but had been able to hold out and even to break out of the ring. They were liberated by the column pushing its way through to Xauen. Mola and his *Regulares de Larache* joined the column and dealt Abd-el-Krim a "terrible punishment" on 29-30 September. Mola was replaced at Dar Akobba by Lieutenant Colonel José Miaja Menant (he had once been Mola's captain and now commanded the Battalion of San Fernando), who as a general would go on to declare his loyalty for the Republic in 1936 and become the hero of Madrid's defense. For more on the siege of Dar Akobba, see Emilio Mola Vidal, *Dar Akobba: Páginas de sangre, de dolor y de gloria* (Madrid: Doncel, 1977). Ramas Izquierdo, 204-206. For more on the death in captivity of Lieutenant Federico de la Cruz Lacaci, who was posthumously awarded the Laureate Cross of St. Ferdinand for his actions at Tizzi-Azza on 5 June 1923, see 37.

86. *DOL, Negociado de campaña*, 27 September 1924, 32; and *SHM*, Legajo #54, Rollo 16, *Colección de historiales*, "Campañas de Marruecos, Historial de guerra, 1ª y 2ª Banderas" (3ª Bandera), 179. Cano Velasco, ed., 155, recorded that on 27 September, Targa and Magan in the Lau sector were abandoned.

87. *DOL, Negociado de campaña*, 28 September 1924, 32; *SHM*, Legajo #54, Rollo 16, *Colección de historiales*, "Campañas de Marruecos, Historial de guerra, 1ª y 2ª Banderas" (3ª Bandera), 179-180; and Estado Mayor Central del Ejército, 14. Harris, 137-138. Ramas Izquierdo, 206-208, has details on the operation to reach Xauen.

88. *DOL, Negociado de campaña*, 30 September 1924, 32-33; and *SHM*, Legajo #54, Rollo 16, *Colección de historiales*, "Campañas de Marruecos, Historial de guerra, 1ª y 2ª Banderas" (3ª Bandera), 180-181. Woolman, *Rebels in the Rif*, 137. Ramas Izquierdo, 209-211, gives more details on the operation and battle. See 48 for more on the death of *Alférez* Baldomero de Matos Toda.

89. Subinspección de la Legión, ed., 228. Payne, 214, wrote that after the blockade of Xauen had been broken on 30 September, "he [Primo de Rivera] found that his plans for a general withdrawal had to be delayed because of the anarchy in the command and the supply system. He was eventually forced to court-martial several of the senior officers who had been criticized by Queipo [de Llano], Franco, and others." De Galinsoga, 96.

90. De La Cierva, *Franco*, 82, recorded that 10,000 Spanish soldiers garrisoned Xauen and other small outposts in this sector.

91. Subinspección de la Legión, ed., 228. Traveling on the roads was dangerous for everyone, including Primo de Rivera and General Jordana, who were almost killed in an ambush near Ben Karich while visiting troops at the front. See Harris, 138, and Woolman, *Rebels in the Rif*, 137.

92. *DOL, Negociado de campaña*, 1 October 1924, 3. On the first day of October, the six Legion *Banderas* of the were stationed in the following locations: the Ist and IIIrd *Banderas* were at Dar Accoba/Akobba; the IInd was at Zoco el Jemis de Beni Aros; and the IVth, Vth, and VIth were in Xauen. *SHM*, Legajo #54, Rollo 16, *Colección de historiales*, "Campañas de Marruecos, Historial de guerra, 1ª y 2ª Banderas," 184. Subinspección de la Legión, ed., 228. Cano Velasco, ed., 155.

93. *DOL, Negociado de campaña*, 1 October 1924, 33; Subinspección de la Legión, ed., 228-229; and *SHM*, Legajo #54, Rollo 16, *Colección de historiales*, "Campañas de Marruecos, Historial de guerra, 1ª y 2ª Banderas" (3ª Bandera), 180-181. Ramas Izquierdo, 37, has more on the death of Lieutenant Tomás Peire Legorburu. Woolman, *Rebels in the Rif*, 137, recorded that the Tetuán to Xauen road was so dangerous for Spanish traffic that "on October 1 a column of forty [empty] motortrucks driving back to Tetuan was fired upon, and a majority of the vehicles destroyed." Harris, 139, also has the above mentioned quote.

94. Subinspección de la Legión, ed., 229.

95. Subinspección de la Legión, ed., 229. *SHM*, Legajo #54, Rollo 16, *Colección de historiales*, "Campañas de Marruecos, Historial de guerra, 1ª y 2ª Banderas" (3ª Bandera), 181.

96. Subinspección de la Legión, ed., 229. *DOL, Negociado de campaña*, 2-15 October 1924, 33, recorded that in this period, seven Legionaries were killed and two officers and sixty-one Legionaries wounded. *SHM*, Legajo #54, Rollo 16, *Colección de historiales*, "Campañas de Marruecos, Historial de guerra, 1ª y 2ª Banderas" (3ª Bandera), 181.

97. Subinspección de la Legión, ed., 229-230; *DOL, Negociado de campaña*, 16 October 1924, 33, noted six Legionaries killed, plus two officers and forty-one Legionaries wounded; *SHM*, Legajo #54, Rollo 16, *Colección de historiales*, "Campañas de Marruecos, Historial de guerra, 1ª y 2ª Banderas," 181-182; and Estado Mayor Central del Ejército, 14. Ramas Izquierdo, 212-216, has more details on the battle, as well as on all the officers who distinguished themselves that day. One of the officers mentioned in Franco's battle report was a German *Alférez*, C.L. Carlos Tiede Zeden. This mention would be the first of many, as he would go on to achieve great fame within the Legion, rise to the rank of major (posthumously), and be killed in action (on 11 January 1937) during the Spanish Civil War. In tribute, the XI *Bandera* (*comandante Tiede*) was named in his honor. The Brotherhood of Ex-Legionaries (Ceuta chapter), under the leadership of its president, Captain C.L. Alejandro Zamacola Monis (ret.), paid homage to C.L. Carlos Tiede Zeden, as well as to other fallen Legionaries, at Santa Catalina Cemetery, where he is buried. The date chosen for this moving tribute was the 73rd anniversary of the founding of the Legion. According to an article in *El Faro* (Ceuta), Carlos Tiede Zeden/Zenen was born in Prussia on 23 October 1892 and joined the Legion on 27 June 1921. In addition to the numerous decorations awarded to him by Spain where two Imperial German Iron Crosses awarded for valor during World War I. See Manolo González (M. G.), "Copa de vino español con motivo de LXXIII aniversario de la Legión," *El Faro*, Sunday, 19 September 1993, 15.

98. Morales Lezcano, 236; Harris, 140; Payne, 214; and Preston, 46. Woolman, *Rebels in the Rif*, 138, wrote that Aizpuru was replaced, not because he was incompetent, "but because Primo de Rivera felt personally responsible for the withdrawal" and wanted to assume full responsibility for an operation that was so controversial. Arraras, ed., 156, noted that while Primo de Rivera was in Morocco serving as High Commissioner, he was temporarily replaced as president of the Directory by the Marqués de Magaz (Admiral Magaz). Salas Larrazábal, 159. García Figueras, 202. On 203, the author wrote that the final outcome on responsibility for the Annual disaster came to an end when Generals Cavalcanti and Navarro were absolved and General Dámaso Berenguer was transferred to the reserves. On 4 July 1924, a broad amnesty was granted giving closure to the sad episode that occurred in July 1921.

99. *DOL, Negociado de campaña*, 18 October 1924, 33.

100. Harris, 142. *DOL, Negociado de campaña*, 21 October 1924, 33.

101. *DOL, Negociado de campaña*, 22 October 1924, 33-34; and *SHM*, Legajo #54, Rollo 16, *Colección de historiales*, "Campañas de Marruecos, Historial de guerra, 1ª y 2ª Banderas," 184. This source claims that the day's operation was to evacuate Zoco el Jemis.

102. *DOL, Negociado de campaña*, 23 October 1924, 34.

103. Subinspección de la Legión, ed., 230-231. *DOL, Negociado de campaña*,

24 October 1924, 34, recorded twenty-one Legionaries killed, plus two officers and forty-four Legionaries wounded. *SHM*, Legajo #54, Rollo 16, *Colección de historiales*, "Campañas de Marruecos, Historial de guerra, 1ª y 2ª Banderas" (3ª Bandera), 185-186, has a brief summary of the Legion's contribution to the evacuation of Xauen in October 1924. This source makes the important observation that the Legion not only had to evacuate the soldiers posted in those far-flung outposts but also had to bring back their weapons, munitions, and other matériel useful to the rebels. Because of the high number of dead and wounded, even the "walking wounded" were needed to perform guard duty (at their encampment) and light combat services (not front-line combat duty). Ramas Izquierdo, 216-219.

104. *DOL, Negociado de campaña*, 25 October 1924, 34.

105. Subinspección de la Legión, ed., 231-232. *DOL, Negociado de campaña*, 26 October 1924, 34, gave the final casualty toll as follows: one officer (Lieutenant Manuel Guallar/Guallart Martínez) missing (*sic*), thirty-six Legionaries killed, plus five officers and seventy-eight Legionaries wounded. *SHM*, Legajo #54, Rollo 16, *Colección de historiales*, "Campañas de Marruecos, Historial de guerra, 1ª y 2ª Banderas," 189. *AGM*, Legajo #M-3204, SECCIÓN #1, DIVISIÓN #1, October 1924, 21-22. While the Legion was engaged in heavy combat with the enemy, Colonel José Millan Astray was also in the western zone. The unlucky Millan Astray was once again wounded, this time in his left arm, having it amputated on 28 October because of gangrene. Estado Mayor Central del Ejército, 14. Ramas Izquierdo, 219-223. For more on the death of Lieutenant Manuel Guallart Martínez, see 38.

106. *DOL, Negociado de campaña*, 26 October (*sic*) 1924, 34. This operation almost certainly took place on 27 October, not 26 October as the Legion was at Draa-el-Asef on the 26th. The erroneous date is most probably a typographical error. Barea, 228, has more on the arrival of the Legion in Xauen and what it was like there before the evacuation.

107. *DOL, Negociado de Campaña*, 28 October 1924, 34. Subinspección de la Legión, ed., 249. *SHM*, Legajo #54, Rollo 16, *Colección de historiales*, "Campañas de Marruecos, Historial de guerra, 1ª y 2ª Banderas," 184. This source gives the date for the evacuation of Zoco el Jemis de Beni Aros by the IInd *Bandera* as 22 October, instead of the *DOL*'s date of 28 October. Estado Mayor Central del Ejército, 14, noted that on 27 October, Akarrat and Dardara were evacuated.

108. Estado Mayor Central del Ejército, 14, stated that they encountered strong resistance from the enemy ("*sosteniendo fuertes combates de retaguardia*") during their evacuation, while the following source said it went off smoothly. *DOL, Negociado de campaña*, 30-31 October 1924, 34. Subinspección de la Legión, ed., 249-250.

109. *DOL, Negociado de Campaña*, 1 November 1924, 34-35. Cano Velasco, ed., 155. Subinspección de la Legión, ed., 233.

110. *DOL, Negociado de campaña*, 2 November 1924, 35. *SHM*, Legajo #54, Rollo 16, *Colección de historiales*, "Campañas de Marruecos, Historial de guerra, 1ª y 2ª Banderas," 184, recorded that on 2 November, the IInd *Bandera* was operating in the vicinity of Alcazarquivir (between Larache and Xauen). For the actions of the Ist and IIIrd

Banderas at Miskrela, see 190.

111. *DOL, Negociado de campaña*, 3-8 November 1924, 35. Subinspección de la Legión, ed., 250. On 3 December, the IInd *Bandera* formed the vanguard of Lieutenant Colonel Mola's column to establish a post in Alcazarquivir. De Arce, 181, recorded that on 5 November, after the peninsular troops had been rounded up and sent back toward Tetuán, the five *Banderas* of the Legion were given the task of gathering all the civilians (Spaniards, Jews, or Moroccans) and taking them out of Xauen in trucks specifically prepared for that purpose. Preston, 46.

112. *DOL, Negociado de campaña*, 9 November 1924, 35. *SHM*, Legajo #54, Rollo 16, *Colección de historiales*, "Campañas de Marruecos, Historial de guerra, 1ª y 2ª Banderas," 184, noted that the operation scheduled for 9 November was in the area of Monte Sagrado. The following day, 10 November, the IInd set out to break the siege the rebels had placed on Teffer. The withdrawals in this sector continued with the IInd *Bandera* providing protection for them; on the 15th it was Muises, and Meserach/Mexerach on the 17th. On the 23rd, it provided protection for the evacuation of Tilili and las Torres, and for the rest of the month it encamped in Meserach, from where it covered various *blocaos* on the established defensive perimeter. Subinspección de la Legión, ed., 250, has more on the actions of the IInd *Bandera* during early November. Estado Mayor Central del Ejército, 15.

113. Woolman, *Rebels in the Rif*, 139. Pennell, 168. De La Cierva, *Franco*, 82-83, referred to the evacuation of Xauen as the "withdrawal of the ten thousand." Hills, 137, noted that it was Franco's idea to evacuate Xauen under cover of darkness, and that even though it was a unique concept at the time, Castro Girona accepted it. Crozier, 80, wrote that General Castro Girona was very worried about the evacuation, especially after what had happened to Silvestre in 1921. Avoiding another Annual was uppermost in his mind, and that is why the men never panicked, although they had plenty of reasons to. Trythall, 48, recorded that "details of Spanish soldiers removed the Spanish street names [in Xauen] to save them from the indignity of defacement." Harris, 143, wrote that nothing was intentionally destroyed by the Spaniards, but that they took with them as much portable property as could be carted away, as it was their design to return at a more auspicious date and to once again inhabit Xauen. In August 1926, this was successfully achieved.

114. *DOL, Negociado de campaña*, 17 November 1924, 35; Subinspección de la Legión, ed., 235-236; De La Cierva, *Franco*, 83; Cano Velasco, ed., 155; Estado Mayor Central del Ejército, 14; Barea, 228; and Pennell, 169. Crozier, 81, has Franco's final instructions to his officers and NCOs prior to evacuating Xauen, as well as his conversation with an old Moroccan, who explained to him why the people had turned against Spain and why they supported Abd-el-Krim. Scurr, 15. De Galinsoga, 96-108, has plenty of information on the evacuation of Xauen itself, as well as on the entire retreat from Xauen to Tetuán. He also has Millán Astray's comments on the operation, as well as Franco's own diary entries, which were published in *Revista de Tropas Coloniales* with the title of Xauen the Sorrowful (*Xauen La Triste*).

115. Woolman, *Rebels in the Rif*, 140, recorded that unlike earlier Spanish outposts, which were built on hilltops, both Dar Akobba and Xeruta had been erected below the surrounding hills to make the water supply more accessible to the troops. Needless to

say, when the enemy attacked both positions, the Spaniards came under withering fire from above as well as from all sides. Estado Mayor Central del Ejército, 14.

116. *DOL, Negociado de campaña*, 18 November 1924, 35. Subinspeccion de La Legión, ed., 236-239, gives a detailed account of each *Bandera*'s contribution on this date. The Legion performed admirably on this day, as one *Bandera* covered the withdrawal of the other in echelon. See 250-251, for the actions of the IInd *Bandera* during the second half of November. *SHM*, Legajo #54, Rollo 16, *Colección de historiales*, "Campañas de Marruecos, Historial de guerra, 1ª y 2ª Banderas" (3ª Bandera), 190. Woolman, *Rebels in the Rif*, 139. Cano Velasco, ed., 155-156. Harris, 146, has more on the actions of the IInd *Bandera* during November. Ramas Izquierdo, 224-229, has more on the retreat from Dar Akobba to Xeruta. For more on the death of *Alférez* Manuel López Hidalgo, who was posthumously awarded the Laureate Cross of St. Ferdinand for his actions in the battle, see 48-49.

117. Woolman, *Rebels in the Rif*, 139. Cano Velasco, ed., 156. Subinspección de la Legión, ed., 239. Trythall, 48. De La Cierva, 238 (photo 3), noted that a detachment of light tanks (Renault *FT-17*) were used to cover the evacuation from Xauen to Zoco el Arbaa, with three of them destroyed by the enemy. As the mountainous terrain was ill-suited for tanks, the role they played was probably more psychological than practical.

118. *DOL, Negociado de campaña*, 19 November 1924, 35. Subinspección de la Legión, ed., 239-243, has all the details of each *Banderas* actions in the battle to evacuate Xeruta. *SHM*, Legajo #54, Rollo 16, *Colección de historiales*, "Campañas de Marruecos, Historial de guerra, 1ª y 2ª Banderas" (3ª Bandera), 190-191. Woolman, *Rebels in the Rif*, 139, wrote that at Xeruta, General Serrano (one of the column commanders) and "more than a thousand of his men were struck down." Furneaux, 129, noted that General Serrano was shot dead by a sniper and that General Federico Berenguer was wounded in the same location. Scurr, 15. Ramas Izquierdo, 230-238. For more on the death of Legion hero Captain Pablo Arredondo Acuña, who for his actions at Xeruta was posthumously awarded the Laureate Cross of St. Ferdinand for a second time, as well as the Individual Military Medal, see 29-30 and 302-306; for Lieutenants Matías Font Quetglas and José Serena Guiscape, see 38; and for *Alféreces* Francisco Abad López and Francisco Salgués Otero, see 49.

119. Subinspección de la Legión, ed., 243. Cano Velasco, ed., 156. Harris, 144. See Barea, 228, for a vivid portrait of what Zoco el Arbaa was like during the earliest days of the evacuation. Scurr, 15, wrote that following the death of General Serrano only one column was left, and that for three weeks it remained completely surrounded at Zoco el Arbaa. Woolman, *Rebels in the Rif*, 139. Payne, 216-217. Fleming, *Primo de Rivera*, 190, praised the Spanish army when he wrote, "Unlike Annual, however, there was no mass panic and by the 25th most of the units had made it to the mountain fortress of Zoco el Arbaa." Franco had five *Banderas* in Zoco el Arbaa, and from 20 to 30 November he used them to protect its perimeter. They provided security for the encampments, roads, and convoys, suffering thirteen Legionaries killed, plus one officer and forty Legionaries wounded. See, *DOL, Negociado de campaña*, 20-30 November 1924, 35. Harris, 144, noted that General Alberto Castro Girona, along with the advance guard, arrived at Ben

Karich on 19 November, leaving the main body of the army cut off at Zoco el Arbaa.

120. *DOL, Negociado de campaña*, 29 November 1924, 35-36; and *SHM*, Legajo #54, Rollo 16, *Colección de historiales*, "Campañas de Marruecos, Historial de guerra, 1ª y 2ª Banderas" (3ª Bandera), 191-192.

121. *DOL, Negociado de campaña*, 1 December 1924, 36, recorded that on 1 December, the Ist, IIIrd, IVth, Vth, and VIth *Banderas* were in Zoco el Arbaa, while the IInd was in Mexerach (Larache).

122. Subinspección de la Legión, ed., 251.

123. Subinspección de la Legión, ed., 251.

124. *DOL, Negociado de campaña*, 5 December 1924, 36; *SHM*, Legajo #54, Rollo 16, *Colección de historiales*, "Campañas de Marruecos, Historial de guerra, 1ª y 2ª Banderas," 192; and Ramas Izquierdo, 239-241.

125. *DOL, Negociado de campaña*, 7-8 December 1924, 36; *SHM*, Legajo #54, Rollo 16, *Colección de historiales*, "Campañas de Marruecos, Historial de guerra, 1ª y 2ª Banderas," 186-187; and Subinspección de la Legión, ed., 251.

126. *DOL, Negociado de campaña*, 10 December 1924, 36. Subinspección de la Legión, ed., 243-245. This source has much more information on the day's operation, including a *Bandera*-by-*Bandera* account of what each did. Casualties from this source were fourteen officers and 223 Legionaries either dead, wounded, or missing. *SHM*, Legajo #54, Rollo 16, *Colección de historiales*, "Campañas de Marruecos, Historial de guerra, 1ª y 2ª Banderas" (3ª Bandera), 192-194. Ramas Izquierdo, 241-247. For more on the death of Captain Rafael de Rada Peral, see 30; for Lieutenants Federico Aguirre Ibeas, Francisco Albert Arran (medical doctor), and Vicente Parra Gil, see 38-39; and for *Alféreces* Julián Pérez Mañero and Juan González Mumma, see 49-50.

127. *DOL, Negociado de campaña*, 10 December 1924, 36; *SHM*, Legajo #54, Rollo 16, *Colección de historiales*, "Campañas de Marruecos, Historial de guerra, 1ª y 2ª Banderas," 187; and Subinspección de la Legión, ed., 251.

128. *DOL, Negociado de campaña*, 12 December 1924, 36. Subinspección de la Legión, ed., 245-247, has much more on the battle. Casualties: one officer and twenty-five Legionaries. This source mentions the participation of the Spanish air force in the retreat: but unfortunately on this day, the air force began to bomb the *Regulares* by mistake. Harris, 145, has more on the air force. *SHM*, Legajo #54, Rollo 16, *Colección de historiales*, "Campañas de Marruecos, Historial de guerra, 1ª y 2ª Banderas" (3ª Bandera), 194. Estado Mayor Central del Ejército, 14. Ramas Izquierdo, 247-250.

129. *DOL, Negociado de campaña*, 13 December 1924, 36; Subinspección de la Legión, ed., 247-248; and *SHM*, Legajo #54, Rollo 16, *Colección de historiales*, "Campañas de Marruecos, Historial de guerra, 1ª y 2ª Banderas" (3ª Bandera), 195. Sablotny, 288, wrote of seeing Tetuán, the capital of the Spanish protectorate, from behind rebel lines. Furthermore, he claimed that he could see Ceuta and its mountaintop fortress, El Hacho.

130. For the final phase of the retreat from Xauen to Tetuán, see Harris, 145, who recorded that "the Spanish losses on that last day of the retirement were 450 killed and wounded." His total casualty figure was 800 officers and 17,000 men. Woolman, *Rebels in*

the Rif, 140, wrote, "On the last day alone [the Riffians] shot down more than 500 of Franco's rearguard Legionarios." The author was unable to substantiate this information regarding the number of Legion casualties. His (i.e., Woolman's) total casualty figure was around 17,000, like that of Harris. Furneaux, 132, recorded: "The casualties were announced officially as: 1 General [Serrano], 6 Lieutenant-Colonels, 8 Majors, 175 other officers; wounded, 600 officers. 17,000 ordinary soldiers were reported dead or missing." Payne, 215, gives his total casualty figure as 2,000. Fleming, *Primo de Rivera*, 192-194, has the most accurate information on the number of casualties, including an excellent table (5.1) with all the detailed figures. De La Cierva, 240, estimated that less than 2,000 men were lost in the evacuation. Scurr, 15, gave the figure of about 1,000 casualties for the Legion during the entire operation. From the research they have done, I must concur with De La Cierva, Payne, and Fleming that the casualties for the Spanish military were less than 2,000. Preston, 46.

131. Harris, 145-146. There is another paragraph to this speech and Harris has it in his book. Translation by Harris. Gómez-Jordana y Souza, 70-71, has Primo de Rivera's speech in Spanish.

132. *DOL*, *Negociado de campaña*, 14 December 1924, 36-37; Subinspección de la Legión, ed., 251-252; *SHM*, Legajo #54, Rollo 16, *Colección de historiales*, "Campañas de Marruecos, Historial de guerra, 1ª y 2ª Banderas," 187; and Estado Mayor Central del Ejército, 15.

133. *DOL*, *Negociado de campaña*, 15 December 1924, 37; and *SHM*, Legajo #54, Rollo 16, *Colección de historiales*, "Campañas de Marruecos, Historial de guerra, 1ª y 2ª Banderas," 195. Fleming, *Primo de Rivera*, 203-204, has more on the rebellion by the Anjera tribe behind the Estella line.

134. *DOL*, *Negociado de campaña*, 17 December 1924, 36; *SHM*, Legajo #54, Rollo 16, *Colección de historiales*, "Campañas de Marruecos, Historial de guerra, 1ª y 2ª Banderas" (3ª Bandera), 196; and Estado Mayor Central del Ejército, 15.

135. *DOL*, *Negociado de campaña*, 18 December 1924, 36; and *SHM*, Legajo #54, Rollo 16, *Colección de historiales*, "Campañas de Marruecos, Historial de guerra, 1ª y 2ª Banderas," 195, noted that the tribes in this sector had long been loyal to Spain, but had now gone over to the enemy.

136. *DOL*, *Negociado de campaña*, 19 December 1924, 36.

137. *DOL*, *Negociado de campaña*, 20-21 December, 1924, 36. *SHM*, Legajo #54, Rollo 16, *Colección de historiales*, "Campañas de Marruecos, Historial de guerra, 1ª y 2ª Banderas," 195. After this operation, on 21 December, the Ist, IVth, and Vth *Banderas* returned to Laucien, and from there they passed through to Tetuán, finally ending up in Dar Riffien for rest and reorganization. Estado Mayor Central del Ejército, 15.

138. *DOL*, *Negociado de campaña*, 30 December 1924, 36.

139. *DOL*, *Negociado de campaña*, 31 December 1924, 36. Subinspección de la Legión, ed., 513-515, contains a brief listing of the major actions of the Legion during the year 1924. For a brief summary of the major events of the Ist, IInd, IIIrd, IVth, Vth, and VIth *Banderas*, see *SHM*, Legajo #54, Rollo 16, *Colección de historiales*, La Legión, "Acciones de guerra de las distintas Banderas de la Legión (1920-1939)," 3-4, 10, 16, 21-

22, 26-27, and 31, respectively.

While the Legion was in the field, changes within the organization were taking place as well. New amendments and articles were added to the original charter in order to deal with situations and/or conditions that would arise. See, ROC (2-I-1924), CL #2 (6), DO #2 (3-I-1924), (21): Establishing rules and regulations (4 articles) for the transfer of those conscripts who wished to join the *Tercio de Extranjeros* (the Legion) and for volunteers who would not receive the usual enlistment bonus. ROC (26-I-1924), CL #44 (67), DO #22 (27-I-1924), (274): Repealing the statue of last 14 November (CL #513) relating to deserters from the *Tercio de Extranjeros* and determining where they will serve the sentence imposed upon them. ROC (7-II-1924), CL #62 (92), DO #32 (8-II-1924), (417): Approving the rules and regulations (16 articles) by which to govern the promotion of men from the ranks (Legionaries) to the positions (rank) of *alférez*, lieutenant, and captain of the *Tercio de Extranjeros*. ROC (20-II-1924), CL #83 (127), DO #43 (21-II-1924), (552): Deciding (6 points) how to proceed with the vigilance of recruits departing to join the *Tercio de Extranjeros*. ROC (1-III-1924), CL #108 (166), DO #52 (2-III-1924), (705): Deciding on the organization of the two *Banderas* of the *Tercio de Extranjeros* and the four *Tabores* of the indigenous regular forces [the *Regulares*]. ROC (18-III-1924), CL #123 (183), DO #66 (19-III-1924), (843): A pay increase of one *peseta* per day is granted to the Legion.

140. Barea, 229.

141. De Galinsoga, 110. Franco's promotion to the rank of colonel became effective on 7 February 1925, backdated to 31 January 1924.

Chapter 6

The Alhucemas Bay Landings and Abd-el-Krim's Defeat

At the start of 1925, Abd-el-Krim's power in the Spanish protectorate of Morocco had reached its zenith. From this point onward, it would decline as internal problems and a reinvigorated Spanish army would eventually defeat his Riffian Republic. Key ingredients in the Spanish success are the capture and demise of Abd-el-Krim's rival, el Raisuni; the Alcazarseguer landing, which was a precursor to the much larger and more important Alhucemas Bay landings; the rapid decline of Abd-el-Krim's power following his attack on the French protectorate; and the Alhucemas Bay landing, the most momentous event of 1925.

For the Legion, the Alhucemas Bay landings would be one of the most important events in its history, overshadowed only by the Legion's participation in the suppression of the Asturian miners in October 1934 and the Spanish Civil War. At Alhucemas Bay, the Spanish and French military were able to resurrect the concept of combined operations after the Allied debacle at Gallipoli ten years earlier. Alhucemas thus served as the bridge between Gallipoli (1915) and Norway (1940), which then culminated with the most significant amphibious landing in history at Normandy in 1944. The victorious outcome of the Alhucemas Bay landings was the beginning of the end for Abd-el-Krim and his hopes for a Riffian state. For the Legion, it was a welcomed military success after the army's humiliating set back with the retreat from Xauen. For Colonel Franco, Alhucemas Bay meant personal success and recognition as it led to his promotion to brigadier general.

Nevertheless, the situation looked bleak in early January. Abd-el-Krim had driven Spain from the Gomara and part of the Yebala, and although he had failed in dealing the Spanish military another crushing defeat a la Annual, he had achieved a great triumph.[1] Militarily, the situation in the western zone remained relatively quiet, except for the rebellion of the Anjera/Anyera tribe in late 1924, which caused havoc in the areas of the Ceuta-Tetuán-Tangier triangle. Primo de Rivera dispatched two columns: one under the command of Franco in the Ceuta sector, the other under the veteran Morocco campaigner General Saro in the Tetuán sector. In the eastern zone of the protectorate, Tizzi-Azza remained the focus of aggression between Spanish forces and the Riffians, with important battles fought there. Tizzi-Azza was a slugfest, with neither side having sufficient strength to defeat the other. The Legion played no role in these battles. Since Abd-el-Krim's attention had shifted to the western zone in late 1924, the Legion had been transferred there to meet his thrusts.[2] On the first day of January, the six *Banderas* of the Legion were stationed behind the Estella line, with the Ist, IVth, and Vth *Banderas* at the Legion's training camp of Riffien, the IInd at Haira Tuila (Larache sector), and the IIIrd and VIth at Ain Yir.[3]

The Primo or Estella line had been established to eliminate the small and isolated *blocaos* that dotted the landscape throughout the protectorate. It was Primo de Rivera's intention to move these vulnerable outposts behind a strongly defended perimeter. This was accomplished after the retreat from Xauen when the front line in the western zone was situated just beyond the environs of Tetuán. The Estella line not only provided protection for Spanish troops but also deprived the rebels of essential war booty they desperately needed to continue their struggle.[4]

The Legion's first operation of 1925 took place on 2 January when the Ist *Bandera* left its base camp to establish two *blocaos* at Restinga-Hayar. The following day it left for Tetuán, where it served in a garrison role until 6 January, when it moved to R'gaia to perform a variety of essential campaign services.[5] On 4 January, the IVth *Bandera* began to establish several fortified positions at Ain Ganen, suffering four Legionaries dead and seventeen wounded.[6] The "Tigers" of the IIIrd *Bandera* left Ain Yir on 5 January for Riffien and moved from there to the port of Ceuta, where they embarked aboard the *Atlante* for Melilla. Arriving in Melilla on 9 January, they proceeded to the fort at Sidi-Guariach serving in the garrison role. On 19 January, they marched to Ben Tieb, the Legion's major encampment in the eastern zone, from there carrying out their assigned tasks.[7] On 7 January, the IVth *Bandera* occupied a number of positions in Ain Ganen. In a firefight with the rebels, the Legion lost six Legionaries killed, plus three officers and twenty-two Legionaries wounded.[8]

While the Legion was engaged in carrying out its assigned duties on land, its commander in chief, Franco, was planning to prepare an amphibious landing at Alcazarseguer on the Anjera coast with the hope of quickly putting an end to the rebellion there. On 7 January, he reconnoitered the coastline from the deck of the gunboat *Bonifaz*. A few days later he reexamined the coast from the deck of the gunboat *Canalejas*. Finally, 14 January was chosen for the operation. That dawn, a small convoy composed of a gunboat, a coast guard vessel, and three tugs set off from Ceuta escorting six "K-type" landing barges and headed toward their destination of Punta Alcázar. Aboard the six self-propelled landing crafts were the IVth and VIth *Banderas* of the Legion, a unit from the *Regulares*, a mountain battery, and support services. Unable to proceed because of rough seas, the convoy promptly returned to port. Although this first attempt had been unsuccessful as a result of unfavorable weather conditions, the operation would be tried again in March.[9]

From 8 January to the end of the month, all six *Banderas* of the Legion performed their campaign duties, suffering two Legionaries killed, plus one officer and eleven Legionaries wounded.[10]

After driving Spanish forces from Xauen, Abd-el-Krim had one more obstacle to overcome before he could claim himself to be lord and master of the western zone—el Raisuni. El Raisuni, as a Spanish ally, had received excellent remuneration in money and weapons for his loyalty. He remained in his small palace at Tazarut, which Abd-el-Krim sarcastically called "the Madrid of the Jibala," outside the Estella line. Spanish officials had offered to relocate el Raisuni to Tetuán for his own safety, but he refused. Abd-el-Krim's younger brother, M'hamed, planned the attack on Tazarut. It began late on 23 January. Under the command of Abd-el-Krim's old lieutenant, Ahmed Heriro, the attacking force made up of Jibali, Gomaris, and Riffians was able to overcome the sherif's defenders. The battle lasted a few hours before the attackers took el Raisuni prisoner. Suffering from severe dropsy, he had to be carried on a litter first to Xauen and then to Targuist, deep in the Rif. Refusing to eat and wishing to die rather than to live as a slave, he finally did so on 3 April.[11]

CHANGES IN THE LEGION

In February, the Legionaries remained at their previously noted postings performing their typical campaign duties. Although there were no major battles fought this month, the Legion underwent momentous changes as an organization. This reorganization began on 7 February when an ROC (Circular Royal Order) made Franco's promotion to full colonel official with a retroactive date of rank of 31 January 1924. With a third eight-pointed star gracing the cuff of his tunic, Franco, at thirty-one, became the youngest colonel in the Spanish army. The original charter of the Legion stipulated that it be commanded by a lieutenant colonel, but now that it had increased in size and would soon add another *Bandera* (the VIIth) and the *Escuadrón de Lanceros* (Squadron of Lancers, effective post-Franco), it was deemed that a full colonel should command the unit.[12] In addition, the Legion's original organization of September 1920 was modified with the retention of eight machine guns and eight mortars per mortar platoon; four platoons per rifle company, with the fourth platoon armed with six light machine guns; each company to be composed of 216 men; and also proposing the creation of a cavalry *Bandera* (what would come to be known as the Squadron of Lancers, with 150 men).[13]

A week later, the Legion received new uniforms that became regulation by the time of the Alhucemas Bay landings. Some of the clothing changes included a summer battle dress of shirtsleeve, with rank displayed on a "*galleta*" (rectangular patch) worn above the left breast pocket, the Legion's emblem embroidered on the newly added epaulets of the shirt, and the replacement of the "Mills" web gear for one made of brown leather.[14]

A Royal Order dated 16 February changed the Legion's title from *Tercio de Extranjeros* (*Tercio* of Foreigners), to *Tercio de Marruecos* (*Tercio* of Morocco). The name change could also have been because "foreigners" (e.g., the English, Americans, Canadians, and Germans) had not fared at all well in the Legion because of brutal discipline, poor living conditions, language barriers, and dietary differences. In fact, foreigners never constituted more than 10 percent of the Legion, and the great majority of those who could tolerate the harsh life of a Spanish Legionary came from Latin America and Portugal. Therefore, since the Legion was engaged in fighting in Morocco, why not call it the Tercio of Morocco?[15] Even this new name did not last more than a month, as it became *El Tercio* on 2 March. As noted previously, from its inception the corps was always called "*La Legión*" by all those who were members of it, from Millán Astray on down, and thus it has remained to the present day.[16]

The first major operation in March took place on the 19th when the IInd *Bandera* assisted in the occupation of a *blocao* at Handa Hamara. In a hard-fought battle, the IInd's temporary commander, Captain Gabriel Navarrete Navarrete and a Legionary were killed and four Legionaries were wounded.[17]

The previously postponed amphibious invasion of Alcazarseguer, which would lead to the opening of a third front in the struggle against the Anyera rebels, took place on 29-30 March. The invasion column, under the overall command of General Federico de Sousa Regoyos, was composed of the IVth and VIth *Banderas* commanded by Colonel Franco and of a *tabor* of the *Regulares de Ceuta* commanded by Lieutenant Colonel Álvarez Arenas. The operation began late on 29 March when the Spanish navy and air force bombed and strafed coastal villages in preparation for the landing. The land forces arrived at Alcazarseguer aboard the steamer *Vicente la Roda* from which the three battalions transferred to the six "*Kaes*." The armed trawler *Arcila* provided naval protection. The two *Banderas*, forming the vanguard of the invasion force, hit the northeastern shore of the little beach at 0100 hours on 30 March and quickly secured the port. The firepower (artillery) and swiftness of the invaders completely overwhelmed the rebels. The operation was a total success with minimal casualties incurred. In the Legion's case, only one Legionary died and one officer and nine Legionaries were wounded. With Alcazarseguer in Spanish hands, the third front was opened, which allowed their forces to proceed in a southward and westward direction in a campaign that would continue to drag on. More important, perhaps, the Alcazarseguer landing also served as the precursor to the much larger and more important landing at Alhucemas Bay, which would take place that September.[18]

On 1 April, the Ist and Vth *Banderas* were still at R'Gaia; the IInd remained at T'Zenin; the IIIrd was at Ben Tieb; the IVth was now at Kudia Gomariz; and the VIth had returned to the Legion's headquarters at Riffien. For the duration of the month, they remained at these posts performing their usual campaign duties.[19]

With el Raisuni out of the way, Abd-el-Krim turned his immediate attention to internal problems. Harvests had not been as plentiful as expected, and now that the Spanish army was relatively secure behind the Estella line, he was finding it difficult to supply his growing army with weapons and munitions at the expense of the Spanish. Payne observed that the aforementioned situation could have been the chief reason for Abd-el-Krim's decision to strike at the northern sector of the French zone. In spring 1924, he encountered stiff armed resistance from the tribesmen of the Ouergha River valley when he tried to gain control of the region. French resident general Marshal Louis-Hubert Lyautey had always been apprehensive regarding Riffian gains at the expense of the Spaniards. French officials, however, had never been favorably inclined to expressly collaborate with the Spanish, since they were viewed as rivals and the mere perception that they would be linked to a failing power, which the Moroccans had little respect for, would diminish their own repute.[20]

Nevertheless, the French authorities took preventive action along their border. They moved soldiers from Fez to the territory of the Zeni Zerwal tribe, a fertile and critical region regarded as "the breadbasket of the Rif." On 9 April 1925, Abd-el-Krim launched a preemptive strike, sending five *harkas* against French outposts along the Uarga/Ouergha/Wergha River. Caught between the French and the advancing Riffians, the Zerwalis chose to go with the latter.[21]

The situation in Morocco had taken a new direction as Spain's problems with Abd-el-Krim and his rebellion now spilled over into the French sector. Spanish officials, were of course, still trying to bring an end to the rebellion. According to Fleming, during this time (spring 1925) Spanish agents had been discussing a settlement to the rebellion with Abd-el-Krim, but once again it had proved fruitless. He also noted that Primo de Rivera was planning to abandon the entire protectorate except for the *presidios* (Ceuta and Melilla), but that now with Abd-el-Krim's attack on the French, the situation had changed.[22]

The six *Banderas* of the Spanish Foreign Legion were moved around by the first day of May. The Ist *Bandera* joined the IIIrd at Ben Tieb, and the IInd moved to the capital of the protectorate. The IVth and IVth were now at R'Gaia, and the Vth moved to T'Zenin.[23] Also on 1 May, the Legion formed the VIIth *Bandera* with personnel from the other *Banderas*, and from the depot company. Major Gregorio Verdu Verdu took command of the new *Bandera*, and it went to Riffien for further instruction and organization. As its standard, the VIIth *Bandera* chose the arms of Lieutenant Colonel Valenzuela on a white field (represented on the reverse by the Cross of St. James). Also on the same date, the *Escuadrón de Lanceros* was created, with its members coming from the depot company. Captain Pedro Sánchez Tirado commanded the squadron, which remained at Riffien for further instruction and organization. For its standard, the squadron selected the banner the Catholic kings carried during the conquest of Granada. The Squadron of Lancers served in the escort and reconnaissance role during the campaign.[24]

With the Legion's change of name to *El Tercio* taking place on 2 May, the corps was divided into two legions: the eastern zone (headquarters in Melilla), 1st Legion, consisting of the Ist, IInd, IIIrd, and IVth Banderas with Lieutenant Colonel Amado Balmes Alonso commanding; and the western zone (headquarters in Ceuta), 2nd Legion, consisting of the Vth, VIth, and VIIth Banderas (later to be joined by the VIIIth, organized on 1 January 1926) with Lieutenant Colonel Juan de Liniers y Muguiro commanding.[25]

The situation for the French was grave along the French protectorate border as Abd-el-Krim chalked up one victory after another, threatening Taza and Fez and even coming within thirty kilometers of the latter for a time. The government in Paris blamed Marshal Lyautey for failing to stop the Riffian onslaught on French positions. Lyautey, who had been in poor health for many years, resigned, temporarily replaced by General Naulin. Lyautey did remain as resident-general, however. Eventually, Marshal Henri Philippe Pétain, the hero of Verdun, would assume overall command of French forces in Morocco.[26]

Primo de Rivera had declared after the retreat from Xauen that once Abd-el-Krim had finished with the Spanish, he would turn his attention to the French. To date, France had remained indifferent to Spain's difficulties and defeats in Morocco; as long as Spain alone was the victim of Abd-el-Krim's attacks, France would sit tight. Deserters from the Spanish Foreign Legion had often tried to make their way to the French border, expecting succor. Yet French rifles and munitions were prevalent in Abd-el-Krim's army. Now the two European powers, facing a common foe, agreed to cooperate in putting an end to the rebellion. Representatives of the two nations met throughout June and July 1925 to hammer out an agreement on terminating the war. The Franco-Hispano Conference met first in Madrid, then again on 25 July when the parties to the conference reached an agreement, and on 28 July when Pétain and Primo de Rivera met in Tetuán to finalize their plans for a combined operation.[27]

For the Spanish Foreign Legion, the situation remained static and relatively calm. On the first of July, the seven *Banderas* of the Legion were deployed as follows: the Ist was at Dar Quebdani (eastern zone); the IInd, VIth, and the Squadron of Lancers were in Riffien; the IIIrd was at Ben Tieb (eastern zone); the IVth at T'Zenin; the Vth at Laucien; and the VIIth was at R'Gaia.[28] On 6 July, the Vth *Bandera* took part in establishing a *blocao* at el Derxa. In the firefight that ensued, the Legion had one officer and four Legionaries wounded. For the remainder of July and the entire month of August, there were no major engagements as the Legion performed its usual campaign duties.[29]

LANDINGS AT ALHUCEMAS

By September, Primo de Rivera was eager to carry out the amphibious landing at Alhucemas Bay. Franco had been encouraging him for some time to strike at the heart of the rebellion, Ajdir, to bring a rapid closure to this military quagmire in which Spain found itself. As Franco told Primo de Rivera concerning the landing at Alhucemas Bay: *"No sólo es posible, sino necesaria"* ("It is not only possible, but necessary"). It should be noted that the idea for an amphibious landing at Alhucemas Bay was not the brainchild of Franco but had been proposed by numerous military officers since 1909.[30] And though the Spanish had decided on Alhucemas Bay as the location for the landing, Marshal Lyautey preferred a landing in the region of the Lau River in order to reconquer the territory that had been abandoned the previous year and to advance all the way back to Xauen. Undeterred, the Spanish plan was agreed upon, since it would catch the Riffians in a vise formed by the Spanish army moving southward and the French army moving northward. For Abd-el-Krim, there would be no escape from the two pincers.[31]

The formidable task of preparing the plans for the Alhucemas Bay landing was given to the brightest General Staff officers in the Spanish army. Among the most notable planners under the command of General Ignacio Despujols were Colonels Manuel Goded Llopis and Joaquín Fanjul Goni, *capitán de fregata* (naval commander) Carlos Boado, and the younger officers, Lieutenant Colonel Antonio Aranda Mata and Antonio Barroso y Sánchez-Guerra. Franco himself played a major role in the planning because it would be the men of the Legion, the IInd, IIIrd, VIth, and VIIth *Banderas* constituting 18 percent of the invasion force, who would hit the beach first.[32]

It came as no secret to Abd-el-Krim that the Spanish and French were collaborating on an amphibious landing, and that it would most likely take place at Alhucemas Bay. When the French General Staff reviewed and approved the proposed plans, Abd-el-Krim's position became difficult. His armies would soon be forced to fight on four fronts: (1) the reinforced French advancing from the south; (2) the Spanish army pushing west from Melilla; (3) the Spanish army defending Tetuán from the attacks of Ahmed Heriro; and (4) the seaborne invasion about to come on the shores of the Rif. His forces were spread too thinly, and his seasoned regulars were not numerous enough to be present, in effective numbers, on all fronts.[33]

As the targeted date for the invasion loomed ever closer, the three branches of the Spanish military made preparations. The land forces were composed of two brigades. One would leave from Ceuta under the command of General Leopoldo de Saro y Marin; the other would set out from Melilla under the command of General Emilio Fernández Pérez. The navy's ships, under the command of Vice Admiral Yolif y Morgado, were ready and waiting in Cartagena, while the entire air force was distributed between the aerodromes of Ceuta and Melilla.[34]

General José Sanjurjo Sacanell was the man entrusted with overall command for the actual landings. On 20 August 1925, he reconnoitered the western part of Alhucemas Bay by air looking at Riffian fortifications. By the first day of September, all the ships, men, and supplies were loaded and final instructions given to the operational commanders. The operation was set to commence.[35] Abd-el-Krim, however, launched a preemptive and diversionary attack against Spanish lines near Tetuán. He hoped that this attack on the protectorate's capital would delay the Alhucemas Bay landing long enough for autumn's inclement weather to set in.[36]

On 5 September, the two invasion fleets set sail from Ceuta and Melilla toward Alhucemas Bay. General Saro commanded the Ceuta column (9,000 men), and General Fernández Pérez commanded the Melilla column (also with 9,000 men). Colonel Franco, with the VIth and VIIth *Banderas* (aboard the *Jaime II* [VIth *Bandera*] and the *Capitán Sagarra* [VIIth *Bandera*]), served as the vanguard for General Saro's column, while the IInd and IIIrd *Banderas* (aboard the steamer *Antonio Lazaro*), under the command of Lieutenant Colonel Balmes, were part of the column of General Fernández Pérez.[37]

On 6 September, the battle for Kudia Tahar, which had begun on 3 September, began to heat up when the rebels began to pound it heavily with their artillery. Abd-el-Krim's brother, M'hamed, had sent his field commander, Ahmed Heriro, with Abd-el-Krim's army of Jibalis and Riffians to attack the vital Spanish position of Kudia/Cudia Tahar, a critical link in the Estella line. If it fell to the rebels, it would have left Tetuán wide open for artillery bombardment. Enemy artillery reduced Kudia Tahar's defenses to rubble. With casualties mounting, their only cannon destroyed, and the failure of a relief force from Tetuán to break through, the situation was critical.[38] Aware that an attack on Alhucemas loomed, Abd-el-Krim had carried out his threat to attack Tetuán hoping to divert the Franco-Hispano invasion force away from his homeland.

Meanwhile, on 6 September the IInd and IIIrd *Banderas* continued steaming aboard the *Antonio Lazaro*, while the VIth and VIIth *Banderas* aboard the *Jaime II* and the *Capitán Sagarra* continued on their journey toward Uad Lau. In an attempt to obfuscate their intended landing site, the two *Banderas* made desultory landing attempts at the former Spanish positions of Uad Lau, Kaaseras, and Targa. In addition, the warships of the fleet bombarded these same coastal targets.[39] The following day the four *Banderas* of the Legion continued on their journey and threats of a landing along the coast. By dawn the invasion fleet had arrived and was off Alhucemas Bay prepared to land (see Map 6).[40]

At 0600 hours on the foggy morning of 8 September, the invasion began with naval bombardment and aerial bombing and strafing of the invasion beaches of La Cebadilla and Ixdain. In addition to softening up the beaches prior to the disembarkation, the Spanish air force supported the landings by providing reconnaissance, artillery spotting, bombardment, and strafing runs. It racked up 1,462 hours of flying time, dropping almost 150,000 kg (330,000 lbs) of bombs.[41] At 0900 hours, the order was given to board the "K's," which would then be towed closer to the beach. The tugs would cut their lines to the "K's" at about 1,000 meters from shore, and these crafts would proceed the rest of the way under their own propulsion. While naval gunfire raked the enemy coastline, the VIth *Bandera* headed in toward the beach at 1140 hours. Commander Carlos Boado of the Spanish navy preceding the landing crafts in a motor boat, diverted them away from the primary target of La Cebadilla beach toward the adjoining Ixdain beach because the former contained fifty unexploded aerial bombs, which now served the enemy as a mine field. Twenty minutes later, the landing barges ran aground on

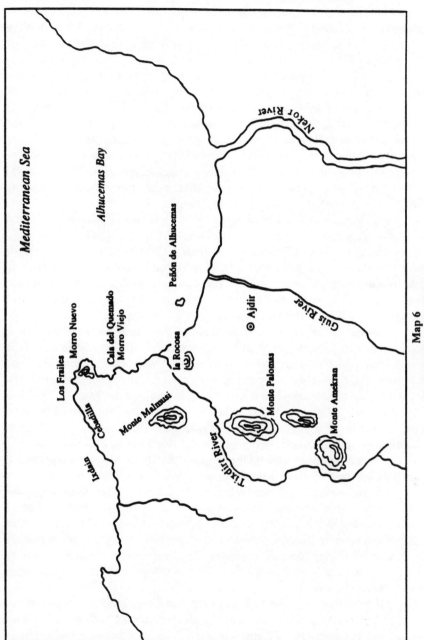

Map 6
The Alhucemas Bay Landings

rocks and shoals. Franco, disobeying a direct order to abort the mission (he would later claim an officer's prerogative on the scene), gave the order for the bugler to sound the call for attack. This energized the Legionaries, who along with the pro-Spanish natives of the *Harkas de Tetuán y Larache* jumped out of their landing crafts into neck-deep water. With their weapons held high above their heads, they waded ashore.

The initial plan called for the *Harkas* to attack head on and on the right flank, while the Legion attacked on the left. Colonel Franco led the VIth (Major Rada) and VIIth (Major Verdu) *Banderas* ashore. The 24th Company of the VIth was arguably the first to reach the beach, with the 22nd Company to its right and the 23rd Company to its left. The machine gun company provided effective fire support for the invasion. The VIIth *Bandera* supported the attacks of the more experienced VIth, and they too achieved their assigned missions. Overwhelmed by the aggressiveness of the attack, the defenders barely resisted and fled, leaving behind a cannon, several machine guns, and their dead.

By sundown on that first day, the Legion had secured Morro Nuevo; the VIth *Bandera*'s standard fluttered from its crest. With over 8,000 men and three batteries having been put ashore, it was obvious that the surprise landing west of Alhucemas Bay had been a success. Abd-el-Krim had been expecting the landing to take place within the bay itself, but the Spaniards fooled him by landing at Ixdain/La Cebadilla, which was less well defended and belonged to the Bucoya tribe, not Abd-el-Krim's Beni Urriaguel.[42]

Aboard the *Antonio Lazaro*, the IInd and IIIrd *Banderas* watched as their fellow Legionaries assaulted the beach. With eager anticipation, they awaited the disembarkation order. They noticed that their ship was heading away from the beach, however, not toward it. Primo de Rivera, aboard the flagship *Alfonso XIII* along with General Sanjurjo, had been notified by radio of the situation at Kudia Tahar. As noted, the Riffians had launched a major attack on the Spanish position of Kudia Tahar in the hopes of eventually reaching Tetuán. The Spanish defenders were holding out, but several attempts to relieve them had failed. In response to this threat, Primo de Rivera ordered the IIth and IIIrd *Banderas* plus a regiment of the army (4,000 men total) to head for Ceuta at full speed.[43]

The following day, 9 September, the IInd and IIIrd *Banderas* continued toward Ceuta, where they were to await new orders. They reached the port of Ceuta the next day and quickly entrained for Tetuán. There, they encamped for the night.[44] Meanwhile, back at the beachhead the VIth and VIIth *Banderas* continued with their work of fortifying and consolidating their newly established lines of defense on La Cebadilla/Ixdain beaches. Enemy cannon and rifle fire wounded five Legionaries that day.[45]

On 11 September, the IInd and IIIrd *Banderas*, under the command of Lieutenant Colonel Amado Balmes, which formed the vanguard of General Sousa's relief column, marched toward Kudia Tahar (see Map 7). From their well-fortified and defended positions, the rebels were able to blunt the Legionaries' initial thrust. Forced to withdraw and reorganize, the Legionaries tried again the next day (12

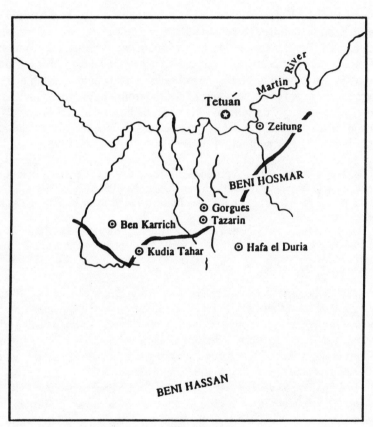

Map 7
The Liberation of Kudia Tahar

September) with Dar Gasi/Gazi as the focal point of their attack. With their usual determination and ferocity, the Legionaries drove the rebels from the surrounding hills and caves at the point of the bayonet. The beleaguered outpost was finally relieved on 13 September. At Kudia Tahar, the enemy left behind 135 dead, along with seventy-four weapons. For the Legion, the casualties had also been high, with one officer, Lieutenant Inocencio Real Herrainz, and twenty-five Legionaries killed. The wounded included Lieutenant Colonel Balmes, a *Bandera* commander, six officers, and ninety-four Legionaries.[46]

The Kudia Tahar survivors, and the Legionaries who had rescued them, marched triumphantly through Tetuán past Primo de Rivera, who had returned to the capital. During the parade Primo de Rivera saw firsthand the odious and barbaric side of the Moroccan campaign. The sight of rebel ears, noses, and heads skewered on the bayonets of the Legionaries who paraded past him greatly disturbed Primo de Rivera, who reprimanded the troops publicly for such actions: the practice subsequently decreased.[47] It should be noted that atrocities took place on both sides. Legion deserter Sablotny personally experienced one such incident while fleeing to Tangier with fellow deserters:

We saw that they brought in Spanish prisoners, former soldiers of active regiments of Spain. The Arabian [sic] warriors delivered them into the hands of the Arabian [sic] widows, that they might avenge themselves. And the fate of the Spaniards in the hands of those savage females was lamentable.

In another room at the side of ours, one by one they were beheaded by the women, and our eyes leaped out of their sockets on seeing that these women had still not been satisfied.[48]

The VIth and VIIth *Banderas* at Alhucemas continued with their fortification work and successfully repelled a determined Riffian attack on 11-12 September. In the aforementioned encounter, the *Banderas* turned back a spirited counterattack by 1,500 Riffians, with 200 of them being *juramentados* (men who have sworn to die in battle). By the next day, the beachhead was secured and men and matériel continued to pour onto the beaches.[49]

For Spain to have successfully landed on the doorstep of Abd-el-Krim's Riffian capital, while at the same time losing their own capital of Tetuán, would have been another black eye to Spanish prestige and honor around the world. One would have overshadowed the other, with Abd-el-Krim reaping the greater publicity. The relief of Kudia Tahar, however, as well as eliminating the threat to the capital, had been accomplished through the actions of the Legion. Once again, when a unit of the army was on the verge of annihilation or a Spanish city was threatened, the High Command turned to the Legion to remedy the situation.

Between 14 and 18 September, the *Banderas* manned their various garrisons, carrying out their typical campaign duties, having three Legionaries killed and twenty-five wounded.[50] The IInd and IIIrd *Banderas*, fresh from their victory at Kudia Tahar, left Ceuta on 19 September aboard the *Escolano* headed for La Cebadilla beach; they arrived and disembarked at Los Frailes beach the following day.[51]

After establishing their beachhead, the Spanish army faced a difficult and costly fight. The Riffians used the harshness of the terrain to maximum advantage. From the beaches of La Cebadilla and Ixdain to Ajdir (Abd-el-Krim's capital), the land is rough and rocky with many peaks and caves. The rebels fired their artillery only at night to make it more difficult for Spanish planes to locate their gun emplacements.[52]

Early on the morning of 20 September, Primo de Rivera disembarked at Cebadilla beach, where he deliberated with Generals Sanjurjo, Saro, Fernández Pérez, and their staffs about the next step to be taken in the offensive. They concluded that the hills overlooking the landing beaches, which were dotted with Riffian artillery, should be the primary target. They selected Morro Viejo, Malmusi Bajo, and the Cuernos of Xauen/Malmusi Alto as the goals for the forthcoming attacks, which were to commence on 23 September. After thorough preparation and reconnaissance, the attack began in earnest at 0730 hours on the morning of 23 September. Colonel Goded's column, which included the IInd and IIIrd *Banderas*, encountered light resistance in securing Cala/Kala del Quemado, Malmusi Bajo, and Morro Viejo. Franco's column faced more difficulty in trying to take Malmusi Alto. Lieutenant Colonel Balmes led his IInd and IIIrd *Banderas* in the battle for Malmusi Bajo. In bitter, bloody fighting, the two *Banderas* suffered six Legionaries killed, plus two officers and twenty-six Legionaries wounded. It was Franco's VIth and VIIth *Banderas*, however, that bore the brunt of the fighting. The Riffians knew that losing Malmusi Alto would leave them wide open for a Spanish thrust toward their capital via the Ajdir plain. In the sanguinary battle for Monte Malmusi, the Legionaries fought their worthy adversaries in vicious hand-to-hand combat. The ferocity of the engagement was reflected by the casualty count for the two *Banderas*: four officers and 40 Legionaries killed; nine officers and 113 Legionaries wounded. Despite these losses, the Legion controlled the 500-meter-high hill by 1055 hours.[53] Fleming noted that this battle pushed the Alhucemas Bay front lines ten kilometers deeper toward the interior of the Rif and also verified the 8 September amphibious landing, securing numerous strategic positions deemed essential for further advances. The Riffians lost 200 killed, one field piece, four machine guns, plus 300 rifles and hand grenades.[54]

From 24 to 29 September, the IInd, IIIrd, VIth, and VIIth *Banderas* carried out their assigned task of fortifying their most recent gains in the Alhucemas sector (Malmusi). Subjected to intense artillery and machine gun fire, the casualties mounted. On 24 September Lieutenant José Casado Bustos died, and on 28 September Major Francisco Borrás Estévez was also killed. In those few days, the Legion suffered two other Legionaries killed, plus two officers and twelve Legionaries wounded.[55]

The final offensive operation of the month took place on 30 September when the IInd and IIIrd *Banderas* under Lieutenant Colonel Balmes formed part of Colonel Goded's vanguard, with its daily mission the occupation of Monte

Palomas. In a bitter struggle, the Legionaries forced the Riffians out of their well-entrenched positions. However, the assault had cost the lives of two officers and six Legionaries; the wounded numbered four officers and thirty-four Legionaries. Simultaneously, the VIth and VIIth *Banderas* advanced after a preliminary artillery barrage. Covered by the machine guns of the Legion, the Legionaries and the *Regulares* pressed forward on las Palomas. The enemy resisted the Legionaries' attack at Loma O, but the Legionaries were able to break through with their automatic weapons and mortars. The attack had cost the Legion five Legionaries killed, plus two officers and twenty-seven Legionaries wounded.[56]

On the first day of October, the IInd and IIIrd *Banderas* assisted in the day's operation, which called for the taking and occupying of Adra/Adrar Sedun/Seddun to expand the perimeter of the initial landings and subsequent advances. In the breakout offensive the Legion suffered one Legionary killed, as well as two officers and six Legionaries wounded.[57]

The Riffians were now on the run as the Spanish forces closed in on Ajdir, Abd-el-Krim's capital. The French were also on the move, reconquering all the territory they had lost along the Uarga River and pressing on with their offensive.[58] Naturally, the Legion was in the forefront of this onslaught on Abd-el-Krim's homeland. Between 2 October and 12 October, the IInd, IIIrd, VIth, and VIIth *Banderas* continued to operate in the Palomas and Ajdir sectors while being subjected to intense Riffian artillery and rifle fire. During these ten days casualties for the Legion were three officers (among them Captain Cuevas and Lieutenant Pardo of the 5/II) and twenty-four Legionaries were wounded. Of greater importance around this time was the capture and torching of Ajdir on 2 October by Spanish forces.[59]

On 13 October, the IInd and IIIrd *Banderas* under the command of Lieutenant Colonel Balmes participated in rectifying the front lines and linking of Calvet, a position called Casamata, and Amekran Bajo. The enemy attacked and occupied Casamata that same night when all those within were either killed or wounded. For the Legion, the casualties were severe. Fourteen Legionaries died; one commanding officer (Lieutenant Vicario), three officers, and twenty-nine Legionaries were wounded.[60] The very next day, 14 October, the IInd *Bandera* recaptured Casamata and occupied it along with Calvet. Until the end of the month, the four *Banderas* in the area carried out their duties of rectification, consolidation, and fortification of terrain conquered as they awaited further orders. While performing these duties, the Legionaries were under constant artillery, machine gun, mortar, and rifle fire. On 17 October, the recently named commander of the IInd *Bandera*, Major Manuel Orgáz/Ordáz Sampayo, died (along with four Legionaries killed and nine wounded) when an enemy shell slammed into Calvet. From 18 to 31 October, the four *Banderas* suffered three Legionaries killed and eighteen wounded.[61]

With a great victory behind him and an end to the Rif Rebellion looming ever closer, Primo de Rivera rewarded his generals (Sanjurjo, Saro, Fernández Pérez, and Despujol) with promotions and himself with Spain's highest decoration, the Grand Cross of the Laureate Cross of St. Ferdinand (which brought with it a huge pension).[62]

Inclement weather had arrived in the protectorate, and operations were markedly reduced on both sides. For the Legion in the Alhucemas sector, this meant carrying out typical campaign duties, with fortification on the top of the list, from 2 November to 31 December.[63] Even though offensives had been greatly diminished because of the weather, casualties continued to mount from rebel attacks. During this two-month period the Legion suffered twelve Legionaries dead and fifty wounded.[64]

SUMMARY

For the Spanish army, and the Legion in particular, 1925 had been momentous. It had begun with the army behind the Estella line after 1924's retreat from Xauen, but with the Anjera tribe rebellion behind the line. During early 1925 the Legion was in the forefront of offensives designed to subdue the rebels. The Legion's amphibious landing at Alcazarseguer in March, which opened a third front in the campaign, was a complete success. The Alcazarseguer landing served as a precursor to the much larger and more important Alhucemas Bay landing in September.

The Legion itself was thriving, and its role as the elite unit of the Spanish army in Africa was clearly demonstrated by the need to increase its ranks. Beginning in mid-February, the Legion underwent an overhaul that included Franco's official promotion to full colonel; the name change from *Tercio de Extranjeros* to *Tercio de Marruecos*, which was shortly thereafter changed to simply *El Tercio*; the addition of the VIIth *Bandera*, as well as the formation of the stately Squadron of Lancers; and the creation of two legions, one based in Melilla (with four *Banderas*) and the other in Ceuta (also with four *Banderas*).

The Rif Rebellion took an important turn in April when Abd-el-Krim attacked French forces in the south. Now he was engaged in fighting a two-front war along with combating famine and disease (typhus) and dealing with a serious lack of weapons and munitions. The beginning of the end would come in September when Spanish forces put an end to Abd-el-Krim by staging an amphibious landing at Alhucemas Bay, his front doorstep, while the French pushed northward from French Morocco. The combined operation at Alhucemas Bay was a total success, one that led Woolman to claim, "The cost not withstanding, Alhucemas was a great victory for Spain—the only definitive one they were to achieve during the whole of the Rif Rebellion."[65]

Hoping to deflect or postpone the impending landing at Alhucemas Bay, Abd-el-Krim gambled and lost when he tried to seize the Spanish outpost of Kudia Tahar. Withstanding a difficult and costly attack, the Legionaries of the IInd and IIIrd *Banderas*, who were diverted from the landing to carry out this vital operation, eventually rescued the defenders. The Legion had parried Abd-el-Krim's desperate lunge toward Tetuán and now he saw that his situation was perilous. With the capture of Ajdir, Abd-el-Krim fled deeper into the Rif, hoping to make the conquest of the Rif as costly as possible for Spain.

NOTES

1. For more on the Riffian situation at this time, see Payne, 217. Vaughan, 6, wrote that in early 1925, Abd-el-Krim "commanded a total force estimated at 80-120,000 men. The effective forces under his command were 6-7,000 'Regulars', an elite corps of hand-picked and trained men." Vaughan also gives an excellent description of the organization, hierarchy, and weapons used by Abd-el-Krim's army, even describing Abd-el-Krim's personal bodyguard: "[Abd-el-]Krim's Body Guard was a unit of snappy, precision drilled men who could even do the goose step!" Pennell, 177-180, gives a very insightful description and analysis of the events taking place inside Abd-el-Krim's emirate in late 1924 and early 1925. Morales Lezcano, 236, called Abd-el-Krim's state "*Dawla Jumhuriya Rifiya*, o Estado autónomo de El Rif [Autonomous State of the Rif]." Furthermore, he declared that it also "received military and moral support from the European Left and from the Islamic world in general."

2. Woolman, *Rebels in the Rif*, 161 and "In Spanish Morocco," 84. De La Cierva, *Franco*, 84. Furneaux, 133.

3. *DOL, Negociado de campaña*, 1 January 1925, 37. Cano Velasco, ed., 156. *SHM*, Legajo #54, Rollo 16, *Colección de historiales*, "Campañas de Marruecos, Historial de guerra, 1ª y 2ª Banderas," 187.

4. Payne, 217. The Estella line did not completely cut off the amount of contraband that made its way to Abd-el-Krim as Woolman, *Rebels in the Rif*, 155, noted that in spite of the Spanish navy's blockade and the Primo line, the rebels were still able to visit Tangier, where weapons could be obtained. Moreover, Abd-el-Krim was able to obtain arms from the *Regulares* who, looking to augment their pay, had sold them to Tangier merchants.

5. *SHM*, Legajo #54, Rollo 16, *Colección de historiales*, "Campañas de Marruecos, Historial de guerra, 1ª y 2ª Banderas," 195-196.

6. *DOL, Negociado de campaña*, 4 January 1925, 37-38.

7. *SHM*, Legajo #54, Rollo 16, *Colección de historiales*, "Campañas de Marruecos, Historial de guerra, 1ª y 2ª Banderas" (3ª Bandera), 196-197. Cano Velasco, ed., 156.

8. *DOL, Negociado de campaña*, 7 January 1924, 38.

9. De La Cierva, 242-243, noted that these "K-type" landing barges, known as *Kaes/Kas* (K's) in Spanish, were bought from the British in Gibraltar by the farsighted minister of war, Juan de La Cierva, prior to the Conference of Pizarra in 1922. Each landing barge was self-propelled and capable of transporting 300 men with all their equipment, as well as a vehicle. They were to also be employed with great success during the Alhucemas Bay landings. Page 245 has a period photograph of the *Almirante Bonifaz*. Eduardo Quintana Martínez and Juan Llabres Bernal, *La Marina de Guerra en África* (Madrid: Compañía Ibero-Americana de Publicaciones, S.A., 1928), 238. Goded Llopis, 158, also added that the "K-type" landing barges were lightly armored (i.e., bulletproof to small arms). *Jane's Fighting Ships*, ed. (1923), 330, has more information on the 1st Class gunboats

Almirante Bonifaz and *José Canalejas*. Subinspección de la Legión, ed., 254. Hills, 138.

10. *DOL, Negociado de campaña*, 8-31 January 1925, 38. *SHM*, Legajo #54, Rollo 16, *Colección de historiales*, "Campañas de Marruecos, Historial de guerra, 1ª y 2ª Banderas," 187, has all the activities of the IInd *Bandera* during the month of January.

11. Woolman, *Rebels in the Rif*, 161-163; Pennell, 178-180; Fleming, *Primo de Rivera*, 210-212; Payne, 217; and García Figueras, 203. Furneaux, 133-136, has a good description of el Raisuni's capture and imprisonment. De La Cierva, 243-244, recorded that Abd-el-Krim gave Ahmed Heriro the following blunt order regarding el Raisuni: "*Cázame al perro*" ("Hunt down that dog for me"). Page 245 has two photographs that depict the final episodes in the life of el Raisuni. Salas Larrazábal, 159-160, wrote that el Raisuni was taken prisoner on January 27 and died on May 4, having failed in his goal of being named the khalif of the Spanish Protectorate of Morocco. He also refers to Ahmed Heriro as "el Chaui." Hills, 138. *SHM*, Legajo #54, Rollo 16, *Colección de historiales*, "Campañas de Marruecos, Historial de guerra, 1ª y 2ª Banderas," 198.

12. De La Cierva, 243, wrote that the command structure of the Legion was changed so that Franco could stay on as its commander in chief. Cano Velasco, ed., 156. De Galinsoga, 110. Payne, 217, observed that through the winter of 1924-1925, the Legion underwent many changes:

The salaries of both officers and men, always comparatively high, were raised even higher. When not in the field, the men of the Tercio ate the best food the Army could provide. Discipline and conduct remained brutal, but *esprit de corps* was improving and executions for insubordination were becoming rarer. Early scandals, such as instances of Tercio officers being shot in the back by their own troops, had all but been forgotten. On the other hand, the rest of the Army, still inadequately cared for, looked on the shock troops with envy and dislike.

De Arce, 181-182, recorded that besides being promoted to colonel, Franco was also awarded his fourth Cross of Military Merit (*Cruz al Mérito Militar*). In addition, at Tauima, the Legion's headquarters in the Melillan sector, a farm was established just like the one at Riffien. Preston, 46; García Figueras, 204; and Scurr, 15. Crozier, 82, noted that Franco was promoted to the rank of colonel based on "battle merits."

13. *AGM*, Legajo #246, SECCIÓN 20, DIVISIÓN 100, contains all the important information on the changes proposed for the Legion and includes such documentation as *Proyecto de plantillas para la futura organización del Tercio de Extranjeros, remitidas por el General encargado del Despacho* (February 1925), a telegram (#24, 6 February 1925), and letter from the Operations Section (*Sección Operaciones*) of the General Staff of the Spanish army in Africa (*Ejército de España en África-E.M.*), between Tetuán and Madrid, dated 9 February 1925, which details the organization of the Legion's units. Furthermore, there is a document entitled *Reorganización del Tercio de Extranjeros* (Reorganization of the Tercio of Foreigners) dated 2 February 1925 that details how the new Tercio was to be organized (composed of two legions, one based in Ceuta and the other in Melilla, and each legion is to be composed of four *Banderas* for a total of 9,000 men), with charts and diagrams. It is interesting to note that the charts and diagrams (for the Tercio, each legion,

each *Bandera*, and the Squadron), entitled *Proyecto de plantillas del Tercio de Extranjeros*, has the word *"Extranjeros"* crossed out, reflecting the name change that took place on 16 February. *SHM*, Legajo #54, Rollo 16, *Colección de historiales*, "Campañas de Marruecos, Historial de guerra, 1ª y 2ª Banderas," 187-188, details the actions of the IInd *Bandera*.

14. Bueno, *La Legión*, 60-63, has more on the changes in uniform and gear, as well as Bueno's drawings detailing the new uniforms. De La Cierva, 243.

15. Subinspección de la Legión, ed., 254. *SHM*, ROC (16-II-1925), CL #37, 59, DO #37 (17-II-1925), 455. This ROC permitted the Legion (or the *Tercio de Marruecos*) to increase its size by 15 percent. *AGM*, Legajo #246, SECCIÓN #2, DIVISIÓN #10, contains a letter dated 19 September 1925 entitled *"Se incrementa la plantilla del Tercio en SIETE Capitanes y VEINTICUATRO subalternos,"* which authorized the Legion to increase its ranks by seven captains and twenty-four subalterns. It was approved by the king by way of a Royal Order. Cano Velasco, ed., 156. Scurr, 15.

16. *SHM*, ROC (2-III-1925), CL #52, 76, DO #316, 48. This ROC not only changed the name from *Tercio de Marruecos* to *El Tercio*, but it also stipulated that its members be called *legionarios* (Legionaries). *AGM*, Legajo #246, SECCIÓN 20 - DIVISIÓN 100, has a copy of the ROC (two pages and dated 2-3 March 1925) with the title *Denominaciones* (Denominations). Subinspección de la Legión, ed., 254; García Figueras, 204; Scurr, 15; and Cano Velasco, ed., 156. On 1 March, the six *Banderas* of the Legion were posted as follows: the Ist and Vth at R'Gaia; the IInd at T'Zenin; the IIIrd at Ben Tieb (eastern zone); the IVth at Riffien; and the VIth at Rio Martín. See, *DOL*, *Negociado de campaña*, 1 March 1925, 38.

17. *DOL*, *Negociado de campaña*, 19 March 1925, 38. Ramas Izquierdo, 30, has more on the death of Captain Gabriel Navarrete Navarrete, who was awarded the Individual Military Medal for his bravery during the battle.

18. *DOL*, *Negociado de campaña*, 30 March 1925, 38. Fleming, *Primo de Rivera*, 204-205, noted that Primo de Rivera referred to the Alcazarseguer operation as this *"modesta operación"* (modest operation), and that the rebellion in Anyera was not extinguished completely until 15 March 1926, nearly an entire year after the landing. Cano Velasco, ed., 156, gave the credit to the IVth *Bandera* (with the 16th Company hitting the beach first, followed by the 10th and 11th Companies) of the Legion, but he failed to mention the contribution of the VIth *Bandera*. García Figueras, 204; and Bolín, 84. De La Cierva, 243, observed that with the success attained by the Spanish at Alcazarseguer, *"Alhucemas era posible"* ("Alhucemas was possible"). This source also has two nice photos of the shoreline and beaches of Alcazarseguer. Page 245 has a period photograph of the *Arcila* which transported Franco to the Alcazarseguer landing. It was aboard the *Arcila* that day that Franco fortuitously met *Alférez de navio* (Ensign) Luis Carrero Blanco who would later rise to become the most powerful man in Spain after Franco himself. Admiral Carrero Blanco was literally blown sky high in his Dodge Dart by ETA (Basque extremists) in Madrid on 20 December 1973. See 479 for more details. De La Cierva, *Franco*, 84-85. Preston, 47. Trythall, 49, wrote that the capture of Alcazarseguer secured the lines of communication between Ceuta and Tangier. Quintana Martínez and Llabres Bernal, 235. *Jane's Fighting Ships*, ed., 332, has more information on the armed trawler *Arcila*. Hills, 143 (n. 28), noted that Alcazarseguer was not the first amphibious operation. He wrote, "In

point of time, therefore, this [the rescue of the Uad Lau garrison in November 1924] must be considered Spain's first essay in combined operations." It is important to keep in mind, however, that whereas Uad Lau was basically an extraction of forces, Alcazarseguer was an insertion on a larger scale.

19. *DOL, Negociado de campaña*, 1-30 April 1925, 38-39; and *SHM*, Legajo #54, Rollo 16, *Colección de historiales*, "Campañas de Marruecos, Historial de guerra, 1ª y 2ª Banderas" (3ª Bandera), 196-197.

20. Payne, 217-218.

21. Woolman, "In Spanish Morocco," 84, wrote that like the Spanish, the French attempted to control their borders by way of a chain of small outposts. Consequently, they had to deal with exactly the same difficulties of supplying and defending these outposts. In dozens of places within the French zone, Annual-like carnage was repeated, with both sides committing horrifying atrocities. For more detailed information on Abd-el-Krim's attack on the French protectorate, see William A. Hoisington, *Lyautey and the French Conquest of Morocco* (New York: St. Martin's Press, 1995), 190-204; Pennell, 185-191; Woolman, *Rebels in the Rif*, 164-179; Petrie, 187-188; Payne, 218-219; Furneaux, 146-200; Estado Mayor Central del Ejército, 16-20; De La Cierva, 244-248; Salas Larrazábal, 160; García Figueras, 204; Llacuna and Polls, 46; and Fleming, *Primo de Rivera*, 229-240.

22. Fleming, *Primo de Rivera*, 215-217.

23. *DOL, Negociado de campaña*, 1-30 May 1925, 39. From the first of May through the 30th of June, the Legion carried out its usual campaign duties with no major battles taking place during the month. *SHM*, Legajo #54, Rollo 16, *Colección de historiales*, "Campañas de Marruecos, Historial de guerra, 1ª y 2ª Banderas," 188, has the details on the actions and movements of the IInd *Bandera*.

24. *DOL, Negociado de campaña*, 1 May 1925, 39. Subinspección de la Legión, ed., 254. Bueno, *La Legión*, 10 and 48-53, has more on the Squadron of Lancers. Scurr, 15.

25. Scurr, 15. Subinspección de la Legión, ed., 254-255. Cano Velasco, ed., 156-157, noted that the new Legion was now composed of "241 commanding officers [*Bandera* commanders] and officers, 56 contract workers [tradesmen], and 7,716 Legionaries, and with 1,370 heads of livestock between horses and mules. The Squadron of Lancers had 159 men and 169 horses, including riding and draught horses. Each *Bandera* had 830 men, and the [each] Legion had a total of 3,450 men." Fleming, *Primo de Rivera*, 212, recorded that with the addition of the VIIth *Bandera*, the new Legion had a total of 251 officers and 7,716 men. Llacuna and Polls, 48. De La Cierva, 255, wrote that the Legionaries themselves referred to the larger unit as "the Legion," and the two smaller (4) *Bandera* groupings as "Tercios."

26. Scurr, 15, wrote that "by June, 43 out of 66 forward posts had fallen and more than 3,000 French troops were dead or missing." Cano Velasco, ed., 157, noted that the French defeat was similar to the Spaniard's defeat at Annual, but that the facts and figures were well concealed, and that Fez was in the same position that Melilla had been in in 1921. Payne, 219. Petrie, 188, noted that "by the end of June, 1925, the forces in Morocco had been increased by some fifty per cent [they originally had 60,000 men], though this had only been rendered possible by the evacuation of the Ruhr [Germany]." Martin Windrow,

French Foreign Legion, Osprey Men-at-Arms Series (Reading, Berkshire, England: Osprey Publications, 1971), 26, noted that "two fresh [French Foreign] Legion battalions were rushed in." Woolman, "In Spanish Morocco," 85, stated that "the French were forced to call up 100,000 reinforcements." Woolman, *Rebels in the Rif*, 177 and 183-185. For more on the actions of the French Foreign Legion during the campaign against Abd-el-Krim, see Douglas Porch, *The French Foreign Legion: A Complete History of the Legendary Fighting Force* (New York: HarperCollins Publishers, 1991), 399-408; Prince Aage of Denmark, *My Life in the Foreign Legion* (London: Eveleigh Nash & Grayson, 1928), 159-204; Major Zinovi Pechkoff, *The Bugle Sounds*, with a preface by Andre Maurois (New York and London: D. Appleton and Company, 1926), 139-193; and George R. Manue, *Têtes Brûlées: Cinq ans de legion* (n.p.: La Nouvelle Societe D'Edition, 1929), 222-235. De Arce, 181, wrote that to try to stop the Riffian onslaught, the French sent "18 battalions of Infantry, 6 squadrons of Cavalry and 12 batteries" to Morocco. Hills, 138. De La Cierva, 251, gave the number of soldiers sent by France to Morocco in order to counterattack Abd-el-Krim's forces as 100 battalions of infantry plus their support services. For more on Lyautey, see Hoisington, 185-204.

        27. Furneaux, 132, has the full quote on Primo de Rivera's comments to journalist Webb Miller regarding Abd-el-Krim attacking the French after he had finished with the Spanish. Gómez-Jordana y Souza, 75-98, has the most complete information on the Franco-Hispano Conference, since he presided at the conference. Quintana Martínez and Llabres Bernal, 240, noted the names of those who participated in the talks. Fleming, *Primo de Rivera*, 247-255. Salas Larrazábal, 160-163, noted that Pétain and Primo de Rivera met in Algeciras. He also has a nice summary of the major points of the agreement. Petrie, 188. De Arce, 182, wrote that the Spanish and French agreed that France would contribute 160,000 men, the majority being colonial troops and attacking from the south (i.e., northward), and the Spanish would contribute 75,000 men, mostly Europeans, who would land at Alhucemas Bay and drive inland and inward (i.e., southward). Scurr, 15, noted that of the Spanish forces in the operation, 18,000 would land at Alhucemas Bay and 57,000 would attack from Spain's eastern zone. Estado Mayor Central del Ejército, 20-21. Arraras, ed., 191. De La Cierva, 247-250. Page 247 has a photograph of those who took part in the Franco-Hispano Conference. García Figueras, 205-206. Llacuna and Polls, 46. Vaughan, 6, gave the number of French participants in the operation as 150,000, indicating that they formed "six mutually supporting columns" with Targuist (Abd-el-Krim's headquarters) as their goal. Woolman, *Rebels in the Rif*, 179-182. Pennell, 196, observed, "The mauling which the Riffis gave the French may have made them euphoric, but it sealed their doom." Preston, 47. Xavier Huetz de Lemps, "la collaboration franco-espagnole pendant la guerre du rif (1925-1927): un mariage d'amour ou de raison?" *Hesperis Tamuda* vol. 29, fasc. 1 (1991): 85-111. Recent scholarship on the relationship between Spain and France concerning the Rif Rebellion.

        28. *DOL, Negociado de campaña*, 1 July 1925, 39; and *SHM*, Legajo #54, Rollo 16, *Colección de historiales*, "Campañas de Marruecos, Historial de guerra, 1ª y 2ª Banderas," 188, deals with the actions of the IInd *Bandera*.

        29. *DOL, Negociado de campaña*, 4 July 1925, 39-40. Also 7 July-31 August 1925. *SHM*, Legajo #54, Rollo 16, *Colección de historiales*, "Legislación relativa a la

Legión," Año 1.925. By ROC of (21-VII-1925), CL #222, the personnel of the *Tercio de Marruecos* was established based on two legions, with four *Banderas* each, and one depot *Bandera*. De La Cierva, 251, recorded that on 25 July 1925, Primo de Rivera named the young Muley Hassan Ben Muley el Mehdi Ben Muley Ismail Ben Muley Hassan to be the new khalif of the Spanish Protectorate of Morocco with his headquarters in Tetuán. However, this information was not announced publicly until a substantial victory against Abd-el-Krim had been won.   Furthermore, on 20 August, Abd-el-Krim's artillery overlooking Alhucemas Bay opened fire on the Spanish-held Peñón de Alhucemas (800 meters away).   An artillery duel between the Riffians' fifty-plus cannons versus the Spaniards' eight batteries (32 pieces) raged for a few hours with serious injuries to Spanish personnel (the commanding officer, Colonel Monasterio, was killed by a shell fragment), but the Spanish gunners were able to silence a few of the Riffian guns. Morales Lezcano, 237, recorded that Muley Hassan Ben el-Mehdi was publicly proclaimed the new khalif (*Jalifa*) on 8-10 November 1925. Woolman, *Rebels in the Rif,* 195. The new khalif was the son of the first khalif. Quintana Martínez and Llabres Bernal, 252, noted that on 22-23 July, General Sanjurjo ordered the battleship *Alfonso XIII* into Alhucemas Bay to shell the Riffian positions. Cano Velasco, ed., 157.

30. Payne, 110, noted that it was first proposed by the then war minister, General Arsenio Linares y Pombo. Fleming, *Primo de Rivera*, 263-277.

31. Arraras, ed., 191, recorded that Marshal Lyautey would later remark that "Franco and Graziani are the two most outstanding soldiers of our time." Woolman, *Rebels in the Rif,* 193, wrote that Lyautey had said the following of Franco: "Spain has only one man in Africa—Franco." Lyautey's complimentary statement regarding Franco's martial skill seems out of character for one who General Gómez-Jordana y Souza said was a "Hispanophobe at heart." See Cano Velasco, ed., 157. Franco had for a long time stated and wrote in his book that Alhucemas was the seat of the rebellion. For more on Franco's thoughts on Alhucemas, and the need for a landing there, see Crozier, 82-84; and De Galinsoga, 110-111. Llacuna and Polls, 47, called Alhucemas Bay "the lung[s] of the insurrection." Manuel Castellanos, *Historia de Marruecos*, vol. II, 4th ed. (Madrid, 1946), 264, stated: "Alhucemas, [was the] key to the Moroccan problem." For the Spanish military's plans for an amphibious landing at Alhucemas, going back to 1912, see Estado Mayor Central del Ejército, Chapter 2; and Gómez-Jordana y Souza, 99-121. On the first day of September, the Legion was deployed as follows: The Ist *Bandera* remained at Dar Quebdani; the IInd was at Yazanen; the IIIrd was now in Melilla; the IVth was at Raremel; the Vth was at R'Gaia, while the VIth and the VIIth *Banderas*, as well as the Squadron of Lancers, were in Riffien in preparation for the Alhucemas Bay landing. See, *DOL*, *Negociado de campaña*, 1 September 1925, 40; and *SHM*, Legajo #54, Rollo 16, *Colección de historiales*, "Campañas de Marruecos, Historial de guerra, 1ª y 2ª Banderas," 188.

32. De La Cierva, 250, stated that Franco told him that while he was preparing the operation, he read as much as he could on amphibious landings, especially the ones that were "tragically frustrated at the Dardanelles," and that the "specter of Gallipoli presided" during the planning phase. It is interesting to note that Manuel Goded Llopis, Joaquín Fanjul Goni, Antonio Aranda Mata, and Antonio Barroso y Sánchez-Guerra all joined the rebels in 1936. Goded was executed during the first days in Barcelona; Fanjul sought refuge

in the Montaña Barracks in Madrid but was executed after the Republicans violently stormed the place; Aranda was in Oviedo (Asturias), where he was able to outwit the radical miners and secured the city for the rebels; and Barroso became one of Franco's personal adjutants, one of the most capable staff officers in his Nationalist army. For more on the Spanish Civil War deeds of the aforementioned officers, see Thomas, and Payne.

33. Furneaux, 201-203, stated that Abd-el-Krim had no fear of the Spanish army, but he was concerned about the Spanish navy, since he had never engaged it in formal battle; they were "an unknown quantity." Abd-el-Krim also believed that the Spanish-French alliance would eventually collapse. Llacuna and Polls, 48.

34. De La Cierva, 251. For more on all the units that took part in the Alhucemas Bay landing, see Appendix H. *SHM*, Legajo #54, Rollo 16, *Colección de historiales*, "Campañas de Marruecos, Historial de guerra, 1ª y 2ª Banderas," 198. Cano Velasco, ed., 157.

35. Woolman, *Rebels in the Rif*, 188, wrote that Primo de Rivera had dropped leaflets printed in Arabic, which stated that the Rif would soon be invaded and that Abd-el-Krim would be captured and punished for his rebellion. The tribesmen were given three days to surrender, but none did. Pennell, 198.

36. De La Cierva, 251-252, observed that Abd-el-Krim had said on more than one occasion that "if they disembark at Alhucemas, I will take Tetuán" ("*Si ellos desembarcan en Alhucemas, yo tomare Tetuán*"). *SHM*, Legajo #54, Rollo 16, *Colección de historiales*, "Campañas de Marruecos, Historial de guerra, 1ª y 2ª Banderas" (3ª Bandera), 199-200. Estado Mayor Central del Ejército, 59-60. Furneaux, 203, noted that Abd-el-Krim had hoped for "the *levante*, the strong gale-force wind which blows down the Mediterranean in September, [which] was due." Arraras, ed., 191, wrote that Primo de Rivera told those who doubted or objected to the invasion, "The wind of the levante will not blow" ("*No soplara el viento de levante*"). This quotation ("*No soplara*") also appears in De La Cierva, 254.

37. Subinspección de la Legión, ed., 255, noted that whereas Colonel Franco would command the vanguard of the Ceuta column (Saro), Colonel Manuel Goded Llopis would command the vanguard of the Melilla column (Fernández Pérez). Cano Velasco, ed., 157-158, noted that on 3 September, the IInd and IIIrd *Banderas* boarded the steamer *Alhambra* in Melilla and practiced a landing at Punta Negri, located west of the city. Before setting sail from Ceuta, the VIth and VIIth *Banderas* loaded their "K's" (K-21 and K-23) with ammunition, food, and other field gear. *DOL*, *Negociado de campaña*, 5 September 1925, 40. The IInd and IIIrd *Banderas* headed for Alhucemas Bay, while the VIth and VIIth *Banderas* set out at 2000 hours toward Rio Martín, where the rest of the invasion fleet awaited. Also on 5 September, the Vth *Bandera*, under the leadership of its temporary commander, Captain Fernando Bernabe Ortiz de Esparraguera, assisted in escorting a convoy to Kudia Menar. In fierce hand-to-hand fighting with the enemy, the Legion suffered two officers, Captain Antonio Cabaledia and *Alférez* José Carrera (*sic*), and eleven Legionaries killed, with one officer and thirty-six Legionaries wounded. Ramas Izquierdo, 250-254, has all the details on the convoy to Kudia Menar engagement. For more on the deaths of Captain Antonio Caval Hevia and *Alférez* José Cervera y García de Paredes, see 30 and 50, respectively. See also De Galinsoga, 111; Crozier, 84; Hills, 138; and Trythall, 50. Rafael López Rienda, *Abd-el-Krim contra Francia: Impresiones de un cronista de*

guerra (Madrid: Calpe, 1925), 240-333, details his personal, eyewitness account of the Alhucemas Bay landings from 5 September, to the capture of Axdir in early October.

38. Woolman, *Rebels in the Rif*, 188-189; Furneaux, 203-204; Estado Mayor del Ejército, 60-62; and Llacuna and Polls, 48.

39. *DOL, Negociado de campaña*, 6 September 1925, 40. Cano Velasco, ed., 158, recorded that from the Ceuta column, various companies from the two *Banderas* boarded their landing crafts and headed toward the beaches of Uad Lau, only to return to the mother ships. This exercise was also repeated at Targa, M'Ter, and Tiguisas. Estado Mayor Central del Ejército, 57-58. De Galinsoga, 112-113. This source, which quotes from Franco's diary, gives an excellent insight into what transpired around Franco during those momentous days.

40. *DOL, Negociado de campaña*, 7 September 1925, 40. *SHM*, Legajo #54, Rollo 16, *Colección de historiales*, "Campañas de Marruecos, Historial de guerra, 1ª y 2ª Banderas" (3ª Bandera), 199. The Ist *Bandera* from its encampment at Afrau also participated in the attack on Sidi Dris in early September. Gómez-Jordana y Souza, 99-151, gives the background to the landing, as well as covering the landing itself. Cano Velasco, ed., 158, wrote that the VIth and VIIth *Banderas* made another landing threat at Sidi Dris on the Temsaman coast (Woolman said this was done by the IInd and IIIrd *Banderas* coming from Melilla) and was also subjected to intense naval gunfire from the combined Franco-Hispano squadron of thirty-eight Spanish and eight French ships. Estado Mayor Central del Ejército, 49-50, 53, and 58-59. The French fleet, which had sailed from Oran, provided protection for the Melilla column. Goded, 182-186 and 193-196, detailed the final orders and preparations for the disembarkation scheduled for the following morning. Of the eight French ships that made up the invasion fleet, three were capital ships: the battleship *Paris* (flagship of Admiral Hallier) and the cruisers *Metz* (ex-SMS *Königsberg*) and *Strasbourg* (ex-SMS *Regensburg*). For more information on, and photos of, the three French capital ships, see *Jane's Fighting Ships*, ed. 1925, 158 and 164, respectively. Woolman, *Rebels in the Rif*, 190, wrote that the original date set for the invasion was 7 September, but the Ceuta column had been detained by unfavorable currents. Primo de Rivera was going to carry out his plan of invasion. He stated, "I promised Marshal Pétain I would disembark, and I will disembark, whatever it costs." De Galinsoga, 113, has "Day 7" from Franco's war diary. Scurr, 16. Arraras, ed., 191, has two nice photos of the "K's" and the support ships at Alhucemas Bay. Fleming, *Primo de Rivera*, 263-285. Preston, 47. Furneaux, 204.

41. *Crónica de la aviación*, 219. The Breguet XIX, one of the most advanced planes in the Spanish air force, flew over the beaches of Alhucemas Bay.

42. *DOL, Negociado de campaña*, 8 September 1925, 40-41, noted that in combat with the enemy, the Legion had suffered three Legionaries killed and fourteen wounded. Cano Velasco, ed., 158, gave the casualty figures for the Legion as four dead and nine wounded. The author also wrote that it was the 21st Company, not the 24th, that first set foot on the enemy beach. Llacuna and Polls, 49-50. Garriga, 50-51. On 50, the author noted that Franco disembarked on La Cebadilla beach. Subinspección de la Legión, ed., 256-257, noted that the VIth *Bandera* was transported to shore aboard the *K.21* and the *K.23*, towed by the tugboats *Ferrolano* and the *Gaditano*. This source also has four

photographs taken of the disembarkation. Ramas Izquierdo, 254-260, noted that because the landing crafts were fifty meters out and thus unable to reach the shore, the tanks brought to precede and support the landing could not be unloaded. Scurr, 16. For all Spanish forces, the casualty count was 124. The ten light tanks (*FT-17*s) were eventually landed at Los Frailes beach. De Galinsoga, 113-117, "Day 8" deals with the Alhucemas Bay landing, and as Franco wrote in his diary, "Those defenders who are excessively tenacious are put to the knife." Estado Mayor Central del Ejército, 59 and 64-67. Goded, 196-200, related that the soldiers ironically named Los Frailes beach Misery Beach (*Playa de la Miseria*); and La Cebadilla, Biarritz. De Arce, 182-183. Petrie, 188-189. Arraras, ed., 192, recorded that Captain Rodríguez Bescansa was the first man to step ashore. José M. Fiestas, ed., *Guía del Museo del Ejército* (Madrid: Privately printed, 1984), 84. Pennell, 199, noted that 5,000 Riffians opposed the Spaniards at Alhucemas. Fleming, *Primo de Rivera*, 285-299. De La Cierva, *Franco: Un siglo*, 255-265. A solid narrative with great photos of the landings. De La Cierva, *Franco*, 89, wrote that the large bombs were subsequently disarmed by sappers from the engineers. Preston, 47-48. Hills, 139. Trythall, 50. Castellanos, 266, described the journey of the "K's" towards shore thus: "The black landing barges raised at the prow, with their strange primitive vessel appearance, plough through the sea producing large amounts of spray." Woolman, *Rebels in the Rif*, 190-191. Woolman observed that "there were special floating docks built specifically for use during the Alhucemas operations." Furneaux, 204-208, noted that Abd-el-Krim was not strong enough to defend every beach in the targeted area, so he gambled on strongly defending Alhucemas and Ajdir. "Like von Rundstedt and Rommel in 1944, Abdel Krim failed to perceive which landing was the real thing and which was the diversion planned to deceive him."

43. Cano Velasco, ed., 158. Subinspección de la Legión, ed., 257. *SHM*, Legajo #54, Rollo 16, *Colección de historiales*, "Campañas de Marruecos, Historial de guerra, 1ª y 2ª Banderas" (3ª Bandera), 200. Woolman, *Rebels in the Rif*, 189.

44. *DOL*, *Negociado de campaña*, 9-10 September 1925, 41; and Estado Mayor Central del Ejército, 68.

45. *DOL*, *Negociado de campaña*, 9-10 September 1925, 41. Llacuna and Polls, 51, observed that on 10 September, the French launched their agreed-upon offensive along the Uarga/Wergha River, catching Abd-el-Krim between themselves and the Spanish. Woolman, *Rebels in the Rif*, 193-194. Goded, 200-206, recounted the arrival and unloading of the Melilla column on 11 September.

46. *DOL*, *Negociado de campaña*, 11-13 September 1925, 41. Ramas Izquierdo, 260-268, gives an excellent narrative of the battle of Kudia Tahar, which includes the instructions given by Primo de Rivera to the troops, an account of the battle by LTC Balmes, and a battlefield report published on 26 September 1925 in the Spanish newspaper *ABC*. For more on the death of Lieutenant Inocencio Real Herrainz, see 39. Subinspección de la Legión, ed., 257-263, also provides a first-rate account of the battle. *SHM*, Legajo #54, Rollo 16, *Colección de historiales*, "Campañas de Marruecos, Historial de guerra, 1ª y 2ª Banderas" (3ª Bandera), 200-202. Estado Mayor Central del Ejército, 62-63, lists all the units that took part in the battle of Kudia Tahar. Goded, 187-192. Cano Velasco, ed., 158. Fleming, *Primo de Rivera*, 299-301. Scurr, 16, noted that of the 200 defenders at Kudia Tahar, 176 had been killed by 8 September. De Arce, 183. For his valor at Kudia Tahar,

Major García Escamez, commander of the IIIrd *Bandera*, was awarded the Laureate Cross of St. Ferdinand. Woolman, *Rebels in the Rif*, 190, noted that Primo de Rivera was so pleased with the fighting spirit of those who survived the siege of Kudia Tahar that he "personally gave each one a cigar and 25 duros [1 *duro* = 5 *pesetas*]."

47. Furneaux, 204. Woolman, *Rebels in the Rif*, 201, has more details on the Legion's parade before Primo de Rivera in Tetuán when they carried various body parts ("severed arms, bunches of ears skewered together, hearts," etc.) impaled on their bayonets. Payne, 220, wrote that the practice of collecting human trophies was typical among the shock troops (e.g., the Legion, not the *Regulares*) during the Rif Rebellion, but it did not agree with Primo de Rivera's idea of civilized warfare.

48. Sablotny, 297.

49. Llacuna and Polls, 51.

50. *DOL*, *Negociado de campaña*, 14-18 September 1925, 41.

51. *DOL*, *Negociado de campaña*, 19 September 1925, 41. Cano Velasco, ed., 158. *SHM*, Legajo #54, Rollo 16, *Colección de historiales*, "Campañas de Marruecos, Historial de guerra, 1ª y 2ª Banderas" (3ª Bandera), 202. Goded, 206-211, chronicles the events that took place at the Alhucemas beachhead between 12 September and 22 September, when unloading the necessary supplies of water, food, and munitions was threatened by the inclement weather. The men were living off canned sardines and seawater-soaked hardtack. The successful landing was in danger of suffering a severe setback because not enough matériel could be brought ashore. Fortunately for the Spaniards, the Riffians lacked the strength to attack during this vulnerable time. Preston, 48.

52. Woolman, *Rebels in the Rif*, 191-192; Pennell, 199; and Fleming, *Primo de Rivera*, 301-304.

53. *DOL*, *Negociado de campaña*, 21 September 1925, 41. Although listed as 21 September in the *DOL*, the battle for Monte Malmusi took place on 23 September. Ramas Izquierdo, 268-272. For more details on the death of Lieutenant José Espinosa Orive, see 39-40, and for *Alféreces* Antonio Lorente de Nó, Julio Jiménez Aguirre, and Antonio Navarro Miegimolle, see 50-51. For their bravery above and beyond the call of duty, Lieutenant José Espinosa Orive and *Alférez* Antonio Navarro Miegimolle were both posthumously awarded the Laureate Cross of St. Ferdinand. Subinspección de la Legión, ed., 263-266, recorded the casualties for the VIIth and VIIIth [*sic*] *Banderas* as sixteen officers and 199 Legionaries either dead or wounded. The VIIIth *Bandera* was not created until 1 January 1926. Cano Velasco, ed., 160. *SHM*, Legajo #54, Rollo 16, *Colección de historiales*, "Campañas de Marruecos, Historial de guerra, 1ª y 2ª Banderas" (3ª Bandera), 202-204. Estado Mayor Central del Ejército, 72-81, has a thorough account of the battle as well as a listing of all the units that took part in the battle. Goded, 210-219, provides an excellent description of the battle and his personal experiences during it. De Galinsoga, 118; Scurr, 16-17; de Arce, 183; Pennell, 199; and Arraras, ed., 192. Payne, 220-221, noted that Abd-el-Krim's forces now began to desert in large numbers. Also see De La Cierva, 267-269; Furneaux, 212; Crozier, 85; Trythall, 50-51; and Hills, 139-140.

54. Fleming, *Primo de Rivera*, 301-305.

55. *DOL*, *Negociado de campaña*, 24-29 September 1925, 41-42. Ramas

Izquierdo, 40, has more on the death of Lieutenant José Casado Bustos of the VIIth *Bandera* and, on 24-25, on Major Francisco Borras Estevez of the IInd *Bandera*.

    56. *DOL, Negociado de campaña*, 30 September 1925, 42. Subinspección de la Legión, ed., 266-267. The casualty list in this source for the IInd and IIIrd *Banderas* was one officer and one Legionary killed, one officer and two Legionaries wounded. For the VIth and VIIth *Banderas* it was two officers wounded, four Legionaries dead and forty-two wounded. *SHM*, Legajo #54, Rollo 16, *Colección de historiales*, "Campañas de Marruecos, Historial de guerra, 1ª y 2ª Banderas" (3ª Bandera), 204. Ramas Izquierdo, 273-275. See 40 for more on the death of Lieutenant Raimundo López García, and 51 for *Alférez* Eduardo Trello/Trelles Moreno. Cano Velasco, ed., 160, noted that in the two battles (23 and 30 September), the four *Banderas* had 182 casualties, the same as had been sustained at Tizzi-Azza. Scurr, 17, added that the heights of Conico and the Buyibar Valley (the Monte Palomas-Monte Conico-Buyibar line) were also captured by the Melilla column (IInd and IIIrd *Banderas*). Estado Mayor Central del Ejército, 82-87, gives the big picture of the operation from planning to execution. Goded, 220-226, provides a detailed narrative of the battle for las Palomas. Also see, Llacuna and Polls, 51; Fleming, *Primo de Rivera*, 306-307; De La Cierva, 269-270; Arraras, ed., 192; De Galinsoga, 119; and Furneaux, 213.

    57. *DOL, Negociado de campaña*, 1 October 1925, 42. On 1 October the seven *Banderas* and the Squadron of Lancers were deployed as follows: the Ist was at Afrau; the IInd, VIth, and VIIth were at las Palomas; the IIIrd was at Morro Viejo; the IVth was at R'Gaia; the Vth was at Riffien; and the Squadron of Lancers was at T'Zenin. Subinspección de la Legión, ed., 267; and *SHM*, Legajo #54, Rollo 16, *Colección de historiales*, "Campañas de Marruecos, Historial de guerra, 1ª y 2ª Banderas" (3ª Bandera), 205. Goded, 226-231, has all the details on the Adrar Sedun operation. Estado Mayor Central del Ejército, 88-91. Cano Velasco, ed., 160. Arraras, ed., 192. Fleming, *Primo de Rivera*, 307.

    58. Scurr, 17.

    59. *DOL, Negociado de campaña*, 2-12 October 1925, 42. *SHM*, Legajo #54, Rollo 16, *Colección de historiales*, "Campañas de Marruecos, Historial de guerra, 1ª y 2ª Banderas" (3ª Bandera), 205-206, recorded that members of the IInd *Bandera* entered Axdir/Ajdir and participated in razing the Riffian capital. Subinspección de la Legión, ed., 267; Estado Mayor Central del Ejército, 91; and Goded, 231-233. Sablotny, 268-269, described Ajdir and the fortifications he saw when he passed through it in 1924. Furneaux, 213, wrote that Primo de Rivera offered the Riffians the opportunity to surrender (within three days), but this offer was not extended to Abd-el-Krim, who had to be punished. Payne, 221, wrote that as their supply of weapons and ammunition began to run out, the rebels swiftly fell back. Scurr, 17, noted that on 8 October, Spanish and French forces linked up at Zoco el Telata. Pennell, 199. Fleming, *Primo de Rivera*, 307-308. De La Cierva, 271-272.

    60. *DOL, Negociado de campaña*, 13 October 1925, 42; *SHM*, Legajo #54, Rollo 16, *Colección de historiales*, "Campañas de Marruecos, Historial de guerra, 1ª y 2 Banderas" (3ª Bandera), 206; Subinspección de la Legión, ed., 268; and Estado Mayor Central del Ejército, 91-93. Cano Velasco, ed., 160. While the IInd was operating in the area in and around Calvet and Amekran Bajo, the IIIrd was in the Ajdir sector and occupied La Rocosa. Goded, 234.

61. *DOL, Negociado de campaña*, 14-31 October 1925, 42-43. Subinspección de la Legión, ed., 268. Ramas Izquierdo, 25, has more on the death of Major Manuel Ordaz Sampayo (commanding officer of the IInd *Bandera*). It is interesting to note that during the Rif Rebellion, the Legion saw four majors (*comandantes*) killed in action, each in command of the IInd *Bandera* when he died. *SHM*, Legajo #54, Rollo 16, *Colección de historiales*, "Campañas de Marruecos, Historial de guerra, 1ª y 2ª Banderas" (3ª Bandera), 206. Goded, 235-238.

62. Fleming, *Primo de Rivera*, 310. Woolman, *Rebels in the Rif*, 195. Sanjurjo would not only be promoted to lieutenant general but also be appointed, on 2 November, the new High Commissioner of the Spanish Protectorate of Morocco, replacing Primo de Rivera.

63. *DOL, Negociado de campaña*, 1 November 1925, 43. On 1 November the Legion was deployed as follows: the Ist *Bandera* was at Dar Quebdani; the IInd at Calvet; the IIIrd at La Rocosa; the IVth at R'Gaia; the Vth at Riffien; the VIth and VIIth were at las Palomas, and the Squadron of Lancers remained at T'Zenin.

64. *DOL, Negociado de campaña*, 2 November-31 December 1925, 43. Cano Velasco, ed., 160. Subinspección de la Legión, ed., 268. This source also contains a brief listing of the major actions of the Legion during 1925, on 515-516. De La Cierva, 272. For a brief summary of the major events of the Ist, IInd, IIIrd, IVth, Vth, and VIth *Banderas*, see *SHM*, Legajo #54, Rollo 16, *Colección de historiales*, La Legión, "Acciones de guerra de las distintas Banderas de la Legión (1920-1939)," 4, 11, 16, 22, 27, and 32, respectively.

65. Woolman, *Rebels in the Rif*, 192.

Chapter 7

The Finale: Ajdir, Targuist, and Peace, 1926–1927

The combination of the Alhucemas Bay landings and the French offensive from the south had made the outcome of Abd-el-Krim's rebellion inevitable. Spain and France's joint military effort was too much for Abd-el-Krim. The Spanish army, with the elite Legion (composed of eight *Banderas* and one Squadron of Lancers) and *Regulares* leading the way, had become an efficient fighting machine. After the retreat from Xauen, Primo de Rivera had seen that the army would be improved through better logistical support and training, which naturally led to an improvement in morale. Dissent within Abd-el-Krim's own ranks, enhanced by lack of food, by disease, and by the military impact of Alhucemas, exacerbated his dilemma. Nevertheless, more fighting and dying lay ahead. The Spanish army needed to push the rebels away from Tetuán and reconquer Xauen, which had been abandoned in late 1924, as well as to drive inland from Ajdir toward the heart of the Rif (Targuist) and into the Gomara. However, 1926 and 1927 were basically years of "mopping up" pockets of resistance and consolidating the conquest of Spanish Morocco.

On the first day of January 1926, the seven *Banderas* of the Legion were strategically deployed: The Ist *Bandera* at Dar Quebdani; the IInd at Ben Tieb; the IIIrd at La Rocosa; the IVth at Riffien; the Vth at R'Gaia; the VIth and VIIth at Palomas; and the Squadron of Lancers still at T'Zenin. In addition, the VIIIth *Bandera* was formed on 1 January, with its members coming from other *Banderas* as well as from the depot company. Major Luis Carvajal Aguilar commanded the unit, which chose for its standard the coat of arms of Admiral Christopher Columbus.[1]

Winter's inclement weather had put offensive operations on hold, but the Legionaries continued to carry out their typical campaign duties throughout the months of January and February, resulting in ten Legionaries killed and twenty-four wounded.[2]

Based on *méritos de guerra* earned during the Alhucemas Bay landings, on 3 February Franco was promoted to brigadier general. At 33, he became the youngest general in all of Europe. As a general officer, he was, however, required to relinquish command of the Legion, which was returned to the newly promoted Colonel José Millán Astray y Terreros. Franco assumed command of what Paul Preston called "the most important brigade in the Army, the First Brigade of the First Division in Madrid, composed of two aristocratic regiments, the *Regimiento del Rey* and the *Regimiento de León*."[3]

By a Royal Order dated 9 February (DO #32), Millán Astray assumed command of the Legion. He arrived in Ceuta on 10 February minus his left arm (which had been amputated in late 1924 after his wounding at Fondak), but having lost none of his typical vim and vigor.[4]

A new Spanish-French meeting took place in Madrid in February to discuss the final phase of operations that would bring about the defeat of Abd-el-Krim. France was represented by Marshal Pétain and his chief of staff, General Georges; Spain was represented by Generals Primo de Rivera and Gómez-Jordana. Of the enemy it was said: "He is very weakened, but we must continue to fight him in order to totally defeat him" ("*Está muy quebrantado, pero hay que seguir combatiéndole para derrotarle totalmente*"). They met again in Uazan on 17 March to finalize the necessary preparations, which were to commence during the first two weeks of April.[5] Militarily, the situation began to heat up in February. With the rebellious Anjera tribe finally defeated, the Spaniards in the western zone once again faced their old nemesis, Ahmed Heriro. Even though he had been driven away from the environs of Tetuán after the battle of Kudia Tahar, he had left several cannons concealed in the caves of the Gorgues mountains, which he now used to shell the city. The guns were wheeled out to bombard the city, then wheeled back into their protective caves when Spanish planes, hoping to spot and destroy them, flew overhead. It was necessary to send in ground forces to clean out the rebels from the surrounding heights. The operation was to begin during the first days of March.[6] According to Payne, Ahmed Heriro's artillery attacks on Tetuán "was to some extent a strategic diversion, for [Abd-el-] Krim had learned of the new Franco-Spanish talks and hoped, by throwing his main weight against the Spanish, to encourage dissention or a relaxation of French efforts."[7]

On 1 March, the eight *Banderas* of the Legion were deployed: the Ist at Amekran; the IInd and IIIrd at Ben Tieb; the IVth at Espinosa; Vth and VIIth at Kudia Tahar; the VIth and VIIIth at Ben Karrich; and the Squadron of Lancers now at Laucien. The Legion's *Banderas* were now evenly split between the eastern zone and the western zone, with the first four *Banderas* (Ist-IVth) in the east, and the last four *Banderas* (Vth-VIIIth), plus the Squadron of Lancers in the west.[8]

The first casualties occurred on 2 March, before the start of the operation, when Legionaries bivouacked at Kudia Tahar were subjected to enemy mortar fire. The attack left two Legionaries wounded.[9]

The force chosen to clear the rebels from the Tetuán sector was comprised of four infantry columns and eleven artillery batteries. The two principal assault columns consisted mainly of the Legion (under the command of Colonel Millán Astray) and the *Regulares* (under the command of Colonel Luis Orgaz y Yoldi), along with two support columns (Lieutenant Colonels Aureliano Álvarez Coque and Eduardo Saenz de Buruaga). The attack began on the morning of 4 March. The Legion's role in the operation began with the Vth and VIIth *Banderas* advancing from Kudia Tahar, while the VIth and VIIIth *Banderas* proceeded from Ben Karrich. Their objective for the day was to capture and occupy Loma Redonda. However, strong enemy resistance and spirited assaults by the Legionaries led to heavy casualties among the attackers; eight Legionaries were killed, and three officers and forty-three Legionaries wounded. Among the injured was the hapless Colonel Millán Astray, who was gravely wounded once again, this time in the face. A determined rebel counterattack, which caused many Spanish casualties, rapidly blunted the overall attack. A follow-up attack was called for the following day.[10]

With Millán Astray *hors de combat*, command of the Legion fell to Lieutenant Colonel Juan José de Liniers y Muguiro.[11] The following day, 5 March, the same four *Banderas* under the command of Lieutenant Colonel Luis Valcazar Crespo set out to seize and occupy Hafa el Baira/Haffa del Duira. The ensuing combat left three officers and six Legionaries dead and three officers and eighty-two Legionaries wounded.[12] The operation continued on 6 March with the same four *Banderas* engaged in "mopping up" what remained of the rebels. The day's mission called for taking and occupying Dar Raiz—accomplished at the cost of four Legionaries killed and thirteen wounded. The next day, the four-day operation to drive the enemy from the environs of Tetuán came to a successful end with Spanish forces capturing Yebel Bu Zeitung, the final rebel redoubt. For the Legion, the casualty list for the day was short, with only two Legionaries wounded.[13]

While the brunt of the fighting was taking place south of Tetuán, another column under the command of Lieutenant Colonel Asensio operated in the Lukus River sector, which was east of Alcazarquivir and just north of the French protectorate, against the Ahl Serif and Beni Isef *kabyles*. Rebel resistance quickly collapsed in both territories, as it did in many parts of the northern Yebala. The most important defection from Abd-el-Krim was in the Beni Hozmar *kabyle*, where the four-day operation had just taken place.[14]

From 8 March to 31 March, the Legionaries continued to perform their usual campaign duties, suffering seven Legionaries dead and nine wounded.[15] In the eastern zone (Alhucemas Bay sector), the military situation was relatively calm because of poor weather. However, the Legion performed small-scale operations (*golpes de mano*). One such operation was carried out against the village of

Ikarrusen, which was situated near the Legion's main encampment in the east, Ben Tieb, where the IInd and IIIrd *Banderas* were stationed. The local tribal chiefs had come together to plan an offensive against Spanish forces in the region. At Ben Tieb, Legionaries had formed a unit called *Hijos de la noche* (Sons of the Night), a "Special Operations" unit ready to strike when called upon by their superiors. At Alhucemas, this unit, under the command of Sergeant Sangiorgio, had performed admirably, infiltrating and operating behind enemy lines, causing destruction to matériel, and inflicting casualties upon their foe. After sundown on the night of 21 March, two units of the Legion's commando group, under the leadership of *Brigadas* (Sergeant Majors) Ramos Torres and Dimitri Ivan Ivanof, slipped out of their Ben Tieb encampment. They reached Ikarrusen late that night and located the house where the tribal chiefs were meeting to make their plans. After "neutralizing" the guards posted outside, they climbed on to the roof of the house and proceeded to drop hand grenades on the stunned plotters, turning the room into an abattoir. Other rebels rushed to their defense, but the Legionaries were able to escape, returning to Ben Tieb with minimal casualties.[16]

Behind the scenes, the Spanish and French High Commands had met in late March to plan strategy for the upcoming spring offensive. As Fleming noted:

In general it amplified the rather vague February 6th convention and committed the Allies to a coordinated push into the Beni Urriaguel from the north, east, and south. These advances were to be swift and incisive undertakings, disallowing a fixed front or the use of heavy artillery. According to Goded, the plan envisioned a radical change in Spanish tactics in that it committed the Army of Africa to blitzkrieg-like mobility and jetisoned [*sic*] the concept of positions and slow, excessively cautious advances.[17]

Realizing that his political and military situation was extremely precarious, Abd-el-Krim agreed to meet the Allies to discuss an end to hostilities. Discussion began on 27 April in the town of Uxda close to the Moroccan-Algerian border in the northeastern corner of Morocco. Neither the Spanish nor Abd-el-Krim—by this time desperate—was very eager to attend, and differences over autonomy of the Rif and the release of Spanish and French prisoners of war (which Abd-el-Krim refused to accept) led to failure. The final push would begin in a few days.[18] In preparation for the upcoming major offensive in the eastern zone, all the *Banderas*, with the exception of the VIth, were concentrated there (see Map 8).[19]

THE FINAL OFFENSIVE OF THE RIF CAMPAIGN

The Spanish High Command had prepared a column in Midar of 15,000 men under the command of General Carrasco; this column would operate parallel to a French division led by General Dosse. In Ajdir, the main starting point, three columns had been organized under the commands of Colonels Emilio Mola, Benigno Fiscer, and Amado Balmes. In addition, a cavalry column under Major

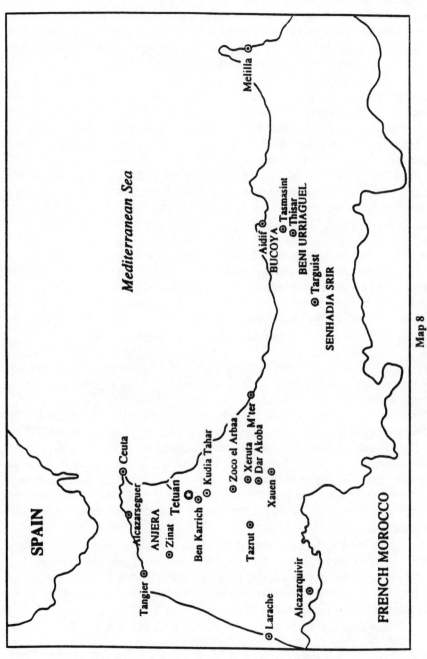

SPAIN

Tangier ◎

Alcazarseguer ◎ ◎ Ceuta

ANJERA

◎ Zinat   Tetuan

Ben Karrich ◎ ◎ Kudia Tahar

◎ Zoco el Arbaa

◎ Xeruta M'ter

Tazrut ◎ ◎ Dar Akoba

Xauen ◎

Larache ◎

Alcazarquivir
◎

Mediterranean Sea

Aidif ◎

BUCOYA ◎ Tasmasint
        ◎ Thisar

BENI URRIAGUEL

◎ Targuist

SENHADJA SRIR

◎ Melilla

FRENCH MOROCCO

Map 8
The Campaigns of 1926

Monasterio and a reserve column commanded by General Dolla were to participate. In all, 25,000 men were involved in the operation. The overall field commander for this major operation was the highly experienced General Alberto Castro Girona. General Sanjuro, *general en jefe* (senior general) in Africa, with his chief of staff, the very capable General Goded, would oversee the entire operation. They relocated their headquarters to Ajdir for this purpose.[20]

At dawn on 8 May 1926, the operation designed to deliver the coup de grace to Abd-el-Krim and his rebellion began. The aforementioned columns, composed of the Legion, *Regulares*, and Spanish army regulars, were to sweep mainly through the *kabyle* of the Beni Urriaguel (Abd-el-Krim's own), destroying all before it. The Ist, IInd, IIIrd, IVth, Vth, VIIth, and VIIIth *Banderas* set out under the command of their respective commanders. Lieutenant Colonels Ricardo de Rada and Luis Valcazar led the combined Ist and IInd *Banderas* (Mola's vanguard), and the IVth and Vth *Banderas*, respectively. The day's operation plan called for the Legionaries to take and occupy Pista Prisioneros, Regbaba, and Afgar. Under cover of their own machine guns and mortars, the Legionaries advanced against the 12,000 well-entrenched Riffians who defended their native soil with great determination and skill. Even after losing a position to the Legionaries, the Riffians were able to counterattack with cannon and mortar fire support. The Legionaries met the Riffian onslaught with ferocity and rebuffed the attack. The Riffians suffered a setback with many casualties and much loss of matériel, but the fight had just begun. It had also been costly for the Legion with 21 Legionaries killed, plus three officers and 112 Legionaries wounded.[21]

The battle resumed early the next day, 9 May, with the same *Banderas* (minus the Ist and IInd) continuing the advance. The Legion's mission for the day was to take and occupy Casa de Mikobian and Loma de los Morabos. After intense preliminary artillery and aerial bombardment, the IVth and Vth *Banderas* moved out to capture Loma de los Morabos. Having done so at the cost of numerous casualties, the Legionaries dug in for the night under violent Riffian gunfire. Simultaneously, the VIIIth *Bandera* forming the vanguard of the column of the center set out from Asgar/Azgar and assisted in the capture of Casa de Nicobian; they too dug in for the night. Casualties were once again heavy as a result of tenacious resistance of the Riffians. For the day, the Legion had two officers and fifteen Legionaries killed, as well as six officers and sixty-nine Legionaries wounded.[22]

On 10 May, the IVth, Vth, VIIth, and VIIIth *Banderas* moved to capture and occupy Position A, houses along the Guis River, and Lomas de Nicobian. In a hard-fought contest, at least on one occasion ending with a bayonet charge, the Legionaries suffered heavy casualties: one officer and twelve Legionaries dead, plus six officers and forty-two Legionaries wounded.[23]

The final day of the first cycle of operations came on 11 May. The Ist, IInd, IVth, and VIIth *Banderas* assisted in taking and occupying Tefras/Tafras. In combat with the rebels, one Legionary was killed and three wounded.[24]

The Ist, IInd, IIIrd, IVth, Vth, VIIth, and VIIIth *Banderas* saw action once again on 15 May when they participated in the day's scheduled operation, which called for the capture and occupation of *cota* (sector) 320 Sidi Yuset/Yussef (el Morabito) and Bab el Arbaa. In the clash of arms with the enemy, the Legion suffered one officer and one Legionary killed, as well as one officer and twenty-four Legionaries wounded.[25]

An important aspect of this 1926 campaign against the forces of Abd-el-Krim in the Rif was the nature of the terrain. The *lomas* (hills) and ravines located within the aforementioned *cotas* (sectors) offered excellent cover for retreating rebels, and in most cases the battle had to be carried at the point of the bayonet. The landscape was sparsely populated with insignificant small villages, unlike the larger villages found in the Yebala beyond Tetuán. The *africanistas* prosecuting the war knew the importance of securing their flanks and pacifying the inhabitants living in these seemingly insignificant positions. They recognized the mistake Silvestre had made in his headlong rush to reach Alhucemas without first securing his flanks or completely pacifying the various tribes in the Rif. Having learned that painful lesson, the Spaniards would now proceed cautiously, but with determination and purpose.

A desperate Abd-el-Krim, hoping to draw Spanish forces away from the Ajdir sector, repeated the strategy used in September 1925. He attacked Kudia Tahar, sending 1,000 Yebalis and Gomaris under the command of Ahmed Budra (his minister of war) and Ahmed Heriro against Wadi Martil, located near Tetuán on 10 May. Six days later, on 16 May, the VIth *Bandera* (21st, 22nd, 23rd, and 24th Companies), under the command of Captain Carlos Rubio, was in the vanguard of a column that had as its mission supplying positions in the Beni-Madan sector. About to cross the Martín River, the Legionaries of the VIth were caught in a shower of lead from the well-entrenched rebels on the opposite bank. Rapidly deploying, the *Banderas*' machine guns and mortars laid down effective cover fire that enabled a company to cross the river and assault the enemy on their left flank. The battle raged with one company after the other outdoing itself in inflicting casualties on the enemy until late in the afternoon when the Legionaries were ordered to withdraw. For the Legion, the casualties had also been serious, with three officers and nine Legionaries killed and fifty-eight Legionaries wounded.[26]

On 17 May, the same *Banderas* in the Ajdir sector, with the exception of the Vth, which had been rushed to Tetuán to reinforce the VIth, seized and occupied Tasograf, Tamasin/Tamasint (Abd-el-Krim's second headquarters), and Sidi Baki, which was located on the other side of the Nekor River. Casualties were light this day, with only one Legionary killed and nine wounded.[27]

By 19 May, the rebel threat to the Spanish capital had been eliminated when the Vth and VIth *Banderas*, integrated into Lieutenant Colonel Eugenio Sanz de Larín's column, broke the rebels' siege of Budara. Soundly defeated, the rebels left behind their ninety-nine dead and twenty-five wounded, along with their weapons, including all their cannons. For the Legion, the casualties were one Legionary killed, plus one officer and seventeen Legionaries wounded.[28]

The following day in the Ajdir sector, the Ist, IInd, IIIrd, VIIth, and VIIIth *Banderas* captured and occupied *cota* 800 and 1140 and made contact with the Melilla column. Visual contact had been made with the Melilla column the day before, but on this day the two columns linked up approximately ten kilometers south of Temasint at Zoco el Arbaa de Taurirt. The Beni Urriaguel *kabyle* had been cut in two from Alhucemas Bay to the French zone. Casualties were light for the Legion, with one Legionary dead, plus one officer and twelve Legionaries wounded.[29]

One week later, on 27 May, the Ist and IInd *Banderas* seized and occupied Monte Madan. In a bitter clash with the enemy, one officer and three Legionaries were killed. Meanwhile, the IIIrd and VIIIth *Banderas* occupied Cudia Chekran and rectified their front line on the Guis River *sin novedad*.[30]

Two days later, the Ist, IInd, IIIrd, IVth, and VIIIth *Banderas* assisted in the capture and occupation of Ain Kamara. Engaging the enemy in sharp combat, the Legion suffered two Legionaries killed, as well as five officers and thirty-two Legionaries wounded.[31]

The final operation of the month took place on 30 May when the Ist, IInd, and VIIIth *Banderas* took part in taking Poblado Kricha while sustaining only one Legionary wounded.[32]

THE END OF ABD-EL-KRIM

For Abd-el-Krim and his Riffian Republic, the end came as the Spanish and French armies closed in rapidly. His government lay in shambles and his quest for independence was finished. Since the Spanish were sure to execute him for what he had done, he knew he would have to surrender to the French. When Spanish forces overran his last headquarters at Targuist on 23 May, they found only his papers, books, and a Riffian flag. Abd-el-Krim wrote two letters, one to General Sanjurjo and the other to French Resident General Steeg (Lyautey's replacement) requesting an end to the bloodshed and a resumption of the Conference of Uxda. To save himself, as well as his family and staff, he wrote a surrender note, which he had delivered to the commander of the nearest French column, Colonel Cora. As a condition of his surrender and protection, he had to turn over all prisoners, which he did on 26 May. The next day, he surrendered to French officials. The European prisoners who staggered into Targuist on 28 May were in deplorable condition. All Spanish officers had been shot in retaliation for Spanish air raids, but over 100 enlisted men survived a cruel captivity. Those who died did so from poor food, typhus, and brutal treatment. On 2 September, Abd-el-Krim, his brother, their families, and their staff were put aboard a French warship for their voyage to Reunion Island in the Indian Ocean. There Abd-el-Krim lived in splendid exile until 1947, when he jumped ship in Port Said and was given asylum in Egypt. He died of a heart attack on 5 February 1963 in Cairo.[33]

With both Abd-el-Krim and the French out of the picture, it was up to Spanish forces to continue their drive through the Rif in order to link up with forces advancing through the Gomara. Woolman wrote that a few of the tribes could not accept the fact that Abd-el-Krim had capitulated; others felt that despite Abd-el-Krim's surrender, they must continue the struggle for their villages. A number of the tribesmen, however, believed that Abd-el-Krim's downfall was the will of Allah, and they accepted the end of the Riffian state with fatalism and without reservation. The Spanish army remained under the firm control of Primo de Rivera. Discipline within the ranks was relatively good, and his orders were unambiguous when he affirmed that the Spanish occupation was to be as bloodless as possible. As a symbol of submission to Spanish authority, each captured rebel was required to surrender his rifle. No pillaging, cruelty, or reprisals of any kind would be tolerated.[34]

From 2 June to the end of July, all the *Banderas* were engaged in performing their usual campaign duties, as well as fortifying the positions just captured. They were moved to wherever they were needed. From spearheading the aforementioned columns to occupying advanced outposts, the Legion accomplished its assigned missions.[35]

On 2 August, the Squadron of Lancers accompanied the IVth and VIth *Banderas* in the capture and occupation of Asba and Taranes, accomplished *sin novedad*. Also on the same day, the Vth *Bandera* took part in occupying Mexe. Likewise, this operation was carried out *sin novedad*.[36]

As Lieutenant Colonel Capaz's drive continued from the Yebala into the Gomara toward Xauen, the IVth and VIth *Banderas*, plus the Squadron of Lancers (under their respective commanders), went right along with him. On 4 August, they participated in the seizing of Fondalillo, Zoco el Arbaa de Beni Hassan, and several other positions in this sector, all without incident.[37]

Retracing the torturous route taken during the retreat from Xauen in late 1924, the Spanish army was now reversing that painful episode as it conquered everything before it. On 11 August, the IVth and VIth *Banderas*, as well as the Squadron of Lancers, took part in the occupation of Dar Acobba, Xauen, and other positions in this sector. As Primo de Rivera had promised during those dark and difficult days in 1924, the Spanish army had returned to Xauen and taken it without a fight.[38] From 12 to 31 August, the Legion carried out its campaign duties, suffering only two Legionaries wounded during this period.[39]

The IIIrd *Bandera*, on 14 September, assisted in the day's operation in the Ketama sector. There, it exchanged gunfire with the enemy, having one officer and one Legionary wounded. For the remainder of the month, the other *Banderas* carried out their usual campaign duties, suffering two Legionaries killed and one wounded.[40] During the latter part of September, a double-pronged attack was launched. General Alberto Castro Girona's columns passed through Beni Urriaguel and then entered the Ketama *kabyle* to the west. Colonel Sebastian Pozas led the northern advance, moving due west from Targuist, and Captain Luis Ostariz led the southern advance into Senhadja Srir from the southeast. Another command under Lieutenant Colonel Capaz came from the Xauen area, hoping to join up with the other two somewhere in the Ketama region.[41]

On the first day of October, the eight *Banderas* of the Legion were deployed as follows: the Ist and the IInd at Targuist; the IIIrd at Imasinen; the IVth at Dar Acobba; the Vth at Teffer; the VIth in Xauen; the VIIth at Punta Pescadores; the VIIIth at Ferrach; and the Squadron of Lancers transferred from Riffien in the western zone to Targuist in the eastern zone. Spanish military operations during the month of October had been extremely successful.[42] Fleming recorded that General Sanjurjo found that of the sixty-six tribes in the protectorate, fifty-five of them had completely surrendered to the khalif, and seven more had partially submitted. Since February 1926, the army had confiscated some 29,447 rifles, 135 cannon, and 199 machine guns.[43]

The Vth *Bandera* was in action on 3 November when it assisted in the day's operation in the *kabyle* of Beni Ider (western zone) to capture Imacegay. Simultaneously, the VIth *Bandera* took part in the capture and occupation of Xajaya and Sedie while having only one Legionary wounded in the operation.[44] The following day, 4 November, the same two *Banderas* were once again in action in the same sector (Beni Ider); Loma Roja was taken at the cost of a single Legionary wounded.[45]

On 6 November, the VIth *Bandera* was able to seize and occupy Buharrat *sin novedad*. Five years earlier (29 June 1921), the "Tigers" of the IIIrd *Bandera* had "covered themselves with glory" at Buharrat, winning their first of two battle ribbons. The next day, 7 November, it was the Vth *Bandera*'s turn to go on the offensive when it captured Telezta Mesla without incident.[46]

The Vth *Bandera*, on 11 November, carried out an arduous march from Telezta Mesla to Luhordia that cost the lives of four Legionaries who died of physical exhaustion. For the remainder of the month, the Legion continued to carry out its assigned duties.[47]

From 2 December to 30 December the *Banderas* carried out their campaign duties without incident.[48] This changed abruptly on 31 December, however, when Legionaries of the IVth *Bandera*, who were escorting a convoy to Abbada/Abada *Nº* 3, were attacked. In hard-fought combat with the rebels, eight Legionaries were killed, plus one officer and three Legionaries received wounds.[49]

The year 1926 had been one of great progress for the Spanish army in "mopping up" pockets of resistance to their authority. Always in the vanguard, the Legion had been in the forefront of all the columns that crisscrossed the Yebala, Gomara, and Rif. In the coming year, 1927, the Rif Rebellion would come to an end when the last of the rebels were either subdued or forced to flee into French territory and peace was declared in the Spanish protectorate.

THE END OF THE RIF REBELLION, 1927

When the final year of the Rif Rebellion began, the situation was winding down with most tribes submitting to the authority of the Sultan. However, deep in the heart of the Rif, Gomara, and Yebala some tribes (e.g., Ketama and Senhaia) refused to surrender. The Spanish army crushed their rebellion in late March. With the typical inclement weather from about October to March, the situation was static.[50]

During the first days of January, General Sanjurjo received a detailed plan of operations that General Goded and his General Staff officers had prepared.[51] Come spring and with it improved weather conditions, the Spanish army would sweep through southern Yebala and the heart of the Gomara, which were yet to be brought under Spanish domination. Before this plan could be implemented, however, a revolt broke out in the southern Gomara led by an Akhamlish *marabout* (religious mystic) named Sel-litan/Slitan.[52]

On 26 March, Slitan with his Ahmas, Beni Yahmed, and Beni Kalid tribesmen attacked the small Spanish outpost of Tagsut in the mountains of Senhadjan. After six hours of combat, the rebels succeeded in overrunning the position, whereupon they put all but one of the vanquished *Regulares* to the knife. The following day Captain Luis Ostariz of the native police set out with 245 men for Tagsut, hoping to capture Slitan. Caught in a rebel ambush near Adman, they all perished. Shocked and stunned by the distressing news, General Sanjurjo and his chief of staff, General Goded, relocated to Villa Sanjurjo on 28 March in order to respond to this alarming situation. Sanjurjo decided to send three columns. Leading the expedition were Colonel Emilio Mola (with the Ist and VIIIth *Banderas*), Colonel Sebastian Pozas (with the IInd and IIIrd *Banderas*), and Lieutenant Colonel Luis Solans. Once again the battle-tested Legion would play a major role in this operation with the immediate participation of the Ist, IInd, and VIIIth *Banderas*. Furthermore, the High Command transferred the IIIrd and VIth *Banderas*, at that time located in the western zone, to Alhucemas (aboard the *Vicente Ferrer*) and then to Targuist, the Legion's base of operations in the region. The Spanish army's plan was for these columns to move slowly and methodically through the woods and valleys of the Senhadja Srir/Senhadjan *kabyle*, cleaning out all foci of rebellion.[53]

The operation began on 1 April, when 7,000 men marched out of Targuist toward the Senhadjan mountains. At the start, success greeted the Spaniards, who were able to conquer the *kabyle* of Beni Bechir before advancing toward Senhadjan. On 11 April, however, a freak blizzard halted operations and forced the men into their mountain bivouacs. For the next three days they were cut off from General Sanjurjo's headquarters back at Villa Sanjurjo. Fearing a major setback at the hands of both the weather and the enemy, as well as being personally concerned for the welfare of his soldiers, Sanjurjo ordered aerial reconnaissance missions on 14 April to help the beleaguered columns. Snow, sleet, wind, and rain took a much heavier toll on the men then did rebel snipers. By 14 April, the blizzard had abated and the columns, having fought off the weather and the snipers, remained intact and prepared to press on with their mission. As noted, this was not the Spanish army of 1921 that had folded in the face of adversity at Annual.[54] Having recovered from the chilly interruption, columns under Mola and Solans resumed their advance toward Sehadjan on 18 April. They occupied the villages of Ugriden, Bu Remdan, Tamezarin/Tamerarin, and Asenjo, which were then put to the torch. The advance continued the following day with the columns reaching Zoco el Arbaa and Imugzen. With the capture of the Bab Tilua (or Tilma Pass) on 22 April, and with the 2nd and 3rd Companies of the Ist *Bandera* in the van of the column, the strategically important village of Taberrant was occupied at 1600 hours without resistance. On the same day, in an attempt to cut communication lines between Targuist and Adman, the rebels attacked the outpost of Sidi Mezquin in Zerkat. The Spanish garrison, composed of forty men from the *Regimiento de Melilla*, defended their position tenaciously. In the end, only four men out of the original forty were left unhurt, but the enemy suffered many casualties, including their leader, Mohan Asdat, an ex-*caid* of Abd-el-Krim.[55]

Mola's and Poza's columns advanced into the Ketama *kabyle* during the first week of May. By 7 May they had attained its complete submission. Slitan and his men fled the area, moving northward toward Xauen, where he established his headquarters at Ankod.[56]

With operations in the Senhadja-Ketama sector drawing to a close, the Spanish army began a new thrust into the central Yebala (the *kabyles* of Sumata, Beni Isef, and Al Ahmas) to extinguish the last remaining foci of rebellion (see Map 9). In late April three columns were organized under the command of General Souza (column of the right, 4,750 men), Colonel Amado Balmes (column of the center, 3,950 men), and Colonel Emilio Canis (column of the left, 5,300 men). This enterprise, under the overall command of the commanding general of Ceuta, General Federico Berenguer Fusté, began on 29 April in the face of strong resistance. Nevertheless, the Spanish columns pressed on to pacify the Beni Aros by 13 May. From there, they proceeded into the Sumata *kabyle*. Resistance from the tribesmen of the Sumata was even stiffer than that encountered in the Beni Aros, and the columns of the center and of the right both required reinforcements to complete their mission. Nonetheless, the Spanish forces were able to occupy and disarm the Sumata *kabyle* by 23 May, with a few diehard tribesmen fleeing southward to fight another day.[57]

With the central Yebala pacified, the columns were fortified. They then proceeded into the southern Yebala. At the time these operations were being carried out in the Yebala, Colonels Mola and Capaz were also in action in the Gomara, moving west. In this operation, Lieutenant Colonel Capaz's column of 5,000 men (including the VIth *Bandera*) was the main column; Colonel Mola (2,500 men including the Ist and VIIIth *Banderas*) and Lieutenant Colonel Sanz de Larín (with the IInd *Bandera*) commanded the reserve.[58]

Because of the viselike operations carried out by the various Spanish army columns in the Yebala and Gomara, by early June the rebels found themselves entrapped in the area southwest of Xauen. The final battles of the Rif campaign were fought in this region with the Spaniards dealing the rebels one sharp defeat after another and shattering their morale.[59]

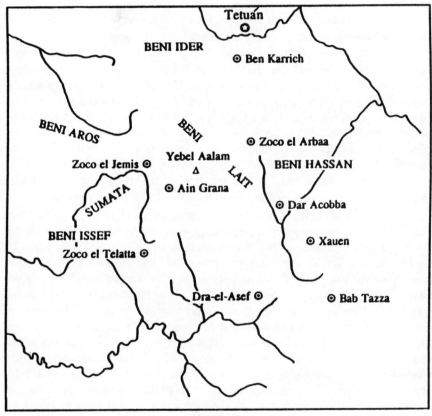

Map 9
The Campaigns of 1927

From its inception, the Legion had insisted on being placed in the vanguard of action, the place of greatest danger, "the place of honor." As expected, the Legion found itself in the forefront of these final operations during the waning days of the pacification of the protectorate. On 15 June, the Legion fought its last major battle of the campaign when the Ist and VIIIth *Banderas*, serving in the van of Lieutenant Colonel Sanz de Larín's column, engaged the enemy in a bitter firefight at Kudia Sebaa. The Legionaries were victorious in their final engagement of the war, with the 29/VIII left occupying the newly conquered position. Casualties among the men of the Ist and VIIIth *Banderas* included two officers (one killed in action, the other, *Alférez* Munar, wounded) and thirty-four Legionaries either dead or wounded.[60]

On 18 June and by Royal Order (DO #134), Colonel José Millán Astray y Terreros, *Primer Jefe del Cuerpo* (commander in chief of the Legion) was promoted to the rank of *general de brigada* (brigadier general). Having attained the rank of general, he, like Franco before him, was required to relinquish command of the Legion. By a Royal Order of 30 June, Colonel Eugenio Sanz de Larín replaced Millán Astray. Millán Astray's promotion signaled the end of the Legion's first chapter, one dominated by Millán Astray and Franco. They had seen the Legion through its initial organization, its early development, and the bloody Rif campaign. Now during the final days of the campaign, a new commanding officer would see the Legion through its first period of peace.[61]

The end of the Rif Rebellion came rapidly when Slitan and his adherents, who were the most stubborn of the rebels, gave up the fight and quickly slipped over to the French side on 8 July. They were never to be heard from again by foreign sources. On 10 July, Spanish forces seized and occupied the hillocks of Yebel Tangaia and Yebel Taria, as well as the Ahmasi (*kabyle* of Al Ahmas) village of Bab Taza/Tazza. It was at Bab Taza on 10 July that Lieutenant General José Sanjurjo Sacanell, the High Commissioner of the Spanish Protectorate of Morocco, proclaimed the complete and total pacification of Spanish Morocco. Sanjurjo wrote: "With the operations carried out today, the last remains of the rebellion have been crushed . . . and the fighting in Morocco has been brought to a conclusion. For the last eighteen years this campaign has constituted a problem for various governments, . . . sapping the nation of its life blood and its moral and economic energies in order to maintain the legacy of pride and gallantry which we inherited from our ancestors—conquerors of a world."[62]

POSTBELLUM EVENTS

With peace declared in the protectorate on 10 July in the "Peace of Bab Taza," the military situation ground to a standstill. Both the *Regulares* and the Legion garrisoned positions recently conquered. *Banderas* were posted throughout the Yebala, Gomara, and Rif, as well as the major towns of Ceuta (Riffien), Tetuán, Xauen, and Melilla (Tauima). Nothing of great importance occurred during the summer months of late July, August, or September. Things began to change in early October, however.[63]

On 1 October, General José Millán Astray y Terreros, the commander in chief of the Spanish Foreign Legion, was paid the highest tribute when by a Royal Order (DO #220) he was named honorary colonel of the Legion. For Millán Astray, this was the greatest honor that could have been bestowed upon him, for the Legion had been his brainchild and his greatest accomplishment. Through his efforts the Legion had grown, developed, and prospered to become the elite fighting unit of the Spanish army.[64]

Besides the honor paid to Millán Astray, the Legion itself was recognized and honored when it finally received its own national standard (the Spanish flag bearing the Legion's motto: "legionaries, to fight; legionaries, to die"). This flag had been hand-sewn by Queen Victoria Eugenia herself and by her ladies-in-waiting. As stated, the Legion was to have received its own national standard in June 1923 when Lieutenant Colonel Rafael Valenzuela Urzaiz was its commander in chief. Certain units of the Legion had been chosen to travel to Madrid to receive this well-merited honor. Valenzuela and the Legion were to be awarded the national colors, which, as Millán Astray had stated, had been "stained with the blood of its Legionaries." But, the furious Riffian attack on the Spanish position of Tizzi-Azza (that cost Valenzuela his life) put this ceremony on hold because the situation in the protectorate was too grave to take time out to hold the ceremony. Now, four years later, and with hundreds more Legionaries and officers having been killed in battle, the Legion would finally be awarded its national standard, by this time not just "stained with the blood of its Legionaries" but drenched in the blood of its Legionaries.

The king and queen of Spain planned to visit the protectorate during the first week of October to present the national standard to the Legion, pass out awards, and tour well-known battlefield sites (e.g., el Fondak and Annual). The royal party left Madrid on 4 October and arrived by overnight train in Algeciras on 5 October. Awaiting them in Algeciras Bay to transport them to Ceuta was the battleship *Jaime I*, which flew the banner of Castile. Disembarking in Ceuta, they were whisked away to Dar Riffien, cradle of the Legion, to preside over the scheduled ceremony. Accompanying the regal couple were Primo de Rivera; Generals Francisco Franco, Dámaso Berenguer Fusté, and Ricardo Burguete; and other dignitaries. Legionaries lined the sides of the road from the wharf all the way to the edge of town. At Riffien, Her Majesty the Queen, serving as the Legion's godmother, was at last able to present the national standard to the Legion. This day the newly appointed commander in chief of the Legion, Colonel Eugenio Sanz de Larín, would accept the banner on behalf of the Legion. In addition, General Sanjurjo, the acting High Commissioner and supreme commander of all forces in Morocco, received the Grand Laureate Cross of St. Ferdinand. The king publicly proclaimed Millán Astray honorary colonel of the Legion. The dignitaries then reviewed the Legionaries present at Riffien (the IVth, Vth, VIth, VIIth, and VIIIth *Banderas*, as well as the depot *Bandera*), in addition to other army units. The royal party continued on to Tetuán on 6 October and then headed off for Villa Sanjurjo (Alhucemas Bay) the following day. From there, the king visited the ruins of Annual. On 9 October, they arrived in Melilla. The king and his party returned to Spain aboard the *Jaime I* the next day.[65]

A week after the Dar Riffien ceremony, *Día de la Raza* (Columbus Day) was celebrated throughout Spain as the "Celebration of Peace" in Morocco. In Spain the government and people rejoiced at the termination of the eighteen-year Moroccan war (9 July 1909-12 October 1927). To commemorate the valor and sacrifice of those who participated in the war, the king decreed that a medal be struck. The reverse of the Moroccan Peace Medal bore the following inscription: "Spain, always disposed to every enterprise of universal civilization, contributed to that of Morocco with the precious blood of her sons and the gold of her coffers. The triumph of her arms and culture of her methods are the foundation of this great work of humanity."[66] These sentiments were not shared by all who served in Morocco, however. Arturo Barea was particularly distressed with Spain's self-appointed mission to bring civilization to Morocco when he wrote:

Why must we "civilize" them if they do not want to be civilized? Civilize them—we? We from Castile, from Andalusia, from the mountains of Gerona, who cannot read or write? Nonsense. Who is going to civilize us? Our village has no school, its houses are of clay, we sleep in our clothes on a pallet in the stable beside the mules, to keep warm. We eat an onion and a chunk of bread in the morning and go to work in the fields from sunrise to sunset. At noon we eat the *gazpacho*, a mess of oil, vinegar, salt, water, and bread. At night we eat chick-peas or potatoes with dried cod. We crack up with hunger and misery.[67]

SUMMARY

During the final campaigns of the Rif War (1926-1927), the Legion continued to serve as the spearhead of the Spanish army in Morocco. With the Riffians on the run following the Alhucemas Bay landings of late 1925, the Spaniards pressed inward into the heart of the Rif, quickly forcing Abd-el-Krim to surrender to French officials on 27 May 1926. His surrender deprived the rebellion of its figurehead. With the exception of a handful of devoted *caid*s who fought on till 1927, the war was over. The eight *Banderas* of the Legion, along with its Squadron of Lancers performed invaluable service crisscrossing the Yebala, Gomara, and Rif, always seeking combat with the enemy.

In its seven short years of existence, the Legion had grown from a motley group of volunteers seeking a paycheck, military adventure, or escape to become the elite fighting force of the Spanish army. John Scurr offered the following as proof of the Legion's fighting capabilities, personal sacrifice, and valor when he wrote that in the 845 battles in which the Legion took part, it sustained casualties of 2,000 dead, 6,096 wounded, and 285 missing. The Ist, IInd, and IVth *Banderas* were collectively awarded the Military Medal, and forty-nine Legionaries independently received the Military Medal. The Laureate Cross of St. Ferdinand, Spain's highest decoration for valor, was awarded to twelve Legionaries.[68]

NOTES

1. *DOL, Negociado de campaña*, 1 January 1926, 43. *SHM*, Legajo #54, Rollo 16, *Colección de historiales*, "Campañas de Marruecos, Historial de guerra, 1ª y 2ª Banderas" (8ª Bandera), 206. The following companies made up the VIIIth *Bandera*: the 29th Company (Captain Manuel Méndez Vigo); the 30th Company (Captain Fernando Beltran de Lis); the 31st Company (Captain Eugenio Calderon); and the 32nd Machine Gun Company (Lieutenant Miguel Ossorio Rivas). Cano Velasco, ed., 160. Bueno, *La Legión*, 10.

2. *DOL, Negociado de campaña*, 2 January-15 February 1926, 44. On 15 February, the IVth *Bandera* relocated from Riffien to Ajdir aboard the steamer *Vicente Ferrer* disembarking at Alhucemas the following day.

3. Preston, 49. Preston recorded that on Franco's promotion, the following words were written (by the Superior Committee of Generals) in Franco's service record: "He is a positive national asset and surely the country and the Army will derive great benefit from making use of his remarkable aptitudes in higher positions." Crozier, 85, noted that in addition to being promoted, Franco was awarded the Individual Military Medal for a second time and was made commander of the French Legion of Honor. De Galinsoga, 121, recorded that in 1940, Marshal Pétain praised Franco by calling him "*la espada más limpia del mundo*" (the cleanest sword in the world). Hills, 141. Trythall, 51-52, wrote that Colonel's Goded and Fanjul were promoted to brigadier general based on war merits along with Franco. Both would be shot in July 1936, Goded in Barcelona and Fanjul in Madrid. Major Ramon Franco, Francisco Franco's younger brother and an accomplished aviator, stole his brother's thunder when he piloted the seaplane *Plus Ultra* (a Dornier *Wal*) across the Atlantic Ocean and touched down in Pernambuco, Brazil, on 2 February, the day before the announcement of Franco's promotion to general. Garriga, 53-56. Subinspección de la Legión, ed., 268, erroneously gives the date of Franco's promotion as 26 February.

4. *AGM*, Legajo #M-3204, SECCIÓN #1, DIVISIÓN #1 (February 1926), 22-23; and *SHM*, DO #32, (10-II-26), "*Destinos*," 361. Scurr, 17. De Arce, 184, noted that Millán Astray would now be commander in chief of the Legion until 18 July 1927, when he would be promoted to brigadier general. Subinspección de la Legión, ed., referred to Millán Astray as "*el manco de Fondak*" (the one-armed man of Fondak). The great Spanish novelist and playwright Miguel de Cervantes Saavedra was known as "*el manco de Lepanto*" because his left hand had been crippled during the sea battle of Lepanto in 1571.

5. Salas Larrazábal, 164. The author in n. 15 gives the names of all the participants at the meeting for both sides. Along with those previously mentioned who represented Spain were José Sanjurjo Sacanell, Manuel Goded Llopis, Luis Orgaz y Yoldi, and Antonio Aranda Mata. These four officers, the cream of the Spanish army, sided with the rebels in July 1936, and the latter two played major roles in Franco's army, while the former two were killed during the first days of the uprising. García Figueras, 209, noted that on 6 February, the *Convenio de cooperación de España y Francia en el Norte de África para el año 1926* (the Pact of Cooperation between Spain and France in North Africa for the year 1926) was signed. Arraras, ed., 192. Payne, 221. Fleming, *Primo de Rivera*, 331-332, has the details of what was agreed upon by the French and Spanish. Gómez-Jordana y

Souza, 156-158. Estado Mayor Central del Ejército, 113-114.

    6. Woolman, *Rebels in the Rif*, 197-198. García Figueras, 209. Fleming, *Primo de Rivera*, 332-333, noted that Heriro's guns had been harassing Tetuán since October 1925. Cano Velasco, ed., 160, recorded that Spanish artillerists had tried and failed to silence the rebel guns by engaging them in counter-battery fire.

    7. Payne, 221.

    8. *DOL*, *Negociado de campaña*, 1 March 1926, 44; Cano Velasco, ed., 160; and Subinspección de la Legión, ed., 269.

    9. *DOL*, *Negociado de campaña*, 2 March 1926, 44.

    10. Fleming, *Primo de Rivera*, 333. A veteran *africanista*, Colonel Luis Orgaz y Yoldi would later go on to play a major role in Franco's army during the Spanish Civil War. When the uprising began, he was able to fly out of Las Palmas in the Canary Islands, land in Tetuán, and take control of the *Regulares*. On 5 May 1941, he was named High Commissioner of the Spanish Protectorate of Morocco. For a brief biography of General Orgaz y Yoldi, as well as Generals Sanjurjo, Mola, Queipo de Llano, Varela, Moscardo, et al., see Eduardo San Martín Losada, *España y su glorioso ejército*, 4th ed. (Madrid: Ediciones S.M.L., 1952), 42-45. *DOL*, *Negociado de campaña*, 4 March 1926, 44. *SHM*, Legajo #54, Rollo 16, *Colección de historiales*, "Campañas de Marruecos, Historial de guerra, 1ª y 2ª Banderas" (8ª Bandera), 207-208. Cano Velasco, ed., 160. Subinspección de la Legión, ed., 269-271 and 272-273, details Millán Astray's fourth battle wound in an account written by Lieutenant C.L. Carlos Tiede Zeden who had accompanied him. Llacuna and Polls, 52, gives the site of Millán Astray's wounding as Beni Garfet. Ramas Izquierdo, 275-277, has full details on the day's action. When Millán Astray was severely wounded, his command was turned over to Colonel Ángel Prats of the 60th Regiment of the regular army. Scurr, 17, recorded that on the morning of 4 March 1926, the VIIIth Bandera seized a hill called Loma Redonda in the Gorgues mountains. Millán Astray ordered that the hilltop be fortified with posts for six machine guns and four mortars, and with forty men. He later returned to inspect the fortifications in spite of incessant fire from enemy emplacements on Hafa el Duira. At 1530 hours, as he neared the first post, he was hit in the face by a bullet that destroyed his right eye, mangled his jaw, and exited through his left cheek. Before being evacuated in serious condition, he still managed to shout, "¡Viva España! ¡Viva la Legión!" *AGM*, Legajo #M-3204, SECCIÓN #1, DIVISIÓN #1 (4 March 1926), 23-24. De Silva, 187-189, noted that besides being known as "the one-armed man of Fondak," Millán Astray was also "the glorious one-eyed man of Loma Redonda." What remained of Millán Astray's right eye is preserved and on public display at the *Museo de la Legión* in Ceuta, along with some of his other personal effects.

    11. Cano Velasco, ed., 160; and Subinspección de la Legión, ed., 275, has the contents of a telegram from Millán Astray to Liniers y Muguiro and the Legion.

    12. *DOL*, *Negociado de campaña*, 5 March 1926, 44; Subinspección de la Legión, ed., 270-271; and *SHM*, Legajo #54, Rollo 16, *Colección de historiales*, "Campañas de Marruecos, Historial de guerra, 1ª y 2ª Banderas" (8ª Bandera), 8. Ramas Izquierdo, 277-279. For more on the death of Lieutenant Joaquín Alonso Rodríguez (at Haffa-el-Duira), see 40; for *Alféreces* Manuel Garzón González (Haffa-el-Duira) and

Gregorio Fernández Aragonés (killed in action at Kudia Tahar), see 51-52.

13. *DOL, Negociado de campaña*, 6-7 March 1926, 44-45; Estado Mayor Central del Ejército, 115-117; and *SHM*, Legajo #54, Rollo 16, *Colección de historiales*, "Campañas de Marruecos, Historial de guerra, 1ª y 2ª Banderas" (8ª Bandera), 208. The "Exploits of El Felipe" had ended. Fleming, *Primo de Rivera*, 333, noted that "El Felipe" was the nickname given by the Spaniards to the cannon the Riffians had used to shell Tetuán for the past six months; it was captured at Yebel Bu Zeitung.

14. Woolman, *Rebels in the Rif*, 198; and Fleming, *Primo de Rivera*, 334.

15. *DOL, Negociado de campaña*, 8-31 March 1926, 45; and *SHM*, Legajo #54, Rollo 16, *Colección de historiales*, "Campañas de Marruecos, Historial de guerra, 1ª y 2ª Banderas" (8ª Bandera), 208.

16. Subinspección de la Legión, ed., 272, gives the date of the operation as 21 May 1926, instead of what I believe to be is the correct 21 March 1926. All operations noted in this source that I know took place in March 1926 have been erroneously dated May.

17. Fleming, *Primo de Rivera*, 335. Gómez-Jordana y Souza, 158-161, has all the details of the agreement.

18. For more information on the Conference of Uxda, see Pennell, 212-214; Furneaux, 221-227 (lists the four demands made by the Allies); Fleming, *Primo de Rivera*, 335-345 (gives an excellent, in-depth account of the conference); Woolman, *Rebels in the Rif*, 198-204; Estado Mayor Central del Ejército, 117-119; Salas Larrazábal, 164-165 (identifies five demands made by the Allies, as well as the names of those who took part in the talks); Arraras, ed., 192; García Figueras, 209; Morales Lezcano, 238; and Petrie, 189. The question of the ill-treatment Spanish prisoners were subjected to at the hands of the Riffians was most germane to the talks. Sablotny, 270, recounted an incident he witnessed while a prisoner of the Riffians in Ajdir: "With the aid of the Red Cross, for the ordinary soldier-prisoners of Spain in the Riff, they brought clothes to dress them—in boats from a nearby cruiser, trousers, coats, and shirts from Melilla." And even though the prisoners were wearing tattered rags, the Riffians deprived them of these new uniforms. "In the presence of many unhappy prisoners, they cleaned arms and cannon with the clothes brought." *DOL, Negociado de campaña*, 1 April 1926, 45; and *SHM*, Legajo #54, Rollo 16, *Colección de historiales*, "Campañas de Marruecos, Historial de guerra, 1ª y 2ª Banderas" (8ª Bandera), 208. On 1 April the eight *Banderas* of the Legion were deployed as follows: the Ist *Bandera* was in the Amekran sector; the IInd and IIIrd were at Ben Tieb; the IVth remained at Espinosa; the Vth was at Dar Harjor; the VIth was at Belabas; the VIIth and the Squadron of Lancers were at Riffien; and the VIIIth was at Tazarines. On 28 April the VIIIth *Bandera* left for Ceuta, where it embarked for Alhucemas arriving the following day.

19. On 1 May the *Banderas* were dispersed as follows: the Ist and IInd *Banderas* were at Malmusi; the IIIrd was at T'Zelata; the IVth was in Monte Palomas; the Vth was at Isli; the VIth was at Dar Harjor; the VIIth was at Buybar; the VIIIth was at Tisli; and the Squadron of Lancers was now at R'Gaia. See *DOL, Negociado de campaña*, 1 May 1926, 45; and Subinspección de la Legión, ed., 275.

20. Emilio Bueno y Núñez de Prado, *Historia de la acción de España en Marruecos (desde 1904 a 1927)* (Madrid: Editorial Ibérica, 1929), 147-148. For an extensive list (a mini Alhucemas Bay landing) on the preparations for the spring offensive of 1926, including air, sea, and land forces, see Gómez-Jordana y Souza, 170-176. Estado Mayor Central del Ejército, 122-126, also contains the complete order of battle for this final push against Abd-el-Krim. Fleming, *Primo de Rivera*, 346, covers the advance of the other major Spanish wing moving from the east (Melilla) toward the heart of the Rif. This wing, in itself composed of three columns—Colonel Miguel Campins (Azib de Midar), Colonel Miguel Ponte (Metalza), and Colonel Sebastian Pozas (starting from the port of Afrau in the *kabyle* of Beni Said)—was to link up with the French (three divisions advancing from the Taza sector) and the principal Spanish column to which I have given primary attention. Woolman, *Rebels in the Rif*, 205.

21. *DOL, Negociado de campaña*, 8 May 1926, 45. Subinspección de la Legión, ed., 276-278, has all the details of the day's battle *Bandera* by *Bandera*. Ramas Izquierdo, 279-285, also contains an excellent description of the battle, as well as a newspaper account written by a journalist for *ABC* (20 September 1926). *SHM*, Legajo #54, Rollo 16, *Colección de historiales*, "Campañas de Marruecos, Historial de guerra, 1ª y 2ª Banderas" (8ª Bandera), 209-211 and 212. Estado Mayor Central del Ejército, 128. Bueno y Núñez de Prado, 148. Cano Velasco, ed., 160, erroneously gives the start of the offensive as 8 March, instead of the correct 8 May. De Arce, 185. Scurr, 17-18. Pennell, 215, gives the Riffian side of the final offensive, including Abd-el-Krim's reaction. Fleming, *Primo de Rivera*, 345, gives the number of Riffian soldiers as roughly 16,500.

22. *DOL, Negociado de campaña*, 9 May 1926, 45-46. Subinspección de la Legión, ed., 278-279 and 281-283 for more on the IIIrd *Bandera* (Occupation of Rechbaba). *SHM*, Legajo #54, Rollo 16, *Colección de historiales*, "Campañas de Marruecos, Historial de guerra, 1ª y 2ª Banderas" (8ª Bandera), 211-212 and 212-213. Ramas Izquierdo, 285-287, also details the actions of the VIIth and IIIrd *Banderas*. See 31 for details on the death of Captain Luis Santa Cruz Teijeiro (19/V), and 52 for *Alférez* Adolfo/Rodolfo Baylón/Baiton González. Estado Mayor Central del Ejército, 129.

23. *DOL, Negociado de campaña*, 10 May 1926, 46. Subinspección de la Legión, ed., 279-280. Ramas Izquierdo, 288-289. For details on the death of *Alférez* Romualdo Domínguez Martín, see 52. Estado Mayor Central del Ejército, 129-130. Woolman, *Rebels in the Rif*, 204-205. Fleming, *Primo de Rivera*, 346-347.

24. *DOL, Negociado de campaña*, 11 May 1926, 46; and Gómez-Jordana y Souza, 176. Fleming, *Primo de Rivera*, 346-347.

25. *DOL, Negociado de campaña*, 15 May 1926, 46; and *SHM*, Legajo #54, Rollo 16, *Colección de historiales*, "Campañas de Marruecos, Historial de guerra, 1ª y 2ª Banderas," 213. Ramas Izquierdo, 52-53, has more on the death of *Alférez* Federico Pina/Pima Monzón. Fleming, *Primo de Rivera*, 347. Pennell, 215.

26. *DOL, Negociado de campaña*, 16 May 1926, 46. Also on 16 May, but on the Ajdir front, the Riffians attacked the IInd *Bandera* at Ain Sedun. They suffered two Legionaries killed and one officer and fourteen Legionaries wounded. *SHM*, Legajo #54, Rollo 16, *Colección de historiales*, "Campañas de Marruecos, Historial de guerra, 1ª y 2ª

Banderas," 213. Subinspección de la Legión, ed., 283-285, has all the details on the "Convoy to Beni-Madan." In addition, there is a congratulatory telegram from Millán Astray to the commander of the VIth *Bandera*. Ramas Izquierdo, 290-292, also has details on the battle. For more information on the deaths of Lieutenants Guillermo Santandreu/Santandereu Babiloni (commanding the 22nd Company that day), Arturo Obanos Ramos, and Eduardo de O'Dena/Odena Loaysa, see 40-41. Estado Mayor Central del Ejército, 131-132. Pennell, 215. Fleming, *Primo de Rivera*, 348.

27. *DOL, Negociado de campaña*, 17 May 1926, 46; and *SHM*, Legajo #54, Rollo 16, *Colección de historiales*, "Campañas de Marruecos, Historial de guerra, 1ª y 2ª Banderas," 213-214. Fleming, *Primo de Rivera*, 347.

28. *DOL, Negociado de campaña*, 19 May 1926, 46. Cano Velasco, ed., 160-161. Fleming, *Primo de Rivera*, 348-349. Woolman, *Rebels in the Rif*, 210.

29. *DOL, Negociado de campaña*, 20 May 1926, 46. *SHM*, Legajo #54, Rollo 16, *Colección de historiales*, "Campañas de Marruecos, Historial de guerra, 1ª y 2ª Banderas," 214. This source gives the number of *cota* 1140 as 1,400. Ramas Izquierdo, 53, also agrees with 1140. Fleming, *Primo de Rivera*, 347-348. Also on this date (20 May 1926), Colonel Poza's column was able to reconquer Sidi Drius and Annual. Estado Mayor Central del Ejército, 133. Woolman, *Rebels in the Rif*, 205. Pennell, 215-216.

30. *DOL, Negociado de campaña*, 27 May 1926, 46-47. Ramas Izquierdo, 53, has more on the death of *Alférez* Adolfo Baeza López, whom *DOL* gave the rank of lieutenant.

31. *DOL, Negociado de campaña*, 29 May 1926, 47. Subinspección de la Legión, ed., 285-286, focused on the exploits of the Ist and IInd *Banderas* under the command of LTC Ricardo Rada Peral (and part of Mola's and Balmes' columns), entrusted with capturing a fortified house in Maaden (Alhucemas sector). *SHM*, Legajo #54, Rollo 16, *Colección de historiales*, "Campañas de Marruecos, Historial de guerra, 1ª y 2ª Banderas," 214-215. Besides giving details on the battle, this source also claimed that the actions of 29 May were the last ones of major importance in the campaign. Ramas Izquierdo, 292-294. Estado Mayor Central del Ejército, 135. Woolman, *Rebels in the Rif*, 205.

32. *DOL, Negociado de campaña*, 30 May 1926, 47.

33. Woolman, *Rebels in the Rif*, 205-207 and 222-224; and Woolman, "In Spanish Morocco," 85. Also see, Pennell, 216-217; Fleming, *Primo de Rivera*, 349-353; Furneaux, 228-239; Payne, 221; and Estado Mayor Central del Ejército, 134 and 137. A Riffian flag, which was captured in Ajdir, is today part of the Africa collection of the *Museo del Ejército* in Madrid. The author saw the flag in Toledo's Alcázar, where the Africa collection was on display in October 1993.

34. Woolman, *Rebels in the Rif*, 209. Estado Mayor del Ejército, 137-139.

35. *DOL, Negociado de campaña*, 2-30 June 1926, 47. Subinspección de la Legión, ed., 287-293 (Chapter 19), has a detailed listing of the activities of each of the eight *Banderas* for the month of June. *SHM*, Legajo #54, Rollo 16, *Colección de historiales*, "Campañas de Marruecos, Historial de guerra, 1ª y 2ª Banderas" (plus the 3ª and 4ª Banderas), 215-218. Fleming, *Primo de Rivera*, 367-369, covers the June phase of the

campaign including the "Raid Capaz" by Major Osvaldo Capaz Montes with 1,000 men through the Gomara. Estado Mayor Central del Ejército, 140-143, also covers the "Raid Capaz." In July 1936, then General Capaz Montes ("Hero of the Rif" and the man who reconquered Xauen in 1926) was serving as commander of the western zone of the protectorate. Hoping to escape having to chose one side over the other in the uprising in 1936, Capaz fled Morocco for Madrid, where he was promptly jailed by Republican forces in the Modelo Prison and subsequently executed. See Thomas, 224 and 404. Woolman, *Rebels in the Rif*, 210-211. Payne, 221.

On 1 June, the eight *Banderas* of the Legion were deployed as follows: the Ist and IInd were at Ikermin; the IIIrd was on the banks of the Guis River (Alhucemas); the IVth was at Ismoren; the Vth was at R'Gaia (as was the Squadron of Lancers); VIth was in Tetuán; the VIIth was at Maluserif; and the VIIIth was at Dar Semuat. See *DOL, Negociado de campaña*, 1 June 1926, 47.

On 1 July, the eight *Banderas* of the Legion were deployed thus: the Ist and IVth were at Ferrach (Targuist); the IInd was at Izugar; the IIIrd at Buxelah/Buselah; the Vth at Riffien; the VIth at Punta Pescadores; the VIIth at Sidi Aixa/Aisa; the VIIIth at Los Altos de Ferrach; and the Squadron of Lancers was still at R'Gaia. See *DOL, Negociado de campaña*, 1 July 1926, 47. *DOL, Negociado de campaña*, 2-31 July 1926, 48. Subinspección de la Legión, ed., 287-293 (Chapter 19), has a detailed listing of the activities of each of the eight *Banderas* for the month of July. *SHM*, Legajo #54, Rollo 16, *Colección de historiales*, "Campañas de Marruecos, Historial de guerra, 1ª y 2ª Banderas" (plus the 3ª and 4ª Banderas), 215-218. Fleming, *Primo de Rivera*, 369-370. Estado Mayor Central del Ejército, 141-142 covers July. *AGM*, Legajo #M-3204, SECCIÓN #1, DIVISIÓN #1 (July 1926), 24, recorded that Colonel José Millán Astray returned to duty in Ceuta (Dar Riffien) on 2 July after being shot in the face on 4 March at Loma Redonda. For the rest of his life, Millán Astray sported a green-tinted monocle over his vacant right eye socket. These monocles, considered treasured mementos by Legionaries, were shown to the author at the *Hermandad Nacional de Antiguos Caballeros Legionarios* in Madrid, and at the *Museo de la Legión* in Ceuta. *AGM*, Legajo #246, SECCIÓN #2, DIVISIÓN #10, contains a telegram from the commanding general of Ceuta to the War Ministry regarding the arrival of seventy-five Legion recruits from America (most probably Latin America). They would be transported from Valencia to Ceuta aboard the steamer *Balmes* and escorted by an officer, two sergeants, and eight enlisted men.

On 1 August, the eight *Banderas* were deployed as follows: the Ist and IInd were at Ferrach; the IIIrd remained at Buselach; the IVth was now at Ben Karrich (outside Tetuán); the Vth was at Alcazarquivir; the VIth was at Tazarines; the VIIth remained at Sidi Aixa; the VIIIth also remained at Los Altos del Ferrach; and the Squadron of Lancers was now in Tetuán. See *DOL, Negociado de campaña*, 1 August 1926, 48.

36. *DOL, Negociado de campaña*, 2 August 1926, 48.

37. *DOL, Negociado de campaña*, 4 August 1926, 48. Fleming, *Primo de Rivera*, 370. *AGM*, Legajo #M-3204, SECCIÓN #1, DIVISIÓN #1 (August 1926), 25 noted that Millán Astray personally took part in the capture of Zoco el Arbaa de Beni Hassan.

38. *DOL, Negociado de campaña*, 11 August 1926, 48. Fleming, *Primo de Rivera*, 370-371, gives the date of the capture of Xauen as 10 August, instead of 11 August. Woolman, *Rebels in the Rif*, 211, also gives the date as 10 August. *AGM*, Legajo #M-3204, SECCIÓN #1, DIVISIÓN #1 (August 1926), 25. Estado Mayor Central del Ejército, 143-146, covers the Spanish drive through the Yebala and the capture of Xauen. It is interesting to note that when Xauen was first taken in 1920 by Castro Girona, it was then High Commissioner of the Spanish protectorate, General Dámaso Berenguer Fusté, who was the senior officer to march in triumph through the city. Now, six years later, it would be his younger brother, General Federico Berenguer Fusté (commanding general of Ceuta) with the main body of the Spanish force, who would have that honor in mid-September.

39. *DOL, Negociado de campaña*, 12-31 August, 1926, 48. Subinspección de la Legión, ed., 287-293 (Chapter 19), has a detailed listing of each of the activities of the eight *Banderas* for the month of August. *SHM*, Legajo #54, Rollo 16, *Colección de historiales*, "Campañas de Marruecos, Historial de guerra, 1ª y 2ª Banderas" (plus the 3ª and 4ª Banderas), 215-218.

40. On 1 September the *Banderas* of the Legion were deployed as follows: The Ist and IIIrd were at Targuist; the IInd was at Izugar; the IVth was at Dar Acobba; the Vth was at Teffer; the VIth was in Xauen; the VIIth was at Zoco el Arbaa; the VIIIth was at Ferrach; and the Squadron of Lancers was at Riffien. See *DOL, Negociado de campaña*, 1 September 1926, 48-49.

41. *DOL, Negociado de campaña*, 14 September 1926, 49. Subinspección de la Legión, ed., 288-293 (Chapter 19), has a detailed listing of the activities of each of the eight *Banderas* for the month of September. Fleming, *Primo de Rivera*, 377. Estado Mayor Central del Ejército, 146-148, covers Spanish army operations in the Rif and Gomara during August and September. Woolman, *Rebels in the Rif*, 212.

42. *DOL, Negociado de campaña*, 1 October 1926, 49. During the month of October, the *Banderas* continued to carry out their typical campaign duties having one Legionary killed and three wounded. Subinspección de la Legión, ed., 288-293 (Chapter 19) has a detailed listing of the activities of each of the eight *Banderas* for the month of October.

43. Fleming, *Primo de Rivera*, 377. Woolman, *Rebels in the Rif*, 212, recorded that only the tribesmen of the Sumata in the Lukus, the Beni Lait in the Yebala, the Gezawa, and the Beni Yahmed fought on.

44. On 1 November the Legion was deployed as follows: The Ist and IIIrd *Banderas* were at Targuist; the IInd was at Tauima (the Dar Riffien of the East); the IVth remained at Dar Acobba; the Vth was at T'Zenin; the VIth was at Riffien; the VIIth was now in Xauen; the VIIIth was still at Ferrach; and the Squadron of Lancers was at Dar Xaui. See *DOL, Negociado de campaña*, 1 November 1926, 49.

45. *DOL, Negociado de campaña*, 3-4 November 1926, 49-50. Estado Mayor Central del Ejército, 149-152, provides the order of battle for the units that took part in the Yebala and Gomara campaigns of November and December. Fleming, *Primo de Rivera*, 378-379, gives more details on the army's operations during November (versus Beni Ider and Beni Aros) and December (versus Beni Lait). He went on to record that on 3

November, near the Beni Ider village of Sarrama, Spain's nemesis in the western zone, Ahmed Heriro, was fatally wounded in battle. Woolman, *Rebels in the Rif*, 212-213. Woolman called Ahmed Heriro "the most impressive leader in the west" and "one of Abd el Krim's most imaginative and intelligent lieutenants." Heriro was shot in the left kidney and died shortly thereafter. His body was carried away by fellow tribesmen, who buried him with honors in the mountains of Beni Aros.

46. *DOL, Negociado de campaña*, 6-7 November 1926, 50.

47. *DOL, Negociado de campaña*, 11 and 12-30 November 1926, 50. Subinspección de la Legión, ed., 287-293 (Chapter 19), has a detailed listing of the activities of each of the eight *Banderas* for the month of November. The only addition to the Legion's original charter (Appendix A) during 1926 dealt with what should be done about the growing number of Legionaries disabled while serving in the Legion. See *SHM*, Legajo #54, Rollo 16, *Colección de historiales*, "Legislación relativa a la Legión," Año 1926, ROC (22-XI-1926), CL #409 (426), DO #264 (591) ("Legionarios"): "Deciding that Legionaries who have been declared incapacitated and are presently awaiting admittance into the Corps of Invalids [Disabled], shall remain on the Command Headquarters Staff of the Corps [Legion] until the proceedings are resolved."

48. On 1 December the eight *Banderas* of the Legion were deployed thus: The Ist and IIIrd were at Targuist; the IInd was at Tauima; the IVth at Dar Acobba; the Vth at T'Zenin; the VIth and the Squadron of Lancers were now in Tetuán; the VIIth was in Xauen; and the VIIIth was at Ferrach. See *DOL, Negociado de campaña*, 1 December 1926, 50.

49. *DOL, Negociado de campaña*, 2-31 December 1926, 50. Subinspección de la Legión, ed., 288-293 (Chapter 19), has a detailed listing of the activities of each of the eight *Banderas* for the month of December. On 293-294 there is a wrap up of the Legion's accomplishments during the year 1926 and a preview of what was to come in 1927. In addition, 516-517 cover the major operations of the Legion for the year 1926. Fleming, *Primo de Rivera*, 379, wrote that by the end of the year, the *kabyles* of Beni Ider, Beni Aros, and Beni Lait had been vanquished. Woolman, *Rebels in the Rif*, 213, recorded that "by the end of 1926, the Spanish had collected 58,000 rifles, 175 machine guns, 119 cannon of various types, more than 5,000 hand grenades."

50. Subinspección de la Legión, ed., 294. Fleming, *Primo de Rivera*, 379, wrote that during the months of January, February, and March, General Sanjurjo did not carry out any major advances. He devoted the majority of his time to overseeing Primo de Rivera's repatriation program (see Woolman below) and reorganizing the army's cavalry and native units in Morocco. Despite these concerns, proposals were being prepared for further operations. Woolman, *Rebels in the Rif*, 213, noted that nearly all the tribes had surrendered and consequently the Spanish decreased the number of troops in Morocco to fewer than 90,000 men. Morales Lezcano, 238, observed that in January 1927 Mohamed V was proclaimed sultan of Morocco.

51. On 1 January 1927 the eight *Banderas* of the Legion were deployed as follows: The Ist and IInd were at Targuist; the IIIrd was at Cardeñosa; the IVth was at Dar Acobba; the Vth was at Megaret; the VIth was at Buharrat; the VIIth was in Xauen; and the

VIIIth was at Ferrach. See *DOL, Negociado de campaña*, 1 January 1927, 51; and *SHM*, Legajo #54, Rollo 16, *Colección de historiales*, "Campañas de Marruecos, Historial de guerra, 1ª y 2ª Banderas," 215.

52. Fleming, *Primo de Rivera*, 379. On 376, Fleming defined *marabout* as "saint." A *marabout* also means "prophet" in other parts of Africa. Woolman, *Rebels in the Rif*, 210, noted that Abd-el-Krim "despised" *marabouts* as "troublemakers."

53. Fleming, *Primo de Rivera*, 379-380. Woolman, *Rebels in the Rif*, 213. Subinspección de la Legión, ed., 295. *SHM*, Legajo #54, Rollo 16, *Colección de historiales*, "Campañas de Marruecos, Historial de guerra, 1ª y 2ª Banderas," 218. Estado Mayor Central del Ejército, 152-155. Scurr, 18.

54. Fleming, *Primo de Rivera*, 380-381. Woolman, *Rebels in the Rif*, 213. Estado Mayor Central del Ejército, 155-156, has all the details on the events of early April, including the number of casualties for both men and beasts. Subinspección de la Legión, ed., has a detailed account of the actions of the five *Banderas* that took part in this offensive: Ist (296); VIIIth (299); IInd (302-303); IIIrd (305); and the VIth (306). *SHM*, Legajo #54, Rollo 16, *Colección de historiales*, "Campañas de Marruecos, Historial de guerra, 1ª y 2ª Banderas" (3ª Bandera), 218-219 and 222-223. Ramas Izquierdo, 41-42, gives details on the death of Lieutenant Gonzalo de Ceballos Albiach, who was killed in battle on 5 April at Kaid-Tulud.

55. Estado Mayor Central del Ejército, 156-157. Fleming, *Primo de Rivera*, 381. Subinspección de la Legión, ed., 296-297 (Ist *Bandera*), 299-300 (VIIIth *Bandera*), 303 (IInd *Bandera*), 305 (IIIrd *Bandera*), and 306 (VIth *Bandera*). *SHM*, Legajo #54, Rollo 16, *Colección de historiales*, "Campañas de Marruecos, Historial de guerra, 1ª y 2ª Banderas," 219 and 222.

56. Fleming, *Primo de Rivera*, 381.

57. Fleming, *Primo de Rivera*, 381-382. This source noted that Colonel Luis Castello, not General Souza, commanded the column of the right. It is the author's belief that Colonel Castello was in actuality the field commander of this column. Estado Mayor Central del Ejército, 161-163, gives a complete order of battle that details all the units that took part in the Beni Aros operation. In the Yebala sector at this time, the IVth, Vth, and VIIth *Banderas*, along with the Squadron of Lancers, were operating. For example, Colonel Balme's column included one *Bandera* (most probably the Vth) and the Squadron of Lancers, while Colonel Canis' column also included one *Bandera* (most probably the VIIth). For more information on these *Banderas* during this time, see Subinspección de la Legión, ed., 518-519.

58. Estado Mayor Central del Ejército, 163-165, contains the order of battle for the units that took part in the Gomara and Ketama operations. Fleming, *Primo de Rivera*, 382. Subinspección de la Legión, ed., 298, 300-301, 304, 307-308, and 518-519, contains a detailed account of the daily activities of the eight *Banderas* of the Legion during the month of May. *SHM*, Legajo #54, Rollo 16, *Colección de historiales*, "Campañas de Marruecos, Historial de guerra, 1ª y 2ª Banderas" (3ª Bandera), 220, and 222-223.

59. Fleming, *Primo de Rivera*, 382. Estado Mayor Central del Ejército, 165-169, provides the details on the order of battle for all the units that took part in the battles fought

during the month of June, including the occupation of Yebel Alam in the Beni Aros on 16 June. For the actions of the *Banderas* during the month of June, see Subinspección de la Legión, ed., 298 (Ist), 301-302 (VIIIth), 304 (IInd at Amiadi), 306 (IIIrd at Badu), 308 (VIth), and 518-519.

60. Ramas Izquierdo, 295-296. The officer killed at Kudia Sebaa was Lieutenant Luis Corbacho García, commander of the machine gun company (most probably the 31/VIII) and, to the best of my knowledge (and the accounts of Ramas Izquierdo), the last Legion officer to be killed in battle. For more on the death of Lieutenant Luis Corbacho García, see 42. Subinspección de la Legión, ed., 298-299 (Ist *Bandera*) and 301 (VIIIth *Bandera*), also describes the battle of Kudia Sebaa. *SHM*, Legajo #54, Rollo 16, *Colección de historiales*, "Campañas de Marruecos, Historial de guerra, 1ª y 2ª Banderas" (3ª Bandera), 220-221, and 223.

61. *AGM*, Legajo #M-3204, SECCIÓN #1, DIVISIÓN #1 (June 1927), 26. *SHM*, DO #134, (19-VI-1927), Vol. II, 907. Along with Millán Astray's promotion to brigadier, Colonel of Infantry Luis Orgaz Yoldi and Colonel of Cavalry Sebastian Pozas Perea were also promoted to the same rank. Subinspección de la Legión, ed., 309. Colonel Eugenio Sanz de Larín officially took command of the Legion on 3 July 1927 (DO #145); in addition, Lieutenant Colonel Ricardo Rada Peral was named commander of the 1st Legion and Lieutenant Colonel Luis Valcazar Crespo was named commander of the 2nd Legion; see 318. Millán Astray's farewell address to the Legionaries can be found on 323. *SHM*, Legajo #54, Rollo 16, *Colección de historiales*, "Campañas de Marruecos, Historial de guerra, 1ª y 2ª Banderas," 223-226, contains the full text of Millán Astray's farewell address to his Legionaries. De Silva, 191-195, also contains the aforementioned letter. Scurr, 18, noted that Millán Astray "had personally fought in 62 actions" with the Legion. Llacuna and Polls, 53.

62. Estado Mayor Central del Ejército, 169-172, contains the details of the final military operations in early July, as well as the complete text of General Sanjurjo's address "To the Army and Naval forces of Morocco" regarding the termination of the war. Fleming, *Primo de Rivera*, 382-383, contains the passage noted in the text. It is a brief portion of Sanjurjo's complete letter and I have used his translation. De La Cierva, *Franco*, 97, noted that Sanjurjo dictated his last General Order of the campaign (the Bab Taza message) to General Goded. García Figueras, 211-213, also has the Bab Taza letter. Arraras, ed., 192 and 195. Subinspección de la Legión, ed., 315-318 and 518-519, contains information on the occupation of Bab Taza, and the participation of each individual *Bandera* and the Squadron of Lancers for the month of July and early August. *SHM*, Legajo #54, Rollo 16, *Colección de historiales*, "Campañas de Marruecos, Historial de guerra, 1ª y 2ª Banderas" (3ª Bandera), 221 and 223. Woolman, *Rebels in the Rif*, 213-214, recorded that "in the first week of July, the Blad l-Makhzen, for the first time in history, included all of northern Morocco. Spanish Morocco, at last, existed in fact as it had for so long on paper." Scurr, 18. The VIIth *Bandera* had the honor of representing the Legion when Bab Taza was occupied on 10 July. Llacuna and Polls, 53. Payne, 222. Morales Lezcano, 238. For a brief summary of the major events of the Ist, IInd, IIIrd, IVth, Vth, VIth, VIIth, and VIIIth *Banderas* of the Legion for the years 1926 and 1927, see *SHM*, Legajo #54, Rollo 16,

Colección de historiales, La Legión, "Acciones de guerra de las distintas Banderas de la Legión (1920-1939)," 4-5, 11-12, 16-17, 22-23, 27-28, 32, 34-35, and 37-38, respectively.

63. Subinspección de la Legión, ed., 317-318. During this time period, the Legion was deployed as follows: The Ist and IIIrd were at Badu; the IInd was at Tauima; the IVth was at Bab Taza; the Vth was at Riffien; the VIth was at Ankod; the VIIth was in Xauen; the VIIIth was at Targuist; and the Squadron of Lancers was at Riffien.

64. *AGM*, Legajo #M-3204, SECCIÓN #1, DIVISIÓN #1 (October 1927), 26. *SHM*, DO #220, (2-X-1927), 19. It is interesting to note that on the same day (and by the same DO #220) that Millán Astray was named honorary colonel of the Legion, Emilio Mola Vidal, colonel of infantry (*Regulares*) the man responsible for coordinating the rebel uprising that began the bloody Spanish Civil War, was promoted to the rank of brigadier general. Subinspección de la Legión, ed., 320. *SHM*, Legajo #54, Rollo 16, *Colección de historiales*, "Campañas de Marruecos, Historial de guerra, 1ª y 2ª Banderas," 227. De Silva, 196. Llacuna and Polls, 53.

65. This footnote covers both the Legion's national standard and the king's visit to the protectorate. *SHM*, DO #220, (2-X-1927), 19. Subinspección de la Legión, ed., 309-310 and 319-321. *AGM*, Legajo #M-3204, SECCIÓN #1, DIVISIÓN #1 (October 1927), 26. *SHM*, Legajo #54, Rollo 16, *Colección de historiales*, "Campañas de Marruecos, Historial de guerra, 1ª y 2ª Banderas," 226-231, has all the details (including the text of all the florid speeches given) on the ceremony held at Dar Riffien on 5 October 1927. Present at Dar Riffien that day was Valenzuela's young son, who represented his father. Woolman, *Rebels in the Rif,* 214. Bolín, 94-95. Llacuna and Polls, 53. Bueno y Núñez de Prado, 157-158. Bueno, *La Legión*, 21, has the photograph taken at Dar Riffien on 5 October 1927, but he erroneously gives the date as 27 April 1927. On 56 there is a photo of Queen Victoria Eugenia presenting the national standard to Colonel Sanz de Larín. Scurr, 18, also has the first photo noted in the above citation, and he identifies those who are pictured: the Bishop of Gallipoli (then residing in Tangier), R. P. Bentazos (who blessed the Legion's flag), Colonel Sanz de Larín, and the highly decorated (Laureate Cross of St. Ferdinand) Captain Fernando Lizcano de la Rosa.

66. Woolman, *Rebels in the Rif,* 214. *SHM*, CL #487, (21-XI-1927), 585-586, has all the information (detailed in three articles) on the Moroccan Peace Medal, including (1) the proposal for its creation; (2) its design, construction, and inscription; and (3) an explanation of who was eligible to receive this decoration. García Figueras, 213-214. Morales Lezcano, 239.

67. Barea, 79.

68. Scurr, 18. Subinspección de la Legión, ed., 323, contains Millán Astray's farewell address to his Legionaries in which he summed up the seven-year history of the corps, mentioning its battle casualties, awards, and heroes. His casualty count was "116 Bandera commanders and other officers killed; 319 Bandera commanders and other officers wounded; 1,871 Legionaries killed; and 5,775 Legionaries wounded."

Chapter 8

Conclusion and Epilogue

Forged in the crucible that was Spain's Moroccan protectorate during the Rif Rebellion, the Spanish Foreign Legion quickly assumed the mantle of Spain's elite military unit. Deriving its name from the historic "invincible Tercios" of the sixteenth and seventeenth centuries who found glory on the battlefields of Flanders and Italy, the *Tercios de Extranjeros* carried on that martial tradition into the twentieth century.

Spain's military power began a slow decline in the mid-17th century and reached its nadir in the Spanish-American War of 1898. During that conflict, the United States, an emerging world power, defeated the Spanish army and navy. Lack of preparedness and internal strife within the military led to its the poor showing during the war. With the only vestiges of empire left for Spain in North Africa, the Spanish Protectorate of Morocco became the focus for those wishing a military career. The field-grade officers who had served in Cuba or the Philippines in the latter years of the nineteenth century were now the senior field commanders of the Spanish army in Africa. They strove to redeem the reputation of Spanish arms. But the problems that contributed to the "disaster" of 1898 persisted in Morocco. Major engagements in 1908-1909 and 1911-1912 revealed the continued military impotence of the regular Spanish army. Besides failing to adapt to the style of warfare employed by the tribesmen of Morocco, the army was riven internally by the split between officers who wanted promotions based on seniority versus those who believed in promotion through "war merits." Spanish military conscripts, with poor training, shoddy equipment, and no stomach for fighting, were not up to the task of campaigning in Africa. This situation would continue until Miguel Primo de Rivera improved the quality of the regular army following the 1924 retreat from Xauen.

During the 1911-1912 campaign, Dámaso Berenguer Fusté founded the *Regulares*, a unit of Moroccan soldiers commanded by Spanish officers. The *Regulares* became the elite fighting unit of the Spanish army in Morocco, and the list of those who commanded its units reads like a who's who of the Spanish army during the first half of the twentieth century: Francisco Franco Bahamonde, Emilio Mola Vidal, José Varela Iglesias, Luis Orgaz y Yoldi, and Juan Yagüe Blanco. Spain's military strategy in conquering the protectorate was to move inland from their long-established coastal enclaves of Ceuta and Melilla into the interior. Between the two enclaves was Alhucemas Bay, a major objective in their campaign to conquer northern Morocco. The *Regulares*, as paid professionals and knowing the terrain, served as the vanguard for advancing armies, whereas Spanish conscripts were used to hold territory that had been conquered. Occupation of the terrain was accomplished through a series of small *blocaos* (blockhouses) that not only were vulnerable to enemy snipers but also proved a hardship for those called upon to man them.

The *Regulares* served the Spanish army very well in its conquest of the interior, but the Spaniards always felt mistrust concerning the loyalty of these indigenous forces. This mistrust of the *Regulares* was eventually justified when elements of the *Regulares de Melilla* betrayed their officers and companions to throw in their lot with Abd-el-Krim during the Annual disaster. Moreover, after Annual, some members of the *Regulares* sold their weapons and ammunition to agents in Tangier, who then turned around to sell them to Abd-el-Krim.

After the end of the Great War, it was Major José Millán Astray's idea to create a foreign legion, similar to its more famous French counterpart, within the Spanish army. A decorated war veteran of the Philippines and Moroccan campaigns, Millán Astray knew that the protectorate would never be pacified if ill-trained conscripts had to be used to combat the savvy rebels on their own turf. That job would require a unit of professional soldiers who would be well paid to put their lives on the line for Spain. Furthermore, as Millán Astray stated, each Legionary would take the place of a Spanish conscript in Morocco. This policy of substituting conscripts with professional soldiers paid to fight and die greatly appealed to the lower-middle and lower classes in Spain, whose poorly trained and equipped sons were being sent to Morocco by the thousands.

Having proposed his idea to the ministry of war in 1919, Millán Astray progressed rapidly toward plans for the creation of a *Tercio* of foreigners. With the government's approval, as well as support from influential sectors of the army, the Legion was officially born on 4 September 1920, although Legionaries celebrate on 20 September, the day the first man joined its ranks. The combination of Millán Astray and his chosen deputy, Major Francisco Franco Bahamonde, was complementary and highly effective. Millán Astray was the heart and soul of the Legion, the "idea man"; Franco was the foundation, the disciplinarian, and the executor. Franco brought his military professionalism to the corps, something lacking in almost all the units of the Spanish army of Africa. The Legion, with its own General Staff and organization, would be unique within the Spanish army. It was able to operate individually or as part of the vanguard units of the regular army during an operation. It was that flexibility that made the Legion so effective and potent during the Moroccan campaign.

Originally, the Legion's organizers hoped that foreigners would flock to join the Legion, but this did not occur in the anticipated numbers. In fact, the Legion was never manned by more than 10 percent foreigners. Nevertheless, through an effective propaganda campaign featuring colorful posters, the Legion attracted sufficient recruits from all parts of Spain. It offered its adherents better food, higher pay, and a distinctive uniform to set them apart from regular army personnel. Moreover, the Legion had separate and better training facilities and attracted the best officers in the military, with the majority coming from the *Regulares*. In return for these benefits, the Legion asked for strict loyalty and total sacrifice to Spain, the king, and the Legion. Harsh, often brutal discipline was imposed on those who broke the Legion's rules and tenets. Millán Astray's personal philosophy regarding the mixing of the Japanese code of Bushido, fervent Catholicism, and most important, an honorable battlefield death was inculcated into the very being of each Legionary.

As the Legion began to grow quickly from its genesis in late 1920, its reputation for blind obedience to orders, determination in carrying out its mission, ferocity in the face of the enemy, and total disregard for casualties grew as well. The Legion slowly but surely equaled, and then surpassed, the *Regulares* as the vanguard of the Spanish army in Morocco. It proved its value in the conquest of the Yebala during the first half of 1921 and the rescue of Melilla from the Riffians who had annihilated General Silvestre's army at Annual in July 1921. Its mere presence in Melilla could be considered a victory, since it restored hope and confidence that Melilla would not fall to the Riffians. For the rest of the year, the Legion led the way in the reconquest of the Melillan command, rolling back the gains Abd-el-Krim had made after Annual. During the years 1922-1923, the Legion continued to push the rebellious tribesmen deeper into the Rif, but at great cost in men killed and wounded. Among the dead were Lieutenant Colonel Rafael Valenzuela Urzaiz, who had replaced Millán Astray as commander in chief of the Legion. He was killed leading his men in battle while trying to break the siege of Tizzi-Azza. Without hesitation or debate, Franco succeeded Valenzuela as commander in chief of the Legion. It can safely be said that Franco, except for the brief period when Valenzuela was in command, was the true power within the Legion. He was always involved, from its formation, commanding it while Millán Astray was away either promoting the Legion in Spain or recuperating from his many wounds. Franco made the Legion his own by instilling in it his brand of stoic professionalism. The Legion became his own private army and would later serve as his Praetorian guard from 1936 to 1975.

In 1924, with Franco's undisputed reputation as a military leader, the Legion was able to flex its political muscle on two separate occasions. The first occurred at the Legion's main encampment of Ben Tieb in the protectorate's eastern zone. During a luncheon hosted by Franco for Primo de Rivera, the officers of the Legion and the *Regulares* expressed their displeasure with his plan to withdraw all Spanish forces to the coastal enclaves and basically abandon the protectorate. Primo de Rivera, as an army general and veteran of the Moroccan

Wars, knew that any undertaking in Morocco would have to be accomplished with the Legion's total commitment. Otherwise, Spain might potentially suffer one defeat after another throughout the protectorate. The outcry such a situation would have elicited from Spanish public opinion, as well as from the *africanistas*, would have been deafening. As a result of the Ben Tieb demonstration, Primo de Rivera modified his policy of abandonment to one of semiabandonment. Through the Legion's power and influence within the Spanish army of Africa, it had successfully reversed national policy concerning the protectorate.

The second instance took place prior to the retreat from Xauen, which was part of Primo de Rivera's plan for semiabandonment in the protectorate's western zone. In a rather vague plot, Franco, along with two other lieutenant colonels and a reluctant General Queipo de Llano, conspired to kidnap Primo de Rivera, his staff, and the High Commissioner and lock them up in Ceuta's *El Hacho* fortress. For this contemplated coup, Franco had volunteered the services of one *Bandera* of the Legion. Needless to say, the plot was aborted when Queipo de Llano refused to participate. Once again, the Legion was involved in a potential strike against the Primo de Rivera government.

It was because of the Legion that the evacuations of all the small *blocaos* in the Gomara and part of the Yebala, as well as the major town of Xauen, were successfully carried out. The casualties had been enormous, but without the actions of the Legion in covering the retreat, the end result would certainly have been another humiliating rout, not unlike Annual. When Primo de Rivera gave his order for the retreat from Xauen, the Legion obeyed.

During 1925 the Legion once again distinguished itself by putting an end to the rebellion in the Anjera *kabyle* by disembarking successfully at Alcazarseguer. The landing of 18,000 men at Alhucemas Bay in September superseded the earlier amphibious landing at Alcazarseguer. The Alhucemas Bay landings dealt Abd-el-Krim's rebellion a mortal blow because it opened a new front. To add to Abd-el-Krim's troubles, Spanish advances in Alhucemas were carried out in conjunction with a major offensive by the French from the south. Spanish troops quickly pushed toward his capital at Ajdir and captured it. He fled to the interior, but he could not escape the inevitable. The Spanish army, along with the eight *Banderas* and the Squadron of Lancers of the Legion, squeezed Abd-el-Krim from all sides. In 1926 he surrendered to French officials, knowing full well what awaited him if the Spaniards captured him. From then on it was just a matter of "mopping up" scattered pockets of resistance. The Rif Rebellion ended in July 1927.

Following the Alhucemas Bay landings and subsequent push toward Abd-el-Krim's capital, Franco rose to the rank of brigadier general and relinquished command of the Legion. Millán Astray once again assumed command of the Legion until June 1927, when he too became a brigadier general. Colonel Eugenio Sanz de Larín served as commander in chief of the Legion during the period of peace that followed the end of the Rif Rebellion.

Though this work on the Spanish Foreign Legion ends with the conclusion of hostilities in the protectorate, peace by no means signaled the end of the Legion. The eight *Banderas* and the Squadron of Lancers continued to serve as a garrison in Spanish Morocco. With the proclamation of the Second Republic in 1931, the Legion disbanded the VIIth and VIIIth *Banderas*, along with the stately Squadron of Lancers in 1932. In October 1934, when the miners of Asturias declared a Soviet-style revolution against the Republic, the minister of war, Diego Hidalgo, at Franco's suggestion, called upon the Legion and *Regulares* to extinguish the revolt. Lieutenant Colonel Juan Yagüe Blanco assumed command of the expedition, which included the Vth and VIth *Banderas*, and sailed from Morocco to Gijón. In brutal house-to-house fighting that left hundreds dead, the Legion accomplished its mission in less than two weeks. The Legion saved the Second Republic from revolution and at the same time gained the hatred and distrust of the Left. The Spanish Civil War (1936-1939) began in Melilla when the garrison there revolted against the Popular Front government. The rebellion quickly spread throughout the peninsula. The Spanish Foreign Legion and the *Regulares*, the battle-tested Spanish Army of Africa, declared for the rebels and essentially became Franco's personal army. This force played a pivotal role in Franco's ability to take over the Nationalist government and see the war through to a victorious conclusion. During the war the Legion grew to eighteen *Banderas*, including tank units, and was in the vanguard of every major battle. Unlike in 1934, in 1936 to 1939 the Legion played a significant role in bringing down the Second Republic.

With its mission accomplished and Franco firmly in power, the Legion's existence was secured, although the force was reduced in size, with *Banderas* XII through XVIII disbanded. All the remaining *Banderas* returned to Africa, where they took part in the battles of Ifni-Sahara in 1957-1958 and prepared to go into action once again in 1975 to stop King Hassan's "Green March" into the Western Sahara. With Franco's death in 1975 and the subsequent election of a Socialist government, attempts were made to do away with the Legion all together or to weaken it by reducing its training budget. Today it is a brigade-size unit (roughly 7,000 strong) with bases in Melilla (I *Tercio*), Ceuta (II *Tercio*), Almeria (III *Tercio*), and Ronda (IV *Tercio*). Peace-keeping duties in Bosnia-Herzegovina (Operation Alpha-Bravo), Albania, and most recently Kosovo as part of Spain's United Nations contingent, have given the Legion a new lease on life, since its existence before was rather uncertain. Presently the Legion is composed of volunteers who relish the opportunity to serve as shock troops for the Spanish army. In 1995 the Legion celebrated its 75th anniversary, and considering the precarious situation in Eastern Europe, it is possible that the Legion will live to see its 100th.

Appendix A

Organization of the Legion

ORGANIZATION

Circular. Most Excellent Sir: In compliance with what was agreed upon in the royal decree of the 31st of the previous month [DO N° 195], by which the groundwork for the creation of a *Tercio de Extranjeros* [Regiment of Foreigners] was determined, the King, God protect him, has seen fit to order that we proceed with the organization of said unit, adjusting itself to the following rules:

1. The *Tercio de Extranjeros* will form a unit of the Infantry arm and will be composed of its own command and administration headquarters, with one depot and instruction company and three *Banderas* [battalions], each composed of two rifle companies and one of machine guns, with the established designations of 1, 2 and 3.

2. This Corps should be employed tactically in the front line and in all operations of peace and war, without limit to that of its military utility.

3. The soldiers will swear the oath of fidelity to the Flag and will remain as Spanish soldiers subject to the Code of Military Justice and to the Ordinances of the Army.

4. The depot company shall have a number of soldiers under instruction that is in proportion to the necessities started by the organization of the units that are to be created and to the typical casualties that shall be produced henceforth.

5. The three companies of manoeuvre in each *Bandera* will constitute the "combat unit" of it, and the administrative command staff of the *Tercio* and the instruction company, the "Representation and depot of the *Tercio*."

6. We shall proceed immediately with the organization of the Command and administrative staff of the *Tercio*, first *Bandera* and depot company; appointing the lieutenant colonel chief of the *Tercio* and the staff of commanders, officers, professionals attached to the Army, the rank and file and contract workers, who figure into the plans that accompany.

7. This *Tercio* shall have its permanent barracks in Ceuta, in which town and in an adequate building to which it is assigned will establish its offices, warehouses and the "Representation and depot," and in it will establish its organization.

8. The instruction of these troops will be given in accordance with the current regulations.

9. The uniform and equipment, while a code of uniformity is developed for this unit, will principally pay attention to being practical, comfortable, attractive and economical, adhering to the following general principles:

> They will use as headgear, sidecap [*chapiri*—the symbol of the Legion] and peaked cap [*teresiana*], being allowed to wear the straw hat in the summer.
> The tunic [*guerrera*] shall be a greenish khaki, with stand-and-fall collar, and pockets. The pants, of the same color and in breeches-style [*granadero*].
> The gaiters, of cloth of the same color as the uniform. The shoes, brown, employing two types, one for the field and another for barracks or camp.
> The cartridge belts, knapsack, haversack, etc., etc., shall be the models used by the Infantry.
> The winter coat shall be the greatcoat [*capote-manta*].
> The commander of the unit, listening to the economic council, will propose to proceed with the uniform as definite. The commanders and officers destined for the *Tercio* will use the one of this Corps.

10. The armament shall be, according to regulation, the same as used by the Infantry, with Hotchkiss [Modèle 1914] machine guns.

11. The technical elements, for liaison, explosives, implements of sappers, etc., etc., shall be those which are assigned to the battalions of *Cazadores* [light infantry] and *tabores* [battalions] of the *Regulares*, and endowment of regimental matériel, of convoys of men and livestock, shall be the one known to be in the conditions that accompany themselves.

12. In the period of the organization of the first *Bandera*, fifty percent of the noncommissioned officers, sergeants and corporals that figure into the plans of

the same and the command staff of the *Tercio*, shall come from the ranks of the Infantry of the Army, and the remaining vacancies of these employments shall be covered with individuals of the *Tercio*, who possess the proper conditions.

13. The posting of the personnel shall be carried out with adjustment to the following pattern:

For the designation of all the commanders, officers and professionals who are to serve in the *Tercio*, shall bear in mind that the procedure shall be of free choice, by proposal of the High Commission; being recommendable conditions, primarily, campaign merits and services, especially those rendered in the territories of Africa, and the favorable report [which will be confidential] of the commander of the Corps, in regards to the conditions of tact, vigor, physical aptitude, and all else that would especially qualify them for the mission which they are about to undertake. The commanders and officers who aspire to obtain posting, shall formulate their petition through the usual channels, documented and informed as it is previously prepared. The instances of those who wish to be posted at the moment of the formation [of the *Tercio*], should be in Tetuán fifteen days prior to the publication of this royal order, with the goal that the High Commissioner can propose with urgency those selected. The commanders and officers of the *Tercio de Extranjeros* shall annually enjoy forty days of leave with full pay. The noncommissioned officers, sergeants and corporals from the Infantry will be able to, from the day of the publication of this royal order, request the vacancies that are expressed in the previous regulation. The applications will be forwarded to the High Commissioner and will be accompanied by the obligatory documents and of a statement, on a separate sheet, in addition to the marginal, on which the commander of the Corps will make his personal opinion evident of the conditions of especial aptitude of the applicant for his new posting, and shall furthermore show how many circumstances he estimates suitable, conducive to the major illustration concerning the personal characteristics, qualities of leadership, vigor and physical aptitude. Said commanders of Corps shall send the applications with the greatest urgency, with the goal that they will be in Tetuán before the fifteen days, beginning with the date of publication of this royal order.

14. The troops destined for the *Tercio de Extranjeros* shall urgently incorporate themselves, transported courtesy of the State and assisted by corporals with the details during the days of transport until their arrival in Ceuta, and all [NCOs, sergeants, and corporals] dressed in their finest; keeping in mind by the Corps, when disposing of their garments, that the cap, tunic and pants, shall be returned to the source of origin.

15. For the settlement of pay of all ranks cited, it will be kept in mind that it will cause definite vacancies in the units of origin at the end of the month in which the transfer is verified; and with the aim that from their incorporation into the *Tercio de Extranjeros*, they will enjoy the benefits of the increased incomes they will now have, they will pass review of incorporation on the day of their arrival to their *Banderas*, being performed by the *Tercio* the reclamation of the differences in pay until the end of the month, passing the responsibility to the Corps of origin, from those which they belonged, with settlement to the situation in which they passed review of the administrative officer.

16. The troops of first and second category and the contracted personnel will undergo medical examination in the same form as provided for the soldiers in the letters n), o), q), of the instructions for recruitment in Spain.

17. For the posting of the individuals of troops of all the Branches and Units who serve on active duty in the ranks, analogous requirements shall be observed which for the troops, except for the urgency in the course of its request, shall be handled normally.

18. The time of permanence in the *Tercio de Extranjeros* shall be considered for all intent and purposes of the law of recruitment as having served in the ranks of the Army.

19. All the postings of the Corps shall be covered with the individuals belonging to same; but for no concept can they be assigned to render other service which will separate them from the ranks of the *Tercio*.

20. The personnel of the troops can be promoted by *méritos de guerra* [battlefield promotions] and in time of peace, by arrangement to the prevailing provisions, and all the employments of first and second categories and to officers of the *Tercio de Extranjeros*, assimilated to the employment of *alférez* [2nd lieutenant] and lieutenant of the Army, figuring solely in the ranks of the same, in the form that and with the rules which in its day determine, without this concept may proceed to form part of the ranks of the Branches or Corps of the Army, nor occupy other postings than those characteristic of the *Tercio*.

Exempted from the aforementioned rule are those that, coming from the ranks of the Army, join up in the period of organization of the *Tercio* with the rank of corporal, sergeant or NCO, who, besides belonging to the ranks of these troops, shall enter into the general ranks of the Branch, in the form which corresponds to them, to the positions obtained.

21. Foreigners, in all positions of employment, and all the categories of troops coming from direct enlistment into the *Tercio*, could be discharged or expelled from it, for obvious ineptitude or unsuitability of his services, by proposal

of its commanding officer, who in turn could employ the same authority to discharge for similar causes soldiers and NCOs coming from the Branches and Corps, which in this case shall pass to the position which corresponds to them in the Army.

22. In the case of an individual being disabled in combat or from its results, he shall be entitled to retirement due to disability or join the Corps of Invalids, under the same conditions as the rest of the personnel of the Army.

23. Foreigners, after two years of service with irreproachable conduct and worthiness, will be issued a certificate which will serve as a basis for the concession of Spanish citizenship in case they desire it.

24. The punishments which shall be imposed on these troops for misdeeds or oversights, shall be those established by the provisional Code of Military Justice and the Code of Conduct for the detail and interior rules of the Corps; furthermore permitting the commanding officer of the *Tercio* to impose the punishment of suppression on the entire or on half of the remaining, which shall be applied to the improvement of the mess, in spite of what was decided upon in article 317 of the same Code and in 291, chapter 12, title 1 of the Rule previously cited.

25. By the Council of munitions and transport materiel of the Corps in the field and entities which correspond, the armament and materiel that figures in the enclosed statements shall be facilitated with all urgency, proceeding of course to its delivery with preference to any other who has solicited, and keeping in mind that this Corps, shall begin to receive its men thirty days from the publication of this royal order.

26. By the Direction of the Horse Breeding and Remount, to proceed in the same form and attending to equal reasons, to the acquisition and posting of the necessary livestock.

RECRUITMENT

27. The *Tercio* shall fill its ranks with foreigners and Spaniards between the ages of 18 to 40 years, admitting soldiers into the ranks, so long as they agree to the terms which the organization of this unit has established, exempting the volunteers with recompense in Africa, as long as they are serving their commitment.

28. The admission of soldiers shall be carried out in the manner which shall be set up later.

29. For admission of soldiers a birth certificate of the interested party will be insisted upon, or in its absence a declaration by the same, in which he can certify the particulars of filiation and nationality to which he belongs.

30. The duration of the agreement to enlist shall be of four or five years, with Spaniards remaining, in case of a call to arms, due to war or abnormal circumstances through which the Nation may be going through, assigned to the *Tercio* in which they would have served.

31. Having completed their first enlistment, they could reenlist for periods of six months, one year, two, three, four or five.

32. The individuals of the *Tercio*, at the moment they sign their commitment to enlist, will remain subject to the Ordinances and the Code of Military Justice, whose penal laws shall be made known to them at the time of said act, and especially articles 286, 287, 288, 289, 290, 291, 319, 320 and 322 of the above-mentioned Code.

INSTRUCTIONS FOR RECRUITMENT IN SPAIN

33. The recruitment of these troops shall be done in accordance with modern methods, employing an active propaganda campaign and facilitating, by rapidness and simplicity, the procedures of enlistment, by which one can reduce to a minimum the documentation that is required of those who solicit entry. For the organization and development of recruitment, the present instructions will be kept in mind:

a) In all the provincial military Governments of the peninsula, of the Balearic Islands and of the Canaries and general Commands of Africa, in the same way as the military Commands which, by judgment of the Captains-general, its importance will require it and the command staff of the *Tercio*, "recruiting centers for the *Tercio de Extranjeros* shall be established," in the charge of an officer or NCO designated by the Town to permanently discharge this service.
b) The Governor or military Commander shall designate the locale, office hours, which shall be daily and name the auxiliary personnel of the troops which will be indispensable, according to the circumstances of the location. He will likewise dictate the orders which he shall consider opportune for the recruitment propaganda, directing himself toward the military Commanders dependent on his authority and interesting the civil authorities of his demarcation, the necessary cooperation for the greatest success to the proposed aim.
c) The officers or NCOs in charge of the recruiting centers shall zealously make every effort to perform their difficult commitment, keeping in mind that the positive results of their efforts principally depend on the interest and enthusiasm which they put forth toward the task which has been entrusted to them.

d) They shall personally deal with the prospective recruits, whom they will inform in detail of the mission of the Corps, duties which they shall be contracted to perform and benefits which shall be provided to them, being lectured on the pertinent articles of the Code of Military Justice.

e) Once accepted in principle the future soldier of the *Tercio*, for his appearrance and first impression of his favorable spirit, shall be informed by the officer in charge the place and time at which he will be medically examined, giving him the corresponding orders of examination, according to model Nº 1.

f) Examined and classified as fit, the opportune agreement of enlistment will be extended to him, according to model Nº 2, and to it shall be attached the certificate of medical examination; documents which shall be carried by the interested party when presenting himself to the Corps.

g) Once the enlistment agreement has been signed by the new recruit, he shall be considered to be a Spanish soldier, subject to the Code of Military Justice, and shall be suitably attended to by the authorities, in regards to billeting and board, and finally, from the moment of his enlistment until that of undertaking the journey to join the colors, he shall enjoy a per diem of 2 *pesetas* for all types of amenities.

h) The incorporation of the recruits shall be carried out courtesy of the State, individually or forming a Corps, and with this aim and trying not to exceed more than three days the stay in the recruiting centers, the Governors or military Commanders remain expressly authorized to expedite the appropriate passports, telegraphically notifying the respective Captains-general and the Commanding General of Ceuta.

i) During the days of travel by train or ship, the recruits shall enjoy a travel allowance of 2.50 *pesetas* per day for travel or a major fraction of six hours, for all kinds of amenities, advancing the total amount of the recruitment center.

j) When the number or quality of the individuals warrant it, at the discretion of the military authority, the expeditions could be accompanied, to Algeciras, by a corporal. He shall enjoy a travel allowance of 2.50 *pesetas* (which shall be paid for by the recruiting center) in addition to the income which he is entitled to, computing in the same manner for the number of days or part used in his round trip and a day of rest in Algeciras.

k) For the costs of materials for the recruitment centers, stamps, registers, recruitment forms, medical examination orders embarkation lists, gratuities for the troop auxiliaries, etc., etc., also to be charged will be amenities and travel expenses corresponding to each enlistment, five *pesetas* per individual.

l) To attend to the previous expenses, the Captains-general of the regions shall order that different armed units, send to the recruiting centers sufficient quantities [of recruits]. They shall be processed monthly with others, balancing them with the charges extended against the *Tercio de Extranjeros*, who will pay for them with all possible speed by the most convenient procedure.

m) The medical examination to which instruction e) alludes to shall be performed by a military doctor whom the town will name, endeavoring to the utmost the continuance of the cited in the performance of this service.

n) The rules for the assessment of *fit* or *unfit* shall be those that receive the current dispositions for these cases, in addition to requiring a robust constitution and a perfectly functioning organic system.   The doctors nominated shall clearly understand that the quality of the services and the places where they are to dispense them requires that these men previously present a guarantee of health and outstanding stamina.

o) The assessments shall be those of *fit* or *unfit*, without the need for technical justifications, other diagnosis nor obligatory assessments.

p) The results of the examination shall be stamped by the own doctor at the bottom of the order for himself.

q) The recruits, upon arriving at their Corps, shall be examined for a second and final time, by a doctor of the *Tercio de Extranjeros*, and his dictum shall be final and unappealable, be it in agreement or disagreement with the first examination.

r) In the case of having passed judgment on the unfitness of the recruit on the second examination, he shall be returned to the place of his enlistment, providing him the appropriate passport requested by the *Tercio de Extranjeros*, which shall be courtesy of the State, and the individual shall go having been given two *pesetas* daily until the end of his journey.

s) To contribute to the propaganda of recruitment, we shall proceed with the writing of printed announcements and the affixing of posters, which shall be acquired and distributed to the recruitment centers by the *Tercio de Extranjeros*.

t) This complex clause deals with recruiting posters and how they will be paid for.

u) Likewise those in charge of the recruiting centers will make arrangements, with the support, if need be, of the authority on which they depend, the affixing of the posters in public or private places judged to be most suitable, such as the waiting rooms in the train stations, offices of steamship lines, police stations, barracks, etc., etc.; but always being watched by a person or entity responsible for its preservation.

v) The recruitment shall commence in thirty days, counting from the date of this disposition.

x) The Captains-general shall of course give the necessary orders for the establishment of the recruiting offices, notifying this Ministry of the number and types of those organized in each region and Corps to which they belong, occupations and names of the officers in charge.

WAGES

34. The commanders, officers and professionals who serve in the *Tercio de Extranjeros* shall receive in addition to their salary, bonuses and other income which they may be entitled to for their service in Africa, an annual bonus which shall be established by the State Budget, and which in the current fiscal year will be 1,500 *pesetas*.

35. The sergeants, NCOs and contractual workers shall enjoy salaries which have been set for similar troops in the other Corps in Morocco, and the monthly leftover funds settled in diagram A, to be reclaimed by days. For the rank and file, salaries shall be those stated in diagram B. Bonuses for enlistment and reenlistment shall be those specified in diagrams C and D.

36. The individual funds for clothing and savings shall take care of these two needs. When the interested party has paid for accessories and equipment received and set up a sufficient savings account to pay for all the equipment, what remains will be handed over to him, at any time, be it at the time of discharge, or to his survivors, in case of death.

37. The Commander of the Corps is authorized to encourage the members of the same of postal savings, under the direction and guarantee of their captains.

38. Inasmuch as the per diem and travel expenses for round-trip travel, as with all the costs of propaganda for recruitment and the five *pesetas* which are given to the recruiting centers for each enlistee, they shall be claimed in writing by a statement of corresponding review, justified with a copy of the charges made by the cited recruiting centers and certifying the costs of propaganda, authorized by the commander in chief of the *Tercio*.

39. Having taken care of the newness of the system being put in place, and keeping in mind that, according to these preliminary instructions, the recruiting centers shall be authorized to admit all volunteers who meet the proper conditions, and how inconvenient it would be to stop recruitment at any given moment, snubbing those individuals who want to join, the commander of the *Tercio* remains authorized to go on enlisting recruits, claiming their corresponding wages, even though the established size of the *Bandera* may be exceeded, with the aforementioned individuals attached to it provisionally or permanently.

40. Once the first *Bandera* has been organized, the High Commissioner shall inform this Ministry when to proceed with the formation of the second and third *Banderas*, at the same time proposing the appropriately needed changes and practical advice with regards to recruitment, payment and way of life of these troops.

41. For establishing the materiel fund, general expenditures and organization of the Corps, excluding personal salaries, the commander of the same shall be exempt from, for the first and only time, *one hundred and fifty thousand pesetas*, which shall be claimed in the bank statement review of next October, and from which, said commander, shall submit the appropriate justification to the unit's administrative office, when it has been organized, for proper review.

42. Separate from daily wages, 1.50 *pesetas* a month shall be claimed per individual in review, for maintenance of the above-mentioned matériel fund.

43. The clothing and savings fund shall be augmented by giving each soldier and NCO, at the time of induction, 225 *pesetas*, to establish his fund.

44. Likewise this Corps shall recognize the corresponding portion of wages, regarding the battalion barracks, offices, entertainment, weapons repairing, machine guns, training ammunition, horseshoes, harnesses, bridles, saddles, farrier's tools, rations of bread and fodder, fuel, lighting, cots, billeting and other costs which these troops may incur, so that for the above-mentioned they will be considered as any other in the Army.

45. These troops shall eat together, earmarking two *pesetas* a day per individual, being charged to their wages, and if need be, at the discretion of the commander of the Corps, set aside for the mess a portion or all of the daily bonus, when this is accrued.

46. Hospitalization owing to the troop shall be reimbursed from their pay at a rate of 0.88 *pesetas*, except in the case where they are justified by wounds, lesions or illnesses sustained in combat, in which case they shall be courtesy of the State.

By royal order I say to H.E. for his information and other results. May God keep H.E. safe for many years. Madrid, 4 of September of 1920.

Vizconde de Eza

Sir . . .

Appendix B

Table of Battle Casualties

Units	KILLED				WOUNDED				General Total
	Chiefs	Officers	Troops	TOTAL	Chiefs	Officers	Troops	TOTAL	
I Bandera	- - - -	29	472	501	1	72	1351	1424	1925
II Bandera	4	16	387	407	2	68	1061	1131	1538
III Bandera	- - - -	20	332	352	5	46	864	915	1267
IV Bandera	- - - -	14	241	255	2	44	775	821	1076
V Bandera	- - - -	15	164	179	2	29	660	691	870
VI Bandera	- - - -	14	210	224	2	31	714	747	971
VII Bandera	- - - -	2	36	38	2	14	199	215	253
VIII Bandera	- - - -	1	43	44	- - - -	6	145	151	195
Squadron of Lancers	- - - -	- - - -	- - - -	- - - -	- - - -	- - - -	1	1	1
General Total	4	111	1885	2000	16	310	5770	6096	8096

Percentage of Casualties for the Legion, 1921-1927

	Chiefs and Officers	Troops	Total
Posted and admitted	960	19,923	20,883
Casualties	441	7,655	8,096
Percentage	**45.94%**	**38.43%**	**38.77%**

War Casualties by Rank

Chiefs and Officers	Killed	Wounded	Total
Colonels	- - -	1	1
Lieutenant Colonels	1	3	4
Majors (*Comandantes*)	3	12	15
Captains	19	58	77
Lieutenants	49	130	179
2nd Lts. (*Alféreces*)	41	116	157
Medical Captains	- - -	1	1
Medical Lieutenants	1	5	6
Chaplains	1	- - -	1
		Total Casualties	**441**

Troops	Killed	Wounded	Total
Sergeant Majors (*Suboficiales*)	7	25	32
Sergeants	42	196	238
Corporals	146	466	612
Legionaries 2nd class	1,690	5,077	6,767
Medics	- - -	3	3
Farriers	- - -	3	3
		Total Casualties	**7,655**

Summary of Casualties

Chiefs and Officers	441
Troops	7,655
General Total	**8,096**

Source: Federico Ramas Izquierdo, *La Legión* (Ceuta, 1933), 18-19.

Appendix C

The Legion's Creed

THE SPIRIT OF THE LEGIONARY is unique and without equal; it is of blind and fierce combativeness, always seeking to close with the enemy to employ the bayonet.

THE SPIRIT OF COMRADESHIP, with the sacred oath to never abandon a man in the field until all have perished.

THE SPIRIT OF FRIENDSHIP is the oath sworn between each two men.

THE SPIRIT OF UNITY AND SUCCOR. At the cry of "The Legion to my aid!" wherever it may be, all will go to the rescue and, with or without reason, will defend the Legionary who asks for help.

THE SPIRIT OF THE MARCH. Never will a Legionary say he is tired until he collapses from exhaustion. It will be the swiftest and toughest corps.

THE SPIRIT OF SUFFERING AND TOUGHNESS. The Legionary will not complain of fatigue, nor of pain, nor of hunger, nor of thirst, nor of lack of sleep; he will perform all jobs, will dig, will haul cannons, vehicles; he will man outposts, escort convoys; he will work on whatever he is ordered.

THE SPIRIT OF SEEKING BATTLE. The Legion, from the individual man, to the entire Legion, will always rush to where firing is heard, by day, by night, always, always, even though not ordered to do so.

THE SPIRIT OF DISCIPLINE. He will carry out his duty, he will obey until death.

THE SPIRIT OF COMBAT. The Legion will ask always, always, to fight, out of turn, without counting the days, nor the months, nor the years.

THE SPIRIT OF DEATH. To die in combat is the greatest honor. One does not die more than once. Death comes without pain and to die is not as horrible as it seems. More horrifying is to live as a coward.

The flag of THE LEGION will be the most glorious because it will be stained with the blood of its Legionaries.

All Legionaries are brave; each nation is famous for its courage; here it is necessary to demonstrate which people are the most valiant.[1]

NOTE

1. For the original Spanish text, see Millán Astray, 23-29. Scurr, 6; and Hills, 143 (n. 26). It is interesting to note that the "spirit of comradeship" of the Legion was not unlike the Mongol's code of law (*yasa*), which "made it a capital offense for a warrior to abandon a comrade in battle." See John Keegan, *A History of Warfare* (New York: Alfred A. Knopf, 1994), 205.

Songs of the Legion

"Official Hymn of the Tercio"
(Song of the Legionary)

I'm a valiant and loyal Legionary
I'm a soldier of the brave Legion;
in my soul an aching calvary weighs
which seeks redemption in battle.
My emblem knows no fear,
my destiny is solely to suffer,
my Standard, to fight with daring
until attaining
victory or death.

Legionary, Legionary,
who gives yourself to fight,
and to fate do you leave your luck,
for your life is a game of chance.
Legionary, Legionary,
with bravery that is unmatched,
if in battle you find death,
you shall always have for a shroud
Legionary,
the National Flag.

We are all unknown heroes,
no one cares to know who I am;
a thousand tragedies, of various types,
life's twists and turns have formed.

Each one shall be what he wants,
my previous life has no importance,
but together we make up the Standard
which gives the Legion
the highest honor.

Legionary, Legionary,
who give yourself to fight,
and to fate do you leave your luck,
for your life is a game of chance.
Legionary, Legionary,
with bravery that is unmatched,
if in battle you find death,
you shall always have for a shroud
Legionary,
the National Flag.

Words: Comandante Emilio Guillem   Music: Modesto Romero

"The Betrothed of Death"

No one in the Tercio knew
who that Legionary was
so audacious and reckless
who enlisted in the Legion.

No one knew his past
moreover the Legion assumed
that a great pain bit at him
like a wolf at his heart
moreover, if someone asked him who he was
he would answer them with pain and hardness.

I am a man who luck
has wounded with the claws of a beast
I am betrothed to Death
who's going to unite in a strong embrace
with such a loyal companion.

When the battle was the roughest
and the fight most fierce
defending his Standard
the Legionary advanced
and without fearing the thrust
of the excited enemy
he knew how to die like a brave man
and he rescued the Ensign
And, as he stained the burning soil with his blood,
the Legionary, in a pained voice, murmured:

I am a man who luck
has wounded with the claws of a beast
I am betrothed to Death
who's going to unite in a strong embrace
with such a loyal companion.

When his body was finally recovered
next to his heart they found
a letter and a picture
of a beautiful woman
And that letter said
. . . "If God calls you one day,
claim a place for me,

for I am soon to find you"
And in the last kiss which he sent
his last goodbye he dedicated to her.

For having gone to your side to see you
my most loyal companion
I became the betrothed of Death
I drew her close with a strong embrace
and her love became my standard.

Words: Fidel Prado   Music: Juan Costa

"Heroic Tercios"
(Hymn of the Legionaries)

Heroic Tercios, valiant Legion,
which knows how to die in the vanguard
they are the pride of our Spain,
your exploits to fight.
Those who were not born in Spain
and blood and life you give for its honor,
sons of Spain are favorites
who have won its exalted love.
Legionaries to fight,
Legionaries to die,
Legionaries to fight,
Legionaries to die.

Long live Spain! valiant brothers
Long live Spain! immortal Legion.
It's a great glory to die for Spain
embracing a sublime ideal.
With the blood spilled by its sons
the laurels shall sprout more luxuriant,
from which we'll make wreaths that Spain
in its august conscious shall lay.

Long live Spain!
Long live the Legion!

If a rough, fierce fight should arise
or if the eagerness for the struggle ceases to exist,
know that you are always surrounded by loving
subtle shades which give you a kiss.
The thought of Spain as a whole
can be seen in the tenuous, fleeting murmuring
that never ceases to caress you
and is around you as you march.
Legionaries to fight!
Legionaries to die!
Legionaries to fight!
Legionaries to die!

Long live Spain!
Long live the Legion!

Undefeated Tercios, Legion of the brave
to the entire world with pride
you could look at, because you
are of the entire world, honor and glory.

Where the fallen have cried in anguish
where a brother gave his life,
where treacheries ask for vengeance
your bravery was always present.
Legionaries to fight!
Legionaries to die!
Legionaries to fight!
Legionaries to die!

Long live Spain!
Long live the Legion!

Words: Antonio Soler   Music: Francisco Cales

Sources: Ramón Moya Ruiz, 9, 12, and 16, and for the words and sheet music, Coronel Juan Mateo y Pérez de Alejo, 179-182, 183-186, and 187-189. Translations solely by the author, except for *Heroic Tercios*, which was translated by the author and Andrés J. Santana, following punctuation of the original.

Appendix E

A Brief Biography of José Millán Astray y Terreros

José Millán Astray, the future founder of the Spanish Foreign Legion, was born on 5 July 1879 in La Coruña in the province of Galicia. He was the second child and only son of José Millán Astray, a lawyer and writer, and Pilar Terreros Segade. Raised in a middle-class family, he entered the Infantry Academy located in the Alcázar of Toledo on 30 August 1894, having just turned fifteen years of age. Taking advantage of an abbreviated course of study, he graduated in February 1896 at the age of sixteen. The newly commissioned second lieutenant was assigned to the 1st Regiment of the King (*Regimiento del Rey Nº 1*) in Madrid. Six months later on 1 September 1896, he was admitted to the Superior War College (*Escuela Superior de Guerra*). His studies were interrupted by the Philippine insurrection. He served there from 1896 to 1897, receiving numerous decorations for combat actions. It has been written that as he left Manila Bay, he saw the need for creating a legion of volunteers, not conscripts, who would be willing to fight Spain's battles abroad. Having returned from the Philippines, he completed his studies and later became an instructor at the Infantry Academy in Toledo.

With the loss of Spain's overseas colonies in 1898, advancement and promotions were to be found in the protectorate of northern Morocco. In Spanish Morocco, Millán Astray commanded indigenous forces, both the native police and the *Regulares*, and through bravery and competence quickly achieved promotions. Having experienced the arduous duty of serving in Morocco and aware of the glories of the French Foreign Legion both in their colonies and in France during the Great War, Millán Astray was now more certain than ever that a special unit of fighting men was needed for service in the protectorate. By 1919, Major Millán Astray had returned to Madrid and there, as a member of the Tactical Commission, was responsible for updating the infantry manuals. The two texts were *Notas para el tiro de aplicación del combate* and *Especialistas de la Compañía.*

In 1919, he approached the minister of war with the idea of setting up a legion of foreigners, based in part on the French model, which would serve as the shock troops of the Spanish army in Africa. He believed that only well-trained and disciplined professionals could handle the hazards and deprivations that were commonplace in Morocco, not conscripts who had no stomach for combating the tribesmen of the Yebala, Gomara, and Rif. With all the necessary governmental approvals given, Millán Astray was promoted to the rank of lieutenant colonel in 1920 and the Spanish Foreign Legion, or *Tercio de Extranjeros*, was born.

With Major Francisco Franco Bahamonde as his second-in-command, Millán Astray would instill in his Legionaries a fervent sense of duty, courage to the point of recklessness, and blind obedience. It was he who introduced the "cult of death" to the Legion, as is reflected in its various mottos and war cries. Legionaries would become the spearhead of the Spanish army, beginning with the Rif Rebellion and continuing to this day. Wounded several times in battle, as well as losing his left arm, right eye, and several fingers on his right hand, Millán Astray would go on to be known as *El Glorioso Mutilado* ("The Glorious Mutilated One"), as well as *El Fundador* ("The Founder"). Promoted to brigadier general in 1927, Millán Astray would keep a low profile during the Second Republic. He traveled extensively throughout Latin America and visited the United States prior to the start of the Spanish Civil War. When the Civil War began in 1936, he was in Argentina but quickly returned to be at Franco's and the Nationalists' side. In the first days of the uprising, he served as the head of the press and propaganda department, but later was named director general of the Corps of Mutilated Gentlemen (Wounded War Veterans). He died on 1 January 1954 having attained the rank of major general, as well as honorary colonel of the Legion. He is interred in the *Cementerio de Nuestra Señora de la Almudena de Madrid.*

Sources: José Millán Astray, *La Legión* (Madrid, 1923); General Carlos de Silva, *General Millán Astray* (Barcelona, 1956); and *AGM*, Legajo #M-3204, SECCIÓN #1, DIVISIÓN #1. This is Millán Astray's personnel file, which contains all the information regarding his military career, it is located at the *Archivo General Militar* in the Alcázar of Segovia. For an vivid portrayal of Millán Astray, see Barea's description of him in *The Track*, 88-91 and 173. A negative depiction of Millán Astray is to be found in an article written by an ex-Legionary entitled "Embajadas Malditas" ("Damned Embassies") and published in a New York anarchist newspaper called *Cultura Proletaria*, 3, Nº 186, Saturday, 4 October 1930, 1.

A Brief Biography of Francisco Franco Bahamonde

Francisco Franco Bahamonde was born on 4 December 1892, in the naval seaport of El Ferrol in the province of Galicia. He was the second son of a naval paymaster who dreamed of following in the footsteps of his forefathers by becoming a naval officer. The Spanish-American War put an end to those aspirations as Spain's overseas empire was lost and along with it the need for a large number of naval vessels and officers. With no opening to be found in the Naval Academy, a position was found for the young Franco at the Infantry Academy in Toledo. He entered the gates of the Alcázar in Toledo in 1907, even though he was underage at the time. Small of stature and build, Franco drilled with a sawed-off rifle and stoically endured the hazing of his classmates. He was seventeen years old when he graduated 251st out of a class of 312 cadets in July 1910 with the rank of second lieutenant. He was assigned to the 8th Regiment of Zamora (*Regimiento de Zamora Nº 8*), stationed in El Ferrol.

After the war of 1898, only Spain's overseas possessions in Africa held promise for a martial career, especially for one with such low class standing. Promotions and decorations were to be had in Morocco, so in 1912 Franco volunteered for service in the newly established protectorate. In February 1912, he disembarked in Melilla assigned to the 68th Regiment of Africa (*Regimiento de África Nº 68*). As a member of the nascent *Regulares de Melilla*, Franco fought against El Mizzian in the eastern zone. Later, in 1914, he transferred to the western zone, where he campaigned against el Raisuni. His personal courage, self-discipline, and military acumen allowed him to earn the respect not only of his men but of his fellow army officers as well. Promotions came quickly for Franco as he became the youngest officer in each rank within the Spanish army. He once said to his superior officers who kept recommending him for medals, "I don't want decorations, . . . I would like promotion." An *africanista* like Millán Astray, he believed in Spain's mission in Morocco. Franco was very different from his fellow officers in that he never imbibed, gambled, or whored, but devoted himself to his work. Always leading his troops from the front, Franco was gravely wounded in the abdomen on 29 June 1916 at El Biutz when he led a charge against a rebel machine gun. Not expected to survive his wounds, he was nearly left behind on the battlefield, but he threatened to personally shoot the doctor if he was not the next man to be evacuated. Sent back to Spain to recover, Major Franco spent the next four years in Oviedo, Asturias, performing garrison duty with the Regiment of the Prince (*Regimiento del Príncipe*). His application to attend the Army War College for advanced military education was rejected because of his high rank. Nevertheless, his encounter with Millán Astray in late 1919 led him to accept his offer to become his deputy in the newly created Spanish Foreign Legion. Franco's well-earned reputation for organization, knowledge of tactics, and *sang-froid* preceded him, and Millán Astray knew instinctively that Franco was the man who could fulfill his dream of forming the elite unit of the Spanish army in Africa.

As commander of the Ist *Bandera* of the Legion, Franco took part in all the major battles in both the eastern zone and the western zone of the protectorate. His thoroughness, combat experience, and bravery under fire brought him to the attention of his superiors. Stanley Payne wrote, "Sanjurjo, his commander in Melilla in 1921-22, twice recommended him for promotion to lieutenant colonel, but this proved impossible until after his thirtieth birthday." The Rif Rebellion, and especially Franco's command of the Legion from 1923 to 1926, magnified Franco's already established reputation, which would pay off handsomely when Franco needed it to back the Nationalist forces during the Spanish Civil War and beyond. During the retreat from Xauen, and particularly at the Alhucemas Bay landing of 1925, Franco surpassed himself, receiving the highest of praise from Marshal Lyautey. Subsequently, Franco was promoted to the rank of brigadier general at only thirty-three years of age. He became not only the youngest general in the Spanish army, but also the youngest general in Europe since Napoleon Bonaparte.

With the Rif Rebellion having been brought to a victorious conclusion in 1927, General Franco was named head of the new military academy in Zaragoza in 1928. There he introduced new military tactics (e.g., the importance of artillery and armor in modern warfare), as well as instilling in the cadets the conservative traditional values he cherished such as honor, duty, and patriotism. In 1930, Franco supported the monarchy at the time of the Jaca revolt. However, he would go on to uphold the laws of the Second Republic from its inception in 1931, to the start of the Civil War, even though the left-wing elements in the cabinet had removed him from command of the military academy and had posted him first to La Coruña in 1931 and then to the Balearic Islands in 1933. During the Asturian miners' strike in October 1934, Franco stood by the Republic and put down the revolt with the use of the Foreign Legion and the *Regulares de Ceuta* from Morocco.

When the Spanish Civil War began in 1936, General Franco was in the Canary Islands. He, along with other officers who were not Republicans, had been posted outside the peninsula. General Emilio Mola in Pamplona declared the coup d'état with the support of other high-ranking officers, but not Franco's. Franco remembered the *Sanjurjada*, the botched attempt by General Sanjurjo in Sevilla in 1932 to overthrow the government, and he waited to see what would happen. Sanjurjo, who had been living in exile in Portugal and had been tapped to head the rebels, was killed in a fiery plane crash. With Mola in control of the northern areas, Franco crossed over to Morocco to assume command of the Spanish Army of Africa (the Legion and the *Regulares*), the best-trained and most-experienced unit in the Spanish army. The Spanish Army of Africa was quickly transported across the Straits of Gibraltar in the first air bridge in history using German and Italian transport planes. With Sanjurjo out of the picture, Franco and the Spanish Army of Africa wwere able to supplant the influence of Mola in the north. The nine generals who made up the Nationalist hierarchy voted to make Franco Generalissimo (and *Caudillo* of Spain) for the duration of the war. Able to create a coalition that consisted of various political parties, the Catholic Church, and his allies Germany and Italy, Franco proceeded to fight a methodical military campaign that not only won him victories on the battlefield but also enabled him to eliminate his political foes. Total victory was won in 1939 at the expense of a devastated and fractured nation. During World War II, Franco declared his neutrality while supporting his former Axis benefactors. He refused to join the Axis or to allow the German army to march through Spain in order to seize Gibraltar. However, to repay his debt to Germany for the *Kondor Legion*, Franco sent the "Blue Division" to fight on their side against the Soviet Union. The *Caudillo* was able to adapt his foreign policy depending on the fortunes of war, taking a pro-Axis approach during the early victories of the Axis, but moving to one that was more pro-Allies when things started to turn against his former patrons. Nevertheless, whereas Adolf Hitler and Benito Mussolini never lived to see the end of the war, Francisco Franco survived to rule Spain for the next twenty years.

A pariah after the war, Franco was able to take advantage of the Cold War. Because Franco was a staunch anti-Communist, the United States drew closer to him, eventually allowing Spain to join the North Atlantic Treaty Organization. Bringing peace and stability to a nation that had known only war and political turmoil, he ensured for Spain a steadily improving economy and standard of living. Franco chose as his successor and mentored Prince Juan Carlos, heir of Alfonso XIII, the last king of Spain. Francisco Franco died on 20 November 1975 and is entombed behind the altar in the basilica of the monument he built for those who died fighting for God and Spain during the "War of Liberation" in the *Santa Cruz del Valle de los Caídos* (The Valley of the Fallen), located in the Sierra de Guadarrama, northwest of Madrid.

Sources: Joaquín Arraras, *Franco* (Burgos, 1938); S.F.A. Coles, *Franco of Spain*

(Westminster, MD, 1956); Brian Crozier, *Franco: A Biographical History* (London, 1967); Ricardo De La Cierva, *Francisco Franco: Un siglo de España*, 2 vols. (Madrid, 1973); Luis De Galinsoga, *Centinela de occidente* (Barcelona, 1956); Fernando de Valdesoto, *Francisco Franco* (Madrid, 1943); Francisco Franco Bahamonde, *Marruecos: Diario de una Bandera* (Madrid, Privately printed, 1922); George Hills, *Franco: The Man and His Nation* (New York, 1967); J.W.D. Trythall, *Franco: A Biography* (London, 1970); Paul Preston, *Franco: A Biography* (New York, 1994); Sheelagh Ellwood, *Franco* (London and New York, 1994); Stanley G. Payne, *Politics and the Military in Modern Spain* (Stanford, 1967); David S. Woolman, *Rebels in the Rif* (Stanford, CA, 1968); A & E's *Biography*, "Franco"; and Arturo Barea, *The Track* (London, 1984), 173-174.

Lieutenant Colonel Franco authored two training manuals while he was a member of the Legion: (1) *Instrucciones generales de paz y guerra* and (2) *Instrucciones generales para el regimen interior del Cuerpo.*

Appendix G

Chart of Enlistment Bonuses

	For four years	For five years
For corporals proceeding from the Corps [i.e., the army], in the organization of the *Tercio*	500 *pesetas*	700 *pesetas*
For Spanish soldiers	500 *idem*	700 *idem*
For foreigners	400 *idem*	600 *idem*

Bonuses will be paid [as follows]: half the amount at the time of admission into the *Tercio*, (i.e., following the second physical examination), and the other half, in three equal amounts, after the completion of each of the first three years of service.

Source: *SHM*, DO #199 (5-IX-20), Tomo III, Tercer Trimestre, L130, 889.

Appendix H

List of All Forces at Alhucemas Bay, September 1925

COLUMN FROM THE WESTERN ZONE (Ceuta)

Command: General Leopoldo de Saro y Marin.
Chief of the General Staff: Lieutenant Colonel Mariano Santiago Guerrero.

- One unit (12) of light tanks (Renault *FT-17s*).
- Three *tabores* of the *harca* (two from Tetuán and one from Larache). 900 men total.
- One *tabor* of the *Mehal-la* of Larache.
- Three *tabores* of Infantry from the *Regulares* of Tetuán Nº 1.
- The VIth and VIIth *Banderas* of the *Tercio* (Legion).
- The battalions of *Cazadores* (Chasseurs) of Africa Nos. 3, 5, and 8.
- One battery of 105 mm howitzers (Schneider model 1913).
- Two mountain batteries of 77 mm (Krupp M96nA).
- One mobile depot with two platoons of infantry and one of artillery.
- One unit with four companies of sappers (two from the battalion of Tetuán and two from the one of Larache).
- One platoon of illumination.
- One platoon of field telephones (with twenty handsets).
- Eight optical stations (heliographs).
- One platoon of engineers (laborers).
- Three radio-telegraph stations (one semifixed and two mountain).
- One mountain supply (quartermaster) company, with 125 charges/loads.
- One field bakery platoon.
- One supply platoon to supervise the provisions depot.
- One platoon of a hundred farm workers from the Quartermaster Corps, to assist

in the unloading of matériel.
- One mountain ambulance with thirty-six litters (divided into three platoons of twelve).
- One field hospital with 300 beds, which includes a platoon of sappers to set it up.
- One hygiene service platoon.
- One platoon of a hundred men from the *Compañía de Mar de Ceuta* (coastal infantry to assist in the disembarkation).
- One platoon of a hundred stretcher bearers.

COLUMN FROM THE EASTERN ZONE (Melilla)

Command: General Emilio Fernández Pérez.
Chief of the General Staff: Lieutenant Colonel Alfredo Guedea Lozano.

- The *Harca* of Melilla (800 men).
- Three *tabores* of infantry from the *Mehal-la* of Melilla.
- Three *tabores* of infantry from the *Regulares* of Melilla.
- The IInd and IIIrd *Banderas* of the *Tercio* (Legion).
- One battalion of marine infantry.
- The battalion of *Cazadores* (Chasseurs) of Africa Nº 16; the 2nd battalion of the Infantry Regiment of Africa and the 1st battalion of the Infantry Regiment of Melilla.
- One battery of 105 mm howitzers (Schneider model 1913).
- Two mountain batteries of 77 mm (Krupp M96nA).
- One mobile depot with two platoons of infantry and one of artillery.
- One unit with three companies of sappers.
- One platoon of illumination.
- One platoon of field telephones with twenty handsets.
- Nine optical stations (two on horseback).
- One platoon of engineers (laborers).
- Three radio-telegraph stations (one semifixed and two mountain).
- One mountain supply (quartermaster) company, with 125 charges/loads.
- One field bakery platoon.
- One supply platoon to supervise the provisions depot.
- One platoon of a hundred farm workers from the Quartermaster Corps to assist in the unloading of matériel.
- One mountain ambulance with thirty-six litters (divided into three platoons of twelve).
- One field hospital with 300 beds, which includes a platoon of sappers to set it up.
- One hygiene service platoon.
- One platoon of a hundred men from the *Compañía de Mar de Melilla and Larache* (coastal infantry to assist in the disembarkation).

- One platoon of a hundred stretcher bearers.

Sources: Estado Mayor Central del Ejército, vol. IV, 38-40. This source also details which units were transported aboard which merchant ship for the Alhucemas Bay landing. Quintana Martínez and Llabres Bernal, 250-251; Goded Llopis, 147-151 and 153-156; and Gómez-Jordana y Souza, 124-127, have the same information. The latter source noted that the total number of men involved on the ground would be 18,165, and 4,028 horses and mules. Ibid. has the following information on the air force's contribution, as well as the navy's.

AIR FORCE

Eight squadrons from Melilla, with forty-eight airplanes.
Four expeditionary squadrons, with forty airplanes.
Two squadrons of hydroplanes, with twelve airplanes.
Total: one hundred airplanes.

It was hoped that two-thirds of the planes would be engaged at any one time, and that 22,000 aerial bombs would be needed. To the air force could be added the following contribution from the navy's air arm:

- twenty-four hydroplanes from the *Dedalo*.
- one captive (barrage) balloon.
- five free-floating balloons.
- two dirigibles.

NAVY

- two battleships (*Alfonso XIII* [Admiral Yolif's flagship] and *Jaime I*).
- four cruisers (*Méndez Núñez*, *Blas de Lezo*, *Reina Victoria Eugenia*, and *Extremadura*).
- two destroyers (*Alsedo* and *Velasco*).
- eight torpedo boats (Nos. *7*, *11*, *17*, *22*, et al.).
- six gunboats (*Canovas*, *Canalejas*, *Dato*, *Laya*, *Lauria*, and *Recalde*).
- eleven armed trawlers (*Arcila*, *Alcázar*, *Larache*, *Tetuán*, *Xauen*, *Uad Targa*, *Uad Kert*, *Uad Lucus*, *Uad Ras*, *Uad Muluya*, and *Uad Martín*).
- twenty-six "K-type" landing barges (Nos. *K-1* to *K-26*).
- four transports (*Almirante Lobo*, *España 5*, *Vicente la Roda*, and *A. Cola*).
- two tugs (*four were available: Ciclope, Ferrolano, Gaditano,* and *Cartagenero*).
- two water tenders (*África* and *Número 2*).

For a complete list of all the ships that took part in the operation, see Quintana

Martínez and Llabres Bernal, 257-259. For more details on the ships themselves, see *Jane's Fighting Ships*, ed. (1923 edition for Spanish ships).

The first wave of invaders to hit the beach at Alhucemas would have had the following supplies aboard their "K" crafts:

- 1,920,000 7 mm Mauser cartridges.
- 4,000 hand grenades.
- 2,000 rifle grenades.
- (Two grenades per 6,000 combatants.)
- 1,800 60 mm mortar rounds.
- 48,000 sandbags.
- 2,400 meters of barbed wire.
- 13,600 cold rations for Europeans.
- 4,000 cold rations for natives.
- (For two days.)
- 20,000 rations of crackers.
- 28,000 liters of water for one day at half ration.*

*To these figures should be added the individual allotment issued to each soldier.

For more information on all the equipment that was loaded for the invasion, (from mules, to cement, to wooden plugs to repair shell holes, to life jackets and savers), see Estado Mayor Central del Ejército, 43-45, and Gómez-Jordana y Souza, 125-127. The latter source also includes the number and sizes (from 15 mm to 155 mm) of artillery shells (including 478 gas shells for the 155 mm howitzer), as well as tents, firewood, and feed for the horses and mules. Quintana Martínez and Llabres Bernal, 266, names the ships that transported the supplies and lists what each individual ship carried, as do Estado Mayor Central del Ejército, 41 and 47-49, and Gómez-Jordana y Souza, 132-133. Woolman, *Rebels in the Rif*, 190, noted that "each Spanish soldier was fully equipped with rations, ammunition, grenades, and a gas mask, and the ships carried large supplies of bombs and poison gas."

Bibliography

I. PRIMARY SOURCES

Archival Sources

Servicio Histórico Militar (*SHM*) (Madrid), Legajo #54, Rollo 16 (Microfilm), *Colección de historiales* (La Legión). This file contains the following documents regarding the history of the Legion:

"Campañas de Marruecos, Historial de guerra, 1ª y 2ª Banderas"
"Historial de guerra del Tercio Gran Capitán"
"La Legión (1920-1939): Acciones de guerra de las distintas Banderas de la Legión (1920-1939)"
"La Legión: Resumen histórico"
"[Laureados] del Tercio Gran Capitán—1° de la Legión"
"Legislación relativa a la Legión (1920-1960)"
"Vestuario: Modificaciones en la uniformidad"

Archivo General Militar (*AGM*) (Segovia)

      a. Legajo #246, SECCIÓN 2ª, DIVISIÓN 10ª. This file contains all available material on the Legion, including background on the formation of a foreign legion (19th century), letters written in favor of creating one in 1919, copies of important entries from the DO, Franco's two training manuals for the Legion, organization charts, telegrams, etc.

      b. Legajo #M-3204—José Millán Astray Terreros
      Legajo #F-1025—Manuel Fernández Silvestre
      Legajo #M-3422—Emilio Mola Vidal
      Legajo #B (*sic*)-284—Rafael Valenzuela Urzaiz
      Legajo #C-138—Alberto Castro Girona
      Legajo #B-3 (Ilustres)—Dámaso Berenguer Fusté

El Serrallo de la Legión, Plana Mayor del Tercio, Archivo General (Ceuta)

Resumen histórico de la Legión/Negociado de campaña/Diario de operaciones de la Legión desde su organización en el mes de septiembre del año [1920] hasta el día de la fecha [1927]. This document (*DOL*) provides a detailed day-by-day account of the activities of all the Banderas that took part in the Moroccan campaign (1920-1927).

Academia de Formación de Mandos Legionarios, *Síntesis histórica de la Legión*, Ronda, 1985.

Resumen histórico de la Legión.

Historial del Tercio Duque de Alba—II de la Legión.

Published Documents

The Army War College, Course at the Army War College, *The Present Situation of Spain in Morocco*. Brigadier General Allison Owen, La. N.G. Memorandum for the Director, G-2 Division, The Army War College, 11 October 1924. Washington Barracks, D.C.: The Army War College Curricular Archives, File Number #288A-80.

Estado Mayor Central del Ejército, Servicio Histórico Militar. *Historia de las Campañas de Marruecos*. Vols. III & IV. Madrid: Imprenta Ideal, 1981.

Ministerio de la Guerra. *Colección legislativa del Ejército: 1920-1927*. Madrid: Talleres del deposito de la Guerra, 1920-1927.

Ministerio de la Guerra. *Diario oficial del Ministerio de la Guerra: 1920-1927*. Madrid: Talleres del deposito de la Guerra, 1920-1927.

Memoires and Letters

Berenguer Fusté, Dámaso. *Campañas en el Rif y Yebala, 1919-1920: Notas y documentos de mi diario de operaciones*. Vol. II. Madrid, 1925 and 1948.

———. *Campañas en el Rif y Yebala, 1921-1922: Notas y documentos de mi diario de operaciones*. Madrid: Sucesores De R. Velasco, 1923.

Roger-Mathieu, J., ed. *Memoires d'Abd-el-Krim*. Paris: Librairie des Champs-Elysees, 1927.

Sheean, Vincent. *An American among the Riffi*. New York: The Century Co., 1926.

———. *Personal History*. Garden City: Country Life Press, 1934-35.

Contemporary Newspapers and Periodicals

Times (London), August and November 1921.

New York Times, August-December 1921.

Cultura Proletaria (New York), 4 August 1930.

El Faro (Ceuta), 19 September 1993.

Books

Aage, Prince of Denmark. *My Life in the French Foreign Legion.* London: Eveleigh Nash & Grayson, 1928.

Azpeitua, Antonio. *Marruecos, la mala semilla: Ensayo de análisis objetivo de como fue sembrada la guerra en África.* Madrid, 1921.

Barea, Arturo. *The Forging of a Rebel.* Translated by Ilsa Barea. New York: Reynal & Hitchcock, 1946.

———. *The Track.* Translated by Ilsa Barea. London: Flamingo, 1984.

Bastos Ansart, Francisco. *El desastre de Annual.* Barcelona: Editorial Minerva, 1921.

Bolín, Luis. *Spain: The Vital Years.* With a foreword by Sir Arthur Bryant C.B.E. Philadelphia and New York: J.B. Lippincott, 1967.

Brennan, Terry, as told to W. J. Blackledge. *Death Squads in Morocco.* London: Sampson Low, Marston & Co., 1937.

de Abenia Taure, Ignacio. *Memorias sobre el Riff.* Zaragoza: Imprenta de Antonio Gallifa, 1859.

Eza, Vizconde de. *Mi responsabilidad en el desastre de Melilla como Ministro de la Guerra.* Madrid: Gráficas Reunidas, 1923.

Forbes, Rosita. *El Raisuni, the Sultan of the Mountains: His Life as Told to Rosita Forbes.* London: Thornton Butterworth, 1924.

Franco Bahamonde, Francisco. *Marruecos: Diario de una Bandera.* Madrid: Privately printed, 1922.

García Figueras, Tomás. *Marruecos: La acción de España en el Norte de África.* Barcelona: Ediciones Fe, 1939.

Goded Llopis, Manuel. *Marruecos: Las etapas de la pacificación.* Madrid: Compañía Iber-Americana de Publicaciones, 1932.

Gómez-Jordana y Souza, Francisco. *La tramoya de nuestra actuación en Marruecos.* Madrid: Editora Nacional, 1976.

Harris, Walter B. *France, Spain and the Riff.* London: Edward Arnold & Co., 1927.

La Legión. Riffien: *Memoria de las obras y mejoras realizadas.* Ceuta: Revista África, 1930.

López Rienda, Rafael. *Abd-el-Krim contra Francia: Impresiones de un cronista de guerra.* Madrid: Calpe, 1925.

Manue, George R. *Têtes Brûlées: Cinq ans de legion.* n.p.: La Nouvelle Societe D'Edition, 1929.

Martínez de Campos, Arsenio. *Melilla, 1921.* Ciudad Real, 1922.

Martínez Esparza, José. *Con la División Azul en Rusia.* Madrid: Ediciones Ejército, 1943.

Mateo y Pérez de Alejo, Juan. *La Legión que vive . . . Episodios de la Legión.* Ceuta: Imprenta África, 1927.

Mellor, Frank H. *Morocco Awakes.* London: Methuen Publishers, 1939.

Meyer, Walter. *Dreitausend Kilometer barfuss durch Afrika.* Stuttgart: Loewes Verlag Ferdinand Carl, 1929.

Mico y España, Carlos. *Los caballeros de la Legión (El libro del Tercio de Extranjeros).* Prologue by Tomás Borras and with various letters from Lieutenant Colonel José Millán Astray, first commander of the Tercio de Extranjeros. Madrid: Ucesores De Rivadeneyra, 1922.

Millán Astray, José. *La Legión.* Madrid: V. H. Sanz Calleja, 1923.

Mola Vidal, Emilio. *Dar Akobba: Páginas de sangre, de dolor y de gloria.* Madrid: Doncel, 1977.

Ortega y Gasset, E. *Annual*. Madrid: Rivadeneyra, 1922.

Pechkoff, Zinovi. *The Bugle Sounds*. With a preface by Andre Maurois. New York and London: D. Appleton and Company, 1926.

Picasso González, Juan. *Expediente Picasso: Documentos relacionados con la información instruida por el señor general de división D. Juan Picasso sobre las responsabilidades de la actuación española en Marruecos durante julio de mil novecientos veintiuno*. Prologue by Diego Abad de Santillan. Mexico, D.F.: Frente de Afirmación Hispanista, A.C., 1976.

Price, G. Ward. *In Morocco with the Legion*. London: Jarrolds, 1934.

Prieto, Indalecio. *Con El Rey o contra El Rey: Guerra de Marruecos*. 2 vols. Barcelona: Editorial Planeta, 1990.

Queipo de Llano, Gonzalo. *El General Queipo de Llano perseguido por la dictadura*. Madrid: Javier Morata, 1930.

Quintana Martínez, Eduardo, and Juan Llabres Bernal. *La Marina De Guerra en África*. Madrid: Compañía Ibero-Americana de Publicaciones, S.A., 1928.

Rodríguez de Viguri y Seoane, Luis. *La retirada de Annual y el asedio de Monte Arruit*. Madrid: Sucesores de Rivadeneyra, 1924.

Ruiz Albeniz, Victor. *Ecce Homo: Prueba documental y aportes ineditos sobre las causas del derrumbamiento y consecuencias de él*. Madrid: Biblioteca Nueva, 1922.

Sablotny, Richard. *Legionnaire in Morocco*. Los Angeles: Wetzel Publishing Co., 1940.

Vivero, Augusto. *El derrumbamiento: La verdad sobre el desastre del Rif*. Madrid: Rafael Caro Raggio, 1922.

Waterhouse, Francis A., in collaboration with Roger Wimbush. *Desert Carrion: An Autobiography of the French Foreign Legion*. London: Sampson Low, Marston & Co., n.d.

II. SECONDARY SOURCES

Books

al-Fasi, Alal. *The Independence Movements in Arab North Africa*. Translated from the Arabic by Hazem Zaki Nuseibeh. New York: Octagon Press, 1970.

Alonso, J. Ramón. *Historia política del ejército español*. Madrid: Editora Nacional, 1974.

Alonso Baquer, Miguel. *El ejército en la sociedad española*. Madrid: Ediciones del Movimiento, 1971.

Arques, Enrique, and Narciso Gibert. *Los Mogataces: Los primitivos soldados moros de España en África*. Ceuta-Tetuán: Imp. Tropas Coloniales, 1928.

Arraras, Joaquín, ed. *Franco*. Burgos and Santiago de Chile, 1938.

————. *Historia de la Cruzada Española*. 8 vols. Vol. 1, Madrid: Ediciones Españolas, 1939.

Asprey, Robert B. *War in the Shadows: The Guerrilla in History*. New York: Doubleday & Co., 1975.

Ayache, Germain. *Les origines de la Guerre du Rif*. Rabat, Maroc: SEMER, 1981.

Ayensa, Emilio. *Del desastre de Annual a la Presidencia del Consejo*. Madrid: Rafael Caro Raggio, 1930.

Balfour, Sebastian. *The End of the Spanish Empire, 1898-1923*. Oxford: Clarendon Press, 1997.

Ball, Robert W. D. *Mauser Military Rifles of the World.* Iola, WI: Krause Publications, 1996.

Baon, Rogelio. *La cara humana de un caudillo—401 Anecdotas.* Madrid: Editorial San Martín, 1975.

Bañon Martínez, Rafael, and Thomas M. Barker, eds. *Armed Forces and Society in Spain Past and Present.* New York: Columbia University Press, 1988.

Benzo, Eduardo. *Al servicio del ejército: Tres ensayos sobre el problema militar de España.* With a prologue by G. Marañón. Madrid: Javier Morata, 1931.

Blanco Escolá, Carlos. *La Academia General Militar de Zaragoza (1928-1931).* Barcelona: Labor Universitaria, 1989.

Boado y Castro, José. *El fusil Mauser español, modelo de 1893; descripción, municiones, accesorios, funcionamiento, nomemclatura, desarme, cuidados que exige, noticias de su fabricación, reconocimientos, tiro de precisión, marcas y empaques, propiedades balísticas y datos numéricos.* Madrid: Tipográfico, 1895.

Boyd, Carolyn P. *Praetorian Politics in Liberal Spain.* Chapel Hill, NC: University of North Carolina Press, 1979.

Bueno Carrera, José María. *La Legión: 75 años de uniformes legionarios.* Málaga: Gráficas Urania, 1994.

———. *Los Regulares: Uniformes y organización de las Tropas Regulares Indígenas de Marruecos.* Madrid: Aldaba Militaria, 1989.

———. *Uniformes de las unidades militares de la ciudad de Melilla.* Madrid: Aldaba Militaria, 1990.

Bueno y Núñez de Prado, Emilio. *Historia de la acción de España en Marruecos (desde 1904 a 1927).* Madrid: Editorial Ibérica, 1929.

Busquets, Julio. *El militar de carrera en España.* Barcelona: Editorial Ariel, 1984.

Cardona, Gabriel. *El poder militar en la España contemporánea hasta la Guerra Civil.* Madrid: Siglo XXI de España Editores, 1983.

Carr, Raymond. *Spain, 1808-1939.* Oxford: Clarendon Press, 1966.

———. *Spain, 1808-1975.* Oxford: Clarendon Press, 1982.

Carrasco García, Antonio. *Las imágenes del desastre: Annual, 1921.* Madrid: Almena Ediciones, 1999.

Castellanos, Fr. Manuel P. *Historia de Marruecos.* Vol. II, 4th edition. Madrid, 1946.

Coles, S.F.A. *Franco of Spain.* Westminster, MD, 1956.

Crónica de la aviación. Esplugues de Llobregat: Plaza & Janes, 1992.

Crozier, Brian. *Franco: A Biographical History.* London: Eyre & Spottiswoode, 1967.

Davidson, Basil. *The People's Cause: A History of Guerrillas in Africa.* n.p.: Longman Studies in African History, 1981.

de Arce, Carlos. *Historia de la Legión española.* Barcelona: Editorial Mitre, 1984.

De Galinsoga, Luis. *Centinela de occidente.* With the collaboration of Lieutenant General Franco Salgado. Barcelona: Editorial AHR, 1956.

De La Cierva, Ricardo. *Francisco Franco: Un siglo de España.* 2 vols. Madrid: Editora Nacional, 1973.

———. *Franco.* Barcelona: Editorial Planeta, 1986.

de la Torre Galán, Julio. ¡La Legión! . . . ¡Esa Novia! . . . Madrid, 1969.

de Mazarrasa, Javier. *Blindados en España, 1ª Parte: La Guerra Civil, 1936-1939.* Nº 2. Valladolid: Quiron Ediciones,1991.

De Silva, Carlos. *General Millán Astray (El Legionario)*. Barcelona: Editorial AHR, 1956.

de Valdesoto, Fernando. *Francisco Franco*. Madrid: Afrodisio Aguado, 1943.

Dupuy, R. Ernest, and Trevor N. Dupuy. *The Encyclopedia of Military History from 3500 B.C.. to the Present*. New York: Harper & Row, 1970.

Eggenberger, David. *An Encyclopedia of Battles: Accounts of over 1,560 Battles from 1479 B.C.. to the Present*. New York: Dover Publications, 1985.

Ellwood, Sheelagh. *Franco*. London and New York: Longman, 1994.

Farragut, Juan (pseud.). *Memorias de un legionario*. Madrid: Imprenta Artística, 1925.

Fermoselle, Rafael. *The Evolution of the Cuban Military, 1492-1986*. Miami: Ediciones Universales, 1987.

Fernández de la Reguera, Ricardo, and Susana March. *El desastre de Annual*. Barcelona: Editorial Planeta, 1968.

Fiestas, José M., ed. *Guia del Museo del Ejército*. Madrid: Privately printed, 1984.

Fleming, Shannon E. *Primo de Rivera and Abd-el-Krim: The Struggle in Spanish Morocco, 1923-1927*. New York and London: Garland Publishing, 1991.

Furneaux, Rupert. *Abdel Krim—Emir of the Rif*. London: Secker & Warburg, 1967.

Garriga, Ramón. *La Señora de El Pardo*. Barcelona: Editorial Planeta, 1979.

Gil Grimau, R. *Aproximación a una bibliografía española sobre el Norte de África (1850-1980)*. Madrid: Ministerio de Asuntos Exteriores. Dir. Gral. de Relaciones Culturales, 1982.

González Iglesias, Manuel. *Los novios de la Muerte*. Madrid, 1968.

Hardman, J. *The Spanish Campaign in Morocco*. Edinburgh, 1860.

Hills, George. *Franco: The Man and His Nation*. New York: MacMillan Company, 1967.

———. *Spain*. New York: Praeger Publishers, 1970.

Hobart, F.W.A. *Pictorial History of the Machine Gun*. New York: Drake Publishers, 1972.

Hogg, Ian V., and John Weeks. *Military Small Arms of the 20th Century*. Northfield, IL: DBI Books, 1985.

Hoisington, William A. *Lyautey and the French Conquest of Morocco*. New York: St. Martin's Press, 1995.

Jane's Fighting Ships, ed. London, 1923 and 1925.

Janzen, Jerry L. *Bayonets*. Tulsa, OK: By the author, P.O. Box 2863, 1987.

Joll, James. *The Origins of the First World War*. New York: Longman, 1984.

Keegan, John. *A History of Warfare*. New York: Alfred A. Knopf, 1994.

———. *World Armies*. London: MacMillan Press, 1979.

Kunz, Rudibert, and Rolf-Dieter Müller. *Giftgas gegen Abd el Krim: Deutschland, Spanien und der Gaskrieg in Spanisch-Marokko, 1922-1927*. Freiburg: Verlag Rombach, 1990.

Laroui, Abdallah. *The History of the Maghrib: An Interpretive Essay*. Translated by Ralph Manheim. Princeton, NJ: Princeton University Press, 1977.

Llacuna, José, and José María Polls. *Novios de la Muerte: Historia de la Legión*. n.p., 1987.

Macksey, Kenneth, and John H. Batchelor. *Tank: A History of the Armoured Fighting Vehicle*. New York: Charles Scribner's Sons, 1970.

Martí, Javier. *La Legión extranjera y El Tercio*. Ceuta: Privately printed, 1997.

Morales Lezcano, Victor. *España y el Norte de África—El Protectorado en Marruecos (1912-1956)*. Madrid: U.N.E.D., 1986.

Olson, Ludwig. *Mauser Bolt Rifles*. 3d ed. Montezuma, IA: F. Brownell & Son, 1976.

Payne, Stanley G. *Politics and the Military in Modern Spain*. Stanford, CA: Stanford University Press, 1967.

Pecker, Beatriz, and Carlos Pérez Grange. *Crónica de la aviación española*. Madrid: Silex, 1983.

Pennell, C. Richard. *A Country with a Government and a Flag: The Rif War in Morocco, 1921-1926*. Wisbech, Cambridgeshire, England: Middle East and North African Studies Press, 1986.

Petrie, Sir Charles. *King Alfonso XIII and His Age*. London: Chapman & Hall, 1963.

Porch, Douglas. *The French Foreign Legion: A Complete History of the Legendary Fighting Force*. New York: HarperCollins Publishers, 1991.

Preston, Paul. *Franco: A Biography*. New York: Basic Books, 1994.

Ramas Izquierdo, Federico. *La Legión: Historial de guerra (1 septiembre 1920 al 12 octubre 1927)*. Ceuta: Imprenta África, 1933.

Rezette, Robert. *The Spanish Enclaves in Morocco*. Translated from the English [*sic*] by Mary Ewalt. Paris: Nouvelles Editions Latines, 1976.

Salas, Delfin. *Tropas Regulares Indígenas*. Vol. II. Madrid: Aldaba Militaria, 1989.

Salas Larrazábal, Ramón. *El Protectorado de España en Marruecos*. Madrid: Editorial MAPFRE, S.A., 1992.

San Martín Losada, Eduardo. *España y su glorioso ejército*. 4th ed. Madrid: Ediciones S.M.L., 1952.

Santa Marina, Luys. *Tras el aguila del César: Elegía del Tercio, 1921-1922*. Barcelona: Planeta, 1980.

Scurr, John. *The Spanish Foreign Legion*. Osprey Men-at-Arms Series, no. 161. London: Osprey Publishing, 1985.

Sender, Ramón J. *Pro Patria*. Translated by James Cleugh from the Spanish novel *Iman*. Boston: Houghton Mifflin Company, 1935.

Subinspección de la Legión, ed. *La Legión española: Cincuenta años de historia, 1920-1936*. Madrid: Leganes, 1975.

Thomas, Hugh. *The Spanish Civil War*. New York: Simon & Schuster, 1961.

Thompson, Leroy. *Uniforms of the Soldiers of Fortune*. Poole & Dorset: Blanford Press, 1985.

Trythall, J.W.D. *Franco: A Biography*. London: Rupert Hart-Davis, 1970.

Turnbull, Patrick. *The Hotter Winds*. London: Hutchinson, 1960.

Windrow, Martin. *French Foreign Legion*. Osprey Men-at-Arms Series. Reading, Berkshire, England: Osprey Publications, 1971.

Woolman, David S. *Rebels in the Rif: Abd el Krim and the Rif Rebellion*. Stanford, CA: Stanford University Press, 1968.

Ullman, Joan Connelly. *The Tragic Week: A Study of Anti-clericalism in Spain, 1875-1912*. Cambridge, MA: Harvard University Press, 1968.

Chapters

Cano Velasco, Fernando, ed. "Las Fuerzas Regulares Indígenas" & "La Legión." *Historia de las fuerzas armadas*. Vol. IV. Zaragoza: Ediciones Palafox, 1984.

Fage, J. D. and Roland Oliver, eds. "Morocco." *The Cambridge History of Africa*. Vol. VII. London and New York: Cambridge University Press, 1975.

Fitzsimons, Bernard, ed. *The Illustrated Encyclopedia of 20th Century Weapons and Warfare*. Vol. VIII. New York: Columbia House, n.d. S.v. "España," by Antony Preston, ed.

Hernández Pardo, Pedro, ed. "Weapons of the Spanish Army through the Ages." *Historia de las fuerzas armadas*. Vol. V. Zaragoza: Ediciones Palafox, 1984.

Journals

Estes, Kenneth W. "New brigade structure cements future of Spanish Legion." *International Defense Review* (May 1995): 68-69.

Fleming, Shannon E. "North Africa." *In Spain in the Nineteenth-Century World: Essays on Spanish Diplomacy, 1789-1898*, ed. James W. Cortada, 91-102. Westport, CT: Greenwood Press, 1994.

Galey, John H. "Bridegrooms of Death: A Profile Study of the Spanish Foreign Legion." *Journal of Contemporary History* 4, no. 2 (April 1969): 47-64.

Huetz de Lemps, Xavier. "la collaboration franco-espagnole pendant la guerre du rif (1925-27). un mariage d'amour ou de raison?" *Hesperis Tamuda* 29, Fasc. 1 (1991): 85-111.

Jensen, R. Geoffrey. "José Millán-Astray and the Nationalist 'Crusade' in Spain." *Journal of Contemporary History* 27, no. 3 (July 1992): 432-441.

Pennell, C. Richard. "Ideology and Practical Politics: A Case Study of the Rif War in Morocco, 1921-1926." *International Journal of Middle East Studies* 14, no. 1 (1982): 19-33.

Scaramanga, Philip K. "The Spanish Legion[:] professional core of Spain's rapid deployment force?" *International Defense Review* (March 1988): 274.

Shinar, Pessah. "Abd al Qadir and Abd al Krim: Religious Influences on Their Thought and Action." *Asian and African Studies* Vol. I, Annual of the Israeli Oriental Society, Jerusalem, 1965: 160-174 (on Abd-el-Krim).

Pamphlets

de Samargo, Juan. *Guía del Museo de la Legión*. Ceuta: By the museum, 1990.

Tercio Duque de Alba, 2° de la Legión. *LXXIII Aniversario, 1920-1993*. Ceuta: Privately printed, 1993.

Dissertations, Theses, and Unpublished Papers

Fleming, Shannon E. "The Disaster of Annual: Spanish Colonial Failure in Northern Morocco, 1902-1921." Master's thesis, University of Minnesota, 1969.

Moya Ruiz, Ramón. *La Legión española: La música de la Legión*. Madrid: Privately printed by the author, n.d.

Shinkarenko, Nikolai Vsevolodovich. World War I holdings. *File Number #CSUZ68020-A*. Hoover Institute, Stanford University.

Magazines

De Sotto y Montes, General Joaquín. "Notas para la historia de las fuerzas indígenas del antiguo protectorado de marruecos." *Revista de Historia Militar* 35, (n.d.): 117-154.

García Serrano, Rafael. "¡LA LEGIÓN! 75 años de trayectoria esforzada y heroica." *Defensa: Revista internacional de ejércitos, armamento y tecnología* 18, No. 204 (April 1995): 50.

Turnbull, Patrick. "Spanish Foreign Legion." *War Monthly,* no. 30 (September 1976): 15-17.

Varea, Bonifacio. "El Pueblo de Hormilla con la Legión." *Hermandad Legionaria,* 7 (June 1991): 13-14.

Vaughan, Ron. "The Forgotten Army: The Spanish in Morocco." *Savage & Soldier* 16, no. 2 (April-June 1984): 2-9.

Woolman, David S. "In Spanish Morocco, Two Berber Brothers Became a Legend in Their Guerrilla War against Two European Powers." *Military History.* February 1994, 12, 14, 16, 84, and 85.

Television

A & E's *Biography,* "Franco."

Encyclopedia

Enciclopedia Universal Ilustrada, 1958 ed. S.v. "Marruecos."

Index

Abad de Santillan, Diego, 7–8
Abbada/Abada No. 3, 200
Abd-el-Krim, Mahammed ben, 42, 54, 165, 170
Abd-el-Krim el Khattabi, Mohammed ben, 55, 81, 82; and Ahmed Heriro, 113, 119; and Alhucemas Bay, 169, 172; and Annual disaster, 41, 42; and Beni Hozmar *kabyle*, 193; and contraband, 164, 178 n.4; decline of, 163; defeat of, 191, 194, 198, 206, 222; and El Raisuni, 165; and Emirate of the Rif, 85, 104 n.49; forces of, 125, 178 n.1; and France, 168, 198, 206, 222; and French zone, 167; and Gomara, 113, 114, 119; and Kudia Tahar, 197; and Melilla, 54; and peace negotiations, 89; and prisoners, 103 n.47, 194; and Russia, 142 n.7; and sovereignty, 104 n.50; strategy concerning, 75, 77, 94; strategy of, 119, 124, 132; and Tifaruin, 91, 107 n.63; and Tizzi-Azza, 105 n.59; and war booty, 142 n.7; and weaponry, 142 n.7; and western zone, 164; and Xauen evacuation, 132; and Yebala, 113, 119. *See also* Riffians
Adalid, Colonel, 129
Adgoz, 92, 93, 114
Ajdir, 83, 94, 176, 207 n.2
Adman, 202
Adra/Adrar Sedun/Seddun, 176
Afarnum, 87

Afgar, 196
Afrau, 86, 89, 90, 123
Africanistas, 7, 59, 83, 84, 85, 93, 111 n.84, 121, 122
Aguada, La, 95 n.10
Agulla Jiménez-Coronado, Eduardo, 50
Ahl Serif *kabyle*, 193
Ahmasi, 204
Ahmas tribe, 201
Ahmed Budra, 197
Ahmed Heriro: and Abd-el-Krim, 113, 119; and Alhucemas Bay, 113; killed, 213 n.45; and M'Ter/Meter, 114; and Tazarut, 165; and Tetuán, 192; and Wadi Martil, 197
Ain Ganen, 164
Ain Grana, 81, 83, 85, 86, 92, 93, 114
Ain Kamara, 198
Ain Razta/Rapta, 137
Ain Sixo, 140
Ain Yir, 140, 164
Air Force, 71 n.46, 114, 144 n.20, 145 n.25, 255
Ait-Aixa, 46, 50
Aizpuru y Mondéjar, Luis, 91–92, 115, 134, 155 n.98
Al Ahmas *kabyle*, 202
Alarcón de la Lastra, Fermín, 88
Alcazarseguer, 163, 164, 166, 177, 180 n.18, 222
Alcubilla Pérez, Antonio, 21, 29 n.19, 33 n.34, 38, 60 n.5
Alfau Mendoza, Felipe, 4
Alfonso XIII, 15, 205
Alfonso XIII, 51, 107 n.63, 255
Alhucemas, 201

Alhucemas Bay: and Alcazarseguer,
    166; and Berenguer Fusté, 79;
    forces at, 253–56; and Franco, 93;
    landings at, 168–77, 182 n.29, 185
    n.42, 187 n.51, 222, 253–56;
    strategy concerning, 75, 77, 93,
    122, 163, 220; and Tizzi-Azza, 84;
    and weaponry, 96 n.13
Alicante, 93
Allende-Salazar, Manuel, 47
Almeria, 93
Almirante Lobo, 125
Alonso Alonso, Siro, 56
Alonso Vega, Camilo, 22
Álvarez Arenas, Eliseo, 166
Álvarez Coque, Aureliano, 193
Amadi gorge, 51
"Amargot," 138
Ambar, 78, 97 n.16
Amekran, 192
Amekran Bajo, 176
Anjera/Anyera tribe, 164, 177, 192
Ankod, 202
Annual: and casualties, 63 n.16;
    disaster at, 42, 44; investigation
    of, 47, 83, 99 n.25; prisoners from,
    83, 85, 96 n.12, 103 n.47; and
    Silvestre, 42
Antonio Lazaro, 170, 172
Anyera tribe, 164, 177, 192
Aranda Mata, Antonio, 169, 207 n.5
Arcila, 166
Arevalo Salamanca, Angel, 33 n.34
Argos/Adgoz, 92, 93, 114
Armament. *See* Weaponry
Armored car, 144 n.20
Army, 1–2, 3, 6–7, 8 n.3, 23, 35 n.45,
    179 n.12. *See also Regulares*;
    Spanish Foreign Legion;
    individual units
Army of Africa, 249. *See also
    Regulares*; Spanish Foreign
    Legion
Arrach-Bel-Hach, 123
Arredondo Acuña, Pablo, 16, 21, 29
    n.19, 39, 137, 138
Arrof, 131
Asba, 199
Asenjo, 202
Asensio Cabanillas, Carlos, 193

Asgar/Azgar, 196
Asturias, miners' strike in, 223, 248
Atalayon, 46, 47, 49, 50
Atlaten, 53, 55
Atrocity, 70 n.44, 174, 187 n.47
Axazar, 55
Ayalia, 57, 75
Azib de Midar, 83, 117

Baba, 82
Bab el Arbaa, 197
Bab el Haman, 82, 135
Bab el Sor, 40, 136
Bab Taza/Tazza, 204
Bab Tilua, 202
Balmes Alonso, Amado, 168, 170, 174,
    175–76, 194, 202
Bandera, 25 n.2, 225. *See also* Spanish
    Foreign Legion
Barea, Arturo, 52, 206
Barge, K-type landing, 164, 178 n.9
Barroso y Sánchez-Guerra, Antonio,
    169
Bas River, 79
Batallón de la Princesa, 54
Battalion of Andalucia, 118
Battalion of Barbastro, 129, 130
Battalion of Segorbe, 134, 135
Battalion of the Queen, 129
Battalion of Toledo, 118
Bel-Hayy, 123
Ben Behasa, 86
Beni Aros, 40, 57, 76
Beni Aros gorges, 122
Beni Aros tribe, 202
Beni Bechir *kabyle*, 201
Beni-bu-Ifrur, 57, 58
Beni-bu-Ifrur tribe, 53, 56
Beni Buzra, 119
Beni Faklan, 56
Beni Hozmar, 119
Beni Hozmar *kabyle*, 193
Beni Ider, 200
Beni Isef *kabyle*, 193, 202
Beni Kalid tribe, 201
Beni Madan, 197
Beni Said, 77, 80, 119
Beni Salah, 128
Benitez, 86, 115, 116, 117
Beni Ulixech, 77

Beni Urriaguel, 196, 199
Beni Urriaguel *harka*, 55
Beni Urriaguel *kabyle*, 198
Beni Urriaguel tribe, 42, 172
Beni Yahmed tribe, 201
Ben Karrich, 41, 119, 139, 192, 193
Ben Tieb: and Annual disaster, 44; base
    at, 84–85, 89, 93, 113, 114, 117,
    164, 166, 167, 168, 191, 192;
    incident at, 120–24, 121, 122, 141,
    146 n.38, 221–22
Beorlegui Canet, Alfonso, 21
Beorlegui Canet, Joaquín, 82
Berenguer Fusté, Dámaso, 53; and
    Alhucemas Bay, 79; and Annual
    disaster, 42, 47; and Legion, 39,
    40, 75; and Melilla, 51; and
    politics, 83; and Raisuni, 54; and
    Ras-Medua, 57; and Ras-
    Tikermin, 58; and *Regulares*, 3, 7,
    10 n.13, 219–20; and *Regulares de
    Ceuta No. 3*, 58–59; and
    repatriation, 79; and royal visit to
    Morocco, 205; and strategy, 37;
    and surrender of Xauen, 123;
    victory of, 213 n.38; and Yebala,
    202
Berenguer Fusté, Federico, 51; and Dar
    Busada, 76; and Mt. Gurugú, 54;
    and Taxuda No. 2, 55; victory of,
    213 n.38
Besiar, 81
Blocao, 37–38, 67 n.32, 220
Blocao, Miskrela No. 1, 80
Blocao, of Dar Hamech, 46, 51
Blocao, of Dar Hamed, 50
Blocao, of El Derxa, 168
Blocao, of Gars, 135
Blocao, of Gómez Arteche, 76
Blocao, of Handa Hamarra, 166
Blocao, of Magot/"Amargot," 138
Blocao, of "Mers Mesla," 82
Blocao, of Mezquita, 49
Blocao, of Peucha, 50
Blocao, of Sidi Musa, 138
Blocao, of Tacuun, 81
Blocao, of Teruel, 87
"*Blocao de la Muerte, el*," 46
Blocao "Intermedio," 46
Blocao Peire, 133

Blocao Solano, 90
Blocao Valenzuela, 116
Boado, Carlos, 169, 170
Bonifaz, 164
Borrás Estévez, Francisco, 175
Bucoya tribe, 172
Budara, 197
Buguencein, 54
Buhafora, 84
Buhafora River, 87
Buharrat, 39, 119, 200
Bu Remdan, 202
Burguete y Lana, Ricardo, 83, 84, 85,
    94, 101 n.38, 205
Buruaga, Eduardo Saenz de, 193
Bustamante, 80

Cabanellas Ferrer, Miguel, 3, 47, 79, 80
Cales, Francisco, 22
Calvet, 176
Campins Aura, Miguel, 210 n.20
Canalejas, 164
"Canción del Legionario," 22, 239–40
Candeira Sestelo, José, 22, 82, 128
Canellas, Major, 116
Canis, Emilio, 202
Capaz Montes, Osvaldo, 199, 202
Carvajal Aguilar, Luis, 191
Casabona, 50
Casa de Nicobian, 196
Casado Bustos, José, 175
Casado Obcola/Casaux Beola, Pedro,
    88
Casmata, 176
Castello, Luis, 215 n.57
Castro Girona, Alberto, 76, 122; and
    final Rif offensive, 196; and
    Gomara, 39; and Ketama *kabyle*,
    199; and Monte Conico, 128; and
    Mt. Gurugú, 54; and Tetuán, 129,
    130; and Xauen, 113, 123, 136
Cataluña, 114–15
Cavalcanti de Alburquerque y
    Padierna, José, 51, 65 n.25
Celebration of Peace, 206
Cendra/Sendra Font, Pablo, 88
Cerdeño, Captain, 129
Ceuta, 41, 44, 76, 125; and Alhucemas
    Bay landing, 172; and Anjera
    rebellion, 164; and Legion, 226;

and O'Donnell, 1; and strategy,
220; strategy concerning, 122, 140
Chemorra, 80
Cirujeda Galloso, Fernando, 21
Ciudad de Cádiz, 41, 44
Cobba/Kobba-Darsa, 119, 141, 146
n.34
Cobos Gómez, Eduardo, 21
Colonialism, 2–3
Compaired Iriarte, Francisco, 78
Conference of Sidi Musa, 92–93
Conferencia de Pizarra, 77, 96 n.11
Contraband, 164, 178 n.4
Corales Romero, Radael, 128
Corbacho García, Luis, 216 n.60
Coronel Cubria, Alfredo, 83–84, 86, 87
Cortéz, *Alférez*, 92
Criado, Díaz, 57
Cuba, 38
Cuban Legion, 52
Cubans, 52
Cudia Chekran, 198
Cuernos, of Xauen/Malmusi Alto, 175

Dacarrak, 136
Dacarrat, 134
Dar Acobba, 49, 53, 55, 75, 89, 137,
199, 200
Dar Busada, 76
Dar Drius: base at, 79, 80, 81, 82, 83,
85, 92, 93; strategy concerning,
113; and tanks, 77
Dar-el-Ata, 140
Dar Gasi/Gazi, 174
Dar Hamech, 46, 51
Dar Hamed, 50, 68 n.35
Dar Hamido, 58
Dar Quebdani: base at, 85, 168, 191;
and communications, 89; securing
of, 80; and Sidi Mesaud, 117;
strategy concerning, 90, 113
Dar Raid, 131
Dar Raiz, 193
Dar Telata, 136
Death, 19, 31 nn.23, 24, 88–89, 237,
246
Defense, in depth, 113
de los Reyes González, Alfonso, 135
Desastre, El. See Spanish-American
War

Despujols, Ignacio, 169
Díaz Álvarez, Teobalde, 60 n.3
Díaz de Rabago, 57, 80
Diego Hidalgo, 223
Dolla, General, 196
Dosse, General, 194
Draa-el-Asef, 82, 135

Eastern zone, 117, 118, 125, 168
Echevarria Esqivel, Pedro, 33 n.34
Echevarrieta, Horacio, 85
El Derxa, 168
El Fondak de Ain Yedida, 40–41, 129
El Harcha, 58
El Llano, 138
El Mago, 136
El Mizzian, 4
El Morabito, 197
El Raisuni, Muley Ahmed: and Abd-el-
Krim, 165; attack on, 39;
campaign against, 76–77; and
Castro Girona, 54; character of, 11
n.16; and Conference of Sidi
Musa, 92; death of, 165; defeat of,
163; and fall of Tazarut, 100 n.29;
and Gomara, 114; and Pact of
Buhaxen, 101 n.38; pact with,
113; protection of, 151 n.69;
retreat of, 82; sickness of, 119;
strategy concerning, 75, 77, 79,
80, 81, 94; and Yebala, 4, 86, 119
Emirate of the Rif, 85
Emsath, 123
Ensat/Emsath, 123
Escuadrón de Lanceros, 167, 168, 177,
191, 192, 199, 200
España, 51, 107 n.63
Espino Rodríguez, Santiago, 52
Espinosa, 192
Estella line, 122, 139, 140, 147 n.39,
164, 177, 178 n.4

Fanjul Goni, Joaquín, 169, 207 n.3
Farha, 90
Farha peak, 86
Fendak Yebel, 138
Fernández Pérez, Emilio, 58, 91, 113,
118, 170, 175, 254
Fernández Silvestre, Manuel, 4, 15, 41,
42, 65 n.25

Ferrach, 200
Ferrer, Major, 50
Figueras Figueras, Felipe, 86, 137
1st Madrid Chausseurs, 2
Fiscer, Benigno, 194
Fontanés, Carlos Rodríguez, 21, 41, 78, 82, 94
Foreigner, 19, 31 n.26, 166, 228–29. *See also* Spanish Foreign Legion, and recruits
IV Machine Gun Company, 82
France: and Abd-el-Krim, 167, 168, 222; and Alhucemas Bay, 177; defeat of, 181 n.26; and Maghreb, 4; and Morocco, 2; and Spain, 2, 3–4, 167, 168, 169, 182 n.27, 191, 192, 194; strategy of, 181 n.21; and surrender of Abd-el-Krim, 198; and Uarga River, 176
Franco Bahamonde, Francisco: and Ain Sixo, 140; and Ainyir, 140; and Alcazarseguer, 164, 166; and Alhucemas Bay, 93, 175; and Alhucemas Bay landing, 168–69, 170, 172; and Ambar, 78; and Anjera rebellion, 164; and Azib de Midar, 117; and Bab el Haman, 135; and Beni Salah, 128; and Ben Tieb incident, 121, 122, 146 n.39, 221–22; career of, 247–49; and Ceuta, 164; character of, 14, 27 n.8, 220, 247, 248; and Cobba/Kobba-Darsa, 120, 146 n.34; and commander's cat, 98 n.22; and creation of Legion, 14–15, 21; and Dacarrak, 136; and Dar Drius, 92; death of, 249; and Draa-el-Asef, 135; formation of, 220; and Garusin, 133–34; and Gorgues massif, 131; and guerrilla warfare, 79; and *Junteros*, 84; and Legion, 220, 221, 223; as Legion commander, 89, 106 n.60; and Legion command structure, 179 n.12; and Legion uniform, 35 n.44; and Lyautey, 183 n.31; and Melilla, 41, 45, 49, 50; and Millán Astray, 14, 247, 248; and Mt. Gurugú, 53; and Mt. Uisan, 56; "Passivity and Inaction," 143 n.16;

and Primo de Rivera kidnapping plot, 130–31, 152 n.78, 222; promotions, 141, 177, 192, 207 n.3, 222, 248; and *Regulares*, 7; and *Regulares de Melilla*, 247; reputation of, 207 n.3, 248; and Riffians, 76; and Rif Rebellion, 59; and royal visit to Morocco, 205; schooling, 247; and Sidi Mesaud, 118; and Solano, 124–25; and Spanish-American War, 247; and Spanish Civil War, 248, 249; and strategy, 79, 93, 136–37; and Tafersit, 115, 116; and Taranes, 132; and Tetuán, 129; and Tifaruin, 90, 91; and Timisal, 132; and Tizzi-Azza, 115; and weaponry, 70 n.44, 97 n.16; wedding of, 110 n.78; wounded, 248; and Xauen, 123, 132, 141; and Yebel Combo/Cobba, 124; and Zoco el Arbaa, 132, 137
Franco Bahamonde, Ramon, 207 n.3
Franco-Hispanic Conference, 168, 182 n.27
French Foreign Legion, 7, 245
Fundador, El, 13. *See also* Millán Astray, José

Galey, John H., 7
Gallego Cuesta, Isidro, 80
García Fuentes, Colonel, 119
García Margallo, Juan, 1
García Uria, 117
Gars, 135
Garusin, 133–34
Gas, 144 n.20
Georges, General, 192
Germany, 4
Gibraltar, 35 n.43
Goded Llopis, Manuel, 169, 175, 196, 201, 207 n.3, 207 n.5
Gomara, 24; and Abd-el-Krim, 113, 114, 119; and El Raisuni, 114; and final offensives, 202; and Mahammed Abd-el-Krim el Khattabi, 54; Riffien infiltrations in, 122; Spanish defeat in, 163; strategy concerning, 39; victory in, 55

Gómez Arteche, 76
Gómez-Jordana y Souza, Francisco, 150 n.62, 181 n.27, 183 n.31, 184 n.40, 192
González Carrasco, Colonel, 139, 194
González Hontoria, Manuel, 77, 94 n.3
González Tablas y García Herreros, Santiago, 41, 45, 47, 50, 76, 81
Gorgues mountains, 125, 129, 131
Government: and Annual prisoners, 85; and *Conferencia de Pizarra*, 77; and Moroccan strategy, 79; and Primo de Rivera, 91–92; and Sanjurjo, 249; and strategy, 75; strategy of, 94 n.3. *See also* Politics
Gracía Bastarrica, Luis, 16
Granja/Huerta de los niños, 49
Gran Peña, 81
Great Britain, 1
Guedea Lozano, Alfredo, 254
Guerrilla warfare, 75, 79, 124
Guis River, 196

Hafa el Baira/Haffa del Duira, 193
Haira Tuila, 164
Hal'il gorge, 115
Hamuda, 84, 86, 87
Hamud-Beveasa, 87
Handa Hamarra, 166
Harkas de Tetuán y Larache, 172
Hauma Beni Bara, 76
Hayera Tuila, 140
Helalech, 82
Heli/Hal'il gorge, 115
Hensura, 131
Hidun Road, 49
Hijos de la noche, 194
Hoj, 125, 149 n.50

Ibuhasen/Ibujaren gorge, 120
Igueriben, 42, 44
Ikarrusen, 194
Imacegay, 200
Imasinen, 200
Imugzen, 202
Issen Lassen, 83, 117
Istiguen, 78
Ivanof, Dimitri Ivan, 194
Ixdain, 170

Jaca revolt, 248
Jaime I, 205, 206
Jaime II, 170
Juan Carlos, 249
Juan de Jaunes, 96 n.13
Juntas de Defensa, 15
Junteros, 84

Kaaseras, 170
Kaddur-Ben-Ab-Selam, 58
Kadur, 58
Kala, 82, 128, 129, 134, 138
Kala Bajo, 128
Kaseras, 55
Keri Kera, 139
Kert River, 4, 53, 58, 77, 79
Ketama, 199, 202
Ketama tribe, 201
Kobba Darsa, 119, 141, 146 n.34
Kondor Legion, 249
K-type landing barge, 164, 178 n.9
Kudia Gomariz, 166
Kudia Kobo, 126
Kudia Nich, 126
Kudia Sebaa, 204
Kudia Tahar, 170, 172, 177, 192, 193, 197
Kugushev, Serge, 142 n.7

La Cebadilla, 170
La Chaif, 80
La Cierva, Juan de, 47, 75, 77
Larache, 3–4, 76, 79, 83, 114, 129, 136, 140
La Rocosa, 191
Laucien, 168, 192
Lauria Immedian, 80
Lau River, 114, 119, 122, 169
Legion. *See* Spanish Foreign Legion
Liniers y Muguiro, Juan José Pérez de, 55, 168, 193
Lizcano de la Rosa, Fernando, 78, 144 n.20
Loma de los Morabos, 196
Loma Gris, 87
Loma Negra, 57, 130
Loma O, 176
Loma Redonda, 193, 208 n.10
Loma Roja, 86, 87

Lomas de Nicobian, 196
Los Frailes, 174
Lucas, Enrique, 90
Luhordia, 200
Lukus River, 76, 193
Lyautey, Louis-Hubert, 167, 168, 169,
    183 n.31

Magan, 119
Maghreb, 4
Magot/"Amargot," 138
Malmusi Alto, 175
Malmusi Bajo, 175
Malo, El, 50–51
Marabtech, 82
Marichalar y Monreal, Luis, 15
Martínez de Campos, Arsenio, 1, 47, 52
Martínez Esparza, José, 80, 98 n.22
Martínez Zaldívar, Pompilio, 21, 38, 60
    n.5
Martín River, 197
Marzo, General, 55, 76, 81
Mas Mula, 40
Maura, Antonio, 47, 75
McGregor, Donald, 52
Mehal-la, 82, 124
Melilla: base at, 82; early conflict in, 1;
    early gains in, 3; and El Mizzian,
    4; and reconquest, 44–58; and
    Regulares, 7; and Spanish Foreign
    Legion, 59, 64 n.21, 221; strategy
    concerning, 113, 220
Melillan Command, 43, 48
Mellor, Captain, 6–7
Mensora, 82
Mercader, Enrique Lucas, 83
"Mers Mesla," 82
Meter, 83, 85, 86, 114, 119
Mexe, 199
Mexerach, 82
Mexerah, 138
Meyahedi, 138
Mezquita, 49
Miaja Menant, José, 153 n.85
Military Directorate, 91
Military Medal, 94, 105 n.59
Millán Astray, José: and Ambar, 78;
    and Beni Aros, 57; and Buhafora,
    83–84; career of, 245, 246;
    character of, 27 n.8, 220; and Dar

Hamido, 58; death of, 246; and El
    Raisuni, 76–77; and Franco
    Bahamonde, 14, 247, 248; and
    Gomara attack, 39; and Hamuda,
    83–84; journey to Madrid, 49; and
    Junteros, 84; and Legion, 220;
    Legion colonel (honorary), 205;
    Legion commander, 192, 222;
    Legion creation, 13–14, 19–20, 26
    nn.3, 7, 220, 246; and Legion
    music, 22; and Legion
    organization, 16; and Legion's
    name, 25 n.2; and Legion uniform,
    35 n.44; and Melilla, 41, 45, 46,
    49, 50; philosophy of, 15, 26 n.7,
    221, 246; promoted to brigadier
    general, 204; recuperation of, 53;
    and *Regulares*, 7; retirement of,
    84, 94; and Rif Rebellion, 59;
    schooling, 245; and Tafersit, 83–
    84; and Tayudi, 83–84; and
    Tazarut, 81; and Tetuán assault,
    193; and Tizzi-Azza, 83–84; and
    Viernes, 83–84; and western zone,
    79; wounded, 51, 69 n.36, 156
    n.105, 193, 208 n.10, 211 n.35,
    246
Miskrela, 80, 134, 136
Mola Vidal, Emilio, 123, 153 n.85,
    194, 201, 202, 220, 249
Molins, *Alférez*, 93
Monasterio, 196
Monte Abarran, 42
Monte Argos, 51
Monte Arruit, 44, 47, 54
Monte Conico, 128
Monte Madan, 198
Monte Magan, 55
Monte Malmusi, 175
Monte Mauro, 58
Monte Palomas, 175–76
Moore de Pedro, Joaquín, 16
Mophan Asdat, 202
Morabo, 133
Morales, Gallego, 57
Morato, Gómez, 86, 87, 137
Moroccan Peace medal, 206
Morocco: geography of, 38; and Spain,
    2–3, 4, 5, 9 n.6, 219
Morro Nuevo, 172

Morro Viejo, 175
Moulay Abd-al-Hadid, 4
Mt. Gurugú, 46, 50, 51, 53, 54
Mt. Uisan, 56–57, 57
M'Ter. *See* Meter
Mula Tahar, 132
Mulay el Mehdi, 92
Muñiz, 134
Muñoz Crespo, 39
Muñoz Grandes, Agustín, 3, 149 n.49
Mura Tahar, 136

Nador, 47, 51–52, 53, 56, 65 n.24, 113
Navarrete, Lieutenant, 116
Navarrete Navarrete, Gabriel, 166, 180
    n.17
Navarro y Caballos Escalera, Felipe,
    45, 47, 54, 65 n.25
Navy, 91, 114–15, 164, 166, 170, 178
    n.9, 184 n.33, 255
Neila, General, 50
Nekor River, 197
"Novio de la Muerte, El," 22, 241–42

O'Donnell, Leopoldo, 1
Olavide Torres, Ignacio, 16
Ordáz Sampayo, Manuel, 176
Oregon, Colonel, 128
Orgáz/Ordáz Sampayo, Manuel, 176
Orgáz y Yoldi, Luis, 193, 207 n.5, 208
    n.10, 216 n.61, 220
Ortega y Gasset, 65 n.24
Ortiz de Zárate, Joaquín, 22, 40, 88
Ostariz, Luis, 199, 201
Ouergha/Uarga River, 167

Pact of Buhaxen, 101 n.38
Palomas, 191
Pardo Ibáñez, Justo, 16
Past, 19
Peire, 133
Peñas Acayat, 90
Peñas Carbonell, 124
Peña Tahuarda, 86
Peñon de Alhucemas, 96 n.13
Peñon de Vélez de la Gomera, 80, 94,
    96 n.13
Peñon Rocoso, 130
Pérez García, Miguel, 22
Pérez Mercader, Emilio, 84

Pérez Tajueco, Joaquín/Jacinto, 92
Pétain, Henri Philippe, 168, 192
Peucha, 50
Picasso Commission, 47, 83, 99 n.25
Picasso González, Juan, 47
Pintado, Lt. Colonel, 90
Pintos Ledesma, Guillermo, 2
Pista Prisioneros, 196
Poblado Kricha, 198
Politics, 75, 77, 83, 85, 130–32. *See
    also* Government
Polo Martínez-Valdés, Carmen, 110
    n.78
Ponte, Miguel, 210 n.20
Pozas Perea, Sebastian, 118, 199, 201,
    210 n.20, 216 n.61
Prado, Núñez de, 135
Prieto, García, 85
Primo de Rivera y Orbaneja, Miguel:
    and Alcazarseguer, 180 n.18; and
    Alhucemas Bay landing, 168, 172,
    174, 176–77; and Army, 219; and
    atrocities, 174, 187 n.47; and Ben
    Tieb incident, 120–21, 141, 147
    n.39, 221–22; and Conference of
    Sidi Musa, 92, 93; and Estella
    line, 164; as High Commissioner,
    134; and Madrid meeting, 192;
    and Pétain, 168; plot to kidnap,
    130–32, 152 n.78, 222;
    pronunciamento of, 91–92, 94;
    and Spanish army, 198; and
    strategy, 113, 114, 121, 122, 143
    n.17, 150 n.63, 167, 191; and
    Xauen, 113, 132, 139–40, 150
    n.63
Primo line, 122, 147 n.39
Prisoners: from Annual, 83, 85, 96
    n.12, 103 n.47; dispute over, 194;
    ill-treatment of, 198, 208 n.10
Promotion, 7, 11 n.24, 15, 219, 228,
    245, 247. *See also specific
    individuals*
Punta Pescadores, 200

Queija de la Vega, Baltasar, 38, 60 n.3
Queipo de Llano, Gonzalo, 126, 130,
    152 nn.78, 79, 222
Quesil, 138

Rada Peral, Ricardo, 123, 139, 196,
    216 n.61
Raisuli. *See* El Raisuni, Muley Ahmed
Ramos Torres, 194
Ras-Medua, 57
Ras Muturaka, 81
Ras-Tikermin, 58
Real Herrainz, Inocencio, 174
Redemption, 20
Regbaba, 196
*Regimiento de Caballería de
    Alcántara*, 52
Regimiento de Melilla, 202
Regulares: and Ambar, 78; and *blocao*
    of Gars, 135; defection of, 42, 64
    n.22, 220; and eastern zone, 125;
    formation of, 3, 10 n.13, 219–20;
    and Garusin, 133, 134; quality of,
    7; and Spanish Civil War, 249;
    and Spanish Foreign Legion, 59,
    61 n.10, 221; and Tagsut, 201; and
    Tetuán, 193; and Tirines, 124; and
    Xauen, 22
Regulares de Alhucemas, 84, 91, 115,
    131
Regulares de Ceuta, 41, 46; and Beni
    Aros, 57; and Legion, 58–59;
    loyalty of, 45, 64 n.23; and
    Alcazarseguer, 166; and Asturias,
    248; and Baba and Sugna, 82; and
    Casabona, 50; and Melilla, 51; and
    Mt. Gurugú, 53; and Tirines, 124;
    and Tazarut, 81
Regulares de Larache, 153 n.85
Regulares de Melilla: disloyalty of, 41,
    45; and Franco, 247; loyalty of, 64
    n.22; and Sidi Mesaud, 118; and
    Tifaruin, 91; and Tizzi-Azza, 84,
    88; and Viernes, 84
Regulares de Tetuán, 38, 76, 82
Reina Victoria Eugenia, 120–21
Repatriation, 79
Restinga-Hayar, 164
R'Gaia, 164, 166, 167, 168, 191
Rif, 86, 94, 197
Riffians, 2, 52–53, 54, 58, 77, 79, 81,
    86–87, 89–90, 92, 113, 114–15.
    See also Abd-el-Krim el Khattabi,
    Mohammed ben

Riffien: base at, 53, 79, 85, 168, 191;
    headquarters at, 166; training
    camp at, 164
Rif Rebellion, 59
Rif War, 62 n.11
Rio Martín, 140
Riquelme, José, 55, 126
Robba el Cozal, 136
Rodriguez Fontanés, Carlos, 21, 41, 78,
    82, 94
Rokoba Adia, 82
Rubio, Carlos, 197
Ruiz-Trillo, Leopoldo, 83
Russia, 142 n.7

"Sacred Forest," 140
Salcedo, Colonel, 90, 91
Saliquet, Colonel, 82
Sánchez Guerra, José, 83, 85, 96 n.12
Sánchez Suárez, Manuel, 118
Sánchez Tirado, Pedró, 167
San Enrique, 57
Sangiorgio, Antonio, 138, 194
San Juan de las Minas, 53, 75
Sanjurjada, 249
Sanjurjo Sacanell, José, 7; and Afrau,
        123; and Alhucemas Bay, 169,
        175; and final Rif offensive, 196;
        and French, 207 n.5; and
        government overthrow, 249;
        honored, 205; and Larache, 79;
        and Melilla, 41, 44, 49; and
        Moroccan pacification, 204; and
        Mt. Gurugú, 53, 54; and Nador,
        51, 65 n.25; and Ras-Medua, 57;
        and Sel-litan, 201; and Taxuda,
        56; and Taxuda No. 2, 55
San Miguel Rasilla, Juan, 33 n.34
Santiago Guerrero, Mariano, 253
Sanz de Larín, Eugenio, 197, 202, 204,
        205, 216 n.61, 222
Sanz Perea, Justo, 88
Saro y Marin, Leopoldo de, 58, 164,
        170, 175, 253
Sebt, 53, 56
2nd Depot Rifle Company, 82
Sedie, 200
Segangan, 53, 55, 113
Selaca, 81
Selalen, 81

Sel-litan/Slitan, 201, 202, 204
Semsa, 128
Sendra Font, Pablo, 88
Senhadja-Ketama sector, 202
Senhadja Srir, 199
Senhadja Srir/Senhadjan *kabyle*, 201
Senhaia tribe, 201
Serilla/Seriya/Sevilla, 139
Serrano Orive, Julián, 81, 119, 120, 123
Sevilla, 139
Shinkarenko, Nikolai Vsevolodovich, 142 n.7
Sidi Abderrahaman, 82
Sidi-Ali-Musa, 86
Sidi Amaran, 49
Sidi Baki, 197
Sidi Dris, 185 n.40
Sidi Guariach, 86, 164
Sidi Hamed, 47, 49, 51
Sidi Hamed el Hach, 46
Sidi Mesaud, 84, 89, 90, 117–18
Sidi Mezquin, 202
Sidi Musa, 46, 92, 138
Sidi-Salem, 58
Sidi Yuset/Yussef, 197
Silvela, Luis, 85, 86, 91–92, 94
Silvestre, Manuel Fernández, 4, 15, 41, 42, 65 n.25
Silvestre line, 113
Slitan, 201, 202, 204
Solano, 90, 119, 124–25
Solans, Luis, 201, 202
Soler, Antonio, 22
Sousa Regoyos, Federico de, 166
Souza, General, 202
Spain: and France, 2, 3–4, 167, 168, 169, 182 n.27, 191, 192, 194; and military, 219; and Morocco, 1–8, 2–3, 4, 5, 9 n.6, 195
Spanish-American War, 1, 219, 247
Spanish Civil War, 223, 246, 248, 249
Spanish Foreign Legion:
    accomplishment of, 206; and
    Army, 179 n.12; and atrocities, 70
    n.44, 174, 187 n.47; and
    Berenguer Fusté, 75; and *blocao*
    defense, 67 n.32; casualties, 32
    n.28, 69 n.36, 235–36; and Ceuta,
    226; command structure of, 165,

179 n.12; cost of, 69 n.40; creation
of, 7–8, 13–25, 220, 246; creed of,
237–38; disabled members of, 214
n.47; and discipline, 221, 229; and
echelon withdrawal, 139; emblem,
34 n.38; 1st Legion of, 168; and
foreigners, 19, 31 n.26, 166, 228–
29; and Franco, 220, 221, 223;
importance of, 118; increase of,
46, 65 n.26; marching, 35 n.46;
and Melilla, 59, 64 n.21, 221; and
Millán Astray, 13–14, 16, 19–20,
22, 25 n.2, 26 nn.3, 7, 35 n.44,
199, 205, 220, 222, 246; modern,
223; name of, 15, 25 n.2, 166,
219; officers, 20, 33 n. 31;
organization of, 16–22, 28 n.15,
29 n.17, 53, 110 n.83, 160 n. 139,
165, 168, 181 n.25, 225–34;
posting of, 227, 228; and press, 29
n.16; and promotion, 228; reasons
for joining, 16–17; receives
standard, 205; and recruits, 16–17,
19, 20, 30 n.22, 31 n.26, 32 n.28,
33 n.30, 49, 52, 69 n.41, 70 n.43,
101 n.33, 142 n.7, 166, 221, 229–
32; and *Regulares*, 59, 61 n.10,
221; reputation, 221; and Rif
Rebellion, 59; 2nd Legion of, 168;
songs of, 19, 22, 239–44; and
Spanish Civil War, 249; and
strategy, 139; success of, 59; and
Tauima, 69 n.39; training, 21–22;
uniform of, 20–21, 22–23, 33 n.
31, 35 n.44, 165–66, 226; and
wage, 30 n.20, 33 n.33, 228, 232–
34, 251; and weaponry, 8 n.3, 23,
35 n.45, 70 n.44, 77, 144 n.20, 158
n.117, 185 n.42, 226. *See also*
Army
Spanish Foreign Legion: Ist *Bandera*:
and Abbada, 132, 133; and Ain
Kamara, 198; and Alhucemas Bay,
169; and Ambar, 78; and
Amekran, 192; and Azib de
Midar, 83, 117; and Bab el
Haman, 135; and Beni Said
region, 80; and Benitez, 115, 116;
and Ben Karrich, 139; and Ben
Tieb, 114, 117, 167; and *blocao*

Peire, 133; and Buhafora, 83–84; and Buhafora River, 87; and Casabona, 50; and Ceuta, 41; and Coba/Kobba-Darsa, 119–20; creation of, 21; and Dacarrak, 136; and Dacarrat, 134; and Dar Drius, 76, 78, 79, 81, 82, 83, 92, 93; and Dar Quebdani, 89, 90, 168, 191; and Dar Riffien, 21, 33 n.36; and Draa-el-Asef, 135; and El Llano, 138; and Ensat/Emsath, 123; and Garusin, 133–34; and Gomara, 202; and Gorgues massif, 131; and *Granja/Huerta de los niños*, 49; and Hamuda, 83–84; and Hoj, 125, 149 n.50; and Issen Lassen, 83; and Istiguen, 78; and Kala, 134; and Kert River, 58; and Kudia Kobo, 126; and Kudia Sebaa, 204; and Loma Roja, 86; and Melilla, 45, 47, 82; and Meyahedi, 138; and Miskrela, 134, 136; and Monte Madan, 198; and Mt. Gurugú, 53; and Muñoz Crespo, 39; and Nador, 53; organization of, 21; and Peñas Carbonell, 124; and Peña Tahuarda, 87; and Poblado Kricha, 198; and Ras-Medua, 57; and Restinga-Hayar, 164; and R'Gaia, 164, 166; Rif campaign final offensive, 196, 198; and Riffien, 164; and Rio Martín, 140; and San Juan de las Minas, 75–76; and Segangan, 55; and Sel-litan/Slitan revolt, 201–2; and Sidi-Ali-Musa, 86; and Sidi Dris, 185 n.40; and Sidi Guariach, 86; and Sidi Mesaud, 90; and Solano, 124; and Tafersit, 83–84, 84, 85, 87, 115; and Tafersit-Bu Hafora, 87, 88; and Taranes, 132, 139; and Targuist, 200; and Tauriat-Azzus, 117; and Tauriat Uchan, 83; and Tayudi, 83–84; and Tazarut, 40; and Tenafe, 134; and Tetuán, 164; and Tifaruin, 89; and Timisal, 132; and Tirines, 124; and Tisgarin, 129; and Tizzi-Azza, 83–84, 85, 87, 116; and Uad Lau, 23;
and Viernes, 83–84; and Xauen evacuation, 132, 133; and Xeruta, 137; and Yarda, 140; and Yebel Combo/Cobba, 124; and Zauia de la Abada, 77–78; and Zinat, 139; and Zoco el Arbaa, 120, 132, 137–38, 139; and Zoco el Jemis de Beni Aros, 140

Spanish Foreign Legion: IInd *Bandera*: and Adra/Adrar Sedun/Seddun, 176; and Afarnum, 87; and Ain Kamara, 198; and Ain Razta/Rapta, 137; and Alhucemas Bay, 169, 170, 172, 175, 253; and Ambar, 78; and Arrof, 131; and Azib de Midar, 83, 117; and Bab el Sor, 136; and Beni Said region, 80; and Beni Salah, 128; and Benitez, 116; and Ben Karrich, 41; and Ben Tieb, 84–85, 93, 114, 117, 191, 192; and Buhafora, 83–84; and Casabona, 50; and Ceuta, 41, 125; creation of, 21; and Dar Drius, 76, 78, 79, 81, 82, 83, 85, 92; and Dar-el-Ata, 140; and Dar Quebdani, 90; and Dar Riffien, 23; and Dar Telata, 136; and El Fondak de Ain Yedida, 129; and Fendak Yebel, 138; first battle, 38; and Gomara, 202; and *Granja/Huerta de los niños*, 49; and Haira Tuila, 164; and Hamuda, 83–84, 86; and Hamud-Beveasa, 87; and Handa Hamarra, 166; and Hayera Tuila, 140; and Issen Lassen, 83; and Istiguen, 78; and Kala, 138; and Kert River, 58; and Kudia Tahar, 172, 174; and Larache, 129, 136; and Los Frailes, 174–75; and Magot/"Amargot," 138; and Melilla, 45, 46, 47, 82; and Monte Conico, 128; and Monte Madan, 198; and Monte Palomas, 175–76; and Mt. Gurugú, 53; and Nador, 53; organization of, 21; and Poblado Kricha, 198; and Quesil, 138; and Ras-Medua, 57; Rif campaign final offensive, 196, 198; and Riffien, 168; and Robba

el Gozal, 136; and "Sacred
Forest," 140; and San Juan de las
Minas, 75–76; and Segangan, 55;
and Sel-litan/Slitan revolt, 201–2;
and Serilla/Seriya/Sevilla, 139;
and Sidi Mesaud, 90, 118; and
Taatof, 140; and Tafersit, 83–84,
89, 115; and Tafersit-Bu Hafora,
87, 88; and Tahar Varda, 132; and
Taixera, 134; and Targuist, 200;
and Tauriat Uchan, 83; and
Tayudi, 83–84; and Tazarut, 40;
and Tetuán, 23, 41, 167; and
Tizzi-Azza, 83–84, 116; and
T'Zenin, 166; and Viernes, 83–84;
and Xauen evacuation, 133; and
Yuma-el-Tolba, 140; and Zauia de
la Abada, 77–78; and Zinat, 126,
128; and Zoco el Jemis de Beni
Aros, 136
Spanish Foreign Legion: IIIrd *Bandera*:
and Abbada, 132, 133; and
Adra/Adrar Sedun/Seddun, 176;
and Afrau, 123; and Ain Kamara,
198; and Ain Sixo, 140; and Ain
Yir, 164; and Ainyir, 140; and
Alhucemas, 201; and Alhucemas
Bay, 169, 170, 172, 175, 253; and
Argos/Adgoz, 92, 93; and Azib de
Midar, 117; and Bab el Haman,
82, 135; and Beni Aros, 57; and
Benitez, 117; and Ben Karrich, 23,
139; and Ben Tieb, 114, 164, 166,
167, 168, 192; and Besiar, 81; and
blocao Peire, 133; and Buharrat,
39, 200; and Ceuta, 125; creation
of, 21; and Cudia Chekran, 198;
and Dacarrak, 136; and Dacarrat,
134; and Dar Acobba, 49, 53, 55,
75; and Dar Hamido, 58; and Dar
Raid, 131; and Dar Riffien, 23;
and Dra/Draa el Asef, 76; and El
Llano, 138; and Gorgues massif,
131; and Gran Peña, 81; and
Hamuda, 87; and Heli/Hal'il
gorge, 115; and Imasinen, 200;
and Kala, 82, 134; and Ketama,
199; and Kudia Nich, 126; and
Kudia Tahar, 172–74; and La
Rocosa, 191; and Los Frailes,

174–75; and Mensora, 82; and
Meter, 83, 85, 86; and Mexerach,
82; and Meyahedi, 138; and
Miskrela, 134, 136; and Monte
Conico, 128; and Monte Palomas,
175–76; organization of, 21–22;
and Peñas Acayat, 90; Rif
campaign final offensive, 196,
198; and Riffien, 79, 191; and
Selaca, 81; and Selalen, 81; and
Sel-litan/Slitan revolt, 201–2; and
Semsa, 128; and Sidi
Abderrahaman, 82; and Sidi-
Guariach, 164; and Sidi Mesaud,
117, 118; and Sidi Musa, 138; and
Tafersit, 115; and Takun, 81; and
Talambo, 89; and Taranes, 132,
139; and Tazarut, 40, 81; and
Tenacot, 82; and Tenafe, 134; and
Terinos, 89; and Tetuán, 125; and
Timisal, 132; and Tizzi-Azza, 115,
116; and Uad Lau, 83, 85, 87, 89;
and Xauen, 132, 133; and Xeruta,
137; and Zauia de Tilili, 82; and
Zinat, 126, 128, 139; and Zoco el
Arbaa, 41, 132, 137–38, 139
Spanish Foreign Legion: IVth *Bandera*:
and Abbada/Abada No. 3, 200;
and Adjir, 207 n.2; and Afrau,
123; and Ain Ganen, 164; and Ain
Kamara, 198; and Alcazarseguer,
164, 166; and Bab el Haman, 135;
and Beni Aros, 57; and Beni
Salah, 128; and Benitez, 86; and
Ben Karrich, 139; and Ben Tieb,
114, 117; and Buhafora, 83–84;
and Ceuta, 125; and Dacarrak,
136; and Dacarrat, 134; and Dar
Acobba, 200; and Dar Drius, 92;
and Dar Hamido, 58; and Dar
Quebdani, 85; and Dra/Draa el
Asef, 76, 82, 135; and El Fondak
de Ain Yedida, 129; and El Llano,
138; and El Mago, 136; and
Espinosa, 192; and Fondalillo,
199; and Garusin, 133–34; and
Hamuda, 83–84; and Hensura,
131; and Kala, 128, 129, 134; and
Kala Bajo, 128; and Kudia
Gomariz, 166; and Kudia Nich,

126; and Loma Gris, 87; and Mensora, 82; and Meyahedi, 138; and Miskrela, 134, 136; and Monte Conico, 128; and Monte Magan, 55; and Peña Tahuarda, 86; and R'Gaia, 167; Rif campaign final offensive, 196; and Riffien, 53, 164; and Sidi Mesaud, 84, 117, 118; and Sidi Musa, 138; and Tafersit, 83–84, 86, 87, 89, 115; and Tafersit-Bu Hafora, 87, 88; and Taranes, 139, 199; and Tayudi, 83–84; and Tenafe, 134; and Teruel, 87; and Tetuán, 130; and Tizzi-Alma, 93; and Tizzi-Azza, 83–84, 87, 92, 93, 115; and T'Zenin, 168; and Uad Lau, 75, 79, 81; and Uta-Lecha, 134–35; and Viernes, 83–84; and Xauen, 83, 133, 199; and Xeruta, 137; and Yarda, 140; and Zinat, 126, 128, 131, 139; and Zoco el Arbaa, 132, 137–38, 139; and Zoco el Arbaa de Beni Hassan, 199; and Zoco el Jemis de Beni Aros, 140

Spanish Foreign Legion: Vth *Bandera*: and Ain Grana, 85; and Argos, 114; and Argos/Adgoz, 92; and Ayalia, 75; and Bab el Haman, 82, 135; and Beni Aros, 57; and Beni Ider, 200; and Ben Karrich, 139; and Besiar, 81; and *blocao* Solano, 90; and Coba/Kobba-Darsa, 120; and Dacarrak, 136; and Dacarrat, 134; and Dar Akoba, 89; and Dra/Draa el Asef, 76; and El Derxa, 168; and El Llano, 138; and Ensat/Emsath, 123; formation of, 55; and García Uria, 117; and Hensura, 131; and Hoj, 125; and Imacegay, 200; and Kala, 82, 134; and Kudia Tahar, 192, 193; and Laucien, 168; and Luhordia, 200; and Mexe, 199; and Meyahedi, 138; and Miskrela, 134, 136; and Peñas Carbonell, 124; and R'Gaia, 166, 191; Rif campaign final offensive, 196; and Riffien, 79, 85, 164; and Selaca, 81; and Sidi Abderrahaman, 82; and Solano,

119, 124; and Taimutz, 139; and Takun, 81; and Talambo, 89; and Taranes, 139; and Tazarut, 81, 82, 83; and Tazza, 119; and Teffer, 200; and Telezta Mesla, 200; and Tenacot, 82; and Tenafe, 134; and Terinos, 89; and Tetuán, 130, 193; and Tirines, 124; and Tisgarin, 129; and T'Zenin, 167; and Uad Lau, 93; and Xauen, 86, 87, 133; and Xeruta, 137; and Yarda, 140; and Yebel Combo/Cobba, 124; and Yebel Ejizyan, 89; and Zauia de Tilili, 82; and Zinat, 131–32, 139; and Zoco el Arbaa, 132, 137–38, 139; and Zoco el Jemis de Beni Aros, 81, 140

Spanish Foreign Legion: VIth *Bandera*: and Ain Grana, 85, 86, 92, 93, 114; and Ain Sixo, 140; and Ain Yir, 164; and Ainyir, 140; and Alcazarseguer, 164, 166; and Alhucemas, 201; and Alhucemas Bay, 169, 170, 174, 176, 253; and Alhucemas Bay landing, 172; and Bab el Haman, 135; and Beni Madan, 197; and Ben Karrich, 139, 192; and Buharrat, 200; and Coba/Kobba-Darsa, 120; and Dacarrak, 136; and Dacarrat, 134; and Draa-el-Asef, 135; and Fondalillo, 199; formation of, 83, 94; and Garusin, 133–34; and Gomara, 202; and Kala, 129, 134; and Miskrela, 134, 136; and Monte Malmusi, 175; and Mula Tahar, 132; and Palomas, 191; and R'Gaia, 167; Rif campaign final offensive, 196; and Riffien, 83, 166, 168; and Sedie, 200; and Solano, 119; and Tagasut, 122, 124, 125, 128; and Tagusut, 117; and Talambo/Talambot, 123; and Taranes, 139, 199; and Tazza, 119; and Tenafe, 134; and Tetuán, 193; and Xajaya, 200; and Xauen, 85, 133, 199, 200; and Xeruta, 137; and Zinat, 139; and Zoco el Arbaa, 137–38, 139; and Zoco el Arbaa de Beni Hassan, 199; and

Zoco el Jemis de Beni Aros, 87, 89
Spanish Foreign Legion: VIIth *Bandera*: and Alhucemas Bay, 169, 170, 172, 174, 176, 253; formation of, 167, 177; and Kudia Tahar, 192, 193; and Monte Malmusi, 175; and Palomas, 191; and Punta Pescadores, 200; Rif campaign final offensive, 196, 198; and Tetuán, 193
Spanish Foreign Legion: VIIIth *Bandera*: and Ain Kamara, 198; and Ben Karrich, 192; companies of, 207 n.1; and Cudia Chekran, 198; and Ferrach, 200; formation of, 191; and Gomara, 202; and Kudia Sebaa, 204; and Loma Redonda, 208 n.10; and Poblado Kricha, 198; Rif campaign final offensive, 196, 198; and Sel-litan/Slitan revolt, 201–2; and Tetuán, 193
Spanish Foreign Legion: XIIth *Bandera*, 68 n.35
Squadron of Lancers. *See Escuadrón de Lanceros*
Steeg, General, 198
Sueiro Villariño, Alvaro, 21
Sugna, 82
Sumata *kabyle*, 202
Sumata tribe, 202

Taatof, 140
Tabuarda, 86
Tacuun, 81
Tafersit, 84, 85, 86, 87, 89, 113, 115, 116
Tafersit-Bu Hafora, 87
Tafras, 196
Tagasut, 122, 124, 125, 128
Tagsut, 201
Taguel Manin, 46
Tagusut, 117
Tahar Berda, 81
Tahar Varda, 81, 132
Taimutz, 139
Taixera, 134
Takun, 81
Talambo/Talambot, 89, 123

Tamasin/Tamasint, 197
Tamasusin, 80
Tamezarin/Tamerarin, 202
Tangier, 4, 140, 164
Tank, 77, 78, 97 n.16, 144 n.20, 158 n.117, 185 n.42. *See also* Weaponry
Taranes, 132, 138, 139, 199
Targa, 170
Targuist, 198, 199, 200, 202
Tasograf, 197
Tauima, 52, 69 n.39
Tauriat-Azzus, 117
Tauriat-Buchit, 58
Tauriat Hamed, 58
Tauriat Hamed/Uchen, 57
Tauriat Uchan, 83
Tauriat Zag, 58
Taxuda No. 1, 54, 55, 56, 57
Taxuda No. 2, 55
Tayudi, 84
Tazarut: Abd-el-Krim's attack on, 165; attack on, 58; attack on Legion at, 82; base at, 83; fall of, 100 n.29; Marzo's attack on, 40; Millán Astray's attack on, 76; Sanjurjo's attack on, 56; and Spanish Foreign Legion: Vth *Bandera*, 82; strategy concerning, 79, 80, 94
Tazza, 119
Teffer, 200
Tefras/Tafras, 196
Teijeiro Pérez, Jesús, 89–90
Telafta, 57
Telat, 57
Telezta Mesla, 200
Tenacot, 82
Tenafe, 134, 135
Tercio de Extranjeros, 15. *See also* Spanish Foreign Legion
"Tercios Heroicos," 22, 243–44
Terinos, 89
Terrero López, Suceso, 50, 51, 68 n.35
Teruel, 87
Tetas de Nador, 51
Tetuán: and Ahmed Heriro, 192; and Alhucemas Bay landing, 172; and Anjera rebellion, 164; attack on, 129, 193; base at, 41, 125; as capital, 1; diversion at, 169; and

Estella line, 164; and Kudia Tahar, 170; strategy concerning, 114, 122
Tetuán-Xauen road, 122
Tiede Zeden, Carlos, 155 n.97
Tifaruin, 89–91, 92, 107 n.63
Tifasor, 56
Tilma Pass, 202
Timisal, 132
Timyats, 80
Tirines, 124
Tisgarin, 129
Tisingar-Sbu Sbaa line, 77
Tistutin, 113
Tizzi-Alma, 93
Tizzi-Azza: and Abd-el-Krim, 105 n.59; and *Africanistas*, 111 n.84; base at, 93; captured, 84; 1924 conflict in, 164; convoy to, 116; danger to, 89; as forward post, 85, 141; provisioning of, 92; relief of, 115–16; siege of, 86, 87; strategy concerning, 94, 102 nn.39, 40
Tlat, 56
Treaty of Fez, 4
tribes of, 24
Tuero, General, 51
Tuguntz, 78
Turnbull, Patrick, 19
T'Zenin, 166, 167, 168, 191

Uad Lau: and Alhucemas Bay landing, 170; base at, 55, 75, 79, 81, 83, 85, 87, 89, 93; convoys to, 119; fortified line from, 76
Uarga River, 176
Ugriden, 202
Ulad-Dau, 53
Uta-Lecha, 134–35

Valcázar Crespo, Luis, 21, 58, 115, 119, 193, 196, 216 n.61
Valenzuela Urzaiz, Rafael, 7, 60 n.5, 84, 85, 87, 88, 89, 102 n.39, 105 n.59, 205, 221
Vara del Rey y Herran, Adolfo, 16, 29 n.19, 69 n.41
Varela Iglesias, José Enrique, 3, 7, 121, 146 n.38, 220
Verdu Verdu, Gregorio, 167
Vicente Ferrer, 201

Vicente la Roda, 166
Vicente Puchol, 125
Victoria Eugenia, 205
Vidal y Pons, Antonio, 78
Viernes, 84
Villalba, Major, 115
Villalba Riquelme, José, 15
Villanueva, Miguel, 85, 94
Villarreal Enitau, Marcelo, 29 n.19
Villa Sanjurjo, 201
Villegas Bueno, Emilio, 53, 55
Vives Vich, Pedro, 89
Vizconde de Eza, 15. *See also* Marichalar y Monreal, Luis

Wadi Martil, 197
Wad Lau, 119
Water, 38, 95 n.10
Weaponry: and air force, 144 n.20; and Alhucemas Bay, 96 n.13, 185 n.42; and army, 8 n.3, 23, 35 n.45; and Franco, 70 n.44, 97 n.16, 142 n.7; increase in, 77; and Legion, 23, 35 n.45, 226; and mountainous terrain, 158 n.117; and Riffians, 144 n.20
Weather, 137
Western zone, 119, 122, 164, 168
Weyler Nicolau, Valeriano, 83, 116
World War I, 4
World War II, 249
Wrangel, Peter, 142 n.7

Xajaya, 200
Xarquia Xeruta, 38, 61 n.6
Xauen, 113–41; attack on, 4; as base, 200; base at, 83, 85, 86, 87; fortification of, 76; recapture of, 199; retreat from, 132–41, 222
Xauen/Malmusi Alto, 175
Xauen road, 61 n.6
Xeruta, 137

Yagüe Blanco, Juan, 3, 7, 220
Yarda, 140
Yazanen, 56
Yebala, 4, 7, 37, 119, 122, 163, 202
Yebel Bu Zeitung, 193
Yebel Combo/Cobba, 124
Yebel Ejizyan, 89

Yebel Tangaia, 204
Yebel Taria, 204
Yolif y Morgado, Francisco, 169
Yuma-el-Tolba, 140

Zaragoza, military academy at, 248
Zauia de la Abada, 77
Zauia de Tilili, 82
Zeluán, 47, 54
Zeni Zerwal tribe, 167
Zerkat, 202
Zinac/Zinat, 126, 131, 139, 140
Zoco el Arbaa: advance on, 202; attack
     on Legion near, 38, 61 n.6; base
     at, 41, 49; and Castro Girona, 136;
     combat at, 120, 132; and Xauen
     retreat, 137–38, 139, 158 n.119
Zoco el Arbaa de Beni Hassan, 199
Zoco el Arbaa de Taurirt, 198
Zoco el Had, 49, 50
Zoco el Jemis de Beni Aros, 40, 81, 87,
     89, 136, 140
Zoko el Had, 56
Zoko el Had de Yazanen, 56
Zona, de retguardia, 113
Zona, de vanguardia, 113

About the Author

JOSÉ E. ÁLVAREZ is Assistant Professor of History at the University of Houston—Downtown. Born in Marianao, Cuba, he came to the United States in 1961. He is a member of the Society for Military History and the Society for Spanish and Portuguese Historical Studies.